YOU'RE BETTER THAN THEY THINK YOU ARE

SIR ROD ALDRIDGE

YOU'RE BETTER THAN THEY THINK YOU ARE

JOHN BLAKE

Published by John Blake Publishing,
2.25 The Plaza,
535 Kings Road,
Chelsea Harbour,
London SW10 0SZ

www.johnblakebooks.com

www.facebook.com/johnblakebooks ⬛
twitter.com/jblakebooks ⬛

First published in hardback in 2018

ISBN: 978-1-78606-573-5

British Library Cataloguing-in-Publication Data:

A catalogue record for this book is available from the British Library.

Design by www.envydesign.co.uk

Printed and bound in Great Britain by Clays Ltd, Elcograf S.p.A

1 3 5 7 9 10 8 6 4 2

Papers used by John Blake Publishing are natural, recyclable products made from wood grown in sustainable forests. The manufacturing processes conform to the environmental regulations of the country of origin.

John Blake Publishing is an imprint of Bonnier Books UK
www.bonnierbooks.co.uk

In memory of my mother and father,
and
for my grandchildren, Florence, Atticus and Annie,
who are the future.

CONTENTS

ACKNOWLEDGEMENTS

I would like to thank my wife, Carol for her encouragement in writing this book. She has lived through every draft and must be relieved to see it finally published.

My children, Debby, Michael, Jennifer and Robert have all contributed massively both in terms of real-life stories and also in commenting on the content.

It meant a great deal to me to be able to reflect the comments from my mother about us as a family and her insight into my early years. Sadly, she passed away before the book was published but had lived to the amazing age of 101.

I have also had a great deal of help from my cousin Sonia and her husband Chris on the family history, ably assisted by my father's brother Peter and his wife Ann.

My thanks to Mike Harding both for a lifetime of friendship and the actions that he took to get the 'Class of 64' back together. The observations of 'the lads' on our school life are telling.

The contributions from John Scotford and Steve Wilkins, who I worked with at CIPFA for many years, have enabled me to capture a very key part of my career that completely changed my life.

Similarly, my thanks to Mike Burr and Rich Benton for their input. As a team, along with Roger Brier, the four of us had the courage to put everything on the line to conclude the management buyout which proved to be the start of the Capita story.

I am similarly grateful to the input from Lynn Chidwick who was my PA for over thirty years and has been on the complete journey with me.

I wanted to write this book in recognition of the team that built Capita, many of whom are still working for the company, and who placed their trust in us for their careers and their livelihoods. My thanks to John Tizard for commenting on the various drafts, particularly on Capita and the development of the outsourcing industry.

Of course, none of this would have been possible without the involvement and input of Paul Pindar, Paddy Doyle and Gordon Hurst. We were a great team and led the development of a new industry in the UK.

At a time when Capita is going through a difficult period for the first time in its thirty-year corporate history, it is easy to forget the successes of the past and the massive contribution of all those involved. I am proud to have been a part of that history and this is as much their story as mine. I hope that I have done them justice in my portrayal of it.

My thanks to Julia Fawcett, the CEO of the Lowry, and to Stephen Crocker for their input and the time we have shared in working together in my role as Chair of the world-class arts centre in Salford.

Similarly, to my team at the Foundation who have changed the lives of so many young people through our work and continue to do so every year.

I want to acknowledge the support given to me by Stafford Hildred in producing a great deal of the material which provided early drafts of the book, and to Rob Green for the patience that he showed in working with me in getting this project concluded. Similarly, to Toby Buchan of John Blake Publishing for his professional guidance and support.

I should make it clear that any omissions or inaccuracies in the book are totally down to me, and that this is my interpretation of events.

This is my story and I hope you enjoy reading it.

INTRODUCTION

Writing this book has taken far longer than I expected. The process has raised mixed emotions in me. Naturally, there have been lots of wonderful memories and stories about things of which I am incredibly proud. Equally, some events have been painful to recall requiring me, in some cases, to deal with things I had left behind in my thoughts many years ago. More than once I have had to ask myself, why am I doing this? The answers have remained the same.

This book is for my family.

I don't come from a background of wealth and privilege. My parents were ordinary, working-class people. My father was a sheet metal worker in a factory for most of his working life but after being made redundant at a late age, he started a painting and decorating business. He worked hard to provide for his family, and my mother made sure that home was everything that we needed it to be. The way that she managed money, controlling the household expenditure so that bills were paid on time, was truly impressive. She ran systems to be admired. They bought their own house in 1938, something that was quite rare for a young couple of their standing at that time, and when I came along nine years later they made sure I had the very best that they could afford. I have nothing but respect for all of the effort that they put into making sure that we were a happy and strong family unit.

The way that my parents had been brought up, the hard times through the war years and the austerity of rationing, made them appreciate everything that they had, everything that they worked hard to buy, but it also limited their belief in what they were capable of achieving. They were of a generation that tended to accept their lot in life. For all their hard work, they knew their place. They really didn't believe that they should aspire to be anything more than they were. No one expected more of them; no one thought they could do better. As long as they were happy, there was nothing really wrong with that.

I refused to accept that way of thinking. I never knew my limit or my place, never wanted to stand still and forever wanted to take a couple of steps beyond. That's why this book is for my family, particularly my own children, who have been on this journey with me and for my grandchildren whose lives stretch out ahead of them. They mean everything to me. I have come a long way in the last 50 years but I think it is always important to remember your roots. So I wrote this for them to be able to take a look back at where I came from, because my background is part of their background, too.

This book is for the friends and colleagues I have worked with.

I have seen great success and achieved many things of which I am immensely proud but I didn't do it all on my own. I have had the privilege to work with some truly remarkable people. One of my greatest skills has been in building teams of talented people who work well with and for each other. I set out to achieve this in all that I do and it is fundamental to much of my own development. It is fantastic to see what can be achieved when a group of individuals starts to work together as a team. Seeing them spark off each other to fulfil their own potential is a hugely satisfying experience and when it all comes together, the sky's the limit.

At Capita, this was particularly true. The way that we grew the business from a start-up under the noses of many large and established players was very special, as was the pace of growth we achieved. It is testament to what determination, passion and inner belief can deliver. I think it is important that the people who helped to make that happen are properly recognised. It may be that an official history of the company will never be written but my version of how the company started and became a market leader is in this book. I hope I give due credit to the wide range of people who were involved throughout the business.

The same applies, of course, to those with whom I worked in the public sector at the start of my journey. They supported me in the development of my career and set me on course to build a company that was ultimately able to service their needs. I learned so much from these colleagues, many of whom were pioneers of great change both locally and on the national scene.

More recently, with the Aldridge Foundation, in sponsoring the Academies and in working with organisations such as the Lowry, I have met and worked with people who have changed the lives of so many others for the better. That has been a true privilege.

After leaving Capita, there was no way that I could simply retire, sit back and do nothing. That's just not me. The wonderful thing about eventually becoming involved in the Academies Programme was that I could use all of my experience in working with local and central government, as well as years of business acumen, for the benefit of the young people who are our future. I would not, however, have got very far without the teams of talented people who taught me so much about the world of education that was previously completely unknown to me. This book gives me the chance to acknowledge the roles that they played.

This book is for our students.

Of all of the things that I have done, I would say that my work of the past 12 years as an Academy sponsor has been the most rewarding. There can be no greater sense of achievement than helping others to achieve their true potential. That is especially true in education. I make no excuse for emphasising throughout this book that a good education gives you choices. This should be the right of every individual, but that hasn't always been the case, and certainly not in the challenging communities where, as a Foundation, we choose to work. Neither was it the case for me.

I failed my 11-plus exam and was subjected to a standard of education more designed to encourage marking time rather than to challenge me to grow. I did not go on to the local grammar school where a better education and better opportunities appeared to flow naturally. At the time, that was a disaster for me and still haunts me today. You might now be thinking, 'Give it a rest, Rod – that was sixty years ago!' but I've never been able to forget the feeling of outrage and the belief that I had been written off before my life had really even begun. We need to wake up to the fact that this is still happening to many students today.

The gap that is so apparent between those that have and those that have not felt wide when I was a boy but today it is even wider. There are whole communities where one can see the adverse social impact this is having. This injustice affected me then and it still rankles now. The education system was divisive and it carried through into working life where there was a sense of inevitability that potential employers looked more favourably on those who had achieved traditional academic excellence – many saw themselves as part of the same 'set'. There have always been people who have underestimated me, people who have failed to believe that I could achieve what I was aiming for. Proving them wrong has always been one of the things that has driven me.

Aldridge students are encouraged to reach for the stars and to stretch the boundaries of what is achievable. I am a firm believer in the adage that 'It's not where you come from that matters but where you want to get to that counts.' Providing our students with the best possible education in top class facilities, as we do now, gives them the confidence to believe that anything is possible. We major on developing enterprising attributes and entrepreneurial instincts in our students which will increase their employment opportunities through preparing them for the world of work of tomorrow. Many will not wait for a job but create one through starting a business. Equally, in our family of academies we are now seeing young people going on to university as a natural progression if they choose to do so, from areas where their schools previously didn't even have a sixth form. And in 2013, a very talented young lady became the first Aldridge student to be awarded a place at Oxford University. Many others have followed in her footsteps since.

Education, encouragement and self-belief are what we offer our students and for them more than anyone else reading this book, I hope they embrace the mantra that has always spurred me on:

YOU'RE BETTER THAN THEY THINK YOU ARE

SIR ROD ALDRIDGE, OBE

1

IN THE BEGINNING

Many great things have happened in my life, but my most remarkable good fortune came right at the start, when I was born into a wonderfully warm and loving family.

Since then experiences in life have taught me the crucial importance and great benefits of the family as an institution. The longer I live, the more I consider just how lucky I was to come into the world as the first and only child of a decent, kind and hard-working couple called Len and Doris Aldridge.

Home was an immaculately kept semi-detached house named 'Lendor': No. 38 Foredown Drive, in Portslade, then a fast-growing area of the coastal town of Brighton and Hove. I lived there from the day I was born in Hove at 4 pm on Friday 7 November 1947 until the day I first got married at the age of twenty-two.

My mother's parents lived nearby at No. 65. She had two sisters: Joyce lived in Brighton and Phyllis, who was the wife of a sergeant major in the Army, was abroad for long periods. My father's mother lived in Portland Road, Hove and his two brothers, Alf and Peter and his sister Dorothy all lived locally. With so many relatives close at hand we had our own little community and enjoyed regular meals and get-togethers.

Yet I always felt I had something extra as well. Although my mother and father and I were happy to be members of that growing collection of individuals who were either Aldridges or Taylors (my mother's family) we were also a rock solid little unit on our own. We enjoyed the frequent, enlarged family occasions, but my mother and father and I were extra special to each other. It wasn't anything that was talked about, but I always felt supremely safe and happy with just the three of us from a very early age.

My parents were born within a year of each other midway through the First World War, my father on 21 July 1915 and my mother on 16 June 1916. She was eighteen when they met at an Oddfellows (local friendly society) dance at the Cliftonville Hall. It turned out that they even lived in the same road, my father at No. 344 and my mother at No. 257.

My mother recalled: 'I went with my friend Olive and two brothers came over and asked us to dance. That was Len Aldridge and his older brother Alf. Len asked me and we found we both loved dancing and got on so well together on the dance floor. He was lovely and I fell for him. I knew straight away, "This is the one".' The courtship was happy but, in those very different pre-war times, the couple were very carefully controlled by their parents. My mother said: 'We were walking out together for three years or more but I always had to be in by ten o'clock. If we weren't back on time my father would be standing in the street. He was so strict. He would curl up if he could see the way young ones carry on today, living together after they have only just met.' I think my mother and father were meant for each other. They were a great partnership and I am certain neither of them ever had eyes for anyone else.

My parents married on 31 July 1938. Remarkably Alf and Olive also fell in love and later also got married! It must have been quite a night at the Cliftonville Hall. My father worked for Harringtons, a local coach-building firm. He started on an apprenticeship straight from school when he was just fifteen and became a highly skilled metalworker who put many of the important finishing touches to the coaches that had earned Harringtons a national and international reputation.

There were to be no peaceful early years for my parents, as World

War Two began in 1939. My father joined the Army soon after war was declared and served in North Africa and in India. I don't know a lot about what happened to him, because he very rarely talked about it. Sadly, I believe he had a very bad time and the war took a terrible toll on his health. By the time he came home, although he went straight back to work in the factory, he was not a well man.

In our family we were all working class and proud of it, but we had a big work ethic and were always striving to do better. My parents owned their own house, which was quite unusual in those days. The house was bought for £750 when they got married before the war. They paid a deposit of £20 and had a mortgage, which my mother said my father worked: 'All the hours God made' to pay. My mother insists Foredown Drive was 'A very posh road'.

Portslade is near Brighton, which is associated with fun and became notorious as a venue for couples seeking a divorce in the days when proof of infidelity was required. A receipt for an overnight stay in a hotel or boarding house, sharing a room with someone other than your spouse, would usually do the trick. It also became known for clashes between the 'Mods and Rockers', gangs of youths who fought running battles on bank holidays in the sixties. Hove was more upmarket with wider roads and many palatial homes where lots of wealthy people lived. Then there is Upper Portslade where we lived. My mother classed it as a 'posh' area, whereas Lower Portslade had many 'rough areas'. As a youth, when trying to impress people about where I lived, I said that I lived in, 'Portslade, near Hove actually!'

My parents were determined to own their own home. Often they would say to me: 'It's better to have a mortgage and buy your house than to waste money on paying rent to a landlord.' It was part of their upbringing and it became part of my upbringing as well. My parents' mortgage came from the Oddfellows, the long-standing friendly society that played a big part in their lives. My father played cricket for them on a Sunday and the family went to watch and would bring a picnic. Our family included Uncle Lou, who was a local secretary of the Oddfellows. He used to keep parrots and had one in each room of his house.

My father worked very long hours in the factory. He put in a lot of overtime to earn enough money to keep the family going. He worked there with great diligence and dedication and it was hard, manual work. He was also a union representative, and served for over twenty years as the local branch secretary for the National Union of Sheet Metal Workers & Coppersmiths. My mother had worked before I came along, at Ronuk, a local firm that produced floor polish. She gave that up when she got married. During the war she went back to work and also found herself at Harringtons, where they were kept busy helping to provide parts for Spitfires.

I know all mothers love their babies, but my mother was completely devoted to me from the moment I arrived, even if I was the wrong sex! My mother said:

I had always loved dressing up and I really wanted us to have a girl. When Rodney was born I loved him straight away and I used to dress him up. He was born in one of the best nursing homes in The Drive in Hove. Nowadays mothers are in and out the same day, but it was different then. I was in the nursing home for a fortnight. Rodney was nearly eight pounds when he arrived. He was a very good baby. He had such lovely hair. Although he was my son, I always say he was so pretty. When he was small I used to dress him all in white. My husband's sister Dorothy made all his clothes and she made him some beautiful white romper suits. We had a lovely pram and I was out with him one day and a lady came up to me and she said, 'Excuse me do you ever let him get in the coal box?' Just because he looked so perfect!

I was Christened Rodney Malcolm Aldridge, apparently named after HMS *Rodney*, the British battleship famous for sinking the *Bismarck*, the pride of Hitler's fleet! My mother might have been disappointed that I wasn't a girl, but my dad's father was absolutely delighted. I was the only Aldridge boy at the time and he told my mother he was very pleased that his name was going to be carried on. Unfortunately, Benjamin Aldridge was the grandfather I was destined never to get to know. He died when I was just two years old so I never had the chance to talk to him about his extraordinary military career. While almost all of my relatives lived and worked in pretty ordinary jobs in the Portslade area, Benjamin had a very successful career in the British Army.

He enlisted as a humble private in 1911 and rose through the ranks to become a quartermaster sergeant in the Royal Sussex Regiment. He obviously had the ability to manage a large number of people. Between the two world wars this difficult and demanding job took him from postings like Bermuda, Jamaica and Trinidad in the West Indies to spells in India and Singapore. It also involved being in Malta for two-and-a-half years and a commission with A Company, serving near the Panama Canal.

The family went with him and my Aunt Dorothy was born in Jamaica and Uncle Peter in India. My granddad was away from 1919 until 1936, before returning to live in Hove. Old army records pay fulsome tribute to Benjamin's industrious, loyal and high standard of service throughout his colourful career, and a prized family heirloom is the silver kettle he won for playing hockey. It must have been a very dangerous game the way they played it. In one match he was hit in the mouth and had several teeth knocked out! I am proud to say that I now have the silver kettle as Uncle Peter gave it to me for my seventieth birthday.

When I discovered my grandfather had done all this it made me wonder years later if I had inherited some of his drive and energy. Evidently he firmly believed in careful preparation and diligent hard work. They are certainly traits I've been happy to find in myself and to follow.

I am very grateful to my cousin Sonia for providing this fascinating information. With her husband, Chris, she has diligently researched our family history. What I find surprising is that after all of that travelling the family returned to Hove and was able to settle down without the wanderlust returning in later life.

My first public appearance came when I was pageboy at the wedding of Sonia's parents, my father's younger brother Peter and his wife-to-be Ann. I was only two-and-a-half at the time, but the experience of being a pageboy was an early example of my parents' determination that everything had to be perfect in our family. I was dressed for the part and rehearsed endlessly for the role. This involved me walking up and down the hall at home under careful guidance of my mother, who was holding a towel attached to her waist to represent the train of the bride's dress.

My parents were wonderfully caring and determined we would always do our absolute best. They were concerned never to look foolish, consequently my world was never about taking risks: if you couldn't do something well, then you didn't do it. So you practiced in case you made a mistake and showed yourself up, an early lesson I have never forgotten.

My Aunty Ann recently recalled my performance as a pageboy: 'You were perfect in every way. The wedding was at St Leonard's Church, which is large with a huge aisle so there was a long walk. You held my train and did your job beautifully. You were dressed completely in white: white shirt, white trousers, white socks and even white shoes.' Uncle Peter added sharply: 'All that was missing was a halo!'

Peter's quick sense of humour was something he shared with my father and, according to my uncle, it was my father who was the driving force behind organising family occasions. 'Len was a lovely chap,' said Peter. 'He was great at getting people together for a cricket match or a family picnic. He was a fun person and when he got older he looked just like you do now,' he told me.

Ours was clearly a family that enjoyed doing things together and I grew to appreciate this. Every Thursday we would all go to Nannie Aldridge's house, 344 Portland Road, Hove, the family home since 1936. My Nan was a very strong personality who kept the family together with No. 344 very much the hub of the Aldridge family. It involved two changes on the bus to get from Foredown Drive to Portland Road, but it was worth it for a tea that included wonderful cream cakes and jam doughnuts. At the time my Aunt Dorothy was also living there with her daughter, Brenda, and so with my Aunty Ann and my cousin Sonia it was a pretty full-on time.

We watched Eamonn Andrews presenting *Crackerjack* on TV. This was a great treat as we didn't have a television in our house until much later. One downside was my nan's budgerigar which she would release and allow to fly freely around the room. I hated this, as it would suddenly swoop and attempt to land on your head!

Sometimes we would also go down on a Saturday evening when other members of the Aldridge family would come. It would culminate in us playing card games such as 'jingles' and 'chase the ace'. I liked this because I seemed to win and I would take my winnings back home and store them in my drawer, regularly counting the money I had in my 'bank'.

We also watched television series such as *Dixon of Dock Green*. I still recall the phrase from Sergeant George Dixon of 'Evening all', as he saluted to the camera. There was also *Quatermass*, a BBC science fiction series which really frightened the life out of me.

My mother's parents moved to a house just up the road from us at No. 65 Foredown Drive in 1940 because they wanted to be closer to my mother. I called my maternal grandfather Poppy or Pop – a term that my own grandchildren use for me now – and he used to take me to school and collect me. We spent a lot of time together and he meant a great deal to me, regularly coming to watch me play football for the school team. My mother looked after my grandparents, effectively acting as a housekeeper. This created tension between my mother and father and was one of the rare things they argued over. Another was my mother wanting rooms redecorated and the outside of the house painted. This had a great effect on me and could well have been the beginnings of my sense of wanting to 'outsource' tasks. I could never see the sense of my father using the two weeks off he had from working in a factory to be up a ladder painting the house.

Sundays were all about having tea at home with Nan and Pop. We would always have tinned salmon. There would probably also be strawberries and cream to follow or some of my mother's incredible trifle.

It was also my task to go up to see Nan and Pop at least twice a week when I came home from school. Often I would spend Saturday afternoons there watching *Grandstand* with Peter Dimmock. My grandfather loved a bet on the horses and a neighbour across the road, Mr Royston, had an account with a local bookmaker, which meant that Pop could put bets on by telephone from Mr Royston's house without

Nan knowing what he was spending! I was also grateful to Mr Royston as I recall watching the 1958 World Cup Final between Brazil and Sweden on his TV, seeing for the first time the skills of the young Pelé.

Another memorable meal was when my father would return home on his bicycle having been down to the seafront to bring home a crab, and cockles or winkles. I can clearly remember sitting around with a needle removing the cockles from their shells. Some of the less memorable meals were bubble-and-squeak, which appeared on a Monday to use up the food from a Sunday. Yuk! I can still smell it today!

My birthday is two days after Bonfire Night and my dad used to make a huge fuss of the occasion. We would have a big bonfire in the garden with the whole family. It was a very important event in my life when I was younger. My dad made the Guy from old clothing and stuffed it with paper along with the occasional firecracker to make you jump as it burned. The Guy had pride of place in the kitchen, sitting on a chair for two weeks leading up to the event. It was very scary if you went into the kitchen with the light off and forgot the Guy was there. My father loved everyone to be happy. Sometimes he would laugh so much he had watery eyes, which is another trait I have inherited.

Christmases were always great family occasions. We were sent to bed early so the grown ups could enjoy themselves drinking and filling the stockings with presents from 'Father Christmas'. My cousin and I would pretend to be asleep, but could hear everything that was going on.

One Christmas I remember well is 1958. My father took my cousin Andrea and I along with my uncle to see Brighton and Hove Albion play Fulham at the Goldstone on Boxing Day. It turned out to be historic, because there was a record crowd of 36,747. As young children of eleven and ten respectively we were moved over the heads of people to be allowed to sit on the area between the pitch and the terraces. We had a great view and I was able to see the wonderful Johnny Haynes and the legendary Jimmy Hill close up. Brighton won and we walked home to Foredown Drive as very happy people.

It sounds idyllic and in many ways it was, but there was also a very cautious side to my parents, which I feel was particularly restrictive in my development. I was not encouraged to make friends. I did not do some of the normal boyish things, such as join the cubs or scouts. My parents did everything to ensure the three of us had a very safe existence. In essence, they did everything they possibly could to protect me. Yet it wasn't easy being an only child. Looking back I think it was quite claustrophobic. Being born just after the war, I believe that they had wanted to have children for quite a time. I soon learned I meant everything to them. It was quite a responsibility and put pressure on me to perform at my very best in everything that I did at every stage of my life.

It was a protected, positive environment designed to give me all I needed. Visitors to our house were not welcome unless my mother was aware well in advance that they were coming or had been specially invited.

At the front of the house was a small lawn, immaculately kept with a border of flowers around it. The doorstep had a brass sill that was religiously cleaned by my mother every day so you could see your face in it. Woe betide any visitor who the stood on the gleaming brass when they entered. I was trained from an early age always to step carefully over it and one of my schoolmates still remembers the telling off he got for standing on it!

The front sitting room was only used for special occasions when we had guests. It was never used by the three of us, unless my father was redecorating the family room. The red lounge suite was covered in white sheets and the curtains left partially drawn to ensure that no sunlight could get through to fade the precious furniture. When the sitting room was used for special occasions, like Christmas or birthdays, it became a very lively space.

Going round the house again in my mind I can remember how the atmosphere changed when we got our first television set when I was thirteen years old. It was around the time that ITV started. There were no rentals for us. My mother had saved up for weeks so that we could buy a TV outright. The new PYE set had pride of place in front of the French windows, which were never to be opened again. It was where we watched together the first ever episode of *Coronation Street* in December 1960. A particular favourite was *Sunday Night at the London*

Palladium with Bruce Forsyth, a wonderful person, who I later had the pleasure of meeting socially and playing golf with. This also became the home of many sporting memories that I watched with my father, including England winning the World Cup in 1966, Manchester United winning the European Cup at Wembley for Sir Matt Busby, Chelsea beating Leeds in the FA cup Final and Celtic winning the European Cup. Together we watched some of the fights between Muhammad Ali and Sonny Liston and I remember watching Buzz Aldrin and Neil Armstrong walking on the moon in 1969.

Meals were always taken together. I can remember how pressurized this felt. If I did not want to eat the food on my plate it was virtually impossible to leave it without having a heated discussion. On reflection, the important thing is that we had time together as a family and talked about various things that were going on in our lives. Only when I went to work at sixteen were family meals restricted to evening meals.

The table had the ability to be enlarged to house bigger gatherings or for card evenings. It was also used for my father and me to complete large jigsaw puzzles. I can still remember the one we had of the Coronation and the crowd scene as the Queen returned to Buckingham Palace in the state coach. The joy on people's faces was fully apparent and it was very difficult to piece together.

My parents were not heavy disciplinarians. I was rarely smacked, The looks on their faces got their message across very effectively. I knew when I was in danger of stepping out of line. If this approach failed I was sent to my room, which only became a real punishment once we had a TV!

Surprisingly, my parents both smoked, which horrified my mother in later life and she was very hard on all of my own children who participated in that 'filthy habit'. My father officially gave up smoking because of his heart issues. However, I caught him more than once afterwards having a crafty smoke in his shed. He would quickly throw the cigarette away, hoping that I had not seen him. It was always the smell on the clothes that gave it away.

Before I went to school in the morning my mother would go over my times tables, which I learned forwards, backwards and through different permutations thrown at me. I credit her for developing my love of numbers. Her unrelenting drive to ensure that I came top in the weekly tables test still leads me to be a supporter of getting the basics right. She also used to go over the list of twenty words I had to learn for a weekly spelling test. The numbers came much easier to me than the spelling and that's still very much the case today.

The kitchen had a larder in it, which, believe it or not, was used by my mother as a safe haven whenever there was a thunderstorm. We used to sit in the larder playing cards until the storm passed. She was very scared of thunder and lightning which may have originated with the fear associated with the noise of bombs dropping in the war. One story goes that she walked up the road to check on my Nan and Granddad after a raid when the streets were in the total darkness imposed by blackout regulations. Only when she saw the street in daylight did she realise that she must have walked around the edge of a huge bomb crater. One wayward footstep and she would have plunged into a massive hole filled with jagged debris.

My parents' careful approach meant that you saved up for things. HP (hire purchase) was not a feature in their world. They thought, 'Why pay the interest? Wait until you can afford it!' At first the only item on long-term credit was the mortgage and my mother was an incredible manager of money. She saved money in jam jars, keeping a different jam jar for each household bill, always ensuring there was enough in the jar to pay the bill when it arrived. Even latterly, at one hundred years of age she did a monthly bank reconciliation and woe betide you if you were the one in the family who had not presented a cheque that she had issued for a birthday or Christmas gift.

Upstairs, the spare bedroom was used by my father as an office for his union work. Also in this room was an old gramophone on which my father played vinyl records while working on his trade union books. He spent a great deal of time in this room and any union member who visited the house was rapidly directed upstairs and rarely invited into the lounge. If the branch chairman came, the front room was opened up for him, as he was considered important by my mother.

At the front of the house was the bathroom and to the left of this was my mother and father's bedroom, which was very traditionally furnished with two large free-standing wardrobes and a dressing table in the bay window. I recall it most for the times that my father was in bed recovering from various illnesses that he had and the long conversations we had or the games of cards we played. The view from the window was great in that you could see down to the sea in the distance and all the way up and down the road. From the window you could also see that the gardens were well kept. Any garden not kept to a high standard was talked about.

My room at the top of the stairs was my domain. There was an airing cupboard one side of a fireplace and a cupboard that housed all my clothes and toys on the other. Growing up as an only child I designed games where I played both the home and away team. One involved a balloon and kicking it athletically over my head, giving me the opportunity to dive onto the bed as a goalkeeper to make a save, the wall along by my bed being the goal. The resounding thud on the bed brought shouts from downstairs, with the warning that I would crack the ceiling in the lounge.

To the left of my bed was a bedside table on which there was a radio, which was a birthday gift from my parents. It was my window to the outside world. I listened to boxing matches involving Henry Cooper and the commentary of Harry Carpenter, football games, *The Archers* and to Radio Luxembourg. And I was a Radio Caroline fan. I also, of course, listened to John Arlott's wonderful, rich commentaries on the Test matches. My bedroom window looked out onto the garden, with the long ladders that my father used to decorate the house propped up against the wall. The ladders proved to be a wonderful home for birds to make their nests and provided an amazing opportunity viewed from behind the curtains to see eggs hatched, the young fed and then to see the moment when they first flew and left the nest.

I spent hours in this room building up my stamp collection, reading my football books and cutting pictures out of the newspapers that would go into my scrapbook with the hope that I would one day get them autographed. This covered both football and cricket and proved to be the most effective way for me to learn the map of the UK through finding out where the clubs' home grounds were. I linked these with the relevant geography for the area, such as where ports were or coal fields. It also taught me about where the major cities were and the seaside towns similar to Brighton. It enabled me to calculate the miles that The Albion had to travel to play its next game. I could name the players in the team photographs and individual pictures without reference to the printed words beneath them.

I lived for Sundays when my father took me to the park to play cricket. He was a good cricketer, but it did not stop me from hammering the ball around the park, forcing him to run after it while I ran up and down the wicket aiming to make a fifty or, even better, a century.

The garden was always kept tidy. There was a large piece of grass to one side and a smaller one to the left with a path going the whole of the way up the garden to the top where there was a space for potatoes to grow. From this small area my father fed us all every year with potatoes, carrots, peas, beans, beetroot, tomatoes, swede, cabbage, broad beans, strawberries, raspberries and rhubarb. He also grew flowers such as sweet peas and chrysanthemums and grew plants like wallflowers and marigolds from seed. I was allocated a small space as my garden where I planted various crops mirroring my father's efforts. I didn't really take to this. Playing with a ball was far more fun.

To me the garden was a sports pitch to enable me to develop my football and, most importantly, cricket skills. Here again I invented a game where I was both the bowler and batsman. The stumps were set in a wooden block made by my father and placed about halfway down the path. I placed a deckchair behind the stumps to act as the wicketkeeper. With my bat in my left hand I would run up and bowl and as it bounced back from the wall I changed my bat from my left to right hand to be ready at the crease to play a shot. The run-up would depend if I were mimicking Freddie Trueman as a fast bowler or Jim Laker as a slow offspin bowler. When my cousin Keith came to visit we had a more conventional game of cricket, but the fence was always four runs and anything over the fence into our poor neighbour Mr Smith's garden was six runs and out!

It was a wonderful world to me. There was also a wall outside the house near the road where, at that time, no cars were parked. I used to throw the ball hard against the wall and react to the speed it came off to catch it, which was why I was very good at fielding. My practising paid off even if it was in a world of my own. I suppose it sounds weird now, but I didn't know anything different.

Over time the garden shed was replaced by a garage that housed the Vauxhall car my father bought, and it became his workshop when he was made redundant. He would take in panel-beating jobs and it also housed all his painting and decorating equipment. It was also the space where he 'built', rather than bought, my Christmas presents. He made me a fire station where the doors opened together, similar to a real fire station and it even had a pole for fireman to come down. Best of all was a fort that he designed and built with a practical feature that the cowboys and Indians could be stored inside by lifting up the top of the fort and using a built-in space below. My mother approved of this as this meant my room was kept tidy. It even had a working drawbridge. The pleasure this gave me was endless.

I look back on my childhood with massive fondness. I know I was loved very much. My parents helped in every way they could. I do now see it was a limited and isolated period, but I was happy with my own company as a young boy and even today I like my own space. During these years I thought a lot about what I was going to do when I grew up and how I was going to emulate the successes of my idols. Unfortunately, I never did open the batting for England at Lord's or captain Brighton & Hove Albion at the Goldstone Ground!

My mother did everything for me. There was always food on the table and the house was kept in an immaculate condition. She was a hard taskmaster but did a great deal to keep me focused on my studies at every age! I was very, very lucky because I felt safe and loved. I had a sort of fantastically safe underpinning that I believed would protect me from any eventuality.

One of my earliest memories is of my first day at St Nicholas School in Portslade. I was immaculately dressed, and photographs convince me that my mother really did want a girl, because there is a very feminine look to some of the things I was wearing! Until then I had been very carefully protected. I was very cautious about just about everything in life. Everything that I did at school was a shock because I had never spent very much time with other children. I remember the surprise of that first day and I can recall my mother standing anxiously at the door of the classroom, not really wanting to let me go in. She told the tale that she went shopping in Brighton because she was too upset to go home. But after she had gone I found it was quite exciting meeting new people in a new environment. I think I quite enjoyed it, frankly.

It was very clear that some of the people I met at school were very different from us. It was a bit daunting for a while and I was always fairly quiet and withdrawn in class. It was such a change. My home was very warm and loving and we were very important to each other. I think my father wanted more children but I am not so sure my mother did. It would have been interesting to see what changes the arrival of a brother or sister would have made to my life. I sense it would have helped me a lot because the responsibility of being an only child has been quite onerous. I have always felt it my job to be there for my parents. Strangely, I still don't feel free of that. It is part of me in the way I act towards people and is what I taught my own children. I believe passionately in the family unit and I believe you have a responsibility to respect your parents.

My parents certainly gave me everything they possibly could. My education was always a top priority for them from as long ago as I can remember. As an investment in me they even bought a complete set of *Encyclopaedia Britannica* from a door-to-door salesman. This was very expensive for them, but they wanted to me learn and develop in ways with which they felt they couldn't help. The books were fantastic, opening a whole new world, and they instantly gave me a resource where I could go and find out about things. My father even persuaded my mother that they should be paid for on hire purchase, going against an important part of their 'safety first' financial philosophy.

They went without a lot of things because of me, but clearly these were sacrifices they were happy to make. There were quite a lot of restrictions designed to keep me away from any hint of possible danger. I wasn't allowed to go on school trips, for example. In their way they were not being unkind, this was all part of their protection and at the time I understood that.

Portslade was a very comfortable place in which to live and to grow up. We would visit the beach in Hove on occasions even though my mother intensely disliked being out of her comfort zone. I shared my mother's views about the seaside. I hated the pebbles on the beach and the fact that sand only appeared close to the water's edge, which was not a place I ventured too close to. The best things were the ice creams and the noise of the sea. I still love that sound today. My father was a good swimmer and regularly went for a swim during the summer. I never saw my mother in a swimsuit or going into the sea. I eventually learned how to swim at the age of twenty-six. Consequently, the seaside does not hold great memories for me, although being helped by my father to sail boats on the nearby, and hugely popular, Hove Lagoon are treasured times.

I hope I'm not making my childhood seem too harsh and austere. My parents' generation had been through a great deal of hardship. Times were tough in those post-war years. Food rationing did not end until 1954 when I was seven years old, although my mother insisted on using real butter rather than margarine, as she saw this as symbolic of being 'better off'!

We always did lots of things together as a family. One of the treats was to go out to the cinema in Brighton, where the large blockbuster films were on a very wide screen, and I particularly remember *South Pacific* and *Oklahoma*. We were also great fans of Norman Wisdom films. It was a big treat to go to see a film and we would look forward to the prospect for days.

I also have some wonderful memories of some brilliant holidays, spending weeks with my Uncle Bert and my Aunt Emily along with their daughter Margaret on the farm that he managed just outside Henfield. I would help with feeding the chickens and pigs that they kept. We even made the feed of a mixture of bread and water in large buckets in their huge kitchen. My greatest excitement was when I joined my uncle on the tractor during haymaking. Lunch was cheese sandwiches with pickle and an apple or orange. They were long special summers, and I remember watching the sun rise and set.

We were also fortunate to have holidays abroad, which were certainly unusual in those days. My uncle Tom served abroad in many different parts of the world including Nairobi and in Germany. When he was in Germany it gave the extended family the opportunity to visit my uncle, my Aunt Phyllis and my cousin Andrea for holidays. This was quite an incredible experience for us. We left on the train from Brighton Station to London and then caught another train to Harwich where we took the ferry to the Hook of Holland and then across to Germany. I recall carrying a very small suitcase, presumably to enable me to feel grown up. The customs officer played his part by marking the case with chalk in the same way as they did our family luggage. It was such an adventure going to sleep in a cabin and waking up in Holland. I remember watching the coat hanger on the back of the cabin door swaying viciously as the boat bobbed about on the crossing.

My uncle was stationed in Münster and we visited the area where there was a dam that had been attacked by the British wartime bombers, known as the 'Dambusters'. We obviously spent a great of time in the Mess, the home of all the British soldiers, however with my uncle being a sergeant major we were afforded many special privileges. When later he returned home to complete his service in England, stationed in Bulford in Somerset, we also had some great times there on the compulsory two-week holiday that my father was forced to take, when the entire factory closed for the period. When my uncle left the services the couple ended up buying a house in Three Bridges, near Crawley; he paid for it outright from his Army settlement. We even had great holidays there with my cousins Andrea and Elaine, despite the fact it was only an hour's journey by car from our home. Amazingly, twenty years later I was to take that journey in my own car every day when I went to work for Crawley Urban District Council as an accountant.

Childhood is very precious and my parents did everything they could to give me a happy one. I had some great times when I was growing up and by the time I was seven or eight I had another interest that helped me to experience things outside of home and family. I discovered that I could dance and this talent proved to be a game changer for me, in more ways than one.

2

MY DANCING
YEARS

I can't say I recall it too clearly, but my first step into the world of ballroom dancing must have been taken when I was just seven. It would have a profound influence on my life for the next fifteen years and in many ways it shaped me as a person. Dancing most definitely increased my belief in my own ability, which flowed over into how I thought, acted and the goals that I set myself and went on to achieve in other areas of life.

My parents had met each other going to dances and it was one of the great joys they shared together, with evenings at The Regent Ballroom in Brighton dancing to the Syd Dean Band, as well as at The King Alfred in Hove. In the 1950s, the TV series *Come Dancing*, hosted by Judith Chalmers and David Jacobs, was a regular television treat enjoyed by millions. My mum and dad loved the show, but they really preferred to dance themselves rather than watch others. I took an interest in dancing early on and my parents encouraged me to try it. To a shy young boy, it seemed like an exciting new adventure. I took to it straight away.

Fortunately, I inherited some natural ability as well as my parents' passion for music and movement and with help from them I took my first simple dance steps at home. My mum and dad were both delighted at my enthusiasm. Acting as my dance partner, Mum loved to show me steps and help me keep in time to the music.

My parents took me to join a local dance school that had been recommended to them. The lead teachers of the school were Monica and Jimmy Priestly, who held classes at the Cliftonville Hall in Hove, the home of the Oddfellows, where my mother and father had first met. The Priestlys were a wonderful couple. Jimmy had sustained a serious leg injury during the war and had a plate in his leg just above the knee, yet he could still glide around the floor.

I was full of trepidation when I first joined, but I enjoyed myself almost immediately. To my great joy I soon found that, with Monica and Jimmy's help, dancing was definitely something I could do and enjoy.

Of course I realised that most boys my age wouldn't have dreamed of learning to dance. It was seen very much as a 'girlie' activity, so I definitely didn't advertise my new hobby to my schoolmates. But the news soon got out and people made jokes. I was nicknamed 'Waltzing Matilda'! Even some members of my immediate family pulled my leg about it. I never really minded the teasing because I had found something I enjoyed that allowed me to express myself.

I was involved with 'Old Time Dancing', which is now known as 'Modern Sequence Dancing'. This involved learning a sequence of dance steps which were repeated over and over again. There were more than twenty such dances but the most well-known were the Veleta, the Military Two Step, the Magenta Tango, the Boston Two Step and the Mayfair Quick Step.

I can see now that taking up dancing was completely out of left field, but I have never been afraid of going my own way. As soon as I realized how much I enjoyed it, I started not only to take dancing exams, but also to go in for competitions, which appealed to my competitive nature. Dancing exams enabled me to measure the improvement that I was making over various levels. The awards you received were bronze, silver, gold, gold bar, gold cross and the national award, which effectively recognised that you had 'arrived' as a dancer. I passed the national award exam on 20 September 1958 at the age of eleven.

These exams were highly stressful to me. All the students had to turn up at the same time and to wait their turn, and when your name was called you went into the hall. The examiner sat at the end, behind a table. My partner on these occasions was Monica Priestly who, given that I was only nine at the time, was several feet taller than me. I had to perform three dances in front of the examiner, who was both watching your feet and writing notes all through the performance. At the end of this I returned to the small room to await the result. Luckily I passed all of them on the first attempt, several at highly commended level. There was usually a celebration event at the school when you received your award, and the dreaded handwritten report that pointed out your faults was sometimes difficult to read! Good results for the school were celebrated because it attracted more students.

One happy early discovery was that the vast majority of the other young dancers were girls. There were one or two other boys but there were lots and lots of girls, which I loved. I soon found myself very much in demand in the dancing world. It was a world where it was common to see two girls dancing together for lack of male partners, so to have a boy and a girl partnering each other was seen as something special. I felt special and I liked that.

My parents insisted I had to be dressed properly. Initially I used to wear smart trousers, white shirt and a black bow tie. When I was a little older I would be in a full tail suit. You had to look right; it was all part of the presentation and very important. I loved it. I enjoyed performing. It took me into a completely different world, where I felt safe and successful.

My first tail suit was provided by Broadley Brothers in Hove, but as I grew taller I had to have them made in London. I recall travelling up from Brighton by train on Saturdays to a tailor in Savile Row to have several fittings for a brand new tail suit. These suits took a hammering as they were carried around in a suitcase to numerous events in numerous towns, along with my partner's dress which had a large cover to accommodate its many layers.

Quite quickly I started winning dance competitions and that really boosted my confidence. There were different age ranges for these competitions that went from under-twelve and then progressed to twelve-to-sixteen, before the senior level. Most competitions had two or three rounds followed by a semi-final and final and for each round you danced three different dances. The three or four adjudicators would stand in the middle of the floor, as with modern sequence dancing; unlike modern ballroom dancing, the contestants moved around the outside of the floor. The final would normally consist of six couples with prizes for only the first three. Your objective here was to be placed first by all the adjudicators. I was schooled to smile throughout and look confident, irrespective of the sweat pouring off my brow and all of the exertion making it difficult to breathe!

I practiced twice a week, once in a general class and then in a private lesson with Jimmy for an hour. I became more and more accomplished as a result of his teaching. The need to express myself through the music brought me out of my shell and helped me to develop as a person. This was a really different world and contrasted sharply with my more 'closed' home life. All of a sudden I was in a wider world where I could dance in front of a lot of people with complete confidence because I knew I was good. It was a way of getting over my shyness, because when you dance you need to show your emotion. At any level it is impossible to dance with someone that you do not enjoy spending time with, whether it is on the dance floor, in the practice studio or when travelling to competition venues.

Dancing is a very emotional activity and as I grew older I really enjoyed this aspect of it, using it as an outlet for my emotions. Today when you look at some of the dancers on TV's *Strictly Come Dancing*, a programme that I love, you can see the bond of trust that appears and there is no doubt that a relationship develops. I never went to a youth club like other kids because it really did not appeal to me to socialize in that way. I never met girls at school because I went to an all-boys school, so my only way of meeting girls was in the world of dancing, where I felt confident and competent.

My mother fondly remembered my early dancing days and said:

Rodney's dad and I always loved dancing. We were both so pleased when it turned out that Rodney liked it, too. And it was wonderful that he was so good at it. He was an excellent dancer and he went on to represent Sussex. We were over the moon and we always thought, 'He must get it from us!'

When he was younger he used to come in the evenings

dancing with us and we encouraged him to have a go himself. As soon as he started dancing classes he was off! It was wonderful he was so good at it and I think it helped him in other ways. I noticed when he was at school, when he went up to get a prize he was the only boy that went up with his back nice and perfectly straight. The dancing really helped his posture.

Rodney went on dancing until he was a grown man. Then he gave up competitions and pretty well stopped dancing. We travelled miles and miles to competitions altogether. I have marvellous memories of his dancing days. It was wonderful to have something we could all do together. He worked very hard and did such a lot of practice to make him as perfect as possible. He is very determined when he sets his mind on something.

My first dancing partner at the dance school was Marilyn Tyson. I was eight years old and she was nine. She lived near us in Foredown Drive. Marilyn was slightly taller than me and had ringlets in her hair.

My talent was soon noticed and my parents were approached to see if I was prepared to partner a very talented girl called Cheryl Fletcher. She had been dancing very successfully with another girl. Her parents took her dancing very seriously, with her mother making all of Cheryl's spectacular dresses, and they decided that for her to progress she needed to dance with a boy. I was selected as a suitable partner and, after the inevitable bust up when her current partner was told, our partnership began.

We danced very successfully together for several years and won many competitions. The two most notable achievements we had were to win the under-twelve South of England Championships, held in Lewisham Town Hall, and then to finish third in the All England Championships, held at the Lyceum Ballroom in London. That was quite an achievement as even at that age it was a very competitive field. The winner was Richard Gleave, who went on to have an illustrious dancing career, becoming a world champion and receiving an OBE for services to dance in 2012.

Dancing was also quite a bitchy world in some ways. One of the most bizarre things that happened was when I was banned from the dance floor at the age of thirteen! My mother and father and Cheryl's parents had put us forward to do demonstrations at parties and local functions in Brighton and Hove. One venue where we regularly danced was hosted by Douglas Reeve, a legend in the city who fronted *Tuesday Night at the Dome* and was famous for playing the massive theatre organ in the Corn Exchange. The venue was packed out every week with over 1,000 people and we were booked to come on at around 8 p.m. to perform two numbers. It was very exciting changing backstage with all the other performers and peeping through the curtains to see the place fill up. We even featured on the billboards for the evening.

Cheryl and I waited in the wings on either side of the stage, listening for Douglas Reeve's organ music to start. The demonstration was designed for us to meet in the middle by way of a series of interlocking steps before going into our dance routine. This was quite a nerve-racking performance for a thirteen-year-old. We were a great success and were always asked to do a third dance as an encore.

Our parents were paid expense money for the travelling and perhaps a bit extra for our time, not that my partner and I knew anything about it. Evidently this contravened our amateur status under the rules of the Professional Dance Association. All of a sudden the dancing authorities came down on us like a ton of bricks. We were banned from performing for six months! There was a lot of rivalry and jealousy in dancing and I think we must have fallen victim to that.

Although Cheryl and I danced together for quite a while, the ban from dancing took its toll and the break from competitions seemed to change our relationship. I remember meeting up with her at Hove Town Hall for a dance event a month or so into our ban and we realised the two of us weren't quite right together any more and it was time to move on.

One amazing subsequent coincidence involved the guy who supported Douglas Reeve and played the piano, an elderly chap called William Clark. When I turned up at the age of sixteen to work at East Sussex County Council as the postboy, I walked into the section responsible for making all the cheque payments and who was there as head of the section but the same William Clark. Neither of us ever referred to our roles at *Tuesday Night at the Dome*.

24

Moving on in my dancing also involved moving teachers to Les and Audrey Abernethy-Lewis. This was not easy as Jimmy had taken me a long way, but if I was to improve it was clear that I needed a teacher who was considered to be a bigger force in the dance world. Les Abernethy was that person. He was in great demand as a judge on the national scene.

While there was no transfer fee involved in dancing, I was definitely seen as a catch for their rival school, the Landa School of Dancing. There was a girl there whom they considered was perfect for me, who again had been dancing with another girl. Her name was Sylvia Candy. She was very talented, probably the best partner I ever had. And she was gorgeous! We were both fourteen and danced together for two years, winning lots of competitions. Sylvia was a very pretty girl with wonderful blue eyes and a great smile. I was very much attracted to her, but there was never any reciprocation and she would dash off to see her various boyfriends after the competitions. There came a point where I wasn't happy with the situation and it became increasingly difficult between us. This began to show on the dance floor, where it was obvious to others, including our teacher and the judges, that we were not enjoying dancing together, which led to us splitting up.

By this time I was approaching sixteen, which meant I had to move on to the totally different world of the adult age group. My priorities were also changing with my O Level studies at school and later leaving school to start work. However, I still enjoyed dancing and continued to attend the classes held by Les and Audrey at Portslade Town Hall. During my partnership with Sylvia I had competed against a girl called Ann Fellingham. She had a group of male friends associated with her then dance partner who went to Hove Grammar School and came along to the Town Hall to learn how to dance. This was the very school that I would have attended had I passed my 11-plus.

Immediately I met the grammar-school pupils I felt inferior intellectually, and they were quick to react when they learned I went to Portslade Secondary School. My salvation was my dancing, because they all had two left feet and were struggling to pick up the steps, much to their annoyance. Compared to them I seemed like Fred Astaire! So on the dance floor I was superior, while they subsequently went on to

Cambridge and Oxford universities. I can honestly say I would eagerly have changed places with them. My relationship with Ann developed and she became my dancing partner, then my girlfriend and ultimately we married.

Dancing undoubtedly changed my life in so many different and positive ways. During my competitive career I danced all over the country, although mainly in London and the South East. Venues included Lewisham Town Hall, The Lyceum, Kensington & Chelsea Town Hall, Hastings, Margate, Ramsgate, Butlins at Bognor Regis, Bromley, Slough, and Birmingham. Of course, there were also more local venues in and around Brighton, such as the Carfax in Horsham, at Worthing Pavilion, Glebe Hall in Hove and at Portslade Town Hall.

There were three very special venues where I danced which I will always remember. These were the ACE Club in London, the Tower Ballroom in Blackpool and the Royal Albert Hall.

The ACE Club competitions were for two age ranges: over-sixteen years of age and for the over-forties. It was always held on a Sunday at what is now the Tavistock Hotel in Tavistock Square and it was the place where all the leading couples came from all parts of the country. It was also attended by many of the leading adjudicators and teachers of the day, so it was a good place to get noticed. Ann and I were fortunate to win there on four or five occasions, which was very special to us. It was also a special place because it was one of the venues where my father came to watch us.

The Tower Ballroom in Blackpool is very special indeed, particularly as we all now see it on TV on *Strictly Come Dancing*. Every contestant wants to get there to dance in this amazing place. The British Championships were held there each year. I went twice, once as a Junior and once as a Senior. On both occasions we did not perform well but the experience was unforgettable, although I was never very keen on Blackpool itself!

Perhaps my biggest thrill was dancing at the Royal Albert Hall in front of an audience of over 5,000 people for the annual national final of the Butlin's Veleta competition – yes, just one dance. The noise levels from the audience were incredible as was the floor itself to dance on. Ann and I were privileged to experience this on four occasions. We first had to go to a regional heat and two couples were selected to represent Sussex in the finals. The winner also won the right to a week at any Butlin's Holiday Camp which, believe it or not, was a real incentive as it was a free holiday.

We went once to the camp at Ayr and once to Bognor Regis, but did not take up the options on another two occasions. Over 150 couples turned up at the Royal Albert Hall and for this event and there were twelve judges. For the first round your names were announced along with which county you were representing. The organisers insisted that we got there two hours before the event to rehearse walking down from the stairs to the right and left of the stage as your name was announced and to get safely down the forty steps onto the floor. What immediately struck us both was the sheer size of both the venue and the floor itself, which was heavily sprung. Supporters from our dance school, including of course my mother and father, would travel up to the event from Brighton by coach to cheer us on and they would have three reserved boxes. We always hoped that their coach was not delayed just in case we were knocked out of the event before they arrived. The game here was to ensure that you were noticed by the judges, who, given the number of competitors involved, would have less than a minute in the early rounds to make up their mind about you.

Our coach, Leslie Abernethy, was selected to be a judge on two or three occasions, which was considered an honour and guaranteed us at least one vote. It was always our ambition to get to the final six couples because you were announced and walked down the steps in the centre of the hall with your coach. Sadly, we never quite made it and our best performance was to get into the last twelve which, out of over 150 couples, was an acceptable performance.

I regret giving up competitive dancing at the age of twenty-two. With the ability that I had, it was too young to do so. I loved the adrenaline rush of performing, hearing the crowds shout your name or number and the elation of hearing your number called when you won. It is just a great feeling to go up to collect the trophy and to know all that hard work has paid off.

However, with the need to focus on developing my career, and studying for my accountancy exams, dancing was just taking too much of our social time and we needed to develop friends outside of that world.

With the increased popularity and attention given to ballroom dancing nowadays, I think that, had it attracted the same attention then, I would have considered going down the route of becoming a professional dancer – perhaps ultimately as a teacher. But then many other things that have happened in my life would most definitely not have occurred.

I couldn't see the Chairman of a FTSE 100 company dancing at The Royal Albert Hall! But I'm getting ahead of myself. Dancing was a wonderful adventure but I must return to growing up...

3

GROWING UP

Dancing provided an exciting break from my somewhat closed family circle. At home we rarely ever had any visitors from outside the family and I was not encouraged to invite friends around. It was made very clear to people by my mother that it was not acceptable to just 'drop in' or 'turn up' unexpectedly. Similarly, my mother would never answer the door even to the postman, until she was fully dressed and wearing make-up!

The exception to this rule would be my grandfather, Poppy, who would come down from No. 65 every day and pick up the newspaper that was delivered to us so that he could read it and select the horses to bet on. We could always hear him coming down the side passage of the house whistling as he walked or singing happy birthday on the appropriate dates. There was a fixed routine about our family life that was all part of the feeling of perfection, order and security. Good manners were drummed into me. Always be polite, insisted my parents. They were not religious, but I can remember saying grace before meals. Childhood memories are happy memories and I owe a great deal to my parents for the start in life that they gave to me.

My mother was in charge of our finances, while my father earned the money. This again had a profound influence on me because her management of the domestic accounts demonstrated to me the importance of running a household properly.

This was a well-run operation. Fresh bread was delivered, as was milk – dispensed daily by a milkman who knew all the families on his round. The coal was delivered by the coalman carrying sacks over his shoulder and emptying the sacks in the coal-hole. Burning coal was supplemented by smelly paraffin heaters placed around the house that were obstacles to my football games and in constant danger of being pushed over, and therefore a real fire risk. Our open fire required regular visits from a chimney sweep, but was handy for toasting bread or crumpets for tea.

Even soft drinks like lemonade, soda and cider were delivered, with attention being paid to the empty bottles, as you got money back on them! It was all a largely efficient system where everything came to your house at different times. Of course, the insurance man from the Tunbridge Wells Equitable came to the door to collect the premiums for general insurance and health cover every month. The insurance man's son, Les Hamilton, is now a local councilor on Brighton & Hove City Council.

I think in some ways I have underestimated my mother, possibly because as a boy I was closer to my father. I think my mother may well have been more influential than I thought. She was quite a tough cookie, who controlled the housekeeping with great skill. For instance, we knew we would never be in debt and could never imagine ending up in court with money problems. She was very careful with money, as I suppose she had to be. She made my father decorate the house on a regular basis and keep it perfect. I remember overhearing conversations about sexual relations being suspended until the front room was redecorated!

She did all housework herself and everything was always immaculate, but she never went near the garden. Her tasks comprised cleaning, shopping, and preparing food, apart from breakfast, a meal my father always prepared. She was the lynchpin of our financial lives.

I can still remember some elements of rationing from when I was a boy. I can recall the eggs being put into water to keep them fresh. I was brought up with the belief that you never threw food away. My mother would serve up leftover food a second time and make soup stock from a chicken carcass. I cannot face such extremes as that, but I am the first to recognise that there is so much food wasted with the 'past sell-by dates' game played by supermarkets. The kind of food banks that exist nowadays were not around when I was growing up but, had they been, my mother would have been tempted to pay them a visit – needs must – although she would never have admitted to doing so. She would not have wanted to be seen to be accepting handouts.

I was brought up to be careful with money, as we had to be. We were not like the posh people living in expensive houses. We were hard-working, honest people. We knew our place, and were content. We were well aware that we were never going to be posh. There was a belief that it just wasn't meant to be that way.

While my cautious nature with money comes from my mother, I did not adhere to her principles entirely. As I grew up I decided, 'If I can afford to meet the loan repayments or mortgage then sometimes I would rather have something now than later.'

We didn't have normal things that other people had, such as a television or a car, for a long time, because of my mother's parsimony. Even my Pop and Nan had a TV before we did. We didn't have this and we didn't have that, because my parents wouldn't make such commitments. Who is wrong and who is right? I'm still not sure.

My mother taught me, and later all of my children, how to play card games, from 'rummy' to 'whist' to 'jingles' and 'chase the ace'. Not only was this great fun, but it taught all of us to count in our heads the cards that we had left over at the end of each hand. Even as a centenarian, she was a fierce competitor at the card table, earning the reputation as being 'Deadly Doris'.

Bizarrely she even taught me to knit! Why did she do that? I would spend hours sitting there doing 'knit one pearl one'. Maybe it was company for her as she sat there knitting herself. Apparently I had a favourite yellow jumper that I made. No wonder my Uncle Tom used to suggest that I needed to go into the Army to make a man out of me.

My dad meant everything to me and I idolised him. I did so much with him, particularly in my early years. I think he was more innovative and creative than my mother. He was also braver and more ambitious. He always cycled to work in the factory at Harringtons. He would go off on his bike waving goodbye, and I would be waving back. He rode the bike home for his lunch every day and I would meet him at the bottom of the road – we both came home for lunch. I really looked forward to the moment I first saw him come peddling along the Old Shoreham Road and turn into Foredown Drive. We would walk up the road together and discuss each other's events of the day.

In my earliest years he used to bring home a comic for me and I eagerly anticipated the latest antics of *Roy of the Rovers* and his team, Melchester Rovers. We would talk a lot together, about all kinds of things, including sport. If they were busy at work he would probably not come home until six or seven o'clock, which meant that in the winter months he would arrive on his bike in the dark. When overtime was available there was seemingly no choice for him but to do it, as it was an opportunity to earn extra money, but I was struck by the very long hours that he worked. The summer holiday dates were always fixed so that Dad and all the other employees had to take their breaks when the factory closed down.

I remember seeing some of his work when I visited the factory and realised that he was clearly very skilled at his job. I did not like the factory: it was noisy, dirty and the work was physical and arduous. He never missed an opportunity to drum into me that I needed to work hard at school in order to avoid following in his footsteps.

He used to organise events for the social club and I would accompany him. One such an event was an annual flower show and there was a monthly whist drive, where we would go on ahead to arrange all the tables. My role was to change the two large cards, which were positioned on each side of the room, to show the suit of trumps for each round. If insufficient people turned up to complete a table of four I was invited to join them. It was a real treat, although it taught me how some people took the game very seriously. The biggest treat however, was that if we managed to get the room set up in good time my dad and I were able to play a frame of snooker on a full-sized table.

My dad was really the person I looked up to for what he had achieved and what he stood for. I know that he was not as successful as he would like to have been, but he was hard working and kind and he always had time for me. He loved sport and that is something I inherited from him. He couldn't always afford to buy me things, although when I was ten years old he gave me an interesting choice of birthday presents. He told me that I could either have a budgerigar or a desk. And I chose the desk! That shows what was going on in my young mind, doesn't it?

That was my very first desk and it used to be by the French windows, which opened onto the lawn. I remember, however, that it was moved to make way for the television, when it eventually arrived. I was very proud of the desk. It was an upright piece of furniture with a pull-down flap to act as the work surface. The gift of a desk for my tenth birthday was a turning point in my life. I never regretted rejecting the budgie!

I loved my dad very much but I was scared of him in some ways, and I would definitely never do anything to hurt or upset him. He only had to raise his voice and I would react instantly. Not that I was badly behaved, but if I didn't do the studying I was supposed to be doing he would let me know about it and I would soon buckle down. It was very rare that he got cross, and generally speaking we were just very happy people. Yet my dad was like me, he had quite a temper if something annoyed or roused him. He could go along being perfectly calm for most of the time and then, just occasionally, all of a sudden something would upset him. Then you had to stand well back.

I don't think he was in good health for a long time and he went through some quite depressed periods. My Aunt Ann, who was a nurse, tells me that he had stomach ulcers but that nobody would believe his claims of illness. She said that he would sit on the floor in great pain but the doctor said it was all psychological, and that there was nothing wrong with him. It got to such a stage that my aunt and my mother took him to Southlands Hospital to see a specialist. Ultimately they decided to operate and he seemed to recover, but the same problem reoccurred. One day my mother came home to find him lying on the floor. Apparently his ulcers had perforated, a life-threatening occurrence, and he was rushed to Hove General Hospital and operated on. I recall visiting him there.

It was at the time of Munich air disaster in February 1958. The terrible crash claimed the lives of several Manchester United players, people I had followed in my football annuals (my favourites were Duncan Edwards and Tommy Taylor). Football was a great love that we shared and we discussed this awful tragedy while my dad was slowly recovering from his operation. With him not working, of course, there was an added strain on the family budget.

My dad was usually happy and easy-going, but I suspect that he wasn't completely happy with his life. I think he felt he should have achieved more. His job was not particularly well paid and life was often a struggle, particularly as my parents liked to maintain high standards. While Dad was very practical and good with his hands and this was how he earnt his living, he was also very bright and had a talent for dealing with people. The war interrupted his life and career and I believe prevented him from reaching his full potential. A lot of his ambition was channelled into me and I always wanted to do well to please him. My happiest memories are those of doing things with my dad.

One of my earliest recollections of being with my father's family was in 1953, when we watched the coronation together at my uncle Alf's house. Alf was my dad's older brother. He was quite successful and was the first in the family to have a car. When they came to see us in Foredown Drive, Alf would park on the road and come in to the house while Aunt Olive would stay in the car. I thought this was very strange, even then. Anti-social comes to mind! However, the family simply accepted it. People would go out of the house and talk to her. My mother would take a cup of tea out to her and pass it through the car window, meanwhile buses would be driving around her car! How weird is that?

Education for me started at St Nicholas Infant School, situated about thirty minutes' walk from my house. You approached it by walking along Old Shoreham Road, a very busy main road that passed Victoria Park, where I was to play a lot of sport over the years. Most days my mother would take me and my Poppy would collect me. At the age of seven I moved to Benfield Primary School, which was even closer to home.

I did quite well at Benfield until it came to writing essays. We had to do an essay every Monday and I was absolutely dreadful at this. I was fine at arithmetic, but creative writing was not my thing at all. Other subjects were mainly okay, but I really struggled when trying to create a story, particularly essays. I had a fear of writing for a long time. I hated to see my exercise book came back with lines through words I had misspelt. This affected my confidence. I just couldn't think what to write, so my father used to help me out. He would write an essay out for me at home and I would take it to school and hide it under my arm and just copy it out. I used to lean right over the papers so no one could see I was copying. There were a lot of people in the class, and it's still a wonder to me that they didn't notice what I was doing.

Our ruse worked well for a time, but then I had a major problem when my father was rushed to hospital. Suddenly I didn't have anyone to write my essay. My Uncle Jim stepped in and wrote one, but his style was massively different from that of my father, meaning that I was in danger of being found out. Luckily, I got away with it but there was a suspicion hanging over me for a while and some of my previous essays were examined.

My indifferent progress at school was frustrating for me. I was upset because I really wanted to do well at my studies for my parents' sake, and they desperately wanted to do anything they could to help me. I remember we had study cards from school, which had arithmetic questions on one side and the answers on the other. To prevent students seeing the answers a piece of paper was stuck over them. I have vivid memories of my mother, my father and me getting a chair in our lounge and holding the cards right up to the light so that we could read all the answers!

My parents did everything possible to help me, but I struggled throughout my school years. I am convinced that I suffered because of the lack of good teaching. There was a massive struggle at home to persuade me to read books, rather than my *Roy of the Rovers* comics or my football annuals. In an effort to interest me in reading they bought me books by writers of the classics as Christmas presents. I don't think they ever read Dickens's novels themselves, but for some reason thought that reading *A Tale of Two Cities* would improve my vocabulary. They meant well.

My early education has a lot to answer for. I enjoyed myself at Benfield, playing sport and, in the final year, being given monitor duties which involved the distribution of milk each playtime. As

I approached the end of my time there, however, there came a real disaster. It was the worst thing to hit my family.

I failed the 11-plus!

I had been feeling reasonably confident when I took the test, but it all went horribly wrong. By the time the big exam came round, even though I still struggled with essays, I was good at maths and I was doing much better at most subjects and everyone expected me to pass. But I failed and it was horrendous. I knew I had let down the people I loved and that I had also let myself down.

There were three parts to the 11-plus and I got through the first part. The second part was more difficult and news came in a letter that I had failed. I recently revisited the school where I took the exam as part of the work that I now do with my Foundation. While the building had been extended, to my surprise much had hardly changed. The hall was exactly the same and I stood there in a cold sweat on the very spot that my desk had been for the exam, some fifty-seven years earlier.

I felt awful at the time. There were only five of us in our group who didn't get through. We had to stay at our school when the others went up to the grammar school for the final examination and the 11-plus interviews.

It was terrible. I felt so ashamed. Instead of going to smart Hove Grammar School as expected, I was going to a grim secondary modern: Portslade County School for Boys. My headmaster, Mr Whiting, told my mother on the day that I left Benfield, he was convinced I would do well in life whatever I decided to do. It's a pity that the staff under his leadership had not shown similar conviction in the way that I had been taught.

Poppy was desperately disappointed. I remember just afterwards I was walking down Foredown Drive with him when he saw some neighbours approaching us. He actually made me cross the road and I knew that he had done so to avoid discussing my failure with them. The 11-plus was such a cruel exam because if you failed it you felt you were written off as an individual. It was obvious to me that it deeply affected my parents. They wanted me to be successful in life and this was considered a mortal blow to that objective. A lot was expected of me and I had let them down. The other members of the family were surprised as well and all of them struggled to come to terms with it. It was a real shock to us all.

Ironically, I found that it provided me with a huge incentive to prove people wrong.

Portslade County School for Boys looked a grim and unforgiving place and my early days there were not a happy time. It was a much larger school and of course I went in on the bottom rung. There was a lot of bullying and nervous new boys like yours truly were easy targets. In one part of the playground there were wartime air-raid shelters still in existence, would you believe! As a traditional induction, older boys would push newcomers like me inside there and huge six-foot guys would come in behind you and thump you and slap you around as a welcome treat! It taught me how to talk my way out of things, which I managed to do on a number of occasions. I found befriending them at least made them think twice before bashing the daylights out of you. It was quite a difficult time for me.

My father came to one of the early parents' evenings. I had persuaded him that I was doing well and in the top group. This was far from the truth, because in fact I was initially nearer to the bottom group! It was just the way the room was set out that made me look like a high flyer. My dad soon worked that out and he was not a happy bunny! The class sizes were large, of about thirty-eight to forty kids, and for a time I almost sank out of existence. I was never confident in class, and I was not the sort of person to put my hand up immediately to answer a question. I was always much happier at the back of the room, where you could get lost, than in the front, where you were so much more conspicuous.

But it was not all bad news. One great, happy and very positive thing came out of my arrival at Portslade. I made friends with a boy called Mike Harding and we remain close to this day. He was another new arrival with a similar background to mine. He lived just around the corner from me in Benfield Close and was an only child like me but, unlike me, both his mother and father went out to work.

We met on the first day at secondary school. Mike didn't come home for lunch but we would walk to and from school together every day. He became the brother I never had. After we left school we went on to work together in three different places. He's been my best man and Godfather to my son Michael. The date of birth of his son, Richard and my youngest son, Robert, is the same: 7 July. Mike shares the same date of birth – 31 May – as my daughter Debby, and amazingly my latest granddaughter, Annie, was also born on that date! It's a very close relationship and it was important to me, very important. It still is.

Having a friend was exciting for me. Even my overprotective parents were delighted to accept Mike. Inevitably, I went round to his house more than he came round to mine. We played cricket outside his house in the road where there was a convenient lamp post to act as a wicket. In the winter or if it was raining, we would play cricket indoors. Our style was cramped by the arrival of his grandfather from Canada, who lived in the house for a number of years. While this stopped indoor cricket our attention moved to the quarter-size snooker table that Mike had in his lounge. I cannot tell you the fun we had playing this game. His grandfather joined in and proved to be a very competitive player. The winner stayed on and we had trouble in getting him off the table.

The same table doubled up as the home of 'Benfield Rangers', Mike's Subuteo team, who played against my team, 'Foredown Drivers', on many occasions. Our school friends Don Peters and Tom Lammiman also had teams and we would play them at home and away. All my matches were away from home, as playing Subuteo was not allowed at No. 38.

Mike and I shared a love of cricket and football, watching games involving both Sussex County Cricket Club at the County Ground Hove, and Brighton & Hove Albion at the Goldstone Ground. For both sports we used to collect autographs for the scrapbooks that we both put together. We would spend holidays down at the Goldstone Ground and across at Hove Park watching the players train and collect their autographs after they had finished training. Some were very accommodating and some were plain nasty, but overall it was great fun. Once Liverpool came to Brighton for training along the seafront and on the beach. This was a great opportunity to see the great players such as Ian St John up close and to meet the one and only Bill Shankly.

For cricket autographs we arrived at the ground immediately after school to see the closing overs. During play we needed to get to the back of the pavilion but there was a retired guy on patrol checking for membership passes. The challenge, therefore, was to get around him. Various tactics were used but I am sure that over the years he was way ahead on points! Once the players came out after the game, the chase was on to get your scrapbook signed rather than that of the twenty other hopeful scrapbook owners who surrounded the player. Mike had an advantage, in that he was a foot taller than me. One trick was to establish where the player's car was parked and to wait by the passenger door.

Matches against touring sides were an enormous attraction and I recall the games at the County Ground against the mighty Australians. Two of my most prized autographs were of Richie Benaud and the great Sir Don Bradman. My father also took me to see the great West Indians when I was ten. The team included Sir Garfield Sobers and Wesley Hall. My youngest son Robert remembers me taking him to see the West Indians when he was about the same age and him getting autographs from Brian Lara and Curtley Ambrose.

Big Mike was allowed inside our family circle. My parents decided he was safe, I guess. I believe he gave me a lot of help. We watched out for each other. Both of us were very cautious in character. I believe that if he had been outrageously confident and I had been cautious it wouldn't have worked. Our parents were not friends, but acquaintances who already knew one another. Mike and I apparently first met when we were both in prams. His mother was miffed because I came first in a Mother-and-Baby competition!

That friendship changed my life at a stroke. It let in the outside world in a big way. Mike had never been in the habit of going out in large groups so he was not so different to me. He was in things like the scouts and he did go off to camp, but at heart we were two quite similarly deep-thinking boys. In walking home together, we would speak of a whole range of things such as what job we wanted to have, whether we would move away from Portslade and what sort of person we would marry.

One of us managed to get a copy of *Lady Chatterley's Lover*, a book that had been banned from the bookstalls. We sat in Mike's lounge reading through it with considerable amusement and disbelief. We had a dictionary near to hand to check out some of the words that we did not understand, but a number of them were not to be found in our conventional English dictionary!

Making friends with Mike was an amazing experience for me. It was such a huge change to have someone my own age to share everything with and I still feel I was lucky that he is such a good guy. I remained quite self-contained but the friendship with Mike was very important and in time it led to other friendships, particularly as I progressed into the school's sports teams. We had a very successful football team and I played at right-back with Mike at left-back. As well as cricket, I represented the school at football, athletics and basketball.

Mike and I would listen all day to Test match coverage on the radio, on the Third Programme, with commentary from John Arlott. The only way that we could receive the signal was to run the aerial high up near to the ceiling. We would regularly score every ball bowled and every run taken at a Test match. We would be sitting there from 11 a.m. until close of play at 6 p.m. We even took our lunch and tea when the players took theirs!

Mike was one of many friends I made at school and some of us recently met up to recall our young lives. It was a pleasant and very nostalgic occasion and to be honest, it made me think again about some of my long-held resentment at not getting a fair deal from my secondary school. I've always felt that I was on the back foot because I failed the 11-plus and was therefore thrust into the second division of education. I've been angry for a long time about that early failure, and it has haunted me all my life, particularly in later years when I began to achieve things and became successful.

I wonder why on earth should one test at the age of eleven ever have been allowed to become so important to a young person's whole life? It's ridiculous and it's wrong. When I failed I hated to let my parents down and I've long believed I was unfairly treated, like so many who fell foul of that once-crucial, unfair exam.

Rolling back the years with old friends was simply joyous, but through the wistful recollections of so many shared experiences from more than half a century ago I realised that most of them remember Portslade County School for Boys much more warmly and positively than I do. Happily, all of them have forged fulfilling and successful lives.

Victor Mower, who trained as an engineer with BT, reminded me how fortunate we were to leave school at a time when jobs were very much more widely available than they are nowadays. 'I could have done half a dozen different jobs,' said Vic. 'The world was your oyster in those days. These days a lot of people are too frightened to give up any job. I know everyone has more money and more possessions but I think things are worse, not better for young people leaving school today. We were the fortunate ones.' I later found out that one of our group, Keith Hughes, went on to be an engineer working on Concorde and moved to America as part of his job.

The 11-plus failure did not seem to impact so heavily on the parents of my friends as it did in my case. Tom Lammiman, who had a career with British Rail, said: 'It just happened. My mum and dad were hard-working people who were much more focused on their son finding employment and bringing in money than in whether he had passed or failed the 11-plus. I soon landed a job.'

Geoff Parker, who also trained as an engineer with BT, passed the first two parts of the 11-plus but then failed the interview, and it was an ordeal that has haunted him ever since. He said: 'It was harsh failing at that last hurdle. I think that has stayed with me through the rest of my life. Ever since I've always hated interviews.'

Geoff reminded me of an incident at Benfield, our junior school, where a girl in our class was found to have contracted polio. This was catastrophic and he and I were instructed by the teacher to carry her desk out to be incinerated. The teacher kept well away. I put my cap in the desk as we carried it. I was going to leave it there, assuming it would be infected, but the teacher said: 'No, take it out!' So much for health and safety! I recall this incident and remember the horror on my mother's face when she heard of my involvement.

Although I felt inferior to others because of my poor education, I don't think my friends feel quite the same but an old school pal, Don Peters, who was a very good sportsman, has his own bitter memory. He said: 'I was picked as twelfth man for one of the Sussex junior cricket sides and another chap never turned up. I got the nod and went on to the field. Then I was shattered because the other chap arrived very late and they called me straight off and put him on. It was just because he was a Brighton grammar-school boy. Portslade seemed to be out of the stream.' Don went on to work in his family's successful greengrocers business in Brighton.

I still feel aggrieved that we had no proper career advice but my friend Chris Bowyer, who passed the 11-plus, pointed out: 'At the grammar school it was no different. It was like a world of its own. When it came to leaving we received no help with deciding on what career path to follow.' Chris qualified as a chartered accountant, working for a small firm of accountants in the City.

So, with Mike and I going on to work in local government and Phil Plumber becoming a civil servant, we all did well, despite our lack of career advice.

Dancing and sport were the two big things in my life and they were quite separate. I preferred it that way. My friends at school didn't see me dancing but they knew about it. Sometimes the news of success in a dancing competition would be in the paper and I would find myself talked about and teased. I didn't mind too much. I got used to it. On the football field I would sometimes get a ribbing and that was a different matter. The old temper might come up and although I was quite controlled, I was very competitive. Playing at right-back my specialty was the sliding tackle, so woe betide a left winger that riled me, as that form of tackle gave me time to catch you and take man and ball. I had a strategy of letting my opponent know that I was marking him early in the game. Both my sons remember me shouting for them to take the same sort of approach when I was standing on the touchline watching them play for Charterhouse!

Mike has a slightly different recollection. He said:

We were both full-backs in the football team and we took no prisoners. When we were playing for the school team coming second was simply not acceptable to Rod. There was one occasion, when we were playing the Knoll School, I will never forget. There was a lot of rivalry and matches between the two schools could get competitive and quite dirty. There was a lot of kerfuffle and commotion going on and the ball went up the other end of the pitch. When I looked round there was a guy laying out flat on the ground. Rod had got to him. Rod was very uncompromising and focused and dedicated on winning for the school.

Rod was quite a serious child. I don't think we misbehaved a lot at school but Rod would always be prepared to defend his corner. If we were at the local recreation ground and any bigger kids came along, he would always stand up to them if there was any problem. But generally we had a very quiet upbringing. We enjoyed our sport but we also spent quite a lot of time studying. Our young lives were all very sport oriented. It was a nice childhood we had. We both had very caring parents who were focused on helping us to do well and get qualifications.

There was a rough element at school. They used to rough up newcomers, but Rod and I learned to survive and even to get on with the rougher lads. We stuck together and formed a friendship that has really stood the test of time.

We both did quite well at school. There were four or five of us who competed quite closely on various subjects each year to see who could come first, second or third in the end-of-year exams. We were at the top of the A stream, whereas if we'd gone to grammar school we would probably have been at the bottom of the C stream.

Overall I believe we survived and grew up in spite of school, not because of it. I did quite well but I came out with only four O Levels and I had to re-take English. We were not stretched or developed at school. We just existed and we had some very good teachers and some very poor teachers. I will always be grateful to the two maths teachers – Mr Broadbent and Mr Davies. I learned so much under their tuition that I think changed me for the better. They were phenomenal. They gave me a love of numbers that I still have today. I really loved maths. But French lessons were a complete nightmare. Nobody ever passed

French at the school. Nobody. Not just in my year, not in any year! So why was I taking French? I had studied French for three years without any real understanding at all. I got the lowest grade. In the oral exam the examiner stopped part-way through our 'conversation' and said: 'Why don't we just continue in English? We might have a better chat that way!' Why was I forced to waste time on French when I could have been studying something else? That's what makes me angry.

For me, no teacher, apart from the maths teachers, ever switched me on to learning. I quite enjoyed history and geography as subjects but in English and French I just was dead. I think we had teachers who were not very good at their jobs. I was particularly hopeless at woodwork, which was very disappointing and frustrating. My father could do anything with his hands and I can do nothing. Yet I had to sit through woodwork despite being absolutely appalling at it. I can remember a tray I made, where you had to have a dovetail joint and I was so hopeless I ended up putting nails in the dovetail! My only memory of successfully achieving something with my hands is attempting to play the recorder. I tried to copy the finger movements of Mike next to me, which meant I was effectively always one note behind him. The telling moment was when I was asked to play a solo.

I suppose they were trying to teach me in a rounded way how to do things. But I think we were averaged down and not up. In my experience there was no thought of raising aspirations, or any efforts to inspire, just a gloomy acceptance that whatever was going to happen was inevitable.

I enjoyed myself, even though I now feel let down by the system. It's only later in life that I fully realised that I was totally cheated out of a decent education, which is every child's right. I believe that I was massively shortchanged by the school. I can't blame my parents because there was nothing that they could have done about it. That was how schools were in those days for 11-plus failures. Ever since I have realised this truth I have been angry about it, which I have used to my advantage, but at the time it was just the way things were.

Things seemed fine. I was a prefect. I was captain of football. I played in the first XI in football and cricket as well as playing for the school basketball team. I represented the school at the school athletics held at the Withdean Stadium. We had regular sporting fixtures against local schools such as Cottesmore, Hove Manor, Knoll, St Lukes and Stanmer. There were four houses in our school: Arundel, Pevensey, Lewes and Bramber. I was elected by the students in my house to be the captain of Arundel in my final year, which was a source of great pride to me.

I was caned several times, for speaking out of turn or for defending things I thought were injustices. The headmaster, Mr Beal, generally administered the cane and other teachers had a rubber slipper known as 'Fido'. They whacked you hard and it was bloody painful. The worst times were when they slippered the whole class and because it was alphabetical I was first! I had a bit of weight on in those days so I was quite tight in the trousers and I could really feel it. Some would attempt to run away and I have vivid images in my mind of the teacher chasing a child the length of the room, swinging the slipper at different times in an attempt to hit the mark.

There was one incident which all of us can remember that occurred in the technical drawing lesson. One of our fellow students, Miller, was a particularly annoying boy who slouched in his chair and had a bag of grapes to his right, grabbing a handful at regular intervals and stuffing them into his mouth. One day he said something out of turn to the teacher, Mr Parkinson. This appeared to be the final straw and 'Parky' simply picked up the technical drawing board and smashed it over Miller's head. We all watched in amazement as the board split in two. We were worried for Miller because he was the centre-half in our football team and we had an important game coming up. This assault did not seem to bother Miller, who simply blinked and shook his head, proving that the centre-forward he was about to mark in the next game had no chance! On a serious note, the teacher in today's world would rightly be banned, which should have been the case then. But this was Portslade.

4

STARTING OUT
IN LIFE

If I'd passed English language first time I would have had five
O Levels, which would have been a very good result from my
school. As it was, I managed just the four passes. My grades were not
bad. I got a grade 1 in maths, grade 2 for history and geography, with
grade 3 in physics and, of course, the inevitable grade 9 in French. It
was the failure in English language that was the real problem. Most
things I planned to do required passes in English and mathematics.
And so did the job I'd been offered!

There was no thought at any stage that I might go to the grammar
school to do A Levels and a university route was pure fiction. The
only option at sixteen for most of my class was to get a job. The only
question was where. For me, working in a factory was not an option!

Not surprisingly, the formal career advice offered by the school
was nonexistent yet somehow I managed to identify three options
ahead of leaving school. Mr Davies, our maths teacher, said as I was
good at numbers a possibility would be to work in a bank. He knew
someone in the local branch of Lloyd's in Boundary Road, Portslade,
and he kindly arranged an interview with the manager. I could have
fitted quite well into the bank. I could even walk to it from home each
day, which would have delighted my parents. I never ever seriously
pursued it, precisely because the job was just too close to home, and
I felt I needed to put some distance between my home and my job.

Working in a bank in Portslade would have suffocated me. I may not have been a wild rebel, but I had to get out of town for my first job, even if I was still coming home every night.

Another job with a firm of chartered accountants was a possibility and I was interviewed by the partner of a small Brighton outfit. With my love of numbers, I felt that I could have risen to become a qualified chartered accountant. They offered me a salary starting at £320 p.a. but something about the cosy little set-up said 'No'. I found it too claustrophobic. I needed to join a larger organisation with more potential.

So I took the third option, which was local government. I applied for a job with East Sussex County Council in Lewes in the Education Department. As luck would have it when I received the letter inviting me for interview it was for a post in the Treasurer's Department. I got the job, but the position was not exactly glamorous. I was to be the department's post-boy!

The decision to take the job was helped by the fact that my best friend Mike Harding had been offered a job in the Department dealing with vehicle excise licenses, something that used to be handled by local authorities before the DVLA was set up. This meant that we could travel together every day and was a great relief to my parents. Mike's friendly presence made commuting much easier. We were both keen to get started and so we left school on the Thursday and started work on the following Monday. Some of today's youngsters have a gap year. We had a gap weekend!

I bought my season ticket from my annual starting salary of £250 a year. We had to get a train from Portslade into Brighton and then from Brighton to Lewes every day. This felt a world away from home and it represented my first steps towards independence. The job most definitely meant starting at the bottom, yet for me it felt just right. There was something about the solidity of a local authority that appealed to me.

I accepted that other new recruits joining from school with better qualifications than mine would go in at several grades higher than me. There was nothing I could do about that in the short term but the point was that, even at this early stage, they would be thought of as being future management potential, whereas I was not. I realised that my way forward was to gain a qualification as a professional accountant. It would be my passport for the future. If I was qualified, I knew I could go and work anywhere in the country, for any local authority, health authority or whatever. I became completely focused on qualifying as an accountant.

One incident that deeply upset me at the time was associated with the need for me to give a character reference to support my job applications. I asked my dad to do so and I was shattered by his response. He said he did not consider himself adequate to give me a reference for my first job. He said: 'You're applying to do a professional job and I'm a manual worker, I can't do it.' I was not sure this was right but I got a strong sense that it was more about my father 'knowing his place'. I was unhappy. In fact I was very angry. I said to him: 'If you're not good enough for a reference then I don't want to work for such an organisation.' But I did need a job and so we had to find an alternative.

My mother persuaded a local lady, Mrs Cave, who was a JP, to write a reference for me. My Uncle Jim, who was in a professional job working for British Rail, also became a referee. The whole depressing process was somehow symbolic of our lack of awareness of the wider world. Even today this sadly still exists with some of the students at our academies. They have no 'route map' that enables them to get into certain professions, particularly careers within the medical, legal and financial services.

I was sixteen when I started work, though by today's standards I seem to have been much younger in my outlook on life. I am amazed when I look back at how naive I was. Young people today seem so much more confident than I was at that age. My parents were still all-important to me and I discussed everything with them, especially my first job. Their view was that they quite liked the public sector because there was a real sense of a career path along with a pension and stability, which is perhaps a little ironic considering the way things are today in local government.

I found the transfer from school to work a pretty traumatic change. I had never worked before – for me there had been no paper round or any part-time job like other children did in the holidays. Work was a very new experience and I was quite shocked by the length of the day and the freedom that you had. I was instructed to perform very menial tasks and some people treated me with disdain, while others were fairer. Some took me under their wing and helped me. Perhaps they were aware of my floundering naivety and felt sorry for me. I also had a real issue with self-confidence due to a bad acne problem on my face. This embarrassed me and compounded my shyness, forcing me to look away from anyone who was talking to me.

The Treasurer's Department of the County Council was where I worked. There were clearly lots of highly intelligent people working there, while as the post-boy I was considered to be the lowest of the low. Still, my parents were happy that I had got what they considered to be a good, safe job, which was 'white collar' and not in a factory. I'm not sure how they dealt with the fact that I was just a post-boy. They didn't talk about it and stuck to the line that: 'Rodney has got a good job with the council.'

The first day was very daunting. I felt totally out of my depth. Fortunately, there was a kind and thoughtful guy there whom I shall never forget, called Andy Copping. He worked in the Salaries and Wages section, next door to the post -room. Andy looked after me. I knew straight away that I didn't want to stay in that post and I needed to get promoted. However, one of the first things I had to do was to explain to Andy that I had not passed my English Language O Level and therefore did not have the required five. He encouraged me to re-sit English, as without it I would clearly be condemned to be post-boy for some time.

In fact, the post room was a very good place to work if you wanted to learn how the County Council operated. As a post-boy you see a great deal, which I soon worked out this was quite an advantage. I did all the filing generated around the building so I saw all the files on people who worked for the council, including even the confidential ones for senior people. I went into everybody's rooms and collected the post. People ignored me if they were talking and often they were discussing fascinating things. I worked out how to make friends, plus I learnt a lot about how to deal with senior people.

My arrival in the workplace opened my eyes considerably. From the start I was fascinated by my new colleagues. I slowly realised I was very good at summing people up so that I could position myself to get on with them. It was a valuable self-taught lesson in working life.

I had no thought of leaving home and getting a place of my own, or flat-sharing as other youngsters in my position might have done, since my parents and my home were still a hugely important part of my life. In my spare time perhaps I should have simply been out enjoying myself but I still had my dancing, was a regular supporter of Brighton and Hove Albion, and I began studying to get myself on the ladder for promotion.

There were three of us in the post room, working for different parts of the Treasurer's Department and we made a great team. As well as Mike and myself there was a guy name Douglas Hall who was a real character. We had good fun. At lunchtimes we used to go to the social club and play table tennis, which inspired a life-long interest in the game.

The Law Courts were next door and sometimes at lunchtime we used to take our sandwiches and watch the cases. We would sit there eating, fascinated by the real human stories that unfolded in front of us and pleased that we weren't in the sort of trouble we heard discussed in such amazing detail. We saw murderers sent down and many prosecuted who were only two or three years older than ourselves.

Many of my work colleagues fascinated me, especially some of the most senior ones. Mr Jones, the County Treasurer, for instance was a very aloof and imposing figure of six-foot plus. He had his own personal entrance into the building direct from the car park and was very rarely, if ever, seen around the office – in fact, because I was the post-boy he probably saw more of me than he did anyone else.

In many ways, being post-boy was an interesting role. If I was filing papers (I hated filing and still do today), I could look at information and find out all about people's details. It was fascinating. I learned a lot about the organisation, about process and how the administration worked. I had to deal with demands that were sometimes unreasonable, like being sent out to buy cigarettes when it was raining, but I had to go and do as I was told. Once I settled in I realised it was a good outlet for me to work in and I began to see how my career could develop.

In my spare time I watched Brighton play and continued playing cricket for Portslade Cricket Club mainly in their second and third elevens. I still enjoyed dancing very much but I never talked to anyone at work about it, so it seemed that I still had a separate life and I valued this. Even Mr Clark did not appear to connect the post-boy to the act that performed before the interval at the Dome. Perhaps he also enjoyed his double life! I realised that studying was to be my way of earning more money and getting promotion. Being ambitious, this was always in my mind, as was how I acted and whom I befriended in the organisation.

Mike and I retook our O Level English and passed it in the November. To progress further, because I did not have A Levels, I had to pass a Local Government Examination Board, Clerical Division Examination before I could start to take the Chartered Institute of Public Finance and Accountancy (CIPFA) examination as a prerequisite to qualifying as an accountant. After studying at Lewes College in the evenings I passed in June 1965. This gave me a salary increase to £350 p.a. and enabled me to enroll for the correspondence course to study for the Intermediate level of the accountancy qualification.

Local government was an excellent employer because it gave me an apprenticeship and funded some of the costs. I was earmarked as somebody who was actively studying to better himself. If you passed 'Intermediate', you were immediately recognised as somebody who was going somewhere. Even though I was still only the post-boy, I had demonstrated that I was somebody who had brains and ambition.

Of course, life doesn't always run smoothly. Early on in my time in the postroom I had a very unfortunate incident. A lot of people were paid in cash, so the whole payroll added up to an awful lot of money. Every Thursday the post room became the dispenser of the cash and was closed for a period from 9 a.m. to 1 p.m. Four teams of four or five people sat and sorted all the cash to go out to all the employees. It was my role as a five-foot, ten-inch post-boy to go with Mrs Ricketts, the lady responsible for this process, to collect the money from the bank. It was carried in bags fitted with a special button under the handle that you were instructed to hold in once the bag was closed. If you released the button the alarm went off and smoke or tear gas was supposed to come out to foil any robbers. I had been told repeatedly never to release the button.

I was never quite sure how it all worked but on one unforgettable occasion, after collecting the cash from the bank, I inadvertently released the button. I was walking along up Lewes High Street back to County Hall with Mrs Ricketts and suddenly this horrific noise started screaming out. We had to crouch down in a shop entrance to open the bag full of cash and stop it. Thankfully, no smoke or tear gas came out, but I still felt it was a disaster. When we got back Mrs Ricketts had to report the incident to the Head Cashier but she was a supporter of mine, and explained it away as a fault with the button on the bag.

Another black mark for the post-room occurred later. The three of us (Mike, Douglas and I) had to frank all the post. Somehow we made a mistake and franked a load of ordinary letters for three shillings and sixpence, which was way more than the price of an ordinary stamp in those days! To our horror, a significant number of the envelopes were returned by the recipients as an illustration of the waste of public money. We were hauled over the coals by the Assistant County Treasurer.

Another disaster occurred when Douglas was dashing across the road to the post office at the end of the day to get there before it closed. Mike and I were following, and to our horror, the big post-bag he was lugging opened and fell from his shoulder. Letters were strewn onto the road and were blown all over the place. Mike stopped the traffic while Doug and I scrabbled around chasing the letters down the road and returning them to his bag. We were seen by various senior members of staff on their way home. Some found it amusing but the boss of the Establishment Department, Mr Horace Nellare, did not. He required an explanation of our actions the following morning.

In spite of these calamities I was promoted. After spending about eighteen months as the post-boy I was moved into the Establishment Department which was responsible for the payment of salaries and wages. I assumed responsibility for the weekly payroll of all the cleaners, the ambulance staff and the agricultural staff. The details of their pay were recorded on a form that then had to be taken down to the Punch Room where the data was input onto the enormous ICL computer. Punching in the data were an army of scary women who would eat you alive with their comments. I had the habit of blushing, which was not helpful, as it seemed to intensify their attention.

I learned just how important salaries are to people. The day after payday provided an immediate way of calibrating your accuracy levels. If you got anything wrong then the buzzer outside on a reception desk would ring. A member of staff would go out and return with the dreaded pay reference. If it was one of mine, out I would go to be faced with an angry voice saying, 'You got my pay wrong.' The ambulance staff were the most demanding, what's more they had a complicated overtime agreement and were people you didn't mess with. Some complainants turned up at the door while others would ring in to query things. The one telephone sat on the shelf between the Head of the section and his deputy. When it rang the office went silent and it seemed as though everyone was listening to how I dealt with the complaint. I found these experiences a huge incentive to getting things right first time!

I liked the fact that it was all very smart and orderly at work. I was proud to be employed by the County Council. I bought a suit to wear for the office, and I think I only had the one. I always wore a white shirt and a tie and I would never be seen open-necked. It wasn't thought of as formal, it was just that everyone dressed smartly. There were definitely no 'dress down days' in those times but smoking was very prevalent in the office.

After a year in the Establishment Department I began to believe I needed to broaden my experience and move. I would never be considered for the Accountancy Section, responsible for recording all the amounts spent on services and received from Government. This team prepared the Council Budget and worked closely with the County Treasurer and the Deputy County Treasurer. Even as a post-boy I dreaded going into that room. It felt a cold and uncomfortable place to work.

So I turned my attention to the Head of Audit, Peter Godfrey. One of his teams would audit the payroll work that I did and I built a relationship with them. One day Mr Godfrey asked if I had thought about getting experience in audit. Effectively he was looking to poach me. I naturally expressed my keenness to move and was soon appointed an audit assistant dealing with welfare and social services, and getting another increase in salary.

I befriended a person in the section more senior than me called Terry Jones, a Welshman and a real character. He collected old coins and stamps and we played golf together at lunchtime down at the Priory, where there was a nine-hole pitch-and-putt course. It was very competitive and was a source of much banter in the office, both before and after we played.

One of the roles audit performed on a weekly rota basis was to sit in the Assistant Treasurer's office and open the post. With Terry's seniority he was on the rota, but I was not. One Thursday, Peter Godfrey called me into his office and said that he was aware that I was friendly with Terry and wanted to explain to me why he had been dismissed that day. I was shocked and very upset to find that apparently Terry had been taking cheques that had been returned in the post, altering the payee, and then paying them into his account. It was a stupid thing to do because there was absolutely no way that he could have got away with it as the person returning the cheque would have been chased up. Nevertheless, he must have been so desperate for money to put his whole career at risk. I never saw Terry Jones again but inspired by him I continued to collect first day covers. These are special stamps or envelopes from the first day that a stamp is issued, or colourful pictorial franks used to cancel the stamps. First day covers celebrated things like England winning the World Cup or Sir Francis Chichester becoming the first person to sail single-handed around the world. They have always been hugely collectible items, with some becoming very valuable.

Amazingly, even on £350 a year I had cash in my pocket after I had paid for my season ticket, and I still felt well off. I don't honestly understand how. I gave my mother some money every week for my board, but that was always a source of great embarrassment on my part. We never had a formal arrangement because even at that stage I was doing everything I could to save money. I was always a great saver. . I would put as much as possible of my spare cash into the Trustee Savings Bank in Hove, making regular visits on a Saturday. I sense that I understood money, and its importance for having a happy life, but I don't think I had any entrepreneurial ambitions in those days. In my mind back then there was a clear divide between being a Labour supporter and a Conservative supporter, and the distinction was simple: Conservative people ran businesses and Labour people worked in them. My father was a lifelong Labour man and I was always more than happy to follow his lead.

But I was a firm believer that I was here to do something with my life and not merely mark time until retirement. I did not want to have a job where I was obliged to work weekends or evenings. My intention was to get myself in a position where I had a choice over what I did, unlike my father's situation, where others controlled his fate. All that I now needed to do was to plan how to get myself in a position to achieve this aim.

My 'other life' in the dancing world was progressing well. I eventually joined forces with a shy young girl called Ann Fellingham. She wasn't what would be considered a top dancer and had danced with another girl in the juniors, where she took the male role. Not everyone thought the new partnership was a good idea, but I had become friendly with Ann and, with what might well have been an early demonstration of my dogged determination, I insisted that she and I should dance together.

Deep down I knew that the right decision would have been to find a top London dancer to be my partner: someone as good as, or better than myself. I should also have gone to a leading dancing school and then I would have greatly developed my skills. Instead I stuck with what I knew in Brighton, because it was safe and fitted better with my work and studying. Ann was a good dancer, but I was considered to be exceptional and many thought we weren't correctly matched. Ann and I became a good team and we won a lot of competitions together. It was a great source of pride to both sets of parents. It was her mother and father who usually drove us to competitions as they had a car (my parents did not get a car until much later).

Ann's father was the deputy headmaster of a special needs school in Portslade. In many ways he played a bit on my inferiority complex, but I could dance and was the partner to his daughter, whom he adored.

However, he was very helpful when I needed his advice regarding re-taking my English language O Level. It is very challenging to do a re-take when you have left school. I had to go to night school, as did Mike Harding, before I sat the exam again. Ann's father was very supportive as I prepared for the exam, particularly in the way he managed to give me more confidence in structuring my essays. Happily I passed English language this second time.

But the event that still haunts me from those teenage years happened in the spring of 1966, just before 'World Cup fever' gripped the nation. My father came home from work with the grim news that he had been made redundant. At the age of fifty this was very serious for him. He had fifteen years of working life ahead of him, but doing what? I had picked up from the various union meetings that took place in the house that something was going on. Thomas Harrington's, the coachbuilders, was a family-owned business and the family had decided to sell to the Rootes Group. My father was now redundant after working there for thirty-six years and it was a terrible blow for him. Overall, some 200 people lost their jobs.

The effect on my dad was traumatic. He was absolutely shattered at the loss of the only job he had known, and was certainly one of the first to be made redundant. My mother always maintained that his being union secretary made him particularly dispensable. Four years later the factory closed down and everyone was out of a job, with the new owners moving the business to a different part of the country.

It was probably one of my first experiences of workers v. employers: us against them. It was evident that the workers felt passionately about the company, but equally obvious they had to work long hours involving overtime to get a reasonable living wage. What the situation taught me was very useful later in life when dealing with Unison, the union involved with the outsourcing business I built in Capita. My approach was always to be open and honest with people, even when it could lead to them being made redundant. Treat them with respect and never forget that behind every employee there is an extended family that relies on that person to provide a home. Above all, never take a person's pride away from them. This is what Rootes did to my father.

But what my dad didn't do was collapse, and he refused to even try to live on the dole. He did something positive. He had a redundancy payout and he may have signed on for a short period, but in spite of the stress that this brought to our lives and the effect it had on his health, he was determined to keep working and he started a business at the age of fifty. This was my first exposure to entrepreneurship and to the determination that an entrepreneur 'has to succeed'. It most definitely affected me and added to my determination never to get myself in a position where someone could treat me so badly.

Dad set himself up as a painter and decorator because he had always done those sorts of jobs at home and was very good at them. He went out and knocked on doors and found clients. My Uncle Alf helped. Alf was in the building business and he may have given him some work, but then my dad got work from different sources and quite soon from word of mouth. It was a very tough job, with long hours often spent working outside. So he swapped long hours working indoors in a noisy factory to working all hours up ladders in all weathers.

I don't know how much redundancy he got, but bizarrely he and Mum used a lot of it to put central heating in our house. It seems a curious thing to do, but the house was very important to both of them. In our time of adversity he had increased the value of the house and our comfort, and there was no further need for coal fires or paraffin heaters.

It was a very difficult time for my dad. There were arguments. I think he felt upset and lost because he had been at Harrington's since he was fifteen. It was a sad year for the family and particularly for my dad because his mother, my Nanny Aldridge, died in late1966. Consequently this was also a very emotional time for the Aldridge family, as my Nan had been the lynchpin in keeping them all together and in check. With her gone, things fell apart and some of the tensions came to the surface very quickly, taking a time to heal.

My father worked hard at his new business and always kept food on the table, but his redundancy left a feeling of deep injustice that still resonates with me today. My mother's contribution was to get a job and she became a part-time tour guide for Green's, a successful cake-mix factory based along Portland Road in Hove.

Soon afterwards Ann and I were an item, becoming boyfriend and girlfriend as well as dancing partners. Ann worked in The Drive, Hove, as a secretary to a firm of solicitors. Like me she was an only child and I think we got on very well together because of this, but it was certainly not a relationship that modern teenagers would recognise. I know that I wasn't a conventional teenager with a conventional teenager's lifestyle. My routine was very set. I went to work. I came home. I studied. I went dancing. I did not have a wild social life, nor did I go to clubs, or even to youth clubs. Frankly, I didn't want to.

I suppose what I had was stability, and the dancing sustained that. We practiced once a week at Portslade Town Hall and there were usually competitions at the weekend, sometimes on both Saturday and Sunday. To be in a final and know you're good was fantastic. Winning and taking home the trophy was wonderful. My parents rarely travelled to see the competitions because they didn't have a car, so it was great to take the winner's cup home for them to see. I would leave it by my bed and wake up to it in the morning.

But always there was studying and more studying. Even when we were being driven to the dancing competitions, I would often be doing my reading in the back of the car, not entering into distracting conversation with my fellow passengers. I rarely went out during the week because of the mountain of work driven by the programme of study that came with the correspondence course from the Rapid Results College.

Basically, I don't feel that I really developed as a youngster. I think compulsory Army national service would have been a great opportunity for me – I just missed that, much to the relief of my mother. Above all, I know that I would have loved the university environment: working hard and playing hard would have worked well for me. All the same I can recognise now that I was a deep thinker and an intense anger was building up in me. I always wanted to be successful, and not just at dancing.

I was determined that the way to boost my career was by qualifying as an accountant but that was only the beginning of the journey. The good thing about local government is that it is effectively an apprenticeship, but I also needed that professional accountancy qualification with the

Chartered Institute of Public Finace and Accountancy (CIPFA), the professional accountancy body for people working in public finance.

There were three parts to the accountancy qualification. This required me to set myself a very demanding schedule. Some people were selected to study at university for three months, but this was restricted to a few high flyers. In my position all the studying was in my own time and on my own with access to a tutor via the Rapid Results College, whom I never saw or spoke with. I would work in my bedroom from the time I got home from work at Lewes, until 8 or 9 p.m. Sometimes I would come home and go to bed and then my father would wake me up at 8 or 9 p.m. and I would work until midnight. And if I didn't do that he would get me up at maybe 6 or 7 a.m. and I would work for an hour or two before I went to catch the train. Another method I used was to study in the office for a couple of hours before returning home, with only the cleaners to distract me. It almost became an obsession with me. My father built me a very large desk for my bedroom that enabled me to fall out of bed into the chair, spreading out my piles of books that covered each of the eight papers that I needed to pass in one sitting!

As long as I stayed in local government my money would go up every year with increments from the grade that I was on and it would increase every time I passed an exam or was promoted. The world of local government stretches everywhere in the country and the options that were presented very much appealed to me.

I took the Intermediate exam in May at the Bishopsgate Institute, near Liverpool Street Station. I felt in control of my nerves that first morning until I walked into the loo and said good morning to myself in my reflection in the mirror. So it was a big day when on 1 September I received the letter telling me I had passed. That was the Intermediate accountancy exam of the Municipal Treasurers & Accountants (which later changed its name to CIPFA) out of the way. My salary went up, and I was delighted and I felt that all of my hard work was starting to pay off. I then enrolled for the next part of the exam and the process started all over again.

The first person that I told of my success apart from my mother, who was at home when the post came, was my father, who I found up a set of ladders painting a house in Melrose Avenue, Hove. He was delighted and I recall that we all went out to celebrate in the evening.

With this news under my belt, I thought that it was time for me to move on from East Sussex County Council. A position was advertised in the Accountancy Division of Hove Borough Council. In those days it was not Brighton and Hove Council, the two were separate local authorities, with Brighton having a County Borough status and Hove being a District Council. The Hove offices were in Western Road, opposite the Town Hall that I had danced in on many occasions. I went for the interview and was offered the job, but something did not feel right. After thinking long and hard overnight, I called to turn down the job. I must say that this gave me nightmares for many months, as so many people back at Lewes kept asking me why I had decided not to take it.

A short while after this a similar role was advertised at the County Borough of Brighton, which was considered to be a much more prestigious local authority. I applied and was appointed as an Accountancy Assistant in May 1968 on a salary of £1,260. It was to prove to be both a traumatic and career-changing move. Many times during the thirty months that I was there, I wished I was still at Lewes. When I was running to catch the post with my letter accepting the role a dog jumped up and bit me. I ended up in hospital to get the wound treated and have a tetanus injection. Perhaps the dog was on my side and trying to tell me not to accept the job!

However, the letter did get posted and when I turned up at the Town Hall on 8 July it proved to be a rude awakening for me. It was a high-flying local authority. I had been in the protected and much slower world of a County Council working in audit, and was thrust into the cauldron-like atmosphere of a County Borough, where you were much closer to the end customer. The office was divided into five teams of five people led by a Principal Accountant. It also had a separate team that looked at the economic impact of decisions taken for all of the services. There were highly talented people everywhere and many went on to be treasurers or chief executives of other local authorities or health authorities.

The Accountancy Division was run by a tyrant named Frank

Kefford, who was most definitely not a supporter of mine. He made my life hell. Very early on I was in the men's loo doing what one does in a loo and Kefford came in to stand at the next urinal to me. Bearing in mind I had only just started there, he turned to me and simply said: 'Are you numerate?' My immediate reaction was to look down and then say: 'Yes thanks!'

The Treasurer was a wonderful chap called Reginald Morgan, who was a legend in local government finance. He was the reason why high-flyers wanted to come to Brighton to work with him. I had entered the big league. But I wondered, was I capable of performing at this level?

My role was to look after the financial affairs of a number of committees providing services in my town. This meant that I had both to prepare estimates for the year ahead and close the accounts, showing the actual expenditure and income. To do this I had to work with the chief officers of the relevant services, who were all 'big characters'.

Take the Fire Brigade for example, where I had to visit the Fire Chief at the headquarters in London Road. The immediate thing that struck me was the style of the chief, who clearly treated the place as his home, even wearing his slippers during our conversation and receiving his tea on a silver tray.

I had to look after the Entertainments and Publicity Budget covering iconic venues such as the Dome where I had danced as a boy and the Royal Pavilion, the world famous Volks railway along with the North Road slipper baths and the Saltdean Lido. It also covered the much sought-after beach huts set along the beach and the money collected from the 15,700 deckchairs!

I also looked after the Parks and Gardens budget covering the takings from the municipal golf courses at Hollingbury, Waterhall and the Dyke. Naturally, this involved making regular visits to check on performance and to test out the product. On one occasion, a member of the audit team that looked after the Parks and Gardens activities asked to come with me on a visit when I had planned to see the Director. It turned out that they suspected that he had a private garden where he was growing produce for resale. We duly tuned up in the Head of Audit's car and parked in the reserved space. The meeting took its normal course around budgets and performance, coming to an end after about an hour. As we got up to leave the Director turned to Head of Audit, Mr Lee, and said: 'By the way I have put some cabbages and lettuces in the back of your car. I hope you enjoy them.' I could hardly contain myself while he turned white, red and ended up green.

The oddest to deal with was the Cemeteries and Crematoria budget, where I dealt with the main superintendent who was a jubilant man, which seemed out of character for his role. He spent a great deal of time explaining to me that when putting together the estimates of income, he factored in how a cold winter would be good for business, meaning he could outperform his budget.

Once I had put together the estimates and supporting papers for each of these I was scheduled to sit down with 'Keff', who would basically challenge my assumptions and aim to 'take me off at the knees'. At least that is how it felt when I came out from each of the sessions – really quite demoralizing.

It was a great office and we had great fun together going out regularly on Friday night pub crawls around the excellent pubs in Brighton, ending up with a curry. As a new boy on one of these occasions I encountered the induction given to all new recruits. We were all eating our curry but I noticed that one by one people got up from the table, saying that they needed the loo. The waiter clocked this and accepted the first five's disappearance but began to panic when a further three went off. At that point I was the last one there and he worked out that the toilet could not hold nine people. The bill was rushed to the table and the waiter stood over me while I paid. When I got up and left the restaurant all of my colleagues were sitting on the wall outside waiting for me to appear, to give me a drunken round of applause.

One of the team had the great idea that we should buy one subscription to *Playboy* magazine and pass it around the office for each of us to read. A list of people's names was attached to it in the same way that we did for the *Local Government Chronicle*. The *Chronicle* was most sought after on a Friday for the jobs adverts, while the girlie-picture magazine *Playboy* was sought after for many different reasons. Each person had to sign and tick the list and pass it on to their colleague. This was going well until by mistake Kefford's name was put on the *Playboy* list. When it arrived in his office with messages on it saying things such as: 'Please read quickly and pass on, but look at page 10!' the balloon went up and we were all summoned to Keff's room for him to deliver a message about how unprofessional it was for senior people to act in this way. Kefford's office overlooked the sea and after he completed his 'sermon on the mount' one of my colleagues commented that he had counted three ships that had gone past the window during Keff's lecture, which shows how seriously he was taking the reprimand.

Unfortunately, the change of job badly affected my studies. As the date of the exam for Part 1 of my 'Final' loomed, I realised that I had neglected them. The extent of this only became apparent when I received the letter from the Institute confirming the outcome. I had failed all four subjects. This was a hammer blow, as I had obviously been appointed at Brighton on the understanding that I was intending to qualify, as was expected of all people in that section. I had to explain to Keff what had happened, which was rather tricky because in some ways it was down to how he had treated me!

The council turned up trumps, agreeing to help by covering the cost of me going on a revision course. It was held at the London School of Economics over a week. It meant staying for a week in London, which I enjoyed tremendously. The face-to-face teaching I received had an amazing impact. The exam dates were on 5 and 6 November, the venue again being the Bishopsgate Institute. Luckily my twenty-first birthday was the following day on Thursday 7 November! Things fell into place when I retook the exam and with great relief I heard in January that I had passed it.

I know of many colleagues who struggled with the Final Part 2 of the exam and many gave up, leaving them only part qualified. I was determined that this would not happen to me and I would achieve the five-year goal that I had set myself to qualify as an accountant.

While I was contemplating another year of the Rapid Results College's correspondence course, a wonderful offer appeared. My employer, Brighton Council, offered to send me on a day release course to Southampton University, effectively giving me a day off a week to study. Although this meant a long weekly journey, the pass rate of students attending the course was so high that this virtually guaranteed passing and finishing my studies. Three other colleagues were also enrolled and so we agreed to take it in turn to drive our respective cars, sharing the cost of petrol.

I have to say that the journey was not a pleasant experience and it meant long days. During the winter with rain, snow and fog it was challenging. But the course lived up to its reputation. The lecturers were incredible, particularly the ones covering Economics and Audit. Homework was set and studying for me continued every day back at home. When I came to take the exam I felt as confident as one could feel.

My revision technique had become highly tuned and involved reducing my lecture notes to key points, which ended up in a small notebook I carried around with me all the time. In the end I had a photographic memory of the points, leaving the main job of getting it down on paper for the examiner to mark. I still have a sinking feeling when I walk past the Bishopsgate Institute by Liverpool Street Station even today.

Exams really bring out the worst in people. I recall many leaving to go to lunch in tears after the first paper. Some would not return for the afternoon session, but it was clear how important it was to pass the exam. It was their meal ticket for both themselves and their families. Sitting in rows of desks you faced that moment of truth when you turned over the paper to see what delights the examiner had set you. Relief was immediate if the work you had put in sifting through past papers to detect likely trends had paid dividends, and you had therefore 'guessed' correctly about the questions. However you would despair if you struggled to find five out of ten questions to answer.

The Accountancy paper inevitably has a question where you have to produce a complete set of accounts including a balance sheet which, of course, needs to balance. It was a wonderful feeling if it did but frustrating if it did not. It was drummed into us not to spend a disproportionate amount of time doing this or you would not complete the requisite number of questions for a pass mark. This discipline was hard to keep under exam pressure.

In the period between the exam and the result, one minute you convinced yourself you had passed and the next you believed that you had failed. I even had dreams where I saw myself opening the envelope and the elation that followed because I had passed or the nightmare expression on my face when I had failed. Sometimes I even woke up thinking it had all been real.

You were aware of the day that the letter with the result would arrive. There were various stories, such as that you could tell immediately if you had passed because the envelope would be thicker, since it contained your application for membership of the Institute. Inevitably when I heard the postman and saw the thin envelope, I feared the worst. Luckily the myth was wrong because when I opened it the first word I saw was 'Congratulations'.

The first thing that went through my head was that in just six years, or ten if you go back to my 11-plus, I had come from being thought of as a failure by everyone, to becoming a fully qualified accountant. This exam was considered to be the equivalent to a degree, an achievement of which, when I was at Portslade County School for Boys, the 'system' never considered me capable.

I refer to this in speeches as proof that at the age of twelve there was clearly something positive going on in my head, but that the teaching I received never stimulated my brain to be able to connect with it. It took the determination and drive that I had to bring it out of myself in the hours that I had studied in that small bedroom on the desk made by my father, who had never stopped believing in me. It also meant that I was now a long way from being a post-boy, and that it was local government that had enabled me to make this journey. For that, I will always be grateful. My salary increased again and I was now a marketable commodity for the first time in my life. Pass me the *Local Government Chronicle*; local government here I come!

On the Monday morning, I was congratulated by all my colleagues in the office and much to my delight the Treasurer, Reg Morgan, came up to see me at my desk rather than me going down to his room, which was the normal process. His words to me summed it up perfectly: 'Congratulations, Rodney, you now have a licence to practise for the rest of your career. You need to start the process of learning how to use it.' He was dead right!

I have been fortunate to work with some excellent people during my life but Reginald Morgan would be the first that I came across in my career up to that time. His great innovation and forethought encouraged the start of the 'Brighton Festive', which now, forty years on, is a major event in the city. While I was there he also started the thinking around the Brighton Marina, which is now a massive commercial success. If Brighton had continued to have this calibre of CEO over the years, the city would have developed to a far greater extent than it has today. He had the ability to get the facts out of you not by fear but by asking simple, open questions. You felt a need to then give him all of your inner thoughts or doubts about the matter in hand. I made the mistake once, of saying in an explanation to him that: 'This was the way that it was done last year,' implying that this must surely mean that it is correct now or that I had merely followed it 'parrot' fashion without applying my professional judgment to it.

Needless to say I never used that line again, even to this day. Linked to this he also said: 'I will always back your judgment if you do something and have good reasons for doing it even if in hindsight this proves to be wrong. But if you choose to do nothing because it is the easy way out, you're not the man to work for me and I will never back you.'

Times back then just seem very different to life today. There were so many things that we couldn't do then that are natural to us all today. If you wanted to get hold of a person the only way was to call his office or home phone number, the latter of which is rarely used now. The telephone box 200 yards away from my house in Foredown Drive was a huge asset, because we never had a phone in the house until I was fifteen years old, and this was used principally for my father's union work. We were restricted on usage because if he could not pass the charges on to the union, he had to pay for the calls himself. The nightmare scenario was that of arriving at the nearby phone box to make a vital call, and being beaten to it by another person. If your wife was pregnant you kept coins by the side of the bed ready to rush out to call an ambulance.

Today you merely call a person's mobile and no matter what they are doing or wherever they are in the world you can speak to them. The lack of accessibility had a great effect on how you ran your life back then. Add to this the fact that there were no computers, no World Wide Web and no emails and a reliance on fax machines, and it is amazing what we achieved.

Effectively, a person could disappear, only giving a broad indication about when they would arrive back home. This world appealed to me as I could 'drop out' without explanation. People talk about the 'Swinging 60s' but I seem to have missed out on that excitement. I can remember my twenty-first birthday party. I'm afraid it was a very sterile occasion, even though the day before I had finished my exams for the second part of my accountancy qualification. By today's standards, it was a family-led celebration held in the canteen at Harrington's with background music, sausage rolls and sandwiches. It was not a collection of young friends getting plastered, mainly because I didn't have lot of friends, nor did I go to any wild parties, which apparently happened in Brighton.

I did, however, have a fascination for London. Even as a teenager, I enjoyed taking a train from Brighton to Victoria and spending the day just wandering around the sights in London. Ultimately I would spend most of my working life in London and have always enjoyed living there. I would visit the Houses of Parliament, queuing to get a place in the gallery for Prime Minister's questions. From there I would walk along the embankment to see the Crown Jewels in the Tower of London, I would then get the Underground to Piccadilly Circus and visit the area around Soho.

There was always the fascination of the 'dark side' of London, especially Soho. I remember my first visit to a strip club with the satisfaction of the knowledge that no one knew where I was. I recall the first performer I saw, while sitting in the dark, hoping that the waitress would not come over to ask if I wanted a drink. I had read about the extortionate cost of alcohol at these places, and more relevantly I had blown most of my money on the entrance fee. The background music used by the performer, who proceeded to take most of her clothes off, was 'Delilah' by Tom Jones. Amazingly nearly fifty years on Sir Tom Jones would sing 'Delilah' to the guests at my sixty-fifth birthday party.

It didn't seem appropriate to say anything to him about the strip club at the time.

I didn't have a car until I was twenty years old. I was taught how to drive by my uncle, who was a driving instructor for BSM. I passed my test after the second attempt and thirty expensive lessons. The problem was that I did not have a family car to practise in. Well, we did have a family car by then, but after a disastrous episode involving my driving it around a roundabout with my father screaming at me to reduce my speed and not to overtake, we decided that it was better to put at risk a BSM car than the precious car my father owned. It was destined to end its life in Lewes, when the electrics caught fire.

Before passing my test, I added to my poor record with an incident involving a friend's car, parked at our home while they were away on holiday. The VW was parked out in the driveway and I persuaded my father that I was sufficiently proficient to drive it the short distance towards its resting place down the drive into the garage. Having successfully reversed it onto the road, changing into first gear proved more difficult for me than I thought, and the car careered forward, only to come to rest with the help of the Number 11 bus stop! On examination the front bumper was badly dented. Luckily my father's panel-beating skills came to the fore. He took off the bumper and got to work, skillfully straightening it out. When my friend picked up his car it was in perfect condition and the episode was never referred to again by any of us!

My own first motor was a second-hand Austin 1100. It was anything but a flash car but it changed my life. Having my own car gave me an instant sense of freedom. Otherwise it was buses and trains.

5

DIFFICULT DECISIONS

B y now my relationship with Ann had moved on. We had become very close spending time together dancing. We also went on holidays with Ann's parents, travelling by car to Switzerland and the following year to Austria. These were my first times abroad since going to Germany as a child, and they meant a great deal to me. As time went on it became a natural, logical step for us to get married. Reflecting on this now, it was clearly the wrong thing for us to do and our respective families should have said this to us no matter how difficult this might have been.

I don't want to sound unromantic or disrespectful to Ann but we were more friends who found comfort in each other because of our similar backgrounds as only children than anything else. We stopped dancing when I was about twenty-one because we decided we just didn't want to go on doing it. I was working and studying hard and I had somehow lost my enthusiasm, and once Ann and I had stopped dancing together the hobby that had united us had gone.

This coincided with my qualifying as an accountant. I now had no need to study every night. The whole mix of my world changed and I found it a very destabilising experience. I attempted to keep on studying and applied to take a BSc degree in Economics, again via correspondence course. This was never going to happen as the intensity and drive to do it was no longer in me. I stopped and looked round and thought, 'What's going on here?'

All our savings were really earmarked for a deposit on a house, and even though we both had quite good jobs, money was pretty tight. We bought a fairly new terraced house in a cheaper area of Brighton on an estate called Hollingbury. I think it cost £12,000. I was very proud of it, but it was not in a great area. It was a basic town house with two levels to the front and three at the back to accommodate the garage.

I moved straight from my parents' house in Foredown Drive to the new marital home, as did Ann from her home in Franklyn Road, Portslade. We didn't live together before we got married. We never even considered it. In those days you just didn't, what's more our parents would have been horrified by the very idea. Ann was considered to be a very good person by everyone who knew her, including my parents, who liked her a lot. I felt that there was unreasonable pressure put on us by the older generation to get married and to start a family.

We had a very glamorous wedding in July 1969 with a reception at the Norfolk Hotel on the seafront in Hove. There was an alarming last-minute scare, which we had to deal with on the very day of the wedding. The day before we were due to get married we found that the licence we had to get married in the church was not complete! The documentation was not correct, and it became clear that the powers that be were simply not going to allow us to marry unless we sorted it out.

There had been considerable friction leading up to the event because Ann's father was an outspoken atheist and threatened not to walk her down the aisle if we were to get married in a church. He ultimately relented on this, but made his reluctance known throughout.

We had everything arranged, the guests invited, the reception planned, so this was a real crisis. Ann's father and I had to travel up to London at the last minute to an office near Westminster Abbey to get a special licence, so that the wedding could go ahead. We came up very early on the morning of the wedding by train and it was touch-and-go whether we would be able to make it back in time. Fortunately everything was fine in the end. When I look back on this scary hitch I think maybe it was an omen that things shouldn't have happened!

Mike Harding was the best man and we went away on honeymoon to Bournemouth, stopping overnight in Chichester. While we both loved Bournemouth, and I still do, we came back early because we were not that happy being away from home!

It is difficult for me to recall the memories of the marriage and I am most definitely not proud of how it panned out. I don't feel we were ever deeply in love like newlyweds should be. I am a great believer in instinct and somehow my instinct at the time was that I felt that this was not right. We were two very young, inexperienced individuals with no real basis for our relationship at all. There was no huge problem, but there was no magic between us either. We were not particularly well off but we were not hard up, and we both had reasonable jobs.

The following year I moved to Crawley, promoted to a good job in local government terms. So I was commuting by car each day and that put a bit of a stress on the situation. My move to Crawley District Council was quite a step up. I was appointed Group Accountant, really at Assistant Treasurer level, part of the team taking responsibility for the devolved education service offered in Crawley. This was my first step into the world of education and also involved my working for a period at West Sussex County Council. It was good for my career, but not so good for my marriage.

We both really wanted children, and we were both disappointed when none arrived. If we'd had children, you never know what might have happened. Looking back, we were very young for our ages. Neither of us had very much experience of life, really. The marriage lasted only two-and-a-half years. Perhaps I was never fully committed, if I am honest. It sounds a little cruel but I can actually remember standing at the altar during the wedding ceremony thinking, 'I know I can get out of this if it doesn't work out.' There was a degree of innocence about my feelings, and a shy naivety about both of us. Before I met my wife I was very inexperienced about everything, and had not had any girlfriends previously.

Ann and I clearly weren't happy together but then I met somebody else, a young woman at work called Jacqui Doyle. Unlike my parents, I suppose I was a person who felt that if something's not right you've got to sort it out. There wasn't a huge bust-up in my marriage, but I had met Jacqui towards the end of my time with Ann. I have a ruthless side to me, and I knew that my marriage was not going to work, so recognised that I was not the kind of person who was going to stick around. It was all dealt with very amicably, and there was a coldness of emotion rather than anything else. There was no acrimony in terms of lawsuits, just a division of this and a division of that and we moved on. I don't think it was a surprise to Ann when it happened. We both had a clear sense that we were not meant for each other.

I knew splitting up with Ann would upset my mum and dad, and it did. It wasn't the money side of it that was troubling. Obviously we had to sell the house and divide everything up, but it was an untidy process and I am a very tidy person: I don't like flaws or mistakes, and when you end a marriage you've got to admit you've made a mistake. In those days divorce was not that common and I felt it was still widely frowned upon. Telling my parents was probably the most difficult thing I had to do. Ann and I basically agreed we would go our separate ways.

We slept in the same bed together the night before we parted. In the morning I went off to Crawley to work and she said: 'I'll be out when you come back.' She just left the house that day and that was that. It was quite businesslike. She went home to her mother and father and I was left with an empty house. On reflection, I think my actions towards her were reprehensible but I do have the ability to make decisions, even difficult ones, for that is my nature.

Our assets weren't great. There was the house. I stayed there for a while but it became impractical because traveling to Crawley and then coming back to an empty house wasn't much fun. Eventually, my father helped me decorate the house and we sold it.

The end of my first marriage taught me a great deal about myself. I may sometimes be underestimated by others but once I make up my mind to act, which may not be instant, it will happen in one way or another. Although I never saw Ann again, I know that she remarried and had children. I sincerely hope that she has had a fulfilling life.

I closed the door on Brighton and Hove, only keeping it open to visit my parents in Portslade. For a time this meant restricting my relationship with my aunts and uncles and cousins on the Aldridge side. I could no longer be considered as 'perfect' because I was now a divorcee. I had to get away and rebuild my credibility.

The dancing world that had been a prominent part of my life for fifteen years was consigned to the past and rarely mentioned again. Even my own children today know very little about my achievements and only writing this book has reopened that chapter in my life. My mother and father continued to go to the same dancing club as before, meeting all their old friends along with Ann's parents and I believe Ann too, who took on more of a role in teaching other pupils. Seeing Ann could not have been easy for Mum and Dad.

I dealt with all of that in my own way. I have always been able to compartmentalise things that have happened, using them to create momentum and positive energy to move forward with an added intent of proving things both to myself and others who may have doubts about the decision I took.

6

A NEW LIFE IN CRAWLEY

While my marriage was failing my career was moving on at last. Once I had qualified I began to look for other jobs that would see me promoted. Within the Brighton office this seemed unlikely to me. One of the senior Group Accountants, Hugh Harland, who was responsible for the Education Committee, took a job at Hove Borough Council as Deputy Treasurer. His was a huge responsibility as, apart from Housing, it was the largest budget, covering all the schools and colleges in the city. In August 1970 I put in an application for his former role. I was short-listed, but not appointed.

The *Local Government Chronicle* became a must read every Thursday. Within local government ranks there was definitely a hierarchical rating for different types of local authority. Those working in counties tended to stay in them and would be unlikely to move to district councils, which were considered inferior. County boroughs such as Brighton had snob value, as they had responsibility for all local government services. So while you would move to another county borough or possibly to a county if they would have you, it was unlikely that you would move to a district council.

That same month, August, Crawley District Council advertised for a Principal Accountant, attracting my attention because it was in education. The authority had been granted the right for a delegated scheme of divisional administration of the education service under the Education Act of 1944, to run schools in their area. Another attraction was that the highly respected treasurer, Ted Lynch, was a council member of the Chartered Institute of Public Finance and Accountancy (CIPFA), the very body that had awarded me my qualification. Crawley also had one of the fastest-rising stars in local government, Nigel Palk, who had recently joined the authority from the Institute, as Deputy Treasurer.

The job meant a considerable promotion if I was successful. My best friend Mike Harding was already working there in the same department, having moved to Crawley via Crawley Commission for New Towns once he had qualified. My interview with the Treasurer and Nigel Palk went very well, and I really felt at home with them and the place itself. To my amazement, they offered me the position there and then!

When I got back to Brighton Station the first person I rang from a call box to announce the good news was my father. To my surprise he was slightly concerned, as he felt that I should stay with the Brighton job. This deflated me but I had seen enough to feel that the move was the best thing for me.

I accepted the role and left Brighton Borough Council on 4 October. I had a great leaving do and even felt sad about leaving Keff, but I soon got over that. I had made many friends at Brighton and it would be wrong not to mention them in the context of my career, as our paths crossed many times subsequently when I started Capita. The leader of my team was Ian Marriott, who was supportive of me and taught me a great deal. Ian went on to become a treasurer. Others in the office were John Budd, Peter Hyde (a Gold Medal winner of CIPFA), John Moreland, Derek Harvey, David Poynton (another CIPFA prize winner with whom I would work at Capita), John Cooper, David Stainthorpe, Hugh Harland, John Moore, and Simon Keane.

One of the disadvantages of the new job was the 30-mile car journey to Crawley each day. It was a straight road, the A23, going past Hickstead Showground, although there were no motorway stretches at that time and many dangerous places where people would overtake. I bought a brand new blue VW Beetle as it was obvious that I was going to clock up a high mileage and my Austin

1100 would never have coped with it. The journey was particularly treacherous in the wet, in snow and ice and late at night. I know that lots of people tackle longer journeys each day and I don't know how they cope with it. To turn the corner into my road was a relief, but as Ann and I became increasingly distant, home was not always a warm place to walk into.

I started on Monday 5 October 1970 on a salary of £2,268 but had to refund £70 of my training costs to Brighton Borough Council. Having moved from a traditional town hall with history everywhere, I found myself working in a place where the whole of the Treasurer's Department was on the ground floor of a very modern building. As you walked into the main reception, on the right was the cashiers area, where people paid their rates. Opposite was the establishment section, where all the salaries and wages were processed and employees came to discuss any queries over their pay. Next on the left down the corridor was the accountancy division where I was to be based. This was a large rectangular room with six teams of people. My appointment into a new post made it seven. Opposite this was the audit section and next to that was the Treasurer's office. His deputy, Nigel Palk, had a room two doors down with, in between the two, Mr Lynch's PA Bobby Skinner – the office that was the source of all gossip and knowledge. At the far end of the building was the computer room with the office of the Assistant Treasurer, Ron Hill, responsible for the Honeywell computer and his programming staff. That was it!

One great feature was that every member of staff, on a rota basis, down-tooled at a certain time mid-morning for thirty minutes to travel two floors up to the canteen where, in addition to tea and coffee, delicious rolls were served – sausage or bacon. This ritual was repeated in the afternoons with tea and cake. I cannot see this arrangement surviving in today's local authorities. The canteen also served a great lunch for staff at subsidised rates and had an area for table tennis. I played in the league for the council in Division Five, finishing top of the league averages. It became a ritual to practice for an hour before driving home. My regular opponent was Chris Courtney, one of my colleagues in the accountancy division. I also played against Nigel

Palk, narrowly beating him in the final of the competition, which was probably not good for promotion prospects!

My role was to set up a new section in the finance department to deal with the new responsibilities for education within Crawley. My arrival somewhat put the noses out of joint initially of Tony Pearce and David Fellows, who enjoyed the status of effectively being assistant treasurers and most definitely ruled the accountancy division and the room. My appointment was watched with great interest as I was much younger than them, came from a county borough, and destabilised their domain. To be fair to both of them, this was only a passing phase and they became incredibly helpful. Tony went on to become the Treasurer of Worthing Borough Council.

The knowledge of education and the process of transferring staff would later prove invaluable in building Capita and much later in establishing my Foundation. The role was unusual because it also required me to deal with West Sussex County Council, from where the schools had been transferred and with which there was a residual financial responsibility. I had to visit the offices of West Sussex County Council in Chichester. There I encountered the elitist County culture. I had to deal with some pretty switched-on people and one in particular, Richard Tettenborn, who was then an assistant County Treasurer, regularly reminded me that he was a gold medal winner of the IMTA (Institute of Municipal Treasurers and Accountants), and had come first in the finals of the exam. I always maintained that I came fourth, as only the top three were ever announced! When I eventually ended up working for CIPFA I had the opportunity to look at my exam papers. Overall I did better in some than I thought, but it was very apparent that Richard Tettenborn was miles ahead of me. He ultimately became President of the Institute.

In mastering my new duties, I discovered a trait in myself: I was better at starting things and growing them than being in a static situation, which bored me. I had to get used to new colleagues who, like myself, had been appointed into new roles, such as a Director and Deputy of Education who were housed at Goffs Park in wonderful surroundings. There was a legal team in the Clerks Department along with officers in the Parks Department and Engineers Department. I also had to recruit two people to join me in my team, a new responsibility for me. Charles Pennell joined me from Brighton and Martin Harwood was transferred to me from another section.

The elected council members were, of course, all over this new, high-profile area of activity. Crawley had a wonderful council chamber and meetings of the newly formed Education Committee were held there. On 13 November 1970, the first meeting was pictured in the local newspaper and I was standing next to Nigel Palk in the photograph. This was much to the joy of my Auntie Phyllis, who still lived in Three Bridges in the very house that we had visited on holiday as a family all those years earlier. Sadly my Uncle Tom had died.

Of course, there were a large number of teachers, catering staff and cleaners to be paid and this was the responsibility of the establishment section run by Frank Goring. Within his team, looking after the manual payroll, was a girl by the name of Jacqui Doyle.

I only worked for the council for thirty months, but in that time I met the person I would eventually marry, who would be mother to our four children and with whom I lived for 31 years. While we are no longer together, I owe her a great debt for all that she did and the time that we shared.

Our relationship grew. I was very attracted to Jacqui and found her a very kind person to be with. While it was a sad time at home in Brighton, as my marriage came to an end, I became aware that Jacqui's married life had not been easy either. There were many twists and turns in our relationship before we settled as a stable couple. Jacqui's family was very kind and they warmly welcomed me into their home in Furnace Green in Crawley. On many occasions, rather than drive home to an empty house in Brighton, I slept on the sofa in their living room. Jacqui lived with her mother May and father Eugene, her two sisters Susan and Teresa, and her brother Christopher. She also had a young daughter, Debby, from a brief and evidently very unhappy first marriage. Jacqui had suffered a difficult time with the break-up and she had moved across the country to live with her family and make a fresh start. Debby was just two years old when I first met her. She had been born on 31 May 1969. She was a lovely little girl with blonde hair and freckles. I recall her holding on to her mother's leg, partially hiding from me the first time I met her. I always felt Debby was the child I didn't have earlier. She was adorable. I didn't fear her presence, I embraced it.

My marriage break-up was very difficult for my parents. Typically, they hid some of their feelings from me and tried to put a brave face on what happened. That was not easy for Mum and Dad and I hated to hurt them. Not many people got divorced in those days. Then they had to get used to the new lady in my life. Broken marriages were unusual enough back then, but one minute I was divorced and the next minute I was getting together with a divorced woman, who already had a child! Goodness knows how they reacted to my situation in private but they were never anything other than very supportive during a period of huge change for them and for me.

All the same, I was determined to make a real go of it with Jacqui. We got on very well together. I was happy and knew I was lucky to find her. In view of my seniority in the department, I felt a need to inform the Treasurer, Ted Lynch, of the change in my marital circumstances. It was also necessary to explain to him about my relationship with Jacqui.

Overall, working in Crawley was a good period for me and I enjoyed working with the local authority. Mike working there as well was a bonus, and by then he had moved to Burgess Hill, north of Brighton, with his wife, Helen. I had first met Helen when the three of us worked for East Sussex County Council and it proved to be the beginning of a long and wonderful friendship – I was both best man at their wedding and Godfather to their son Richard.

Jacqui's father Eugene had moved around a lot in local government and was an accountant, having also qualified with CIPFA. They had a wonderful family house, which they had initially rented, then subsequently bought, from the Crawley New Town Commission. They were a tightly knit Catholic family who went to church together every Sunday morning.

Jacqui was the oldest of the children. I was at some times fascinated and at other times phased by the endless interaction in the home. There was always so much going on. There was anger, fierce arguments, doors slamming as people disappeared into their respective bedrooms.

There was a lot of emotion, which I was not at all used to yet there was also something wonderful about the energy and the passion in the place. Birthdays became great occasions and Christmas celebrations were absolutely amazing, as there were so many people and so much fun and laughter. As an only child, this kind of lively family interaction was all so new to me and it was a really great experience. I always vowed from that moment that I would have more than one child. The Doyles really made me welcome.

We had some good holidays together. The local government union at that time was NALGO (National and Local Government Officers' Association) and it had a holiday camp down in Croyde Bay in Devon. We had two very enjoyable holidays there when Jacqui and I joined her family. This was a very precious two weeks for us as Jacqui and I had time to spend with Debby as well as with the rest of the family.

I sold the house I had lived in with Ann in order to move to Crawley to be closer to Jacqui and Debby. I found a nice three-bedroom semi in Ash Road, Three Bridges, for £14,550. Of course, the money I had to buy it with was effectively halved because of my divorce, which meant that the mortgage I required was very high. I recall sitting in the lounge regularising my finances and realising that I was spending more than I was earning. It required me to juggle finances in a way that I am sure my mother had done for years. These were not circumstances that I enjoyed and the only way out of it was to earn more. The opportunity to do this came in a very unexpected way.

My relationship with Jacqui grew and within six months of my buying the house, she left the employment of Crawley Borough Council to move in with me to look after Debby and for us to build a family. Our change in circumstances was one of the reasons for the shortage in money because we had to live on one income, but the struggle was well worth it. Debby was a wonderful bonus in my life. I have always thought of her as my natural daughter. Once I formally adopted Debby it was something that was never mentioned again. For me it was a very natural thing to want to do.

I was still very close to my parents, of course, but my ties to Portslade and Brighton and the rest of the family were loosened. I felt as if I was really growing up at last, but I needed to regroup and be more assertive in my new life. Jacqui and I were very much in love, but money was very tight and we had a lot of bills to pay. The interest rates on the mortgage and bank overdraft were high. Life wasn't always easy. I remember having some very lengthy and troubling conversations with the bank manager at Lloyds about how I was going to pay for everything.

I realised I would have to conserve my money very carefully. I was slow at paying people, even on some occasions resorting to sending cheques unsigned to delay payment. Life was tough and we were living very much hand to mouth. There was one murderous day when interest rates shot up and I thought to myself, 'I just don't know what we're going to do from here onwards.' Still, so many people were in the same boat and somehow we got through it.

One way out of this was to get a more senior job in local government, probably involving a move to work in London. It was highly improbable that I would get promotion at Crawley because all the senior jobs were filled by people who were unlikely to move.

Then two things happened to change our lives for the better. The first was out of my control but the second was opportunistic and perhaps showed the first real signs of my entrepreneurial instincts.

The first change was driven by the Government's reorganisation of local government. One of the effects of this was that the powers delegated to local authorities to run their education service, such as happened at Crawley, were to be withdrawn. This meant that all the schools would be transferred back to the control of West Sussex County Council. Put in simple terms, once the Act of Parliament was passed to create the powers necessary for the reorganisation, I was out of a job. So I had no option but to move on from Crawley.

The second change was nearer to home. When I met up with Jacqui, I knew that her father, Eugene, also worked in local government for the Crawley New Town Commission and was a qualified accountant with CIPFA. We got on well as we spent quite a lot of time together and we realised we had things in common, the most striking of which was that we both wanted to add to our income to fund holidays. On one of our visits to the local pub we both thought of the obvious solution: 'Why don't we use the accountancy skills that we've got to earn extra money?'

We talked a lot about finding extra accountancy work from local firms or small contractors and the opportunity came to us quite by chance. Eugene was at work when a woman called Peggy Westley approached him saying that her son was about to start his own business. She said to him: 'Look, you're an accountant can you help my Tony?'

Eugene talked to me and we decided to meet her enterprising son, Tony Westley. He explained that he was going to set up a business in nearby Gatwick Airport to deal in aircraft parts for airlines. He said there was some input from an American company, which wanted him to start something in this country. The business was to be called Aerotron. We met Tony and the business owner Ron Cannady in a hotel near Gatwick to talk things over. They decided not to appoint their own full-time accountant, asking us to take on the role instead. That was in 1973 and it meant a huge change in my working life. All of a sudden, Eugene and I were doing our full-time jobs during the day and then meeting up with Tony Westley in the evenings to set up his office and everything that went with it.

We soon realised we had taken on quite a task. Eugene and I did all of the recording of invoices raised and the bills paid. We prepared the accounts, chased the debtors, wrote the cheques and Jacqui calculated the salaries. At the start, Aerotron was just a two- or three-man operation but very soon the business began to grow. We started to earn good regular money and it became essential to balancing the household budget.

Not satisfied by this, we became even more ambitious and thought, 'Right we're doing it for Aerotron. We can do accounts for other people.' We soon found other self-employed clients. It was a business that worked on word of mouth, with one sub-contractor leading us to his mates that he worked with, who required similar support. We called ourselves A & D Accountants. That stood for Aldridge and Doyle. It became quite an operation and we both even had some personal clients. I ended up having thirty clients. Apart from Tony Westley's Aerotron company, they were mainly sole traders: builders, painters and decorators and all sorts. There was plenty of work, even though much of it was repetitive and time-consuming. Our clients usually brought their invoices and paperwork to the house in an untidy muddle in a carrier bag and Jacqui would have lots of sorting out to do before I could even begin to prepare their accounts for submission to the Inland Revenue. So, after never having considered working for myself, I now found I was a businessman!

This was the start of a very important time in my life, and I went into it with my eyes open. Being with Jacqui meant I had cut myself off from a lot of people, obviously not my mother and father, but not every member of my family approved of our relationship.

My parents never questioned me. I think they were very perceptive. They encouraged me to enjoy my new life. I realised how much I had been frustrated by my life in Brighton and saw that moving away into a larger family had really helped me to grow. We did more family things. We travelled more. I'd never flown before and we went to Majorca – just me and Jacqui. It was fabulous.

One opportunity open to people working in local government is to earn money by working on the updating of the electoral role. This involved sending out forms to the area that you are allocated and then making sure they are returned and completed correctly. Doing this funded our first fight on Freddie Laker Airlines.

Another major change came about around this time as I was on the lookout for a move. A job was advertised in the *Local Government Chronicle* for an Assistant Secretary role in London with the Chartered Institute of Public Finance and Accountancy (CIPFA). I discussed the post with Nigel Palk and Ted Lynch. The job had another strong attraction and that was the Secretary of the Institute, a man called Maurice Stonefrost. I thought he would be an incredible person to work for, and he was. The problem was that it was outside of the conventional progression that my career would normally take.

CIPFA felt like a very prestigious place to work and I was confident that I could find another job in local government later if I wanted to, in the same way that Nigel Palk had done. So I applied for the role. One benefit was that the Institute's offices were at 1 Buckingham Place, SW1 in an elegant Georgian house only a ten minute walk from Victoria Station, giving me a ninety minute commute door-to-door. It was also, briefly, the home of 'No 6' the character played by Patrick

McGoohan in the cult TV series *The Prisoner*. My interview with the great Maurice Stonefrost was successful and on 25 January 1973 I was offered the job at a starting salary of £3,684 p.a.

Leaving Crawley District Council was not easy. I had made some incredible friends in the thirty months I was there, and the experience had changed me as a person into a family man with responsibilities. Again, many of the people I worked with went on to have great careers and featured in different ways in my life at CIPFA or with Capita. As well as my friend Mike who, believe it or not, I would work with again at CIPFA (and who later had a great career with British Gas), I owe a great deal to Ted Lynch and Nigel Palk from whom I learnt so much.

I started to work for CIPFA on Monday 5 March 1973 and the next ten years were to prove to be my apprenticeship for the most major event that would happen in my career, involving the opportunity to start the Capita business.

Taking on a ready-made family was wonderful and Jacqui and I were very happy together. In 1974, we got married. It was a wonderful occasion and I was absolutely sure I was doing the right thing, second time around. We were married in the Registry Office in Crawley Town Hall, the place where we had first met. My mother and father were there, which meant everything to me but none of the extended family came. Mike was my best man again. We had a reception at the Doyle family house in Crawley and then a family celebration at the Russ Hill Hotel. Life felt good again.

7

WORKING
FOR CIPFA

Working for CIPFA was quite a shock to the system. It felt like another world. I went from Crawley Town Hall to a beautiful Georgian house at 1 Buckingham Place, London. The building was used in opening scenes of the iconic TV series *The Prisoner* when Patrick McGoohan turns up in his Lotus and walks into the house as I did, rather less dramatically, one Monday morning in March 1973. The other big difference was that I had gone from an authority with many thousands of employees to an organisation with just fifty. However, the impact of this widely revered institute was truly national and, in fact, international, with members in far off countries of the Commonwealth.

I joined at a key point in the Institute's development as in 1973 it was granted a supplementary charter by the Privy Council, widening its sphere of operation beyond local government into public services such as health, water, gas and electricity. Much of this was derived from the great changes in public services that were going on at that time. It provided the opportunity for me to learn more about these organisations and to create an even wider network of contacts. At this time the Institute of Municipal Treasurers (IMTA) became the Chartered Institute of Public Finance and Accountancy (CIPFA).

Anyone who had a senior position in finance in a local authority had passed the qualification that I had in order to be elected into CIPFA's membership and have the right to use the letters CPFA. Membership also included many in central government as well as those in the health service. It was one of the six major accountancy bodies in the UK, the most well-known being the Institute of Chartered Accountants, whose members virtually all worked in the private sector.

The secretariat I had joined advised both its members and the public bodies that they worked for across England, Wales, Scotland and Northern Ireland on a range of different aspects. It had a very active regional network, making it a networking body of the highest order.

As a public authority-focused body it was far more entrepreneurial than the Institute of Chartered Accountants. CIPFA's courses and conference programme was sizeable and popular. It had a wide range of services that public bodies bought on a subscription basis, which generated regular income.

Even in 1973 it had built a business around a basic mutual premise that local authorities with a temporary cash surplus could lend money to others that would otherwise be overdrawn. This illustrated the power of the Institute to bring together individual treasurers and their councils, resulting in substantial savings to local authorities. There was also financial benefit to the Institute, which was considered a member of the local authority club rather than part of the commercial market, and it competed very successfully against commercial operations. It was even managed by a panel of senior treasurers who were CIPFA members. The bureau grew to such a size that Ted Lynch, the Treasurer I worked with at Crawley, moved to be its full time manager upon his retirement from the local authority in late 1974.

I was met on my first day by Alan Legg, my new boss. He took me up the stairs to the historic council chamber, and next to this was our office. Our office turned out to be the library, and it contained desks for four people, one of which was mine. So in one move I had gone from having a palatial space at Crawley to a desk in a library with a telephone. There were no visits to the canteen and no escaping from this room for private conversations.

The next floor housed the offices for the Secretary, Maurice Stonefrost, his deputy, Richard Emmott, and the all-important PA, who became a supporter of mine, subsequently typing many of my job applications. On the floors above this were the offices of the Education and Training Department, which was obviously the major work of the Institute. I quickly found out that in the basement there was a whole industry, where people beavered away. The most important of the basement activities was the courses and conferences section, through which the Institute generated massive revenues from the programmes that it administered.

In our room, as well as Alan Legg, there was a girl named Sue Gilchrist, the administrator for all the work we did. One of the first key appointments that we made was to fill the post of a junior, and we appointed a young man called Steve Wilkins. He had previously worked in a tailor's, and we could never understand why he applied to work for a professional institute. He turned out to be a very significant appointment and spent the next thirty-five years of his life working for CIPFA, playing a major role in its development. We became a great team. We had to. There was no alternative.

My role entailed taking responsibility for the control and development of the Institute's Financial Information Service (FIS). It was a huge revenue earner for the Institute, providing twenty-eight volumes of information designed to help members interpret different aspects of services provided by local authorities. It reminded me very much of the *Encyclopaedia Britannica* that my parents had bought for me all those years ago.

In today's world this information would be held online and updated accordingly. But not then, and my role was to keep it updated and to answer any technical queries. It was basically a subscription service with monthly updates going out for many of the volumes. Each of the volumes had a Chair and a working group of around a dozen contributors looking after it, so my network of over 300 contacts throughout the country was amazing. Each working group had the role of updating their volume, and mine was to work with them to achieve this. Once I had the copy it was then my job to edit it and then to ensure that the updates were forwarded to the printing company for production and circulation.

At CIPFA I dealt with people who changed the face of communities throughout the length and breadth of the land, and these were large characters in their own right. They included people like Jack Woodham, who transformed Newcastle, Sir Harry Page, who did the same for Manchester, Francis Stephenson, who was 'Mr Birmingham'. There was also John Patrick who masterminded the development of Oxford, and Geoff Pollard who performed the same role for Bradford and the whole of West Yorkshire. All of them ultimately became presidents of the Institute. There were many others of this calibre, and I was exposed to this network, along with key people in their respective organisations whom I also met and with whom I built relationships. This proved to be an invaluable network when, many years later, I was able to apply it to the formation of Capita. They knew me and trusted me as we had worked together for a long time.

I had some unusual responsibilities. I had to act as a focal point for local authorities advising on the introduction of Value Added Tax (VAT) in the country. The impact of this was very similar to that of decimalisation, where people were frantically searching for information about how they should operate and to what they should apply VAT. Sitting at my desk in Buckingham Place I became the expert that everyone called from around the country to ask for guidance.

CIPFA was also a very entrepreneurial organisation and found many ways of generating revenue. Within our small room we worked out that every local authority needed to implement housing benefit legislation that had been introduced. This required applicants to complete forms to enable a test to be undertaken to establish their eligibility for benefits. We designed a standard form through using the network of contributors to FIS, getting it authorised by the Department of Social Security. We then offered every local authority the opportunity to have these forms overprinted with the name of their own authority. We supplied millions of forms to a large proportion of local government offices. This was a great earner for the Institute.

Our organisation was highly regarded by government. It was regularly asked for its views on legislative changes ahead of them reaching the statute books. This presented me with an amazing opportunity to be involved in the preparation and submission of evidence, working with key chief offices to draft it. This included preparing the Institute's evidence into an enquiry on the effectiveness of New Towns undertaken by the Expenditure Committee of the House of Commons. The Institute's working group for this included all the chief executives of the new towns throughout the country, including Ted Lynch from Crawley, and so my experience there was invaluable. I even attended the House of Commons as the Institute's representative to give oral evidence to the Committee.

One of the first things I was asked to do by Maurice Stonefrost, was to review a book that was being prepared by Dr A H Marshall, on financial management in local government. He was a 'God' in that not only had he transformed Coventry into a local authority that attracted the best brains in the country, but his previous books were textbooks used by all students (including myself) who took the Institute's exams. It was now my role to sit down with this man and comment on the manuscript that he was producing for his next masterpiece! This was a daunting experience, particularly considering the awe in which I held him. He was an amazing person to work with and, to my pride, when the book was published he made special reference to me in the preface. I still have the signed copy to this day.

I intended to have three years at CIPFA and planned then to move on, but before I knew it I was in danger of staying for too long. I was enjoying myself. It was a small, yet formal, environment where a lot of people, considered to be experts in their fields, came to sit on committees advising on current issues of the day, influencing how legislation or standards were drawn up and then implemented.

My initial job was as Assistant Secretary. I was the clerk of many committees, preparing papers for consideration, writing up the minutes and then implementing the actions from the meeting. Much of this work led to the publication of reports or booklets. Many of the issues stimulated the need for courses or seminars, mainly held at the Tara Hotel in London, where delegates from all parts of the country would attend. My role was to design the courses associated with the areas of my work, choose the speakers and then attend the event. This proved an enormous opportunity to meet and to spend time with key people around the country, relationships which again, unknowingly at the time, proved invaluable.

One major event was CIPFA's week-long annual conference. A small team of us from the secretariat had the role of supporting the President and the Secretary with the logistics of the event. It was an honour to be invited to join this team but there was already an inner circle that appeared to go every year. Anyone going needed to be liked, and to fit in with the group. To my amazement I was considered to have those attributes!

My first experience of this was at the annual conference in Scarborough in 1974. Delegates and their wives would start arriving in the various hotels over the weekend, the conference starting at midday on Monday with the opening address from the President. The team from the secretariat (including myself) left 1 Buckingham Place first thing on the Saturday to drive to Scarborough in two estate cars, loaded to the gunnels with equipment and signage related to the various events.

One of the perks was that you stayed in the five-star hotel used by the President and the council members. As the junior I was allocated the task of 'shadowing' the President to ensure that he got to every event on schedule. To lose a President would be a career-shortening event. It also included managing the President's wife, which required all my interpersonal skills. It meant I was on duty from first thing in the morning until late at night. It was a role straddling waiter, manservant and bodyguard.

It was most definitely not helpful to awake with a hangover or miss hearing the bedside alarm. As mine was a larger room than anyone else's in our team, the decision was taken to set up a full bar in my room for late-night drinks. I found that waking up with empty glasses and bottles on the table and the smell of brandy in the air was not a great experience. It enhanced my popularity with the team but naturally not with the President, who could detect my less active brain the following day.

My experiences at the annual conferences, in addition to those held in Scarborough took me to Brighton, Eastbourne, Edinburgh and Harrogate. They include many stories such as the infamous occasion when I lost the Chancellor of the Exchequer of the day in the changing rooms under the stage at the Brighton Dome – the very place where I had danced. This happened when there was a power cut just as he was going to the loo before speaking to the delegates!

By the time of the Edinburgh conference, Mike Harding had joined me at the Institute, our third period of working together. While in Edinburgh, we had an opportunity to play golf at one of the local courses. Unfortunately, our round took much longer than planned, resulting in us rushing through the hotel in our golfing gear with our golf clubs at the same time as our guests arrived for a cocktail function.

After I had been at the Institute for just over a year, to my great disappointment Maurice Stonefrost left to become the Chief Executive of the Greater London Council, ultimately working with Ken Livingstone. The new director, who came from the GLC, was Eric Wood. A restructuring saw a new role for three under-secretaries to be established. The role that interested me was the under-secretary responsible for the research and technical division. I applied for the role and was called for interview. A number of potential candidates had left and others fell away, so eventually I was the last man standing and was appointed in August 1974. My move from Crawley had proved to be the right one, as the legislation that would have put me out of a job in Crawley came into operation in April 1974 under the Local Government Act.

My new role was as Technical Director of the Institute, which gave me responsibility for a division that advised the council on the panels established to advise on audit, accounting, higher education, the Financial Information Service and the activities of the Financial Data Processing Panel. The latter is where the beginnings of Capita emerged eight years later. Each of these panels had an assistant secretary, with a role similar to my previous one. Most significantly, each panel had a Chair and a team of twenty people who were considered to be the most knowledgeable brains in the country on the subject, with many going on to hold very senior positions in local government, health and central government. One of the most active groups was the Audit Panel chaired by Philip Sellers and serviced by Mike Harding. One of the biggest successes was the production and marketing of an audit training package which was sold as a training tool to public bodies. Mike and I travelled the country promoting this.

The job also involved having responsibility for the production of the Institute's journal *Public Finance and Accountancy*, building my contacts with the media, and for stimulating the research activities of the Institute, which involved working with the branches around the country to produce thought-provoking publications on current topics – another useful network.

I worked with Maurice Stonefrost in his new capacity of Director General of the GLC to establish a Management Processes Panel that he chaired. I visited him regularly in his wood-lined offices in County Hall, now the Marriott Hotel, but previously the domain of "Red Ken" Livingston, who had his office next to Maurice. The panel consisted of the heads of the public corporations such as Gas, Electricity, Water, the BBC along with senior civil servants. This gave me enormous insight into the issues facing these industries and access to another network of potential contacts.

The part of the job that drove me to distraction and resulted, thankfully, in my move away from the core work of the Institute was the responsibility for monitoring the Institute's relationship with the other accountancy bodies through an organisation called CCAB: the Consultative Committee of Accountancy Bodies. Here I was expected to sit through long and laborious meetings commenting on drafts of accounting and auditing standards that were drawn up by this body and applied to the presentation of commercial accounts. Although much was not relevant to the public sector, as we moved forward certain aspects became increasingly relevant and yours truly was there to protect the interest of the whole of the public sector. It was serious and important stuff but dreadfully boring and not something for me.

In 1980 the Institute appointed Noel Hepworth as its director. Eric Wood had done a good job, but he was nowhere near the stature of Maurice Stonefrost and the Institute had begun to decline in importance. This situation was reversed by Noel, who had a high profile in local government, having previously worked for Manchester City Council and the London Borough of Croydon. I learned a great deal from Noel and would most definitely put him alongside the most talented people that I worked with. He was most definitely entrepreneurial in the way he thought about things and the Institute was set on a growth path as a result of his appointment. But I was not a 'Noel type' and had I applied for the role of under-secretary under his watch, I doubt that he would have appointed me.

A healthy pay increase on becoming under-secretary meant that my decision to move to CIPFA was the right one. The next issue was, where was I to go next or, alternatively, did I see this as the place where I would work until I retired? The latter was not an option in my mind!

The private work for Tony Westley and many other clients had eased the financial pressures on me. The family benefitted from this in many ways, one of which was a trip that Eugene and I were asked to make to Long Beach in California to visit the offices of Aerotron. Jacqui and her mother joined Eugene and me in what was our first visit to the States. We made this into a two-week holiday, seeing for the first time Disney World, Universal Studios and the Grand Canyon as well as Las Vegas, San Diego and San Francisco.

Aerotron remained our major private client, growing all the time and eventually moving to new premises near to Gatwick Airport. Tony managed to purchase two very large consignments of aircraft parts, which were catalogued and stored in the massive warehouse ready for resale.

A & D Accountants went on for quite a long time and while it brought in a significant amount of extra income, it became more and more complicated to give the necessary time to it, while also doing my full-time job. I was pretty sure that, under my employment contract, I was not really supposed to do this other work but I didn't ask.

To do a full day's work and then come home and do this extra work was not easy. My evenings were tied up with a lot of people coming to the house to see me. The phone was always ringing and it became a nightmare. But it was the way we funded holidays and, most importantly, the school fees for our children's education. Jacqui and I had decided that we wanted the best for them. I had been so badly affected by my own experiences of a poor education that I was determined that they would not experience the same. Private education was a considerable expense that we needed to fund and whilst my main employment earnings had increased, it was by no means sufficient to fund school fees. So the evening working went on for many years.

YOU'RE BETTER THAN THEY THINK YOU ARE

Jacqui and I had had our son, Michael James, on 24 September 1975. This provided some company for Debby and we became even more of a family. I never minded working the long hours it took to provide for them. After wanting children for so long I now had two of them in Debby and Michael, which was wonderful for my parents as well. Debby was first and, for my father, she turned out to be the most magnificent thing that could have happened. I know he had been disappointed not to have had grandchildren earlier. But when I got together with Jacqui, all of a sudden my father had an instant granddaughter and now a grandson. He was so happy.

Looking back, we became increasingly concerned about my father's health from around the time of Michael's birth. I recall at Michael's christening, which we held at Goffs Park Hotel in Crawley in March 1976, he was going through one of his occasional periods of depression. There is no doubt that his two very serious incidents of perforated ulcers, when he almost died each time, had taken their toll. While he continued to work at his business the physical nature of it was beginning to show. I was able to help him with the preparation of his accounts and the submission of information to the Inland Revenue. From this information I could see that he had many regular clients and a role with a local hotel where he took care of various maintenance jobs.

My father was also was incredibly helpful to Jacqui and me with the redecoration work that we needed in the new home we had moved to in Blackwater Lane, Pound Hill. He loved coming to us because it also gave him the opportunity to spend time with Debby and Michael, as well as helping us out. On the DIY front I was a great disappointment to my father. He was incredibly talented practically while I had the equivalent of 'two left feet' in that field. My first steps in outsourcing came where I was prepared to earn the money to enable others more skilled than I to undertake the work.

Around Christmas 1978, my father had a mild heart attack. His doctor advised us that he should not see the children for a couple of months until he was feeling stronger. This proved to be very difficult for him and for us, as explaining this to Debby and Michael was not easy. He was prescribed warfarin to thin down his blood. This also meant that in winter he began to feel the cold, which in turn added to his depressed state. The heart attack meant that he had to sign on with the DHSS, at a very depressing office on Boundary Road near Portslade Station. I went with him and he was forced to sit to wait his turn with people who were out of work and claiming benefit, something he had never done even when he was made redundant. Many, he said, were able to find a job, but were prepared to take a handout rather than try. Coming from a lifelong Labour supporter, this was a very powerful statement.

I recall the day that he received a letter from Social Security declaring that he was eligible for invalidity benefit. The words 'invalidity benefit' hit home to him as it appeared to write him off for good. He had been condemned to join those who relied on state handouts. He continued to do jobs around the house but his major job was to take and collect my mother to and from work at The Alliance Building Society's main office near to Hove Park, where she was a kitchen assistant.

I bought Dad a season ticket for Sussex County Cricket Club to encourage him to watch a game at the County Ground, where he took me many times as a young boy. I recall that summer we saw a great game together involving Sussex in the semi-final of the Gillette Cup which they went on to win that year. My father would be very proud that I am now a vice-president of the club, enabling me to go into the Committee Room, a place where we had only previously watched people sitting on the balcony with their gin and tonics while we drank our pints of bitter.

I went with my father to see his doctor. I felt that he was not getting good medical advice. He had become increasingly breathless. He was under a Dr Chamberlain at Hove General Hospital following his heart attack, and they were confident that he would fully recover. From where I sat it seemed that there was more that they should be doing for him, and so that day in the surgery I was there to get answers. His local doctor examined him yet again and sought to convince me, in his words that: 'Your father will make his three score years and ten,' which seemed in those days to be the measure of success.

Unfortunately, in those days I was not as effective as I am now at getting things done that are important to me. And nothing was more important to me than my father. I remain convinced that had I been so there is a strong chance that my father would have enjoyed a longer life. This weighs heavy on me still today. I believe that the National Health Service let him down badly but that is difficult to prove and it is all too late to change things. If I had then enjoyed my current financial position, I would have taken him through private care and if he needed a heart bypass operation I would have paid for it. This sort of option is not available to many people even today and definitely then it was never considered.

Dad should have lived much longer. His two brothers and sister enjoyed far more years. His older brother Alf died at the age of 101, his sister Dorothy lived until ninety-seven and his younger brother Peter is still going strong at over ninety.

I particularly noticed my father's state of mind when we met up as a family on the Sunday for tea at my Aunt and Uncle's house in Upper Lewes Road. Jacqui, myself and the children had travelled down from Crawley. At this time, Jacqui was seven months' pregnant. We had the usual laughs with my Uncle Jim, who was always a jovial character. My father, however, was very quiet and sat for a large part of the time on his own in another room. This annoyed me, as I felt he needed to 'get a hold of himself' and look on the positive side of things. My last memory of him is waving as he crossed the road with my mother to get in their car. I recall being angry with him and really stressed by the situation, which Jacqui and I discussed on our drive back to Crawley.

It turned out to be the last time that I saw my father alive. Every lunchtime I would ring him at Foredown Drive to see how things were. Next day I was meeting Mike Harding for a pub lunch and we always had a good laugh together over a couple of pints and sandwiches. I decided that day to call my father later. Maybe I was still feeling angry from the previous evening but it proved to be decision that I very much regretted.

For some reason, I decided to leave the office early that day, 12 February 1979. When I arrived home at 5.30 pm, Jacqui met me at the door and told me that my father had died. She had tried to contact me at the office but I was already on my way home. Jacqui has always said that this was the most difficult thing that she had to do in her whole life. Apparently, he had not turned up to collect my mother as he usually did, which was not in character. So she had got a lift home with a friend of hers, only to find my father lying in the hallway. He had had a fatal heart attack and, although the ambulance staff tried to resuscitate him, it was to no avail.

The next two or three days were a blur, doing the things that you are never trained for and always dread, such as registering the death, arranging a funeral and informing people of our sad loss. Jacqui and I stayed at Foredown Drive overnight and until the funeral. One decision that I made and do not regret was that I did not go to see my father at the mortuary. Uncle Jim went to pay his last respects and apparently he looked at peace but had damaged his head in the fall. The saddest thing for me was that in his last minutes he was alone.

The funeral was at the Woodvale Crematorium in Brighton, the place that I used to go to see the director about his budget when working for the local authority. The funeral procession went from my Aunt and Uncle's house at Upper Lewes Road, as my mother did not want my father to leave on his final journey from 38 Foredown Drive. I recall sitting in the chair that my father sat in just days before at the family event to write a message for the wreath. I found the ability to capture in words what he had meant to me.

My job was to look after my mother and that has been my responsibility for the last thirty-eight years. She and Father had been together as a team for forty-one years and now her partner was no longer there. I recall saying to her at the crematorium as we followed my father's coffin into the service, clinging on to each other: 'We do not openly show our grief in this public place. We will do that in private.'

The 'wake' was at the Sackville Hotel, and as usual at these occasions people say things about wishing to see more of each other, rather than just at such sad events, but it never happens. Of course the focus of attention apart from my mother was on Jacqui, who was heavily pregnant and the sadness that my father would never see the child she was expecting.

It was a massive loss to me when my father died. I had lost my compass at the age of thirty-two, but it acted as a spur to me to make sure that I would never let him down. I have never said this before but he influenced my thinking until the very end of his life.

On one Saturday in late October he and I had gone for a walk together. We ended up walking around Locks Hill Park, where we had spent so many hours playing cricket together, including 'test matches' played with a number of my school friends who had wandered over to get a game. It was a football match that happened to be going on at that time, but as we walked around and stood to watch, I gave my father an update on the role that I had at CIPFA and the work that I was doing with Tony Westley. I spoke to him about how unsure I was about what to do next in my career and that I was thinking of starting a business. He told me how he wished that he had left working for Harrington's long before he had been made redundant at fifty and how he regretted that he had not started his own business much sooner in life.

He encouraged me to be braver in my career and not to let the time drift by before it became too late to act. He spoke to me about the release of positive energy he had had when running his own business, as opposed to slaving away in a factory every day of his life. He encouraged me to consider starting a business because, although it was not the normal approach for people of our background, he felt that I was a person who could break this mould and would flourish. He was a perceptive man to the end and this is precisely what I did!

To be honest, I have never really got over my father's death and the fact that he never lived long enough to see the development of Capita, or the subsequent work of my Foundation or, more importantly, my family growing up. I believe in family very deeply and hardly a day goes past when I do not think of my father. When I do things that I am pleased with and others that I am not so proud of, I always ask myself what would my father have said. He was everything to me.

A lasting regret is that my father missed out on the next important occasion in my life. Jacqui and I had a baby girl who was born on 1 April 1979. We called her Jennifer Leonie. Her middle name was chosen in memory of my father.

In 1980 my mum moved out of 38 Foredown Drive, Portslade to live at Flat 1, Kingsgate, 111 The Drive, Hove. Obviously it was a much safer and more suitable home for her, but it was an emotional move for both of us. It finally cut the ties to the house that I was brought up in and the home my mother had cared for so devotedly from the day she and my father had moved in over forty years before.

Life goes on of course. Jacqui and I were determined to enjoy life and we loved family holidays. We went to America two or three times, once more through Aerotron and on other occasions under our own steam. We also visited many European cities and started our life in Portugal.

In fact, after a time I became dependent on the extra money and I even got to the point later of saying: 'Why don't I give up my real job and build this business?' I could see from our experience it would have been possible to build up a good accountancy practice. Jacqui assisted enormously with the business, processing all the salaries and recording many of the expenses, which was a great help. The extra income brought us a lot of good things, but eventually it got to a stage where it couldn't go on.

For many years I worked very closely with Eugene, my father-in-law. Although we worked for long hours mainly at weekends on Aerotron's accounts, we also had a lot of fun together. We regularly mixed these weekends with family events along with a drink or two down at the local pub or a game of snooker at the Conservative Club in Godalming. Overall through this work, we achieved what we set out to do and that was to enhance the quality of life we had as an extended family.

I gave serious consideration to developing A & D Accountants as a main business. However, the thought of having one hundred chaotic small sole traders handing in bags of invoices and paperwork and doing all their books, was horrific. Also, professionally, I wasn't qualified to do this. I had a public sector accountancy qualification and to sign balance sheets along with offering professional advice I would have needed to be a chartered accountant.

Working with Aerotron was an amazing experience. This was the first entrepreneurial thing I had ever done and Tony Westley was the first entrepreneur I had worked with. He was a very astute person, using his knowledge and ability to the maximum. From him I learned about how to manage customers and how to handle customer relationships.

I realised that in order to be successful you need to be extremely careful with your time and effort. You can easily work hard for long unproductive hours and be a busy fool. Tony Wesley was very well organised and everything he did was cost effective. He also had a great instinct for buying wisely. He would buy individual aircraft parts or a whole consignment of stock that would all be methodically referenced and sold at good profits.

Tony Westley is still in Crawley and is still successful. I had enjoyed working for Tony, but in the end it became more and more difficult to keep it quiet from the people at CIPFA, as I started to receive calls from Tony during the day. I was also company secretary of Aerotron, which is a role registered with Companies House and in later years, when chairman of Capita, a journalist who had researched me asked about the role I had with the company.

My two worlds were in danger of colliding. I shudder a bit because I was clearly overstepping the mark and contravening the contract that I had with my main employer. It was potentially a sackable offence. It was edgy at times and it became more and more uncomfortable. The President of Aerotron, Ron Cannady, offered me a job in Long Beach, California, where the main company was. The job would have meant a wonderful lifestyle, but I have never wanted to live outside the UK and I turned it down.

With Tony I knew when it was the right time to leave. He was becoming more and more demanding and I was tiring of the long boring sessions we had with him, watching him drinking his Canadian Club whisky. My relationship with Tony and Aerotron ended as it started, speedily. I recall opening the door to our house one morning only to find a large briefcase on the doorstep. Attached to it was a note, which asked me to return all of the company records that I had in my possession. While we ultimately lost touch in the usual 'Aldridge approach' of moving on, we had ten great years of working together and I was delighted to learn subsequently that the company became very successful, winning the Queen's Award for industry twice. Aeorotron's HQ is now Westley House, a 100,000 square foot warehouse near to Gatwick Airport, far from the run-down offices in Charlwood where it started.

In 1982 a very important person became part of my professional life. We asked a recruitment agency to find an admin assistant for me at CIPFA. Lynn Chidwick (nee Butler) was working at the agency, saw the job spec, took it off the books and applied for it herself! That began a relationship that lasted for 24 years, first at CIPFA and later when Lynn became Employee Number 4 at Capita.

On 23 May 1983 my football team, Brighton and Hove Albion, astonished their faithful fans, including yours truly, by reaching the FA Cup Final for the first time. They had even defeated Liverpool at Anfield. I watched every game on their journey to the final which was a 2-2 draw against Manchester United, famous for the immortal phrase used by the commentator, 'And Smith must score!' Well, Gordon Smith didn't and Brighton lost 4-0 in the replay. Like many a faithful football fan I took it badly. Lynn recalls: 'Normally, Rod would be his warm and friendly self and chat to people in the morning. The day after the replay defeat he went straight into his office and closed the door. It was mid-morning before I ventured in with coffee and sympathy. It was not a good day!'

Football disappointments were not my only problem. As I moved further into my late thirties my career frustration grew. I had realised that setting up my own accountancy business was not the way forward for me and I had reached something of a plateau with my job at CIPFA. I started to think about moving but the Institute was a difficult place to leave.

As the Institute's Technical Director I enjoyed the job because I was working with a great team of people dealing with senior figures in the public sector. Yet somehow it was still unfulfilling because I wasn't running anything myself. CIPFA was at the centre of the public sector, yet it also felt like a backwater where I was floundering. At this time the Institute probably employed about 100 people. My salary was at the level of an assistant county treasurer, with no chance of advancement. The only way was to find a role back in the public sector, but by then I had been at CIPFA for approaching ten years and this was not going to be easy.

I firmly believed I needed to leave the Institute to better myself and I thought it would be easy for me to do so. I was wrong. I applied for more than fifteen jobs without success. It was an unbelievably concerning period in my life and I had many depressing moments, not knowing where this would end for me. I often refer to this in speeches, saying that, unbeknown to me at that time, the greatest opportunity I would ever have in my career was about to appear, pointing out to the audience that had I been successful with any of my applications, the Capita story would never have happened.

When I look back on some of the jobs that I applied for, they all had people in place that I had worked with at CIPFA, but none were prepared to back me for a senior appointment. Yet subsequently all of them did business with me when I started Capita!

The positions that I applied for included Head of Costing Services to the BBC, Assistant County Treasurer of West Sussex County Council, Manager of Audit and Investigations at British Gas, Chief Finance Officer of the London Borough of Lambeth, Assistant County Treasurer of Hampshire County Council, Chief Administrative Accountant to North Thames Gas, Deputy Director of Finance of the Royal Borough of Kensington & Chelsea, Deputy County Treasurer of Surrey County Council, Head of Exchequer Services of Royal Borough of Kingston Upon Thames, and Assistant County Treasurer of Kent County Council.

I shudder to recall that I also went for a job I saw advertised in the *Financial Times* with a company selling financial leasing services to local authorities. While I had no experience of selling or of leasing, I clearly did have the network of local authority contacts, and this would have been invaluable to them. It always saddened me at a time when the private sector was awakening to the opportunities for business in the public sector to see very senior, well-known treasurers taking roles on retirement which effectively saw them being used as front-end salespeople meeting and greeting former colleagues to gain business. I was determined that this would not happen to me.

I was getting interviews, but not being appointed. Looking back, I applied for some quite bizarre jobs, at places where I would have been horrified actually to have worked. I couldn't even get a toe on the ladder. I was told time and time again I didn't have the experience of managing large teams, something that was essential to getting an equivalent salary in another organisation.

A number of conversations took place with senior figures on the Institute Council, whom I had known for years and had worked closely with. They had relied on me in these roles but none were in a position to help me now. What I needed was for one of them to give me a chance in their organisation but I wasn't seen to have the right sort of experience. For me they made great referees but were not prepared to employ me themselves.

I felt stuck. I had a wife, children and a mortgage, which meant that taking a pay cut to get the job I wanted definitely wasn't an option. It was a depressing time. I was heading for forty and I could see people at the Institute not so much older than I was who had long since decided to stay there for the rest of their working lives. I was very frightened of doing that. It was not a good time in my life. I felt I was not developing, not reaching my potential. I again thought of leaving to build up the business I still had outside of CIPFA but then caution stopped me, but I also knew from experience that that was not what I really wanted to do for the rest of my life.

I didn't know then that the greatest opportunity of my life was about to happen, thanks to a Conservative Government led by Margaret Thatcher.

8

CIPFA COMPUTER SERVICES – THE BEGINNING

Yes, in a way Margaret Thatcher of all people, came to my rescue after she swept to power in the 1979 General Election! She came in with the belief that everything in the public sector was inefficient, whereas in the private sector, competition meant that companies needed to be lean and mean to survive. Her mandate, therefore, was to expose this inefficiency in the public sector, and local government bore the brunt of her attack.

High on the agenda were the large, in-house, direct labour organisations (DLOs) which provided blue collar services such as housing maintenance and repairs, collection of refuse, highways maintenance and vehicle fleet management. These DLOs had become large and powerful, with none of their work won on a competitive basis, but given to them as a historic right. Of equal political interest to the Conservative Government, many of the most prominent were in the Labour strongholds of the large metropolitan boroughs such as Manchester, Birmingham and Newcastle. The assault on DLOs also gave Mrs Thatcher the opportunity to take on the unions, who obviously wanted to protect their members who were employees of these organisations to avoid redundancies.

The intent was to use legislation to force local authorities to expose their DLOs to competition with the private sector to win the right to continue providing the services. This created a material change in the way that all local authorities had to think about what they did and was the beginning of the belief that not everything needed to be delivered in-house.

The work I was responsible for at CIPFA involved advising local authorities about the impact on them from such political and economic developments. It meant that I had to stay right at the forefront of knowledge in every area of the work relevant to our members who held prominent positions in every one of these authorities across the country now under political attack. In a sense, it was the very reason for CIPFA's existence, particularly as there was a clear political intent both to extend this thinking to white collar services and to every public body, making local government the testing ground.

Margaret Thatcher was now targeting local government and local authorities, institutions that I believed in. The Institute was centre stage in this and the council wanted to be kept right up to date at all times. Several of the panels that I was responsible for were constantly evaluating the effects of the changes being promoted by the government. The Accounting Panel had, for example, produced an 'Accounting Code of Practice for DLOs' essentially a voluntary code, which translated the legal requirements into practical recommendations for members and officers responsible for the financial management of DLOs. This generated revenue for the Institute from publications and from courses run both in London and regionally.

The Financial Data Processing Panel, chaired by John Scotford, the then Deputy County Treasurer of Hampshire, examined the needs for a DLO computer system to deal with these new requirements. This also seemed to be the perfect opportunity to test the reaction to a standard system approach, since all local authorities were faced with the same requirements and needed to act within prescribed and demanding timescales for implementing the new arrangements. John said: 'Since every local authority faces the same challenge, why don't we do one specification and then make it available to all of them.' John was ably supported by Geoff Pipe, Assistant Treasurer at Birmingham City Council, who became central to our work as it developed. Unknowingly, CIPFA was about to stimulate the beginnings of a FTSE 100 company.

This was at a point where local government was under its greatest attack. I found myself in a remarkable position. I was sitting in the secretariat of a professional institute and I was looking at people working in local authorities who were being repeatedly taken to task by Thatcher. She was attacking almost every possible thing about local government and it was an extraordinary onslaught. She thought the public sector was bloated and inefficient. Basically, she came in with a determined and ruthless agenda. She wanted to dismantle nearly every operational facet of the public sector because she was convinced that it 'simply isn't good enough'. She felt that competition would lead to reduced expenditure and greater efficiency.

Mrs Thatcher decided the best way to get real value for money from local authorities was to make them bid for their own work. She introduced the concept of 'Compulsory Competitive Tendering' (CCT), which shocked the world of local government to the core. The Local Government (Planning and Land) Act of 1980 made competitive tendering of blue collar services compulsory.

Thatcher was saying in essence: 'You might be running the services, but you're not running them well enough. We're going to offer the private sector the chance to run these services. You've got to prove you're good enough to run them more efficiently or they will be moved to the private sector.' It meant that every core function of local government involving these services had to be carefully specified and costed, to allow the private sector to be able to bid for the work. Not surprisingly, the public sector was furious, as the policy effectively obliged them constantly to reapply for their own jobs. Yet opposition was in vain and local government leaders had no alternative but to comply with the Prime Minister's wishes. Although many local authorities had begun to prepare for CCT to be extended to white collar services, covering professional and support services, the Conservative Government under Prime Minister John Major ultimately abandoned this initiative.

It was a pretty fierce attack on the whole system. At the Institute we realised that to have any chance of fighting back successfully, local authorities had to get themselves in a better position to understand the costs of running their services in greater depth than ever before. Early on I could see how this unprecedented challenge also presented a massive opportunity to evaluate how services were being delivered and a new way needed to be developed.

My team at the Institute set out on a three-phased plan to develop a standard DLO computer system. Phase One was to produce a user specification, setting out the basic requirements for such a system. This was completed by the Financial Data Processing Panel in just under three months. The response to this initiative was overwhelming and testament to the powerful position that CIPFA held. Some 154 local authorities agreed to join the Phase Two initiative and to pay a minimum of £1,800 each to join a consortium to finance the production of a functional computer specification. We persuaded the Department of the Environment to put £30,000 into the project and to take an active role, enabling us to claim government support for the initiative. It turned out that CIPFA had sponsored the largest inter-authority co-operative effort of its kind ever to have been achieved in Europe and all this was done from our offices at 1 Buckingham Place.

So we now had a consortium of 154 local authorities of all types with a wide geographic spread, with a broad spectrum of activities and therefore requirements. We had the involvement of accountants, engineers and DLO Managers and a timescale of only twenty weeks to deliver the specification, with a gross budget of £250,000.

In November 1980 we held a 'beauty parade' at the Institute, involving consultants who were keen to undertake the work. We appointed Logica to produce a specification that IT companies could use to write software packages tailored for the CCT bids. A key part of that presentation team was Mike Burr, who eventually joined us in what was to become CIPFA Computer Services. Mike later became one of the 'buy out' team that formed Capita.

It was a considerable achievement that the project was completed by 31 March 1981 on time and within budget. The project had involved over 30 per cent of local authorities and had seen active participation of more than ninety representatives from these organisations. Phase Two participants had received the equivalent of four-and-a-half man-years of expertise and experience for an individual cost equivalent to ten man-weeks of effort. The Specification we produced detailed a computer system to cope with the management and financial control of DLOs, covering the full range of local authority activity, from housing maintenance to highways construction.

It was a triumph for CIPFA and it was going to get even better. Phase Three involved implementation of the system and was completely new territory for the Institute. I recall that we tested out the support for the Institute continuing its involvement through seminars I attended around the country and through a questionnaire that we sent out. It was made clear by those authorities who had participated in the consortium that it would be positively wrong for CIPFA to withdraw at such a critical stage.

It was an amazing experience to see the forms we had sent out for people to sign up, come flooding in each day in the post, supporting us to go with the project. And 27 August proved to be milestone for us all, in that this was the day a letter was sent to local authorities confirming that the consortia arrangements for Phase Three would go ahead.

We announced that we would be prepared to assist in two ways. Firstly, the Institute would act as a central point for those local authorities who wanted to combine with the manufacturer to share the cost of development for a mainframe solution. Secondly, it would help those authorities who wanted what was called a 'stand-alone' system placed on a mini computer that would interface with the mainframe they had. Our role was to manage a consortium designed to provide both a hardware and software solution.

With the help of Logica, we then held discussions with the major manufacturers and suppliers to local government to test out their suitability to respond to the challenge measured on defined criteria, such as presence in the market, customer support to implement and adaptable application packages available. It was important we did this in a measured way since the recommendation of a supplier that failed to deliver systems on time would have direct effect on the reputation of CIPFA. Equally, the non-selection of a supplier had to be managed well with good reasons itemised for the decision, as rejection of their services would inevitably be open to challenge by them. The fact that they had not been selected would not be helpful to their future sales and reputation, and would need to be explained by them to their user base.

As a professional institute we had therefore entered a 'war zone' in the lucrative world of selling hardware and software to local government. All the salespeople in these organisations had bonus arrangements linked to the delivery of quotas and DLO deals presented a serious opportunity to earn large bonuses and to increase market share.

For me this involved entry into the world of these computer suppliers, who were dominated by ICL, which had a 60 per cent share of this market along with Honeywell and IBM. From my days in local government I knew it to be an industry full of slick, well-dressed salesmen with budgets to entertain clients over lunch or at sporting events. In return they had successfully sold local authorities machine capacity that was sometimes in excess of what was needed and also had long-term leases in place, restricting any ability to move away to another supplier.

After these deliberations with the market, we announced that CIPFA's consortia arrangements for an implementation date of 1 April 1982 would focus on the products being offered by McDonnell Douglas Information Systems (CMC) and ICL. CIPFA invited local authorities to join the consortium for a fee of £2,500. For this sum, they were able to take advantage of the discount being offered by both of these suppliers on hardware and software. They could also be involved in the management committees to have a say in the basic specification of the system, and would benefit from Logica's quality assurance procedure.

CIPFA provided education and guidance throughout the development phase, and there was a right to an implementation support at an additional fee, which was considerably lower than that offered to those outside of the consortium. This deal was very cost-effective, as we saw yet again when over one hundred local authorities joined as a result of encouragement by both the Institute and two suppliers who saw it as a challenge to get the largest consortia in place.

The quality assurance by Logica was key as it evaluated the system against the standard specification and accessed the mythology used to develop the solution on offer. This level of scrutiny enabled the Institute to provide a 'seal of approval' to the systems once they were developed. As part of this process, we negotiated on behalf of CIPFA a royalty arrangement in return for the 'seal of approval' for any systems subsequently sold by the two suppliers.

This proved to be a challenge for us to manage as the CMC system was ready on time and CIPFA was able to give it a 'seal of approval' having seen it in operation at Kirklees Metropolitan District Council. Unfortunately, the ICL system was subject to delays and initially did not pass the Logica quality assurance test. With ICL being such a dominant supplier to the market this caused serious ructions involving the intervention of the company's CEO Sir Peter Bonfield, who was in direct discussion with everyone he could find at the Institute, including me, to complain about the process. After some delays the ICL system was eventually passed by Logica and it received our 'seal of approval', enabling the market to decide which of the two solutions to buy. CIPFA had royalties on both!

While I described the computer salesman as being aggressive, overly well-dressed people, it can be said that CMC salesmen took this to another level. The company had come from nowhere as a result of this exercise, and saw it as a major opportunity to challenge ICL's market position. The CMC sales force was a focused bunch of fast-talking barrow boys, who could sell anything to anyone. They set about their task to provide systems which would initially run on a stand-alone machine linked to the mainframe. But ultimately their desire was to replace the mainframe itself, which in most cases was an ICL product.

To support this attack on the market, CMC simultaneously negotiated a deal with the Institute to provide our first in-house machine. This gave them another marketing edge, allowing them to say that if CIPFA had bought one of our machines, it must inspire confidence for you, Mr Local Authority Treasurer, to do the same. CMC put on large sales conferences, at which we were asked to speak; their techniques worked and they built a major position in local government as a result of it.

The CIPFA Council was growing increasingly nervous about the extent of the Institute's involvement and the risk to its good reputation if systems failed, particularly with the financial return it was making. We persuaded the Council that one way of mitigating this was for the Institute to make the specification widely available to other manufacturers, so as to stimulate the widest possible use of the standard specification.

This, however, became another substantial revenue earner for us, as I sold it under a copyright licence. The offer available to these manufacturers was very different to the two consortia. It was stressed that CIPFA would not accept any responsibility for any statements made by these companies about its product, nor would the Institute appraise or endorse the contents on the systems on offer. The copyright licence enabled the company to state, that in its opinion, its produce complied with the CIPFA functional specification.

Notwithstanding these restrictions we found ourselves inundated with requests to meet virtually every supplier of systems to local government in order to negotiate agreements over a copyright licence. The list of twelve suppliers included names not well known today, since many have either been sold or gone out of business. The specification was licensed to Allied Business Systems Ltd, ADP Network Services Ltd, Leasco Software Limited, Business Microsystems, Burrough Machines, RTZ Computer Software, Datapoint, Honeywell, Nixdorf Computers Ltd, NCR and the mighty IBM United Kingdom Limited. In all cases, it was my role to sit in front of executives of these companies to negotiate the terms, which was again a new world for me. It added to my knowledge of their thinking and proved invaluable in the future.

The outcome of all of this was a very lucrative financial one for CIPFA, who had collected consortium fees which more than covered the costs of running the project. The Institute also had a royalty arrangement in place, where it would receive royalties for every system sold across local government, which could involve over a hundred local authorities. The icing on the cake was also the copyright licence that we put in place with twelve other suppliers, each paying around £12,000 for the pleasure of being able to claim association with the functional specification.

What we had effectively been doing under the auspices of CIPFA was to build a business. Many start-up companies stumble because of the inability to understand the market in which they are selling their products. In our case, we understood that market in every detail and what its needs were. Additionally, not only did we have the massive contact base I had developed personally through my nine years with CIPFA, but we had developed a specific client base of more than 154 local authorities who knew us. At the time it was easy to underestimate the value of this network and without a doubt CIPFA did.

The most important task I had to perform during this process was to build a good team to work with. I realised that without the right people, any ambitions I might have would come to nothing. From the start I sensed this could be our springboard to success. The first guy who joined the team was Roger Brier, a CIPFA accountant who had been working for Kirklees Metropolitan District Council and had been involved with the consortia activities. Roger had a deep understanding of the system and of the requirements needed by the local authority to comply with the legislation.

Roger was a bit of a dour northerner, yet he was a bright man, a little younger than me. He was very clever and could think through problems quite quickly. We worked very well together. He had responsibility for the financial reporting side and operated mainly with the CMC consortia. Roger joined as a full time employee in 1982.

The specification was taken up by many agencies in addition to local government. This included the London Transport Executive and West Midlands PTE as well as other transport executives and some local health authorities.

The Chief Executive at West Midlands PTE was Don Colston, who became one of the first clients to back us in a very big way. He awarded us a consultancy assignment to implement the DLO concept in his organisation, which was the beginning of a long-term relationship with Don. We ultimately advised him on the management buyout (MBO) of West Midlands PTE to form West Midlands Travel. Through Don we met Peter (later Sir Peter) Rogers, who was his deputy at West Midlands PTE. Peter went on to become the CEO of Westminster City Council with whom we would have a major contract.

Suddenly this was quite a lucrative enterprise for CIPFA and also a potential problem. The Institute took legal advice and was informed that making profits of such a level was not covered by the Royal Charter. The Institute had put at risk its charitable status. However the Director, Noel Hepworth, could see that this was a route for him to fund the expansion plans that he had for the Institute.

The Institute had already formed another company called CIPFA Services Ltd. This provided a whole range of management consultancy services to local authorities, including advising on major redevelopment programmes. It also worked overseas, particularly in Africa. It was run by a chap with the sometimes unhelpful name of Dick Turpin, who looked amazingly like John Cleese. I got on well with Dick even though over the following eighteen months we were thrust into going head-to-head by the Institute's ideas about how to develop both companies.

The obvious route was for the Institute to form another company, specifically to focus on developing the IT work started by the Financial Data Processing Panel, which had turned out to be by far the biggest commercial operation that CIPFA had been involved with. This change happened in the summer of 1984 when CIPFA Computer Services (CCS) was formed and I was invited to be its managing director.

I should have been over the moon, but the truth was that I was unsure if this was what I wanted for my career! That seems incredible to me now, given how it all turned out. At the time it seemed really risky to move to work for a private company, albeit owned by CIPFA, when I had spent all my working life in the public sector and my plan was to become the treasurer of a local authority. I have nightmares about it now, but I came close to turning the job down. I was worried about what I would do if CCS failed.

It took me a little time to realise that this was far from a dead-end to my career, and rather it was an amazing opportunity that might never come my way again. It also had to be measured against the many unsuccessful applications that I had made to move away from CIPFA.

Lynn Chidwick later called this my 'light bulb moment' and she is probably right. I could see the huge potential of the business and after discussing the opportunity with Geoff Pollard, who was a Past President of CIPFA and a man I respected hugely, I decided to accept the job.

At this point in time, Thatcher's determination to force down costs was going to affect many people's lives and open up huge opportunities for anyone in a position to compete for local government work. It was a chance I had to take. 1984 was also the year CIPFA moved offices to 3 Robert Street, just off the Strand in central London. Strangely, this turned out to be opposite the flat I bought in nearby John Adam Street in 1997.

An enthusiastic young man called Richard Benton joined us in April 1984 from the London Transport Executive. We became involved with him after London Underground showed interest in using the computer system. We liked him straight away and we worked well with him and persuaded him to come and join us. He became our sales director. I liked him because he was very good with people and he could win work. Rich, as he's known, could explain practical aspects of the system very clearly and he could sell things very well.

I always knew the key to our success was to build a great team. The last key executive to join was the same Mike Burr whose work had been so crucial to the design of the specification. We had worked well with Mike, but of course that was when he was still working for Logica. I decided he was exactly the right man to complete the team. In April 1985 he became our marketing director.

Before 1984 I don't think any of us had ever set out to be in our own business. As time went on, we became convinced that we could build something very successful. I think we knew there was a niche in the market and we were quite surprised at the way the business developed. We started to win assignments and projects and the tension came into the system because we were hard-working directors who were responsible for the company, yet all the CCS profits were effectively covenanted back to the Institute. We knew that was going to happen, but we still did not like it because it meant there was not enough investment in the company and there was a ceiling to what we could be paid. If we had been paid according to results we would have been out of kilter with the rest of CIPFA by receiving total earnings higher than those of the director of the Institute!

CCS was set up to own the rights to the specification and the work that came from it, which was really all consultancy driven. We advised people about the implementation of systems. While we were building a business, we were doing so as part of CIPFA. We were doing the whole thing in an environment I knew and there was no personal financial risk to any of us. I was still salaried but it rapidly became apparent that this new business, CCS, could be quite lucrative. I started to resent the fact that we had no ownership in the business. We didn't have any bonus arrangements in our contracts, so we pressed to agree these with the director.

We also started to agree budgets based on the projected future performance of CCS and that produced more arguments. Then I thought, 'Hang on a minute I'm building something here. I haven't got any shares in this. I don't want to be simply on a salary.' So we got into a debate about wanting a stake in CCS, which took CIPFA into very foreign territory. For an organisation with a firmly public sector mentality to give a stake to someone they employed, whom they had asked to set the company up on their behalf, was clearly far too extraordinary for them to even begin to consider. It was simply not in the Institute's psyche to give someone a stake in their business.

So at the end of our discussions they would say a very firm 'NO' to all of my suggestions to move our relationship forward. They would reply with: 'We'll give you a higher salary.' They appointed external advisers charged with the brief to report back to the council on a way forward. This led to more conversations and inevitable delays in reaching a decision, during which time the business was going like a train.

Being a managing director was something I'd not experienced before. The chairman of the Board was John Scotford, who had been the chairman for the Financial Data Processing Panel and had recently been elected to the council. This meant that the business was still guided by people with a public sector background.

The year 1985 marked the hundredth anniversary of CIPFA. I attended the celebration held at Manchester Town Hall on 13 December where the Institute was founded. I received my invitation card from the President, Philip Sellers, with the message 'Have faith' written inside. He was suggesting that I should have faith in the ability of CIPFA to be able to work out an arrangement whereby CCS could remain within the CIPFA family. This was not how it turned out and serious and eventually acrimonious negotiations lay ahead between Mr Sellers and myself.

CIPFA COMPUTER SERVICES – THE BEGINNING

The early years of CCS were exciting times. The income generated was quite remarkable and I was constantly amazed by the potential. We started to work with CMC on developing the DLO system to include packages on Stores, Transport and Plant, Bonus and then offering implementation and training support for these systems to clients that CMC sold to. We won assignments to advise local authorities on their IT strategies involving selection of hardware and the implementation of software solutions. We also had a major contract with London Underground to implement the DLO across the entire network of services. All of a sudden CCS had direct involvement in differing levels of complexity with over 250 public sector bodies.

We also negotiated an agreement with a very forward-looking local authority, West Wiltshire District Council, which set out to license its software to other local and public bodies. Our role was to be a part of the implementation team that came with the package. Effectively by doing so the Institute was signing an agreement, which not only offered maintenance and support, but by its association was giving tantamount approval to the suitability of the product. It was a further illustration of how far the Institute was blurring the lines between the role of the professional body and a commercial concern, particularly as it was Noel Hepworth, the Institute's Director, who was photographed signing the agreement.

Ironically, several years later, Capita bought West Wiltshire Computer Systems, which by then had been moved into a separate company because of the concerns expressed by the District Auditor over the commercial gains it was making and associated contractual risks it was taking should the software fail.

My confidence in the future even allowed me to undertake building a villa in Portugal! When I look back this was amazingly ambitious. We had been on several holidays to the Algarve and Jacqui and I both loved it. We went back again in the summer but this time to a place near Portimão called Serra e Mar, where we rented a house. We had a great holiday and fell in love with the area. We established that there was a plot of land for sale nearby and met with a German called Rolf Rollaper, who effectively owned all the land in Serra e Mar. It is always dangerous to make big decisions while you're on holiday, but we went two or three times in our two weeks' holiday to look. We came home and decided we still liked the idea.

It was a brave move as it required extending the mortgage on our main family home and it was something which none of our family or friends had ever done. However, we wanted to experience the culture of having a second home in another country for all our benefits but primarily for the children. We went back three weeks later to establish if this 'holiday love' for the place was still in us. It definitely was and so we agreed to buy the land and design a house to build on it. Designing it was great fun. I recall us measuring out the size of the villa bedrooms, lounge and bathrooms on the floor of our home in Copthorne to give us a proper idea of how it would all work. We then relayed this back to Rolf and he converted the measurements into a plan. The builders he appointed to build it turned out to be a father and son. Rolf was an amazingly straight character, who helped make it happen. It involved making stage payments, but not before visiting the site to make sure that the work had been done. We designed a pool along with the necessary landscaping of the garden. It proved to be one of the best decisions that we ever made and has provided countless happy memories of the children growing up and for all the friends and the extended family who have been there. It is important to remember that we had to rent out the villa both during the winter and for some of the summer months to be able to afford the additional mortgage. It was special to learn that we had regular tenants who returned year after year as they liked the villa so much.

While this was going on, Roger, Mike, Rich and I had moved towards either opening discussions to take over the business of CCS or for the four of us to leave and start again, but this time owning it. On top of this, Jacqui was expecting our fourth child Robert imminently! Life was full, but it was great. I now felt that I had a career. I had made the transition from public to private.

9

THE MANAGEMENT BUYOUT

Not that life was sunny at CIPFA. The tension between CCS and CIPFA grew and grew and became quite unhealthy and unhelpful, largely because Noel Hepworth was entrenched in his views about the control of the company by the Institute, persuading the council to portray CCS as an extension of the Institute rather than a stand-alone company. I still have enormous respect for Noel, who did a great deal for the Institute, and I see him as one of those people from whom I have learnt a great deal. However, in my view, he was not prepared to be remotely commercial about looking at how the relationship with CCS could work.

The truth of the matter was that we were very valuable to the Institute because our profits were going up and up, which meant they would benefit more and more. The problem was that we didn't feel we were benefitting personally. I faced the risk that if it all went wrong and they wanted to close the company down or to sell it on, then I had nowhere to go.

By this time we were growing and recruiting people. They were good people, but we needed to recruit more senior staff who would come from our competitors or the private sector and the salaries to attract such people would have to reflect this. This caused huge problems with Noel Hepworth and the Institute. Making profits is not something that local government is concerned with.

The senior people at CIPFA mostly couldn't understand why we didn't just get on with our jobs. We got to a stage where we were working hard and the business was showing enormous growth. We felt we wanted to have some stake in it so we went back to them yet again and insisted we would like to have equity. But for CIPFA, a very traditional, hundred-year-old Institute, to accept the concept of giving away, as they saw it, a proportion of a business to the staff, was just unthinkable. There was anger. They didn't see it as an opportunity, they saw it as a great threat. So that suggestion was rejected and the tension grew.

It became increasingly uncomfortable. I can remember doing a presentation in the conference room at Robert Street to the CIPFA Council members about our business because I wanted them to understand what we did. The presentation listed the names of all the local authorities that were in our consortia, the various products that we were developing and the contracts that we had won. At the time it was fairly obvious that there were council members beginning to get worried about where all this was going but many of them were already on our client list! As a consultant you are recommending solutions that you are contractually signing up to deliver, so there are liabilities and they began to get worried and jumpy about this.

On top of that there was the persistent tension that the management team conveyed to council members that we felt we wanted market salaries, a sensible bonus scheme and above all we wanted equity. Our relationship with Noel Hepworth became yet more antagonistic. By this point we were in a separate building, but still very much under the auspices of Noel and the Institute. Indeed, an article in *The Times* celebrating the centenary of CIPFA described the work of CCS as being one of 'seven columns' of the Institute's secretariat.

As a management team we spent quite a lot of time talking about this situation. I think by this point we all believed that there was a real opportunity to build a good business here. We had obviously created a space in a very small way and we were all at an interesting mid-point in our careers. I was facing forty. Mike Burr was five years older, Richard Benton was in his early thirties and Roger Brier was slightly older than him. We were at a time in our lives where we believed we were either going to grasp this challenging opportunity or we might as well go and find something else to do.

We needed a nudge to do something about our ambitions and we received one when I was waiting for a meeting in the lobby to see my bank manager. On the table in the reception area was a book that had been produced by *The Economist* entitled *Guide To Management Buyouts*. I had never heard of anyone in the public sector ever buying their business before, and at the time I didn't even really understand exactly what a management buyout was.

The book had been produced by a firm of accountants called Blackstone Franks. I got a copy and started to read all about exactly what a management buyout entailed. Basically it meant that the management team bought the business from whoever owned it. It shows you how far the world has developed since then because obviously it is a more natural process today. For a management team to plan a buyout is considered in some cases to demonstrate an element of disloyalty. It is seen by some as unfairly exploiting your position.

I read this book and learned a lot. I then decided to go and see the guy who wrote it, whose name was Lance Blackstone. We talked about all the many aspect of different management buyouts, or MBOs as we came to call them. It was fairly apparent quite quickly that it was a very do-able thing. By this time we had a three-year track record. It wasn't spectacular, but it showed we had turnover and profits and we were growing. It was obvious there was a market. Lance Blackstone was very helpful in suggesting we should do something. He introduced me to 3i, a venture capital company. This was another new world for me but I went to see them and it was there I met the 3i executive Paul Pindar. After some discussion and consideration of figures he and his colleagues felt the business was basically backable.

A further issue was also emerging and this was our relationship with CIPFA Services Ltd. This was becoming increasingly tense, difficult and competitive. The dividing line between which company bid for what work was confusing and causing increasing issues. I felt that this situation could only end in embarrassment to the Institute as, in many cases, the clients were its own membership. CIPFA Services had been formed before CCS and held a pre-eminent position in the eyes of Noel.

He also had a closer relationship with Dick Turpin than with myself in that the two had worked together previously at the London Borough of Croydon. I had several long telephone conversations with Dick, mainly in the evenings, suggesting to him that it would be mutually beneficial for us to agree on the need to settle the equity issue with CIPFA. I relayed to him that I had recently met a company that sold consultancy and software services to the public sector, and had floated on the stock market. I said to him: 'We could do that!' He was more risk averse than me and yet he had a greater opportunity than me to benefit from having equity in CIPFA Services, as it was larger than CCS.

Nevertheless, CCS was growing faster and I had no intention of backing off since I knew that my three colleagues were prepared to walk away with me and to start a new company from scratch. The later irony was that several years later CIPFA Services also fell out with Noel and subsequently negotiated a sale to the accountancy firm Touche Ross. Dick and his team had to pay a much higher price for their exit and it did not go as well for the business subsequently.

At the beginning of 1986, because of the growth and success of its trading companies, particularly CCS, the Institute decided that it needed a comprehensive review of the structure. It was clearly heading towards a rationalisation of the businesses. The review was designed to consolidate CIPFA's ownership position while attempting to placate the equity desires of the executives and the concerns that we had about CIPFA continuing to strip all of the profits out of the businesses rather than investing in our growth.

The review was undertaken by Laurie Brennan of New Bridge Street Consultants. He was a very experienced individual and at times must have wondered what he had got himself into, sitting as he was between Noel and the executives of the businesses. It led to a suggestion that a holding company to which the existing companies would be subsidiaries should be set up and called CIPFA Holdings Ltd, with a member of the CIPFA Council as Chair. It was clearly the intention that it would be created to maintain the status quo in the way that the Institute thought about the management of its business. In my appointment letter from Noel dated 1 January 1985 as a Director of the Company it made the statement that: 'The details of any bonus or incentive or equity sharing are still under consideration and discussion.' I am very clear that any movement by CIPFA at this stage on equity would have weighed heavily in our thoughts about going down the more risky route one method of an MBO.

It became increasingly clear that for me this was the opportunity I had been waiting for. If, at my age and with the three colleagues with whom I was working, I did nothing now, I would regret it for the rest of my life. It appeared to unlock all the anger, frustrations and determination I had in me to do something exceptional in my life to prove all the doubters of me wrong once and for all. I am a person who can be easily underestimated.

So the issue was 'how do we make this happen?' My meeting with Paul Pindar at 3i had given me the confidence that we were a backable team, but the question was how to start the process. Paul had little understanding of the public sector and little respect for the people running the Institute. What he could see was that a free-standing business selling services to local authorities could work. Once started, there was no way back and we either completed a deal or I would be sacked. Either way, confrontation with my employer of nine years was most definitely not going to be a pleasant process.

To support the idea of leaving CIPFA, the four of us had worked on plan for a 'start up' business where we assumed that certain members of staff would resign and come with us. It was called "CCS, The Alternative" and handwritten under it were the words "This document does not exist." It involved reliance on our wives for support on admin and the office systems were based on Amstrads. This was also based on a number of the clients deciding to remain with us. That was a high risk strategy, as clearly CIPFA Services would have picked up the residual members of our staff and competed heavily against us with CIPFA backing. We even went as far as identifying potential premises, settling on small offices in Maiden Lane in Covent Garden. These were opposite a Greek restaurant which we sampled to celebrate finding the offices and a pub next door, which seemed to be a winning combination!

There was a clear advantage to us if we could buy the company, as it meant that we would take our three-year track record with us as well as our staff and contracts. This was important, as it meant that our plan to float the business could happen sooner, as you needed a five-year track record to secure entry to the market.

I made a request to the Director and the immediate past President, Philip Sellers, that they should allow the four of us to buy the business. I went to see them and needless to say they were horrified and the meeting did not go very well. Frankly, looking at it coldly and dispassionately now, they probably should have sacked me on the spot, there and then.

What I was bluntly saying was that I didn't want to work with them any longer in the way we were structured. I wanted to buy the business that they owned. In a sense what I was also saying was, 'If you don't sell it to us we are going to go.' It was not an easy situation. The business had contracts with clients, liabilities with leases on buildings and twenty-three members of staff, so for somebody to say, 'I want you to sell it all to me', was a very bold move, particularly to a public-sector based organisation.

The concept of management buyouts subsequently became more acceptable, with in-house teams bidding for work under the compulsory tendering process, but at the time of my suggestion for CCS it was most definitely not a concept to be entertained.

The opposition to my plans from the senior figures at CIPFA was resolute and unanimous, apart from a single encouraging individual: John Scotford. Although he was not a member of the council at that time, John was well respected by them for the role that he had as chair of CIPFA's Financial Data Processing Panel. John was very clear thinking and supportive and we have remained friends to this day. I would like him to provide another view on those extraordinary times.

John Scotford says:

I was around when Rod arrived at the Institute. He was quite a serious guy, quite intense. I got on well with him because he was reliable and he worked hard. I never thought he would go on to create something as amazingly successful as Capita. I don't think anyone did. I definitely did not see it coming. He was just a good person to work with.

128

Rod was supported in setting up the company, but the attitude of the CIPFA hierarchy of Maurice Stonefrost, Philip Sellers and Noel Hepworth soon changed when it became clear to them exactly what Rod's plans were. They were outraged at the idea the new company could be taken away from CIPFA. When Rod said what he wanted to do my view was that 'you're not going to stop him'. I felt there wasn't any way you could stop him if that's what he and his team wanted to do. CIPFA couldn't successfully oppose it because it was going to happen and the best thing they could do was to get the best deal out of it they could. They should never have fought it. They should have struck a better deal than the one they did. They didn't because the three people involved were really anti-Rod.

In the end it got nasty. In a way CIPFA should have been part of it. I don't know why they didn't take a stake in it. Presumably the three of them didn't think it was going to work. There was a personality clash between Rod and the three. Noel Hepworth, Maurice Stonefrost and Philip Sellers were all strong confident men. As they saw it, there was a huge gap between their status and self-belief and Rod, who was way down below them in importance, wanting to do something they didn't agree with. They underestimated him. I underestimated him.

Thank you, John. And thank you for your support when support was pretty thin on the ground. I recall the hours on the telephone that we had in the evenings rehearsing the issues and the tactics to be used to get a resolution of the situation.

A defining moment came when we won a major piece of business in Belfast, Northern Ireland. It was the time of 'The Troubles' and we were awarded a contract to work with Department of Education (DENI) for all the Education and Library boards in Northern Ireland to do a major IT strategy review of their systems and then to implement our recommendations, part of which was to be the new system that we had developed. Our client was a pipe-smoking civil servant called Richard Holmes, with whom we built a long-term relationship.

This was a big consultancy assignment that we were amazed to win, beating off the very strong local competition from Coopers & Lybrand, but it came with many associated risks. There was the obvious threat of the civil violence, which plagued the province at the time. I had to go to Belfast when security was generally on high alert. It was scary around the airport, with army checkpoints on the road and the turnstiles to get in and out of the city centre on foot. But it was a fascinating experience all the same and there was a sense of determination to continue as normal.

CIPFA, both at secretariat and council level, then started to get nervous about the contractual responsibilities that could come from some of these contracts if they went wrong. There was a great deal of negativity from CIPFA, which we felt was unjustified. In business there is always a risk, but it is not something at the time that those in the public sector could calibrate and most definitely not the type of risk that they were familiar with. We faced increasing tension because of the Institute wanting to restrict what we could bid for, but still wanting us to be more and more successful because they liked the profits that we made that helped to fund the expansion plans of the Institute.

In many ways the Northern Ireland contract was the final straw in our relationship with CIPFA. It was a massive contract, by far the most lucrative contract CCS had landed in almost three years of operating for CIPFA. It should have been a cause for celebration, but we were made to feel as if we had done something wrong for taking unnecessary risks. Richard Holmes, our client, came over from Belfast for the opening of the Robert Street offices by Maurice Stonefrost. He sensed concerns in the way he was received by the council members and this convinced me that it was time to make our move.

Armed with the letter from 3i, I went into a meeting with the Director and Philip Sellers to raise the issue of us moving away from CIPFA. At this meeting they asked me to present my proposal to an assembly of the whole council, which comprised more than twenty people. On the day of the meeting I remember sitting at my desk waiting to be called to the Council Chamber. I entered the room and was invited to sit down by that year's president, Arnold Morton, the City Treasurer of Coventry.

I kept to the script that I had prepared. I had no previous experience of presenting in this sort of situation, under this sort of pressure. It was made worse because I was presenting to people I knew, as I had been there nine years by then. The atmosphere felt hostile as I began. Here is what I said to them:

Without a doubt today is a very important and significant day for myself, and for the company that I am responsible for and I would ask you to give careful consideration to what I have to say. I am aware that before getting to this council meeting a number of pre-meetings have been held and no doubt as a result a number of emotions have been voiced. I would therefore ask you to view what I have to say as a business proposition. Can I say from the outset that I recognise things cannot stay as they are? Irrespective of whether you have one, two or three companies, without key decisions on investment, equity and the relationship with the owner there is no future.

When CCS was formed in January 1984 it had three employees, the rights to a functional specification which had already produced for the Institute £200,000, the responsibility for servicing two consortia of local authorities formed to develop a computer system and the responsibility of providing at cost a Bureau service to CIPFA. Nearly three years later that company has approaching thirty employees and has a turnover of £1.5 million, £1.3 million of which is generated by consulting. Over the next five years the executive directors of CCS plan to grow the company four fold, achieved by an expansion of existing services and through the development of complementary areas such as software development. Work now ranges from strategic assignments setting out long-term IT plans to implement, assistance with computer systems and our clients range from local authorities to public utilities and central government. It is the future of that company which is under discussion today.

It is clear from simply reading the respective corporate plans that the business styles and future aspirations of CCS and CIPFA Services are totally different and poles apart in approach. It is our belief that the decision taken prior to this meeting seeking to merge the two companies will not work. I believe that there are a number of reasons for this.

I spelled out the reasons I did not believe in a merger with CIPFA Services as simply and honestly as I could and concluded:

> To merge CCS with CIPFA Services would not be supported by the four Executive Directors of CCS. It would be unacceptable also to our staff, and would dilute the considerable competitive strength that we have developed and harnessed within CCS. I am aware that a merger could be railroaded, but I would suggest for this to be achieved you would have to cut very deeply into the heart of CCS and by implication its people.
>
> As far as the Executive Directors are concerned we cannot allow the tremendous work that has been put into developing the company over the last three years to be diluted and we must look after the best interests of our staff, all of whom have been encouraged to join by ourselves. We therefore ask you to consider a further option, and that is to allow the managers of CCS to go off and form a new company. We want investment and you're not prepared to give us investment. I am able to confirm that we have an offer of funding from 3i. If you support this, we are prepared to offer that CIPFA retains 25 per cent of the business.

I concluded my presentation and suddenly it was very quiet in the room. I think that the Director was horrified and angry that I had the nerve to make the presentation. To put a personal perspective on it, although I presented on my own, I knew that my fellow directors were with me all the way and this was my opportunity to stand up and to assert myself to be the leader of CCS.

I was asked to leave the room. Not surprisingly the outcome of the meeting was that they completely rejected the suggested way forward and the offer. The 25 per cent was seen as irrelevant because: 'You're not going to be successful anyhow and all you want us to have the 25 per cent for is so you can claim association with us, which will give you credibility you will not have.'

Even if the offer had been accepted, the management buyout route was complicated. We would have to change our name and our premises. All the staff would have to transfer, and they therefore had to have the confidence that we were going to pay their salaries. So there were also risks involved for them. As a director of a 'new' CCS I had a conflict of interests. Could I really suggest they all leave and transfer to us and risk losing their pension rights? At first I felt I had no right to do that.

Later on in Capita's days if some employees had come to us and said, 'We want to do a management buyout,' we would have sacked them all on the spot. It's a very dangerous precedent to allow a management team to believe they can buy something. Generally you sell businesses when they're in decline, rather than when they are doing well, so you could have a management team who purposely underperformed so as to create the opportunity for a discussion. We would have acted decisively at that point and brought somebody else in to run the company. My view now, many years on, is that CIPFA should have done that with me and they could have done.

Instead they then decided to continue with the merger route. This meant that Dick Turpin would have become the chief executive of the enlarged business. So as we were under the threat of being merged we decided we would have to do something to counteract that.

With the rejection from the council, I went back to Paul Pindar at 3i to ask if they would back us if we left and help us implement the start-up business plan that we had put together. This was clearly a very risky option but we had had enough of Sellers and Hepworth and I think it was they that even provoked Paul into action about the backup plan. We had already located offices and begun preparing plans to set up our business. The four of us started to grow in confidence. We tried to remain hopeful about the prospects of buying the company from CIPFA, but if that didn't happen we were going to set up on our own.

We began to meet in secret, away from our offices in Westminster, to write our business plan, meeting regularly in room 007 at the Caxton Hotel. Our moods all varied and it was a very emotional time. At times it didn't seem much of a risk at all. I was part of a brilliant team lining up to own a business that we were already running successfully. At other times I worried about the risks I was running, giving up a steady job with a wife and children to support. What I did not know was that I had already burnt my bridges with CIPFA as they planned to sack me and to encourage Mike, Rich and Roger to stay!

After many conversations with John Scotford, I finally went back to Noel and Philip Sellers with two offers in my back pocket from 3i, one to back an MBO and the other a start-up. I said: 'You've now got a choice. You either back us as a management buyout or we will all leave.' The four of us would go and by implication the twenty-odd staff that we had at the time would follow. I let CIPFA know that we had financial backing from 3i to support both routes. If we left they would get nothing for that business and we would start the business up again. It was far better to buy the business, as it would mean we could take with us our three-year business track record, which was very, very valuable. Essentially if we walked away and began again from scratch our track was left behind, but equally it was CIPFA that had lost the opportunity to generate funds for a sale of the business.

It was therefore a stand-off position. We were very clear that we were not going to be merged. Their suggestion was equally blunt to me: 'Take it or leave it.' There was an implied threat but no-one ever went as far as to say to my face: 'If you don't do it you're out.' To sack me would have been a public statement and sent out a lot of negative messages but I have no doubt that even if I had decided to capitulate, my time at CIPFA was over.

It was a very tense period. The wobbles came. You can imagine going home and talking to your wife about risking everything. It was the same for all four of us. We all had families and mortgages and pensions. I pondered the questions: Is this really the right thing to do? Why don't you get another job?

The team spent hours discussing this situation and I got to know their wives and families who were wondering: who is this guy? I had to sell the idea to the wives. My wife knew all about my frustrations and what I was doing and that I couldn't get another job. Jacqui was very supportive, although I'm sure she was worried. I had other positive ideas and I am the sort of person who would have survived, but under no circumstances could we contemplate losing the house as a result of this.

With the news of a backup offer from such a reputable institution as 3i Philip Sellers, with his commercial nous, knew that the game was up. He was also a tough character who was violently against us. He had an annoying phase of saying 'now look here young man' to me. But now the young man he knew was no longer the Assistant Secretary of the Institute, but a man on a mission!

Philip said: 'I'm not going to take this from these people.' He bluntly said to Noel Hepworth: 'We may as well take something for this. We may as well take value now and we'll let them go and we'll compete against them through CIPFA Services. They will never make it so we'll take their money for the Institute.'

The Institute decided that clearly we were people not to be trusted, in spite of our long association. They went down the disloyalty route. They were clearly outraged by our actions and I think they were very close to the boundary of being unreasonable and of being offensive in some of the language they used against us.

We of course had to change our company's name and look for new, larger offices. The ones we had identified in Maiden Lane would not house twenty-three people. The Institute wanted no relationship with us at all and we were not allowed to claim any association with CIPFA.

And then the legal stuff came. Clearly they weren't just going to allow us to walk away without some pretty harsh conditions imposed on us and on what we could do. We had a lawyer by the name of Anthony Fine, who was a partner at Barnett, Alexander, Chart, based in Soho, and was introduced to us by Lance Blackstone. Anthony subsequently came to work for Capita for a period. He helped to set up a company that we established to assist teams from the public sector who won the right to do an MBO around the DLO activity of externalising areas of work such as leisure services or refuse collection.

A large number of people must have known what turmoil was going on, but fortunately it never made the press. They weren't the sort of people to run to the newspapers and, to be honest, neither were we. It was to our advantage to make it appear like a smooth, professional transition to independence, but in the world we live in today it would probably have hit the headlines in the trade press and on social media. We obviously had to talk to our clients in a confidential way. We were saying: 'If we do this would you still come with us?' The staff had to be told at different times what our plans were. It was an exciting and frightening time. But I found that in adversity I became stronger and because it was a cause I believed in, I loved it. I got behind it, we all did. It was four of us against the world and it was very emotional, but we were determined that we were going to come out on top.

Then we had some tough conditions imposed on us by 3i for them to part with the money that was to be invested in us. Although they wanted us and wanted to do the deal, 3i are not a soft touch. If we had failed then it would have annoyed them and hurt them, but it would have ruined us. The investment required by the four us was designed to be at a level where it was a material amount, both individually and collectively.

Subsequently I heard from Paul that when he put a paper to the Board they had initially turned down the proposal, as they didn't think our financial person, Roger Brier, was strong enough, after they'd met the team. Thus the first paper that was put up to 3i by Paul Pindar was rejected. They said: 'This is not backable, we're not going to do it.' To Paul's credit he went away, re-thought it and re-presented the whole idea. I think we had to put more money in the second time but they were finally prepared to back it.

That's when we realised we had started something. Now we knew we couldn't go back but to be honest and blunt we were massively scared of where we were going. CIPFA finally agreed to sell us the company for £330,000. They decided they clearly didn't want us and therefore they might as well take something for the loss of the company now because we were going to go anyway. We could take our existing clients with us, but we were not to use the CIPFA name or to trade on any relationship with it. They were so adamant that they wanted nothing more to do with us that they rejected any thought of keeping the 25 per cent stake in our new company that we had offered them. That is a decision that was to cost CIPFA £2 million, as Capita floated on the USM (Unlisted Securities Market) 18 months later with a valuation of £8 million!

They were actually offensive and personally unpleasant. At the end it was just a question of getting the deal done and getting out. Financially it was a tough call for all of us. 3i's offer was dependent on the four of us putting in a total of £80,000 of our own money. For me, this meant adding an additional £24,000 to my mortgage. This was not an insignificant amount, particularly bearing in mind the sum I had already added to the mortgage to finance the home we were building in Portugal. Looking back on the letter that I wrote to the bank manager at Lloyds in support of this, I realise in hindsight this was a masterpiece of optimism but by then the atmosphere between the four of us and CIPFA was becoming so unbearable that we were hardly speaking to anyone in the Institute.

I was perfectly prepared to put my home at risk to escape, because I knew that I had every intention that Capita would not fail. This was a happy ending to a very tense time. At this juncture my wife Jacqui was expecting our fourth child and it was pretty clear that the bank was serious about what the money meant, because they took a second charge on the house. They left me in no doubt that they would come looking for it if the business failed. I was probably the most bullish of the four of us in terms of taking on the challenge. I think it was partly because at thirty-nine I thought this was the best shot I was going to have so I was going to go for it with everything I had, bearing in mind my recent track record of fifteen failed job applications.

I was also the most vulnerable of the four of us with few escape routes back into local government, which through my actions of taking on CIPFA were now even more restricted. In taking on my employer, I had taken on the establishment.

So we had somebody who essentially could design solutions, we had somebody who could write proposals and sell work, we had another one who could do marketing, and we had me, who understood the markets. That was the team. I picked all those people, I probably don't take the credit for that as much as I should. I picked them by working with them, which I suppose is the best way. I think I'm quite good at recognising people who have talent but, above all, I am good at building teams.

We found new accommodation in the Park Gate building in Tothill Street in Westminster. We basically had no furniture or office equipment, nothing. We did have a name, as Lynn Chidwick helpfully recalls:

> At the time of the buyout of CIPFA Computer Services it was felt that we should distance ourselves from CIPFA by calling ourselves The Local Government Consultancy Ltd. This was the name we tried to register at Companies House, but at the eleventh hour Companies House said we couldn't use it as it implied we had official status or support from local government, which we did not have. It turned out to be a relief that we did not get approval because very quickly we moved beyond the artificial boundary of local government for our clients. So Mike Burr, in his marketing director role, asked everyone in the office for ideas. One of our consultants, Jonathon Rogers, came up with 'Capital Consultants' and proposed a London skyline as the headed notepaper. We, however, felt that we needed to appeal to the whole country, not just London, and Mike suggested knocking the 'L' off and calling it Capita, as that was a Latin name familiar to the public sector (as in *per capita*). He also suggested using Times Roman capital letters to emphasise this and proposed a tag line underneath, not part of the title so Companies House couldn't object, of 'Consultants to the Public Sector' (in Times Roman italic).

Thank you Lynn! I recall we also chose Capita because the IT in the middle indicated we were a technology company and we felt could enlarge those two letters. It was good overall because 'per capita' is a public sector term and so we registered that name. In taking a company 'off the shelf' for the sake of speed, the name of the company we incorporated on 8 December 1986 was Known Ltd, which was definitely not representative of us as we did not see ourselves as having a known limit! This was then subsequently changed to Capita Ltd and the rest, as they say, is history!

The MBO was completed on Friday 13 March 1987. It drove us all much closer together. The process of negotiating the deal had been very emotional and intrusive, with lawyers involved at every turn. It felt very much as though we were the 'meat in the sandwich' between CIPFA and 3i. I had not done anything like this before and neither had the other three. 3i obviously required that we adhered to a number of conditions. They don't just give you large sums of money without clear stipulations regarding reporting, performance and governance. There is a complex contract with them and responsibilities that go with it.

We had twenty-three members of staff who were all transferring to work for Capita. This was a huge vote of confidence on their part. They all had mortgages and families and pensions to worry about. We were the leaders of this new company that they were relying on.

The experience was extraordinary. I wouldn't like to understate the emotional impact the whole uncomfortable extrication from CIPFA had on us. I had one fraught evening when I left the Soho offices of our lawyer, Anthony Fine, feeling so wound up and confused, that I ended up in Victoria. I had walked and walked and I honestly don't know where I went or what I did. I intended to end up at Victoria, but I was so wound up and stressed I think I did it on automatic pilot!

There was a lot of anger around the transfer of our pensions arrangements from the Local Government Superannuation Fund. CIPFA had negotiated rights to be a part of the Wiltshire County Council scheme and all my contributions from the age of eighteen when in local government, plus my nine years at the Institute now resided in that fund. The issue was that, inkeeping with all such funds, there was a pension deficit and my employer had to pay contributions into my pension based on a quinquennial valuation of the fund. I am quite cynical when I hear people talking about pensions being so massively important. I think you should do everything you can to get there and enjoy it, but at thirty-nine it was not the most important thing that I had on my mind. I had obviously been paying into a pension scheme for some time and CIPFA was not prepared for the arrangement with the Wiltshire County Council Fund to continue. They wanted to agree a transfer value which reflected the valuation at that time, meaning any shortfall in my fund would not be made up. There was a lot of 'umming and aahing' about this and in the end to conclude the deal I agreed to take the hit personally.

There were all sorts of emotions going on at the time but we were on this inevitable track. If we didn't go through with it then there was no way back. We got to a point on the day when the deal had to be done. I physically had to get a cheque from the bank manager to the completion meeting to pay for my share of the deal. When we got to the day of the signing, which was Friday the thirteenth of all days, I had to collect all the cheques in and go to the offices of CIPFA's lawyer. I went with Paul Pindar, who had the funds from 3i, to complete the deal. It was a huge thing and that was when my house really was on the line. Each of us had to find the necessary money in his own way. Each of us thought, 'What the hell are we doing here?'

The completion meeting was attended by Phillip Sellers and Dick Turpin. Both of them, I recall, found it a hilarious exercise for some reason. They probably thought that it was easy money for CIPFA. I was surprised when Philip even resorted to reading a passage from the Bible that resides in the office of all law firms as we concluded the final signing of the agreement!

I was angry, but I was also frightened because I honestly didn't know where my career was going. There was absolutely no doubt that this was a wonderful opportunity, but there are no certainties in business. I knew that I had a huge responsibility to seize this chance and make a success of it. The most important fact that comes across to you during a management buyout is that you can't afford for it to fail. You emotionally won't let it fail. It was probably the best time of my life in terms of the development of the business, because we were phenomenal. I think for each of us and definitely for me, it was a last chance. It was an opportunity to do something with great potential. We didn't know where it was going to go to. It was a chance to build something. You never know where opportunities are going to come from, but you've got to recognise them and once you've recognised them you've got to go for it.

We had some very perplexing twists and turns along the way. For example, one of the conditions of the deal with 3i was that we had to have a bank overdraft for the business, and negotiating this provided me with a valuable insight into the way people treat you. I went to Lloyds, which had been my bank since I was sixteen years old, and they wouldn't touch us. We went to several other banks and they wouldn't touch us either, specifically they wouldn't give us an overdraft, which meant that we couldn't trigger the money from 3i. We even considered taking out a loan equal to the overdraft needed and simply logging the money with the bank so that we could comply with the offer letter.

In the end 3i, Paul Pindar introduced us to Barclays and ever since then, for thirty years, they have been Capita's major banker, throughout its growth, its acquisitions and its contracts, all of which generated very sizeable deposits and banking requirements. While they were prepared to give us an overdraft, even they wanted all four of us to guarantee the amount through securing this against our houses. That was a difficult time and two or three of the team, particularly Mike, were running out of patience and getting very nervous about the deal. Certainly two of the four were at times close to walking, even at the last minute! I persuaded them that we should stick with it. So we signed at around lunchtime by which time the staff were in our new offices. I believe we carried some furniture around from our old premises.

Some of the people who were employed by CIPFA Services came round, sadly not to congratulate us or to say 'you're very brave' or even 'good luck,' but to ridicule us. Feelings were quite bitter in some areas. A note had been put out by CIPFA saying what had happened regarding our departure and saying: 'We want nothing to do with them.' I do believe that the phrase: 'Now that the cancer has been cut out we can put all our energies into building our business without them' was used. However, we weren't too worried about bad feelings from ex-colleagues. Indeed it acted as a constant spur to me every day that I came to the office. We were much too euphoric about the future for that. All our current clients had agreed to come with us, which was a very important point. All the contracts were transferred and I was convinced that the future was bright.

We then turned up at our new offices and we suddenly realised that while we had been doing all this work we had changed our name and address – none of our clients knew where we were! We drafted a letter to send out. We had no accounting or cash so I remember queueing up with Lynn at the Post Office on the corner in Victoria and buying 200 first-class stamps to send letters out to say where we were and explain what we were doing. It was phenomenal. We had a party to celebrate, and I can recall going round to everyone at the end of the evening, full of optimism. There was a lot of handshaking and hugging people. We were really up for it.

The celebrations continued when I arrived home I can remember us going out to an Italian restaurant in Crawley to celebrate as a family. Michael was eleven, Jennifer was seven and Debby was seventeen. Everyone was in this new chapter in our lives, and it bonded us together.

The adventure that was to follow over the next twenty years was to prove a legendary process, as very few people have taken a business from a start-up to the FTSE.

10

HEADS ABOVE
THE PARAPET

Friday, 13 March 1987 was a very special day in my life. We signed the deal and the fraught period of negotiations with CIPFA was a thing of the past. At long last, the four of us could focus all our efforts on building Capita as our very own free-standing company.

I have read about people who hold a fear for the number thirteen, and those who have a total fear of Friday the thirteenth. Well, most definitely, after my experiences with signing the deal on Friday the thirteenth I have a fear of neither!

1987 was quite a year for celebrations in our family. Jacqui gave birth to our fourth child, Robert Jonathan, on 7 July. One of the first things that I did was to go to tell Michael of the news at Brambletye School near East Grinstead, and he was allowed home by the Headmaster, Donald Fowler-Watt, to meet his new brother. Michael was the first of our children to board and this move was a very emotional moment for both him and his parents. Michael went on to Charterhouse public school in September.

On 7 November, I celebrated my fortieth birthday with a party at home. Reaching the 'Big Four O' is a time when most people reflect on their life and for me, had I not had Capita and a new addition to the family, I am sure that it would have been a time for a great deal of soul searching. But I now had something to throw myself into, and that is precisely what I did. It was also the year that our villa in the

Algarve was completed, resulting in a very excited family visit to experience it for the first time.

Not that we had much time for celebrations in those early weeks and months of Capita. It was an exhilarating feeling. We hit the ground running hard to keep up with the growing influx of work. There is nothing that can galvanise your efforts more than, after many months of frustration, suddenly finding that you are working for yourself and in control of your own destiny. All four of us felt that surge of relief that we had finally pulled it off. It was heads down with our new company, doubling and redoubling our efforts.

I felt a heavy personal responsibility to the twenty-three people who had followed us from CIPFA Computer Services. It was a huge statement that every member of staff came with us to our new offices at Park Gate, 21 Tothill Street in Victoria. They all believed in the vision that I had set for the company. The team spirit we had was very apparent in the office and obvious to our customers.

CIPFA and CIPFA Services competed against us intensely in those early days. CIPFA also tried relentlessly to ridicule and rubbish us in the market, to whoever would listen. I recall an article in the business and finance section of *The Independent* newspaper on Monday 23 March with the headline, 'CIPFA in knock-down sale'. The piece suggested that the MBO team had got a very good deal, but Dick Turpin in his role of MD of CIPFA Holdings justified this by saying that the business was not offered to anyone else because: 'It was not a very saleable company as it was primarily a people business.' We likewise placed articles in various trade magazines confirming our intention to build the company but holding the line that it was an amicable split from CIPFA, stressing that it had been important to move away as our growth plans were being held back.

In the CIPFA Council there were twenty-three members who were all-powerful and influential in their respective local authorities across the country and one of our main markets was local government. The great thing I had going for me in that particular world was that lots of the key players also knew me. In one capacity or another I had worked with a large number of people in different ways over the previous nine years and established a network of contacts. They knew what I stood

Above: Me aged around eighteen months with my mother and father, Doris and Len.

Below: Portslade County School for Boys winners of the Under-15 League – that's me holding the Cup. We were undefeated for two seasons.

Above: My dancing trophies won in competitions up to under-sixteen level.

Right: My partner, Cheryl Fletcher, and me receiving the trophy as winners of the under-twelve South of England championship held at Lewisham Town Hall.

Above: At the Stock Exchange on the first day of dealings in Capita shares following our flotation on the USM. From left to right: Rich Benton, Mike Burr, myself, Paul Pindar and Roger Brier.

Below: Opening of the BBC Information Centre in Belfast by the Rt Hon. Dr Mo Mowlam, Secretary of State for Northern Ireland, and the Chairman of the BBC, Sir Christopher Bland.

Above: Signing of the Telecom Capita contract with Jim Jackson, BT's Marketing and Business Development Director.

Below: Receiving from Sir Stelios Haji-Ioannou the award made to Capita as winner of the 2003 Royal Bank of Scotland *Sunday Times* Business Award.

Above left: Councillor Sir Merrick Cockell, Leader of the Royal Borough of Kensington and Chelsea, and Sir Rod at the sod-cutting ceremony for the Kensington Aldridge Academy in March 2013.

Above right: Monday, 23 July 2012 – holding the Olympic Torch as part of my participation in the London Olympic Torch Relay.

Below: Receiving my Honorary Doctorate of Business Administration from Manchester Metropolitan University from the Chancellor, Dame Diane Thompson, and the Vice-Chancellor, Professor John Brooks, 17 July 2012.

Above: Dance Champions Dance Summit with Angela Rippon, Arlene Phillips and Lisa Snowdon.

Below: At the celebration of the Foundation's tenth anniversary at Spencer House in London: Khushna Sulaman-Butt stands next to the painting she completed as part of her Fine Art degree from Oxford University. Alongside her are Brendan Loughran, the Principal of Darwen Aldridge Community Academy, and Liam Dargan. Both Khushna and Liam were students at DACA.

Left: The UTC @ Media City based in Salford opened in September 2015.

Right: Kensington Aldridge Academy opened in September 2014.

Left: A view of the playing fields at the Sir Rod Aldridge Cricket Centre, with the Brighton Aldridge Community Academy in the background.

Right: Darwen Aldridge Community Academy, the first of our academies, opened in September 2010. The Darwen Creates business pods are visible at the front of the academy.

Above: Welcoming the arrival of HRH Prince William and Kate Middleton to open Darwen Aldridge Community Academy, the couple's final official public engagement before their marriage.

Below: HRH the Duchess of Cambridge joining a reading lesson with students at the official opening of Kensington Aldridge Academy in January 2015. David Benson, the Principal, is looking on.

for, and what we had already delivered for them through our work on the functional computer specification, at a time when they felt under attack from the government.

Under the terms of the deal the four main clients: the Department of Education in Northern Ireland, London Underground, our work with McDonnell Douglas Information Systems and Honeywell came with us. They had the right not to, but they all chose to transfer because the people working on the contracts were key and were now in the Capita team. It was, nevertheless, a huge compliment that such large organisations were prepared to work with a fledgling company. We also had the rights to the computer specification we had designed and the benefits of the good track record that came through this work.

We won two major pieces of work very, very quickly which was great, but I was well aware we needed to continue winning contracts. We were still a consultancy business at this stage and by then had forty mouths to feed. Invoices issued each month not only paid salaries but the overheads as well, plus we needed to make a profit! Ironically, we never needed the overdraft we had so much difficulty in negotiating as part of the terms of the MBO offer from 3i. From day one we were cash positive. The tremendous initial impetus that we had, along with the amazing team spirit, made us unstoppable.

Both Capita and CIPFA Services became a great source of advertising revenue to the popular trade magazines, including *Local Government Chronicle, Municipal Journal* and even CIPFA's own journal, *Public Finance*. All were read on a weekly basis by our customer base and while it was difficult to track the direct impact on our business from this expenditure, there was a need to show that we were around and most definitely ready to compete.

Every year there was still the CIPFA conference, which I had enjoyed attending when I was part of the Institute. It was a huge event attended by more than 1000 delegates. Since my days on the secretariat, CIPFA had developed a very successful exhibition that sat alongside the conference. For the June Conference, three months after our MBO in March, we took a stand at this exhibition. That instantly raised a lot of Institute eyebrows! It was hilarious to get old colleagues, who were intrigued to hear our side of the story, onto the stand. It was equally reassuring to see how many delegates passed by to wish me well personally, confirming how strong and transferrable my contact base was. Members of the CIPFA Council kept well away for fear of giving us a sign of credibility.

To get some interest going, we put on a competition on the stand, with a prize of a personal computer for the winner. Entry was via a card that needed to be collected from the stand and returned into a 'post box' container, which sat on the corner of our stand. This attracted people to the stand and gave us the opportunity to speak with delegates. It also gave us the names and addresses of people to correspond with post conference about our services. It was apparent that quite a few wanted to win the personal computer, but really did not want to be seen on our stand. So we had many furtive visitors and, much to my amusement, I can still remember seeing a hand coming round the back of the exhibition stand attempting to pop an entry in the box. I saw the hand struggling to find the box and I grabbed it, only to find that it belonged to one of my ex-colleagues from the CIPFA secretariat!

The conference and exhibition were held in Brighton, my home town, at the Metropole Hotel. Our team, led by Lynn, did a 'recce' of the hotel several weeks before the event, and we pulled off an amazing coup. It might sound a little pathetic now, but at the time it was of great entertainment value for the team and a huge PR victory. We established that all the delegates had to enter the conference down a main staircase, which had three large, fully-lit glass display cases. We spoke to the management of the Metropole and negotiated a deal to acquire the advertising rights for all three display cabinets. As a result of this each cabinet had emblazoned in them in huge letters messages about our company. The first said 'Capita, Consultants to the Public Sector'. The next had a list of the services that we offered and the final case said, 'Come and meet the team on Stand 93'. Since on many occasions delegates would be queuing on the stairs waiting to enter the conference sessions, we really did get value for money over the week for our modest outlay. I understand that this really got up a lot of CIPFA noses. Questions were asked from on high, such as: 'How the bloody hell have they done that and who allowed it to happen?' They did manage to have our stand allocated to the most awful place, right in a corner, out of the way.

We still did still some good business there. Rich Benton managed to sign up seven computer manufacturers, who were also exhibiting, to work with us on a standard specification involving new housing benefit legislation. This more than paid for the cost of our stand. Each sale represented about three months' work for a team of three or four people.

The work just snowballed and the momentum was great. We did the exhibition for three years. I can confirm to you that running a stand at an exhibition is exhausting work and a pretty awful way to spend your time.

The bitter breakup with CIPFA was inevitable, but it was still unfortunate. It was sad what happened and it confirmed to me that I am not good at leaving organisations. I had nine years there and made a lot of friends. One of those friends is Steve Wilkins, who I appointed to the secretariat. He is now retired and we are still good friends and play a lot of golf together. Steve said: 'There was a lot of animosity against Rod within CIPFA, particularly when Capita did so well so quickly. I think the people who let the business go were almost seen like the guy who auditioned the Beatles and told them, "You'll never make it."' Steve became a very good friend and while at CIPFA there was a memorable occasion when Jacqui and I, along with Steve and his wife, Bernadette, were invited to a garden party at Buckingham Palace as part of CIPFA's centenary celebrations. I will always recall us meeting Diana, Princess of Wales and shaking her hand.

I worked hard at building a team spirit in the company. It was a sense of: 'We are all in this together.' I found that running a consultancy-style business is not easy. The individuals are by necessity confident people, as they have to go into an organisation and command immediate respect. Equally, they spend large amounts of time away from the base office and their home. I therefore set out on the last Friday of the month for the entire company to have an evening together in a restaurant, just to catch up with them. It was never a very expensive restaurant, maybe a local Italian or Indian, and we took over most of the place with the cost of everything covered by the company. I always thought that when I received the bill at the end of the evening it was probably no more than one day's chargeable time by one of our senior consultants. But the goodwill it created was worth far, far more than that.

I believe it is also very important to take holidays, in order to spend plenty of time with your family. I've never stinted on holidays and in 1988 we took a cruise on the *QE2* to New York and Niagara Falls. It was a wonderful family holiday. Little Robert took his first steps unaided on the ship! Nothing stands still in a family! The next year Debby left home, starting her nursing training at Charing Cross Hospital.

On another occasion we had a family holiday in our villa in Portimão. It proved to be infamous because I took my tape recorder with me and dictated the next phase of our development. These became known as 'The Algarve Tapes' and kept Lynn busy for hours transcribing them.

In business one never stands still either, because if you do you are effectively going backwards. This required me to make some tough decisions. The four of us had come through a lot together and we were certainly a formidable team. However, I always recognised that if someone came along who would improve our team then I must not be afraid to make changes, even if this did put some of the goodwill between us at risk.

One of my strengths, I believe, is that I am a good judge of people, and equally good at building teams. When I see a really talented individual I want him or her on my team. I have no fear of appointing people who may be better than me in some areas of expertise, because overall the only way that I am going to develop is to be challenged. During the MBO process it was clear from discussions with 3i that they were not comfortable with the financial reporting skills within the business. Indeed, initially it caused their board to feel unable to back us. This was Roger's area of responsibility and so once the 3i investment was in place, I knew it was inevitable that the issue would resurface.

To put this into context, Roger and for this purpose myself, were CIPFA qualified accountants and while I always argued my corner with chartered accountants about the relative strengths of the different qualifications, in the end one type of accountant is more focused on the method of operating in the public sector, while the other kind deals with commercial operations. A chartered accountant can sign a company balance sheet and a CIPFA member cannot.

Reality soon kicked in with my exposure to the venture capital boys at 3i. They may provide the money with a smile, but the level of scrutiny and financial reporting required was several notches higher than that of the board of CIPFA Holdings! Similarly, it was clear that they would have a short time-fuse if the business was not performing in line with the agreed financial forecast. This was of personal concern to me, because 3i's balance sheet was a great deal stronger than mine and I still had in my mind the look on the face of my bank manager as he agreed to loan me the money at the time of the MBO.

So, on all fronts, I needed to fix this because in reality if we were to move forward with the growth plans that we had it would become a major issue. During the MBO, I had very much enjoyed working with Paul Pindar. He was clearly a very talented individual and I sensed that he felt frustrated by his role at 3i. Although he got some form of reward (commission or equity options) from the deals he converted, he could not make 'real money', as Paul would see it. So, not long after the MBO in March 1987, I began the process of putting in Paul's mind the possibility of him joining us as our finance director. I became increasingly convinced that he and I could work well together and it would take our growth plans to another level.

This thought evolved and I started talking to people around me like Lance Blackstone, the MBO specialist, and our lawyer Anthony Fine. The feeling from both of them was that Paul was a very talented man, but that I would never be able to persuade him to leave 3i. He was highly successful where he was and was destined to go onto bigger things. I knew I was targeting the right person.

I am a determined man and so I met up with Paul and put the idea of him joining us directly. Of course, he had seen the business plan and he could see the opportunities, but we were still very much in a start-up phase.

Rich Benton recalls:

Roger, Mike and I were taken by Rod to an Indian restaurant on the Buckingham Palace Road one Friday night to meet Paul and resolve whether we could work with him or not. It was supposed to be a meeting for us to have our say, but Paul already had the job offer in his back pocket. If we'd said: 'No' to Paul, he would still have come. Rod was set on him joining us, having decided that Roger was not good enough financially.

Rod and Paul were a good combination. Rod knew the market well and Paul wanted to be rich and he was ruthless and ambitious. Anyone he did not think was performing had no future in the company. He had a pad of accounting paper with a list of names of people who were going to be 'exited'. Part of the deal was that we were all to dilute our shareholdings to create a shareholding for Paul to subscribe for, so he came on board as a significant shareholder. That took some negotiating by Rod.

It would not be unfair of me to say that at the time Paul had very little understanding of the public sector and even less love for it. He thought it was inefficient and ineffective. His thinking was much more along the lines of Margaret Thatcher and therefore he shared the view that it should be dismantled. However, he also recognised that since it spent a great deal of money, there was real potential to make money from it, particularly with the network that I had, and the great potential of the niche that we were in. The terms around Paul joining, particularly on the equity dilution, were tricky. I had no issue in coming to terms with this as I could see the enormous upside of Paul joining us, but I think it is fair to say that the other three were not so convinced initially.

Paul broached the subject with his immediate boss at 3i, Paul Waller, who was beside himself that Paul would even think about leaving, particularly to go to such a small outfit. 3i then made the big mistake of rubbishing Capita's business, to the point of saying it was never going to go anywhere. Paul had the sort of psyche similar to mine, which meant that this was the wrong way to handle him. They missed the point that Paul had decided he wanted to be on the other side of the table and be with a management team that could build a business, where he would have equity, putting him in a place to make capital returns rather than a large salary. He thought Capita was such a vehicle that could achieve this for him, although neither of us believed it would one day grow to become as big as it is.

So, much to 3i's surprise, and not with their good wishes, he decided to accept my offer and leave them with the intent of proving them wrong. History shows that he more than achieved this and that, had 3i decided to hold our shares, Capita would have become their best-performing investment ever made in a UK-based company.

All the time Paul was in discussion with me, I was not aware of 3i's mistaken reaction to Paul about us. From my point of view Paul was not easily convinced. He asked many questions, mainly about our development plans. Overall this was testing out my ambition to grow the business. Much to my surprise he then asked if he could come to my house with Deirdre his wife to meet Jacqui, and for the four of us to have dinner together. It was very clear to me that Paul wanted to see how we lived. He needed to find out if we were people who were really ambitious to achieve great success. Or maybe he just wanted to see what the home of a person who had worked in the public sector for twenty-five years looked like!

Paul was thirty at this point and I was forty-one. He wanted to know if I was a person who could handle success and all its trappings. The meeting at the house went well and my son Michael, who was eleven at the time, still recalls the meeting and in particular, Paul sitting on the floor joining in with the game that he was playing. Paul and I both went away from that evening contented that we could work together and our respective wives were equally supportive. It was quite a vote of confidence for Capita that he wanted to join us, for I was aware that he had lots of other options.

When you do the kind of deals Paul had been doing you get to know the management teams, warts and all. He had views on all the members of our team. I think the fact that we started so well after the buyout and we had won lots of work helped Paul to make his decision. I think he saw the momentum; plus, I did a good job of persuading him!

I always enjoyed working with Paul. He was a very clear, clinical thinker. I instinctively liked him. He had a great sense of humour and he was fun to work with. As a Leeds United supporter, he even had a picture of the Leeds United team of 1971/72 in pride of place on his office wall – always a good ice breaker in meetings. In his own environment he was fiercely ambitious and unashamedly determined to make a lot of money. He is the only person that I know who did a personal balance sheet on the 1 January each year, to ensure that his assets were increasing in line with his aspirations.

All my career had been spent in the public sector, so the first big step for me to move into the private sector and to run a business in which I had a stake, was a big move. But I took to it very naturally and loved every minute of it. I have constantly said to people who have a concern of making such a move that so much of the fear of doing this is all in the mind.

I soon realised how I could use my public sector 'apprenticeship' to my advantage. I recall at the time of the MBO negotiations feeling that this was the greatest opportunity I would ever get in my life and I must make it happen, as such a chance will never come my way again.

Similarly, Paul had seen how, in some of the deals for which he had been responsible, people went on to make lots of money. There he was sitting in 3i as an investment controller overseeing many lucrative deals and he wasn't making money, well not that kind of money. Hilariously, he revealed to us that his only previous experience of the public sector was when, during the summer holidays while at University in Swansea, to earn money he had worked as a dustman, which was not a well-known fact. We, of course, hastened to reassure him that we were not in the blue collar market and had every intention of staying in the white collar market to develop Capita! Despite this, Paul's experience of the dustcarts was to prove invaluable to Capita in a future transaction!

In November 1987, we became a team of five very determined individuals out to build Capita into a highly successful business; all with something to prove.

Of course Paul's arrival as our new finance director impacted on my team, and especially on Roger Brier. The situation became quite difficult because it meant that Roger was no longer centrally involved with the production of the numbers in the business, and effectively became more the operations director, and Roger didn't like that. The three of us – Rich, Mike and myself – tried to persuade Roger to accept this loss of status as he saw it, but there was a huge degree of tension around the place.

Paul didn't make the atmosphere any easier because he is a very direct individual, and it quickly became very apparent that he didn't regard Roger very highly and disliked his attitude. At that time, the one key attribute that Roger had over Paul was a deep understanding of our public sector client base and the way that local authorities operated, which was massively important to us when winning work.

Inevitably, introducing Paul into our team was not easy. Mike Burr was extremely sceptical of him and Rich Benton was unsure. They admired him for what he had done for the MBO, but they were not so sure about accepting into our close team.

I remember the first meeting we had as an enlarged team was in the Caxton Hotel, where, as the Chair of the meeting, I knew I had a problem. There was a great deal of tension in the air and I had to work hard at encouraging discussion. It was a question of moulding them into a team. It was far from an easy task, but somehow I managed to pull it off. Paul very quickly and naturally became my sidekick, my number two, whereas Roger had previously been very much that person.

I had been the managing director of CCS, and became both chairman and chief executive of the new business when we bought it out. Roger quite liked the idea of being the one who was just one step behind, enabling him to adopt a much more controversial and challenging approach. In essence he was a shy man, but he had a great deal of talent and brainpower. I owe a great deal to him, particularly for what he did in the early days of the business within CIPFA. He became the first of the original team to leave in March 1990, not long after we floated.

Conversely, Paul's style was to make his mark, as he had something to prove to himself about the decision to join us. Paul was 'action orientated' and a man on a mission. He and I very quickly became very effective operators, each playing to our respective strengths.

11

FLOTATION ON THE STOCK MARKET

One of the first things we discussed when Paul joined was a suggestion that we float the business on the stock market. We'd been through an MBO, but none of us had ever floated a business. Paul prepared documents with associated numbers attached, which looked very encouraging both for the business and on a personal front. Our financial performance over our short history made encouraging reading and meant that a flotation was possible. It was the three-year track record that we gained from the MBO which was invaluable, as it meant that to float we only needed a further two years of financial results. I believe that this position very much influenced Paul's decision to join us. In its negotiations with us, CIPFA had placed no value on this track record, as they felt we would fail as a company long before flotation became an option! Had we decided to walk away and left the business behind with CIPFA, going down the start-up route, it would have taken us three more years to get to the same position.

With the flotation of Capita as our aim, we set about developing the business to enable us to have the financial track record that would justify such a move. Our objective was to broaden and diversify the base of the business and to build upon our senior team to drive this change.

We had been working for some months with a company called Public Sector Consultants (PSC), a temporary placement business. In

November 1987, we acquired an initial 74.9 per cent of this company, which further diversified the range of services we offered as a group. PSC was based in Birmingham and provided line management and accountancy staff on short- and long-term assignments for local authorities and health service clients. It had a database of individuals who did not want a conventional line management job and were not interested in a consultancy role, but did want assignments where they undertook short-term tasks.

The managing director of this business was Clive Sadler, who held the balance of the company shares, which we bought out in April 1989, prior to our float. Clive was an unusual guy to deal with and regularly used the annoying phrase 'to horse' as a rallying call. I had met Clive before as he was previously a national senior manager for local government at Price Waterhouse, in a team that had offered me a job while I was at CIPFA which I turned down. Another key member in our Birmingham office was David Poynton, who was a senior figure in the health service and eventually became our regional director. I had previously worked with David in local government during my time at Brighton. This move was our first development away from being London based, giving us a presence in Birmingham, with other offices following in Belfast, Leeds and Stockport.

In December of that year I encouraged Julie Fowler, who I had worked with at CIPFA, to join us to be the Director of Capita Training. The idea here was to put on a series of seminars and conferences on current topics, which would not only attract paying customers, but also enable us to attend and promote the broader services of Capita. Julie was well known in the industry, having for fourteen years been responsible for directing the Institute's seminar programme and organising the annual conference. We competed head-to-head with CIPFA's programme of events, and at its peak over 3,000 people attended our events.

Our profile in Belfast was also growing through the assignment that we had with the Department of Education and Library Boards. We had a small but effective team of consultants who worked on both assignments in the province and in London. But we needed a leader for the business. In March 1988, Stuart McDonnell joined to be our managing director. He was well connected locally, which in Belfast was essential, having previously worked with the Industrial Development Board and ICL.

Our management consultancy, which was the core of the business that we bought from CIPFA, was growing well, undertaking projects for clients across local government, health and utilities, with an increasing number of assignments in central government. We also had our work with computer manufacturers, including major projects with McDonnell Douglas Information Systems and Honeywell Bull. In September we added to our senior management team by hiring Brian Kerslake, who had twenty-two years' experience with British Telecom, to become the MD of the consultancy business. Malcolm Fowler also joined from McDonnell Douglas to run our Capita Systems business, which focused on providing services to the computer suppliers.

With the development of Capita and the intention to float the company, there was a need to increase the capacity of our finance team and we decided to appoint a financial controller to assist Paul in his role of financial director. Paul and I interviewed a guy from London Underground who was a qualified accountant in their central team. We had worked with him on the consultancy assignment that we had with them, and Rich Benton knew him well.

After several interviews we had still not convinced him to join us. He was nervous about joining what was a small, start-up business that had just been through an MBO. He was not convinced that we would make it and was concerned about our financial wellbeing. I can recall Paul stepping out of the interview in complete frustration, only to return with the group's bank statements. Paul sat down and actually showed the gentleman the bank statements displaying a very healthy cash balance! Even this did not convince him and he decided to stay with the security of a job with London Underground. I have not named the guy as this most probably turned out to be the worst decision that he ever took in his career, and most definitely the most expensive!

Following this setback, Paul turned to a man that he had trained with at Coopers & Lybrand called Gordon Hurst. Gordon was at Sun Microsystems but jumped at the opportunity to join us. I think his words were: 'If Paul thinks this is a good opportunity, count me in!'

Gordon joined in June 1988 as Financial Controller, which represented the beginning of a highly successful career with Capita that ended with his retirement in 2014. He was made Commercial Director and Company Secretary, joining the Group Board in 1995 and stepped up to Group FD in 1996. He became a key part of the team of four that would take Capita to the FTSE.

In October 1988 we had an unlikely approach from British Telecom. They wanted us to assist them in the development of their local government product entry strategy. Amazingly, the newly privatised British Telecom didn't know how to get into local government! It is important to recognise that at that time BT was effectively considered to be a 'phone company' rather than the IT solution company that it is today. It was a wonderful opportunity for us.

As a tester of our knowledge of the market and of the network that we told them that we had, BT asked us to organise a seminar for them to explain their plans to potential customers. This seminar was to be held at the top of the Post Office Tower, which was not open to the public and so proved a great draw for senior officers from the public sector to attend. I recall going through the list of contacts that I had from my CIPFA days and the early times of the consortia work that we did as CIPFA Computer Services. The list of invitees was impressive as was the response to the event, which attracted a large number of chief officers both at Director of Finance and Chief Executive level.

The plan was to showcase BT as a company and to offer a range of computer-related services to local authorities. The key offering was an outsourcing of the billing arrangements covering printing, enveloping and mailing of all bills and literature connected with the proposed introduction by the Conservative Government of the ill-fated Poll Tax, as it became known. The demands placed on the administration of this exploded three or four fold because a bill needed to be sent to every member of every house.

The objective of the service was to take the pressure away from the internal resources of a local authority. This would avoid authorities investing in costly equipment themselves by using the enormous IT capacity that BT had. Our first customers for a three-year contract were Westminster City Council and the Royal Borough of Kensington

& Chelsea, both of whom subsequently became major customers for the Group in the managed services option that we developed. At the seminar we also trailed the suggestion of extending this thinking to the management of the IT computer facilities.

The response to this initial event was sufficiently encouraging for us to persuade BT to consider setting up a special company to market and deliver these services. We were commissioned to prepare the business plan for this new joint venture and in preparing for it Mike sold every member of staff on to the project, including my PA Lynn and myself!

This company was called Telecom Capita and was launched in July 1990 as a joint venture. This win for us was very, very newsworthy and changed the direction of our business.

We acquired the option over 51 per cent of the equity of the joint venture and they had 49 per cent! It was remarkable that Capita, a new company in the market, had the larger share in an agreement with this giant, but they happily agreed to it. This triggered our move from being a consultancy to becoming a provider of outsourced services under long-term contract.

It certainly shed a new light on the thought that local government is boring. It was a considerable coup and it must have astounded all those back at CIPFA. In fact, BT did apparently seriously consider approaching CIPFA, but having read about our MBO they chose to come to us because we were a more entrepreneurial and ambitious outfit.

The guy at British Telecom that we dealt with was Ken Robey, who was a regional director along with his direct bosses Harvey Parr and Jim Jackson. We were a good team to work with, as we understood the local government market, and we could talk about the problems and opportunities that existed. We knew the right people, so if they wanted an introduction to a particular chief executive or treasurer we could organise that. Amazingly, at that time, British Telecom felt they couldn't do that themselves. We also had the commercial acumen that Paul brought in, being able to structure the arrangements around the joint ventures, many of which were agreed over dinner at Santini's in Victoria.

We started designing products and we worked well together in this rather strange partnership. It was a very bizarre experience. Dealing with such a massive company meant that we entered a world that I'd never known of before. It was even more bureaucratic than dealing with a local authority. Everything was very slow moving, and it became close to impossible to get things approved. Ken Robey used to tell us he was going to have to 'walk a proposal from us around the third and fourth floors to get support for it,' as he put it.

They were nice people, full of goodwill and encouragement, but there were enormous delays getting decisions from them. To a small, fast-moving, entrepreneurial company this was very frustrating. It taught me that as we grew we must strongly resist this level of bureaucracy ever entering our business. It was this culture that ultimately drove the need for BT to completely restructure itself several years later, resulting in mass redundancies.

John Jasper was well known in the computer industry, having worked a great deal with IBM. At Warwickshire County Council, where John was Deputy Chief Executive, he had developed Warwickshire Computing Limited. Paul and I opened discussions with him about joining us to run Telecom Capita and in October 1988 he became a part of our senior management team, bringing a number of colleagues with him.

With the growing trend towards the privatisation of public services, we established Capita Corporate Finance Ltd in January 1988. We provided corporate finance advice to management buyout teams and offered guidance to public bodies on divestment. Paul ran this, as it was very much a crossover between what he had been doing previously at 3i, but with a public sector twist. This again differentiated us from others that could offer this service, particularly as we had been through a management buyout ourselves! We won a number of assignments very quickly, but the most significant was to advise MRS Environmental Services Ltd, the in-house team providing the service, on successfully bidding for the £61-million contract to run the cleansing services of Westminster City Council. A central part of this was a responsibility for rubbish collection around the streets of Westminster, hence my earlier comments about Paul's direct experience of working as a bin man!

So we became a market leader in this new field, all driven by Thatcher's intent to dismantle public sector services, which forced local authorities to consider alternative ways of delivering services. In April 1989, Anthony Fine, the solicitor that we worked with at Barnett Alexander Chart on the MBO, joined us to take over the full-time running of Capita Corporate Finance from Paul. He also took on the role of Company Secretary, a position necessary for the flotation of the business.

To complete our senior team with the flotation in mind, in April 1989 we also appointed our first non-executive director to the Board. I was fortunate to be able to persuade Sir Anthony Wilson to take on the role. He had been partner in Price Waterhouse for twenty-three years and was subsequently the Head of Government Accountancy Services and Accounting Adviser to HM Treasury from 1984 to 1988. It was in this role that I had first met Sir Anthony when I was on the CIPFA Secretariat as Technical Director.

His appointment was the government's first attempt to bring a professional approach to the running of its affairs, and CIPFA was a natural partner to look towards encouraging the trend of training accountants. It was an incredible coup for us to attract such a high-calibre individual to a small company, albeit one that had big ideas. He proved to be a wise counsel to us both in terms of the Board itself but also through the senior contacts that he had at Permanent Secretary level in the civil service as we widened our activities into bidding for work in central government.

This was an amazing period for me. While Capita undoubtedly changed my life, it also took over my life to a dangerous degree at times as all my efforts went into it. I was hugely ambitious for Capita to be a success and, in hindsight, spending so much time on the company changed my relationship with Jacqui and our friends.

At work, all of us played our part and we proved to be an incredibly successful, innovative team that would ultimately lead the change in how the public sector, and in particular local authorities, would choose to deliver services.

Mike Burr, whose commercial experience with Logica was invaluable in winning work recalls:

We were determined to move away from the short-term work and I remember sitting down with Rod to discuss how Capita could develop. We both saw that with the intervention of the Thatcher government, it was timely for local authorities to consider a new approach to how they ran services. In our terms this could see them moving away from buying consultancy to being persuaded to give this responsibility under contract to another organisation to run.

Despite our rapid growth as a consultancy, we were always about three months away from running out of work because of the short-term nature of most assignments. So it took a lot of sales effort to maintain our workload and growth. Being close to the market, we could see the outsourcing of professional services could become an acceptable way of reducing costs for a local authority. The advantage for us in taking on this work was predictability of workload and income, since the contracts would be let for longer periods, typically for five to seven years or more.

As a company, we were always short of consultants to staff projects for new clients and were continually recruiting, mainly from local government. We also began a highly successful graduate recruitment scheme, taking four or five recruits a year over a five-year period. However, our expansion into managed services gave us access to a readily available pool of expertise from staff who would be willing and able, with training, to take on consultancy projects. They were all high quality and the only thing that slowed them down previously was the organisational culture of the public sector they came from. Take the people out of that culture and they flourished.

Mike continues by commenting:

In all our time of recruiting from local government and other parts of the public sector we only ever had one person opt to go back and he regretted the decision. This is what Rod was very good at. He could find and select the right staff, fill them with enthusiasm and inspire them. He changed an awful lot of people's lives for the better. Rod is a private person and I don't think I ever went to his house. Roger was even more closed. Roger and Rod once had quite an angry altercation in the kitchen at Rich's house, so it was probably as well that we didn't get together more often socially. Roger had the intellectual capacity and influence to break up the four of us and he was suspicious of Rod's motives. In the time leading up to the buyout he was full of theories that Rod was going to sell us down the river and do a deal with someone else. Yet there was never the remotest chance of that and we all knew it.

The decision to float led to a huge logistical exercise. At the time it felt like another colossal challenge and it was yet another process that I had never experienced before. We had to appoint a series of advisers for the flotation, all of which inevitably involved a 'beauty parade' process. It soon became apparent that it was more about who Paul and I could best work with both on the float itself and going forward after it. Most definitely in my case, many of the individuals had little or no rapport with my background and the world that I come from in the public sector.

For our Financial Adviser we appointed Hill Samuel Bank and as our broker, Credit Lyonnais Laing, previously Laing & Cruickshank. They were not by any means the largest of the firms we saw, but the key thing was that we were floating on the Unlisted Securities Market, the smallest market, and therefore it was important to work with an organisation that would give us the attention that we needed. Most definitely with the larger firms, while they would say differently, inevitably their fee-earning capacity was with the larger clients that they serviced. To complete the team, our solicitors were Cameron Markby and this started a very long relationship. They were to advise us on many of our early acquisitions.

In very quick order, the business was propelled into the public world of scrutiny by the City, a world that was new to all of us. If one had stopped to think, which at the time we did not, the business only began life in 1984, had been through a management buyout in 1987, and two years later, in 1989, we were floating it as a public company. So in a very short time we were going from being employees of a department in the backwater of a professional institute to offering our business to shareholders on the public market to invest in. Even though I say it myself, this was ballsy, but it was the beginning of what was to prove an amazing adventure for me over the next seventeen years.

We decided to float for a number of reasons. It meant that we could pay down some the company debts and financial commitments that we had following the management buyout and, perhaps most importantly, it would help us to grow the business through using shares to buy other businesses as a way of expanding.

Another reason was that we were able to put in place a share option scheme for key staff as a way of motivating people and encouraging a team. There was always the danger that without this it could lead to an 'us and them' culture, where the directors were seen to be OK thanks to the float but employees asked, 'What has it done for us?' It has to be said that a large number of the senior people in place at this time who received share options did not go on to stay with the company.

I also liked the idea of Capita being a public company as I felt that it brought an added profile and gave weight to the role that we were intending to play with public bodies. Overall however, we all felt that six-monthly reporting to the City brought a certain discipline to the way that we operated that would not be there if we remained a private company.

The whole process was another steep learning curve since, after appointing our advisers, a mountain of information had to be provided to the reporting accountants, Ernst & Whinney, about the financial performance of the business. The drafting of the prospectus involved long meetings with all the advisers, as the document would form the offer to shareholders, and on the basis of the information provided they would then decide whether or not to invest. As directors we had effectively to covenant legally that we were telling the truth about the business and its performance. Putting together the flotation was a marathon task and is why a company should not do it unless they are clear that it is necessary and the business has the capacity to grow in a public arena.

FLOTATION ON THE STOCK MARKET

When the prospectus was published in mid-April 1989 it confirmed that the services offered by the group included:

- Management consultancy
- Information technology consultancy
- Strategic advice to, and conceptual systems design for, computer systems suppliers
- Training courses and seminars
- Temporary placement of accountancy and other professional staff on contract
- Computer services, including facilities management, through a joint venture with British Telecom
- Corporate financial advisory services.

The Group employed 101 staff, with the Group's corporate headquarters strategically located in Westminster along with offices in Belfast, Birmingham, Leeds and Stockport.

A summary of our trading record for the first five accounting periods ending 31 December 1988 as presented by the Reporting Accountants showed that our turnover as CCS had gone from £304,000 in the final ten months of 1984, to £4,301,000 in 1988 as Capita. Our profits rose from £57,000 in 1985, to £747,000 in 1988.

I could only imagine how CIPFA must have felt. They sold the business when it was on a turnover of a few hundred thousand pounds a year and it had very quickly grown to £4.3 million.

Paul and I led on the flotation whilst the other three – Rich, Mike and Roger – ran the business. This was important, as we were floating the business with the stated assumption that profits would grow healthily in line with our published forecasts. The flotation took a great deal of our energy, but our first set of results as a public company would follow very quickly after that and needed to meet those forecasts in the market – welcome to the treadmill!

There was a need to pre-market the stock to potential shareholders to ensure that there was an appetite for the shares in the market. This entailed Paul and I going out to market ourselves to institutions our brokers felt were going to buy an allocation of the shares. I found myself explaining to fund managers what a local authority was, how local government operated and why it was a good market to operate in. I had to spell out the impact of Mrs Thatcher's actions and how it was possible to make money from them. The Capita story had to be told and we captured people's imagination about the potential of the market. We had a good story to tell and I believe we told it well. The take-up was such that there was the need to scale back the allocations that the fund managers wanted in the float. Essentially they bought into Paul and me. My apprenticeship in local government was very valuable indeed because I had a wealth of stories to tell.

Before the float and final calculations were done around the price for the shares, one tricky situation hit us: not everyone was happy for us to float. One such person was the director at 3i who looked after us, and of course 3i was our major shareholder. They felt that we were going to the market far too early in our development and we could command a far higher price for our shares, and by direct implication their shares, if we had another two years of trading under our belt.

Personally, I think that some of this negative feeling was driven by the concern about how Paul had slotted into our operation, which might lead other valuable personnel to defect from 3i. The big issue was to ensure liquidity in the shares, and Hill Samuel required 3i to sell down a proportion of its holding. This involved them selling 400,000 of their shares into the placing that was going to happen. The only way that they would agree to do this was to 'punish' us, the management team, as well, and collectively we were 'forced' to place 250,000 shares of our holding into the market as well. We did not want to sell at that time as we could see the value that these shares could generate as we grew. But to get the issue dealt with, we had to comply with this.

In the flotation it was possible for related parties connected to the management team to buy into shares at the flotation price of £1. I recall the father of my PA Lynn doing so, and later I received a letter from him thanking me for the opportunity and the impact the acquisition of the shares has had on their lives. Similarly, Eugene, my then father-in-law, backed us, as did my Uncle Jim. I was particularly proud of this in view of the way that Eugene and I had worked together to make extra money in our accounting business. He was very supportive of my new venture with Capita and invested in the company despite the risk. I was also enormously grateful to my uncle because of the help that he gave me when my father died. The impact of his decision of his to invest, basically backing me, only became apparent to me when he sadly passed away. My Aunt Joyce showed me a statement of the shares that he held asking what she should do about it. Essentially, he had not sold one share since the flotation and the value of his fairly modest outlay had crystalised into a gain of over a million pounds.

I recall the day that our shares were first listed. Dealings in our shares commenced first thing on 25 April 1989 priced at £1, giving a market captialisation of £8.1 million and the broker put two million shares into the market. The broker took Paul and me for breakfast at the Stock Exchange, to be followed by seeing the first dealing in our shares on the screen when the market opened. The shares went to an immediate premium, which meant that every person holding shares was in the money from day one. After this we met up with Mike, Richard and Roger and had our photographs taken outside the Stock Exchange. I have featured these photographs in the book and I think they show how naive we were about the ways of the city.

The company that we had bought from CIPFA on Friday 13 March 1987 for £330,000 was now valued in April 1989 as a public company at over £8 million. It makes CIPFA's decision not to take the offer of 25 per cent of it, made at the time of the MBO, a rather costly one for them. The current Director of CIPFA, Rob Whitman, did joke with me recently that they were still desperately searching for the share certificate in the vaults!

On the evening after the flotation, I took the family out for a meal to celebrate and surprised them with tickets to see *Phantom of the Opera* which was a hot ticket at that time, with Michael Crawford performing as the Phantom and Sarah Brightman as Christine. There was to be a certain irony much later when I repeated this visit to the same theatre, on the day of my last presentation to the City, when I stepped down as Chairman seventeen years later. Although it was not such a happy occasion, the show was still phenomenal.

One of the great things in our favour was that for a time there was nothing like us on the stock market. At first people didn't know how to describe us or how to categorise us. We were clearly unusual and not a product. We were advising local authorities and the popular conception was, 'They're boring, they're awful so why would I put money into that?' Buying in at the outset is where the money was made and when you are the founding management team floating the business you have a sizeable part of the equity. However, it meant that all your wealth was tied up in one place and it is very difficult to sell shares without 'spooking' the market.

My relationship with Paul proved to be key to the success of Capita. I believe that he needed me and I needed him. I knew how to get the best out of him and he from me. That was the essence of a good partnership. I recognised that from the start, but I was never convinced he saw it the same way. Paul and I nevertheless made a formidable team; I knew the public sector inside out and Paul's knowledge of acquiring companies and structuring deals was a major differentiator of us as a company.

Publicity seemed to enter my life in a big way after this success. I was not at all used to appearing in the tabloids. I was shocked to be sitting on the train the day following the flotation, only to see a women opposite me reading *The Sun* newspaper and the page I was looking at had my photograph, topped by a large headline reading: 'How Rod turned £40,000 into a million.'

I said several outrageous things, which were quite hilarious like: 'I'm not going to change my car,' and 'I'm a modest man, and I just want to get on with the job I'm paid for. We are not planning a party.' In other words, I didn't want people to think I was suddenly going to change. I also said that I got into the office at seven o'clock in the morning. Lynn, my PA, put the article on my desk later with a note attached to the 7 a.m. wording and a large question mark next to it saying: 'When was this?'

People react to things they read in the newspapers in different ways. My son Michael saw the stories about wealth being created and promptly asked for his pocket money to be increased. This I agreed to but with added incentives linked to his academic performance! Life became different and more exciting. Lots of friends and acquaintances bought shares. Whenever we went to cricket or football matches at Michael's school many people asked how it was going and wanted to talk about the share price. A sense of reality soon arrived because on the day Robert, my youngest son, was in hospital for a fairly major operation, news came of a major stock market crash wiping out a considerable amount of the gains on the share price and therefore directly reducing our overall wealth.

I would now like to turn to Lynn Chidwick, who has now retired from Capita, to describe those early days. Lynn recalls:

I was too close to notice a change in Rod at the time, but looking back later I did realise he had suddenly become energised and excited about the potential. He became more and more driven after the management buyout and the flotation. Rod recognised it was not often in life that these sorts of opportunities come along.

Nobody had any idea what ultimately the potential of that business would be. All of us felt involved and many of us got shares. This was the team creation and it was all hands on deck, working long hours very hard. For a long time if anyone asked me what I attributed Capita's success to, I would always say it's basically Rod and the team that he put together. But in fact it's Rod!

In all the time that I worked with him he was very good at building teams. Rod was always the leader. He stayed at the helm. He is really good with people and very charismatic. Right from the outset he had the idea, he had the passion, and he had the drive. People could sense Rod had a vision of where the company was going. He wanted to take the business to the top.

He believed in local authorities and genuinely wanted to do the best for people who transferred to us. It came across. I think they had real respect for the fact that he wasn't just some businessman keen to make money. He wasn't another guy in a flashy suit looking as if he was trying to get rich quick.

Thank you Lynn for those kind remarks. Of course this was only the beginning, because we had floated on a promise of more activity for our shareholders and activity they got in abundance. We developed well as a public company, hitting targets and winning awards.

In November 1990 we were voted Best New Company of the Year, an award sponsored by BBC Radio 4's *Financial World Tonight*. It was based on research carried out into the financial details of nearly 200 UK Companies whose shares had been introduced on the Stock Exchange Unlisted Securities Market (USM) since January 1989. In March 1991, we were voted USM Company of the Year for 1990 at the PLC Awards Dinner held at the Grosvenor Hotel.

It was not surprising that the first member of our team to leave was Roger Brier. He was never really happy after Paul arrived. Roger sold some of his shares and continued to earn an income from the dividends on the remainder of his holding. I don't think he was a man who wanted to make a great deal of money. He just felt he had done enough and he left in March 1991.

Of course we had to explain Roger's sudden departure to the City. The question was: 'If it's such a bloody good idea, why is he going so soon after the float?' We managed to get over that by explaining that the plan was for Roger to work on some of our most major consultancy jobs after leaving us. Then he rather foolishly messed us around. We had a potential client involving a central government contract with HM Treasury. Mike Burr, Roger and I met with the client at the Runnymede Hotel and Roger was in one of his grumpy moods. Basically, he blew it. I recall driving home and spoke to Mike on the 'hands free' car phone, berating Roger's woeful performance. I never spoke to Roger from that moment on. I am not a person to cross.

Mike was the next one of the original four to go. He said he wanted to do other things and he had made enough money. Mike was clearly feeling exhausted and I also believe felt disturbed by Paul's arrival. Increasingly I agreed more with Paul's views around actions that we needed to take with the cost base, and much of this involved the consultancy resource which historically had very much been Mike's domain.

FLOTATION ON THE STOCK MARKET

I owe a great deal to Mike and much of Capita's early development is down to the consulting and commercial experience that he brought to the business, but it was equally clear to me that the time had come for him to move on. My relationship with him suffered as a result of this, particularly around the time that he left the business. Thankfully we have rebuilt some of this friendship and can focus more on what we achieved together. I learnt a great deal from Mike.

On 16 July 1991, just thirty months after floating, we applied to go onto the main official market of the Stock Exchange. At the same time, we sought to raise funds through a placing of shares, giving existing shareholders the right to subscribe on beneficial terms.

We were able to do this because, since our flotation, our turnover had grown from £4.3 million for the year ended 31 December, 1988 to over £20 million for the year ended 31 December 1990. Our profits have similarly trebled from £746,000 to over £2.5 million.

Much of this was due to a very successful period of winning large long-term contracts and an active period of making the key acquisitions that we had stated we would do at the time of the float. The conclusion of these acquisitions was very much led by Paul, using all the experience that he had gained at 3i. Paul was a deal man. The culture that we put forward to the companies that we wished to acquire was that we would act speedily to conclude the transaction, would not play around with the price offered, but we would not enter into a competitive bidding war.

Almost immediately after floating we created a marketing division through the acquisition of Penn Communications in May 1989. We had known Bill Penn, the owner of the business, for over a year through our work with BT, a major client of his company. We saw public relations and marketing as an extension of the services we could offer to local government. Bill, who took an all share deal plus an earn out arrangement, turned out to be a very nervous owner of shares in a public company like Capita, always doubting our ability to make forecasts. Soon afterwards we added Penn PR & Advertising to offer a full service of advertising, public relations, marketing, graphic design and publishing. This was based in Birmingham and its main client was West Midlands Travel, whom we knew well, having worked on a large consultancy project with them and advised the management team, led by Don Colston, on their MBO.

We made a very significant appointment to our Board in August 1989 in the case of Derek Fowler as a Non-Executive Director to join with Sir Anthony Wilson in that capacity. This was now a very strong Board. Before he retired, Derek was Deputy Chairman of British Rail and continued to be Chairman of the British Rail Pension Fund.

I first met Derek when he joined the CIPFA Council during my time on the secretariat. I always recall that Derek seemed a cut above the others on the council, having come from a nationalised industry. His comments were always to the point and people listened to him, including Noel Hepworth! Over time he became incredibly important to me, effectively playing a mentoring role, and he helped me enormously, particularly in learning how to chair meetings. Derek became Deputy Chairman of the Group in January 1991.

He had a great way of describing how to judge the rights and wrongs of decisions. He used a phrase, 'come the inquiry', meaning that you should always judge your decision around how it would play out should any matter come to a point where it would be judged by a court, your employer or even the press. I firmly believe that had Derek still been alive at the time that I took the decision to respond to the Labour Party's request for a loan I would have asked his advice and would not have made the loan.

In December 1989, we added to our marketing division with the acquisition Causeway Communications, a public relations and marketing consultancy incorporated in Northern Ireland who had a major role in the privatisation of Northern Ireland Electricity. Soon after this we acquired the management consultancy arm of Muir and Addy, Chartered Accountants, who were very well connected in the province. This major move into Belfast proved to be of mixed benefit to us. We found the market opportunity for us to grow at the pace that we aimed for was restricted both by the size of the market and the slow pace of doing business there. Maybe it was because of the Guinness!

In May 1990 we concluded the acquisition of J. E. Greatorex, a professional practice of consulting engineers. The business had approaching one hundred people. This proved to be a major move for us and was the beginning of Capita creating one of the largest professional building services divisions in the UK. The company, which was based in Berkhamstead, had been in existence since 1955 and worked extensively in the health sector.

It had a close team of directors led by John Brameld and I remember the very first times that I met the team in our offices at Tothill Street as part of the process to encourage them to join us. It was very apparent that although we had no experience of the property services business we could add a great deal to their organisation through our commercial approach, and they could add to our expertise regarding developing client relationships.

John Brameld joined our main board in June 1990 and again John's background was very different to that of the rest of us, his experience and temperament proved to be invaluable. I have no doubt that he must have wondered on many occasions, when he sat through some of our meetings where we discussed outsourcing, just what he had joined.

We were interested in Greatorex because it had long-term contract assignments lasting two or three years and 30 per cent of its work was in the health service, where we had had limited experience. We also felt that a number of the clients would want to buy some of Capita's other services. Most significantly, it provided the beginnings of our move to be able to offer an integrated selection of back office white collar services, which included property services as an outsourced service.

The joint venture agreement with BT for Telecom Capita granted them the right to subscribe to 51per cent of the equity during 1992. In July 1990, BT indicated that they wanted to terminate the joint venture agreement and the marketing agreement we had with them. This deal resulted in Capita receiving a cheque from British Telecom in full settlement of the arrangement for £1,649,100. I still have a copy of the cheque, as it was another 'game changer' in the life of Capita. A senior employee of BT called Paul and said jokingly in relation to the settlement: 'There's another lorry load of cash on its way over to you!'

Effectively this deal underwrote our flotation on the stock market. We had been paid by BT for the start-up of a business which we now owned. Telecom Capita now had a relationship with over one hundred local authorities through the products that had been developed and had two major long-term contracts, which gave us a market-leading position in a new market called 'IT outsourcing'. As a result of this we had three major business centres in Berkshire, Oxford and Cardiff, all fully kitted out with a workforce that enabled us to bid for other contracts in this emerging market.

John Jasper, the Managing Director of the company, also joined the Group Board. The deal with BT meant that we could consolidate all the turnover and profits of the company into ours, rather than Telecom Capita being treated as a subsidiary in accounting terms.

BT's decision to sell the remaining balance of the business to us, believe it or not, was promoted by the successes that we had had in winning large contracts. The team at BT had a fear of the liabilities that came with these contracts involving the transfer of staff, including redundancy rights and pensions. Several years later these conditions were embedded in TUPE (Transfer of Undertakings [Protection of Employment] Regulations 2006).

The year before, in October 1989, Berkshire County Council had signed a five-year facilities management contract worth £20 million with Telecom Capita, covering the council's mainframe computer and communications operations. The authority had projected a decline in its use of mainframe computing and was attracted by Telecom Capita's offer to build a business centre around the facility along with the possibility of creating of new jobs in the county.

All the staff from the council's Computer Services Division accepted positions with Telecom Capita and as part of the agreement the ICL computer suite was refurbished and redeveloped to become a flagship site for Capita's computer operations, known as the Berkshire Data Centre, which went on to provide services to forty organisations, including a new outsourcing contract with the British Nursing Association.

This first big agreement with a large, prominent county council was very important to Capita. This was a 'ground breaking' deal in the market. At the same time a survey undertaken by Brunel University showed that 85 per cent of computer managers were considering privatising their departments as a result of the DLO legislation.

We spent a lot of time on these discussions to conclude the deal because nothing like this had been negotiated before. There were many questions to answer. How do you transfer a person and take on his employment obligations? If you're employed by a local authority, how do you transfer that employment to another organisation? What happens to your pension? What happens to terms and conditions?

We worked out all the answers and how we could protect people who were transferred with the benefit and help of legal brains at every stage. Pensions were a big issue and people very rightly were nervous. We worked out how you could transfer, but in a sense still keep your pension rights in the local authority fund, where they were with Capita becoming what was termed an 'excepted authority' into the scheme.

For us it was all part of working out relationships, which were non-threatening. We worked with unions to make this happen. In the early contracts the selection process was helped considerably if you won the staff vote selecting you as their preferred partner. We could say: 'You're coming to us and you're going to be the forefront of our business. You've got better prospects with us than if you stay with the local authority. Indeed, if you stay with them, you could all lose your jobs because the work could be won by somebody else.' The essence of our case was that, rather than reducing salaries and wages in the white collar area, we could improve productivity through better business processes, better use of technology and better buying power.

There was a fear that outsourcing would cost jobs. What I would say to that is that ultimately we had to focus on people who were not performing and either help them perform better or encourage them to leave. We had to have better people to transform services. We found many of those situated at a lower level in the organization, whose progression was blocked by more senior colleagues. This situation needed to be addressed rather than left to continue.

The great thing about the public sector, especially local government, is that the network is phenomenal. If you know the network, you can easily get other local authorities to come and look at something. It works both ways of course, so that if it goes wrong everybody knows about the failure as well as the success. The work that I did at CIPFA, all those years of building relationships, was immensely valuable when it came to persuading people to look at what we were offering. After all they had known me for years! I was, therefore, uniquely qualified to be trusted by the people of local government.

My apprenticeship, as I call it, was quite long but it turned out to be enormously valuable. John Tizard is a former local government leader who joined Capita many years later and he said:

> When I joined the company in 1997 there was still a cadre of local authority finance directors and chief executive officers who would always talk in a very positive way about Rod even as Capita was growing into a huge success. This was because they felt that he had come from them and had values they understood. They could have easily thought the direct opposite: that Rod had been a traitor to the cause and gone on to succeed while they relatively hadn't. But they appreciated a track record of promises kept and good deals honoured. Also I think there is something about personal chemistry there that was important and remained important for some time.

The Berkshire deal was signed and we launched it in a big way. Around this time Gloucestershire County Council invited us to bid for the outsourcing of its Honeywell installation. We believed that Telecom Capita was in a prime position to win this contract. Ultimately we were not selected which surprised us and we felt aggrieved about the process they had followed, which we felt was flawed. I therefore arranged to go to see the CEO, Michael Bichard (later Sir Michael Bichard, now Lord Bichard) for a debriefing and to express our concerns. Fortunately, on the train journey down to Gloucester I decided to listen and learn why we lost rather than sound off to Michael about the process. This proved to be an invaluable decision on my part. Not only did his feedback improve our approach to future bidding but more importantly he went on to have an illustrious career in central government, a sector key to our development. Ultimately, Michael became Permanent Secretary to the Department of Employment and Education where Capita were successful in winning three major contracts.

Soon after that Oxfordshire County Council approached us. In the spring of 1991 the CEO of the council, Trevor Vokins, signed a seven-year facilities management contract with Telecom Capita worth £28 million. All 101 staff from the council's central information services department chose to join us. Drawing on the Berkshire experience, Telecom Capita developed the Oxfordshire Data Centre, providing a wide range of computer services.

Quite quickly several hundreds of people were joining us. These were heavy deals. By then we were the market leader by a substantial margin, and three or four more smaller deals followed before there was any real competition.

John Tizard explains:

In a sense what Rod did through Capita, and it remains the case up until today, is become the market leader because he was the first in the market. Capita was able to be ahead of the game with other areas of central government outsourcing and in some of the big private sector deals. There is something there about the entrepreneurial ability to spot the opportunity and to spot the right client. In a sense Rod was able to build that relationship because he had clients who also wanted to build it and because a lot of people in local government were looking at Berkshire and Oxfordshire. There was also political capital in that the senior leadership team, and indeed the politicians, had invested in doing a deal with the team at Capita and so they wanted it to succeed. That's a very good place to start building a market from, rather than from a place where they don't want you. Establishing that initial good relationship was crucial as they became the promoter of arrangement.

Suddenly it wasn't just local authorities looking to us to outsource some of their IT services. Companies House, which is responsible for incorporating and dissolving UK companies, holding all company records and providing records for public access, provided an unlikely opportunity. It was decided to appoint an external supplier and after a short process Telecom Capita was chosen in 1991 to provide facilities, on a three-year contract, giving us a brand new centre in Cardiff.

During the years after the flotation we had moved away from just offering consultancy and started delivering services. It was not just IT either. We began to develop an offering around other managed services.

The start of this journey actually involved a new service. In a joint venture with Serco we won a contract from the Driver and Vehicle Licensing Agency (DVLA) for the sale of personalised registration marks for new vehicles. The contract was only worth £1 million to us but the publicity value was enormous. This operation was run from our Berkshire Data Centre and involved us putting together a telesales operation, which at the time was the largest on-line telesales operation of its type in the UK. The 'Select Registration' scheme offered the buyers of new cars the opportunity to choose their own registration marks, essentially adding a touch more personality to their vehicle. This comprised a letter prefix denoting the registration year, a number of your choice between one and twenty and any three-letter combination. This service proved to be a great success and a major revenue earner to HM Government. For Capita, this contract proved to be the start of our managed services business, which was the major growth driver of the business going forward.

In March 1991, we launched a computerised revenue collection service to assist local authorities in the collection of community charge and national non-domestic rates arrears. This brand new service involved chasing arrears by telephone and was the first of its kind in the market. Whereas Select Registrations was an inbound telesales operation, this was an outbound service, but the equipment and the skills the operators used were similar.

The job was for a Capita operative to establish contact with outstanding debtors using information provided to us by a local authority with whom we had a contract. Names and addresses of debtors were provided to us and fed into what we called our 'powerdillier' computer system to obtain telephone numbers, and then calls were made to individuals directly. To increase the chances of finding a person at home our operators often made calls in the early evening or at weekends. We found that the times that TV programmes *Coronation Street* and *Eastenders* were broadcast to be a very fruitful period for making a call! Very quickly the service had over twenty local authorities as clients.

Capita grew and grew and so did our reputation and our profits. On 24 July 1991 we issued a circular indicating an intention to move to the full market. With the support of Hill Samuel merchant bank we were raising £4.2 million capital through an offer of one new share for six ordinary shares held. The dealings of these shares commenced on 21 August. When Capita became a fully listed company on the stock exchange our turnover had risen to £25 million, we employed 320 people and had eleven sites around the country. Our market capitalisation had quadrupled since the float to £31 million. We were on a family holiday at the time, at the Glitter Bay Hotel in Barbados, and I received a fax from the office congratulating me on becoming the Chairman of a fully listed company, along with a copy of the *FT* ad that had been placed by Hill Samuel Bank Ltd. I recall the celebrations that evening with people we had met on the trip – Andrew and Jacqui Martin and their daughter Heidi. They remain close friends to this day.

Our share price continued to perform very well and we happily kept out of the headlines, busily building the company. That was soon to change as we continued to grow and we attracted the attention of the unions and the national press.

This was a very busy period in my business life but it was equally 'all change' in our family life as well. In 1990 twelve-year-old Jennifer started boarding at Woldingham School, a convent school run by nuns that had a long and imposing drive. It took five minutes to complete in the car, making it impossible to escape on foot! The following year we decided to move from Copthorne near Crawley to a much larger country-style house in Farnham, Surrey. And our older daughter Debby completed her training at Charing Cross Hospital and qualified as a nurse. Michael was doing well at Charterhouse, and because of our move we were now much closer to the school. Four-year-old Robert was developing well and starting to show an interest in golf. He had a set of plastic golf clubs and even at that age you could see that he had a natural swing.

The adventure for us all was set to continue.

12

THE PRINCE'S TRUST AND THE BEGINNING OF MY PHILANTHROPIC JOURNEY

Following the flotation of Capita in March 1989, I decided to get involved with a charity to 'give something back'. My main interests were around education and working with disadvantaged young people. However, it was sport that opened the door for me to the charity world.

Some of my happiest moments have been spent watching my children play sport at school. Standing on the touchline when my son Michael played football for Charterhouse, I got to know a gentleman called John Jarvis. At first we were simply two proud dads and became friends cheering for our children.

While I was embarking on my adventure with Capita, John had been successfully building up a chain of hotels bearing the Jarvis name. He was also a chairman of one of the companies operating under the banner of the 'Prince's Trust' and talked to me about the organisation. John was very enthusiastic about working with the Prince of Wales and the Prince's close involvement with the work of the Trust. He described some of the projects the Trust was involved in, and the conversations sparked my curiosity. I have always been a socially minded individual. I don't like unfairness. I believe in justice and equality and I am convinced everybody has a right to opportunities in life. It is not where you come from that matters, but where you want to get to that counts. I share my father's passionate socialist principles, even though I have never been involved with unions or in frontline politics. At the same time, I don't believe people should get something for doing nothing. I worry about the impact of the benefit culture that exists in many parts of our society. I also feel that people from difficult backgrounds sometimes miss out on the chances offered to the children of the better off.

The young generation is the future and young people deserve a decent opportunity to learn and grow and flourish. John talked a lot about the work of the Trust, which addressed this issue, and I found my interest growing. The aims of the organisation seemed in tune with my own beliefs.

Over an after-match tea at Charterhouse, he said: 'Why don't we set up a meeting for you to come into one of the briefing sessions that they have at the Prince's Trust?' He thought it was time that I took a look for myself and I agreed.

After completing his service in the Royal Navy, HRH The Prince of Wales put his pension into starting the Trust. Since then it has grown and developed enormously by focusing its efforts on helping people with disadvantages. I had always had a high regard for Prince Charles. I could see that some of the things he had done with the Trust had had an enormous, positive effect on the lives of young people, so I said I'd like to do what I could to help. That conversation in 1991 led me to meet the CEO of the Trust, the enigmatic Tom Shebbeare (later Sir Tom), and so began my involvement. It proved to be a truly fascinating and hugely humbling experience over a period covering the next fifteen years of my life. It was also instrumental in my starting my own Foundation in 2006.

I was invited to the Prince's home, Highgrove House, for dinner on 4 November 1993. There was a subtle understanding that if you were asked to such a special event you were going to become a supporter of the Trust. I remember standing with the other guests in a lounge, having been given drinks, and everyone was chatting. Suddenly, I could feel that the atmosphere in the room had changed. Then I realized that

Prince Charles, or 'the boss' as the staff at the Trust refer to him, had walked into the room.

Prince Charles has the enviable talent of making you feel very relaxed and at ease. I recall that two Jack Russell dogs were present as we sat down to have a meal, sitting by his feet. We talked about The Trust and his plans for it and he wanted to understand all about my business activities. He was very knowledgeable about the plight of many young people and very passionate about The Trust and the difference it could make to young lives. I was already a fan, I think, but I soon became much more deeply impressed.

I joined the committee that John Jarvis chaired at The Trust. Other members included Charles (later Sir Charles) Dunstone of Carphone Warehouse, Harvey Goldsmith the theatre impresario, and the late Sir Richard George of Weetabix fame. We were associated with the organisation of some remarkable events designed to raise money for The Trust. The largest was the annual 'Party in the Park for The Prince's Trust', a sellout concert in Hyde Park. The prince attended and the event heightened the awareness of the work that The Trust did for so many troubled young people.

Prince Charles is a remarkable person and his name certainly opens doors. Sporting stars and popular celebrities suddenly become amazingly accessible when HRH's name is used. I soon learned the etiquette of never asking for autographs of our guests or asking them to pose for photographs!

The part of The Trust that I was involved with was really the 'new ideas' end. The Trust was prepared to tackle complicated and controversial social issues head-on without a fear of failure or bad publicity. The Trust took risks with young people that the establishment, particularly the banking system, was not prepared to do. For example, it gave grants to encourage young people to start businesses and provided a mentoring facility from within The Trust family of supporters to mitigate against the risk of failure.

Another new initiative that The Trust promoted was a programme involving the setting up of homework clubs in schools. The Trust's role was to provide the funding for a teacher to stay at the school after hours so as to provide the opportunity for pupils to do extended schoolwork. This proved to be amazingly successful, with hundreds of clubs being formed across the country. It was so successful, that the Department of Education negotiated to take over the running of the programme.

Unfortunately the transfer to the Department was ultimately a decision which The Trust regretted. The programme was never developed to its true potential as it disappeared into the bureaucratic structure of a government department, moving away from the entrepreneurial flair of The Trust. This taught me a great deal and shaped my thinking around the way that Capita ultimately developed. Rather than giving 'the homework club' operation to the civil service machine, it would have been far more appropriate for the programme to have been outsourced to a specialist provider with the government providing the funding. It became clear to me early on that my skills were best used not by attending endless frustrating committee meetings discussing policy, but by becoming involved first-hand with the development and implementation of an idea.

This opportunity emerged from a most unusual source but again, looking back, shaped my understanding of the real issues that were being faced by an increasing number of young people. Most fourteen- to sixteen-year-olds do not have a serious problem at school. They pass their exams and go on to higher education or employment. But for some tens of thousands of young people, school is a real struggle. Underachievement at school can trigger a chain of negative consequences, leading to problems in subsequent years.

The Trust identified a programme called xl, a concept which came from the United States where it had achieved great success in reducing school dropout rates and raising achievement levels. Tom Shebbeare persuaded the Trust Council to implement it in the UK. I was invited to chair the xl Advisory Committee, charged with the responsibility of developing the programme.

Xl was essentially a preventive in-school programme for young people in their final two years of compulsory schooling who are disaffected and at risk of truancy, exclusion or underachievement. It was designed to help teachers calm and deal with disruptive kids without the schools having to exclude them. I came to understand that there is a huge correlation between young people serving custodial sentences and those who have been excluded from school or truanted. I discovered that 93 per cent of young offenders at Feltham Prison had been excluded from school. Home Office research had also shown that truants were more than three times more likely to commit crime than non-truants. At that time, over 9,000 young people were permanently excluded from school in England alone.

These shocking statistics shaped my thinking about how different things could have been in my life had I experienced exclusion at Portslade School for Boys. Xl operated as a club formed within the school, where between twelve and fifteen students met for around three hours every week. It was student-led but guided and encouraged by an xl club adviser, who was chosen by the school for strong teamwork and group facilitation skills. They in turn had a 'Link Teacher' who was a senior member of the school staff.

Overall our responsibility was to co-ordinate the xl programme and xl network while at the same time maintaining a national evaluation framework to ensure quality and consistency. We introduced a national accreditation scheme through the charity ASDAN (Award Scheme Development and Accreditation Network), creating 'The Prince's Trust xl Award' for participating schools. This recognised achievement across the competencies covered during participation in the programme, covering the aspects of: 'improving one's own learning', 'working with others' and 'problem solving'.

We also held annual celebration days for xl club members to acknowledge their success. These were big, joyous events where many young people travelled long distances by coach, train and cars to venues such as the Wembley Arena, to celebrate success and to take part in a day of team-led bonding exercises. For me, it was a valuable introduction into working with schools and children and it shaped much of my thinking around the work I now do as the sponsor of academies.

In 2003 Ofsted gave xl high praise. The programme also proved to be very cost effective. The typical cost of an xl club over a two-year period was just over £5,000. The estimated cost of permanent exclusion to local education authorities was nearly £5,000 per student per year, but the cost of exclusion in terms of damage to the individual and society was incalculable. The feedback from the students presented us with many amazing real life stories. I will always remember one in particular involving a young girl called Ellie who came to one of our events.

Ellie was very bright when she left primary school. But her attendance slipped below 20 per cent and her secondary school predicted she wouldn't sit any GCSEs. At thirteen she started to abuse solvents and alcohol and she was referred to a Drug Abuse Agency which provided support. The following year she was recruited to The Prince's Trust xl club at the school.

Then Ellie faced another setback at the age of fifteen when she was thrown out of the family home. Our xl adviser provided great support during this time and Ellie moved in with her sister in the short term. She completed the xl programme in May 2003 and her attendance had increased to 97 per cent. Ellie achieved a Prince's Trust xl award at gold level. Despite the prediction she would not sit any exams, Ellie sat five GCSE subjects in English, Maths, Computing, Drama and Art and passed them all.

The success of the xl network and its cost effectiveness prompted us to pilot a version of it linked to sport, with one involving rugby clubs and the other linked to football clubs. In these cases, the xl clubs were held at the grounds of the clubs themselves, which essentially were places that students enjoyed going to. In a way, this initiative was the forerunner of the community work around numeracy and literacy that so many of the clubs now do. Indeed, the club I supported as a boy, Brighton & Hove Albion, is very much involved with this, winning awards for its 'Albion in the Community' work.

One amazing by-product of this work for me is that it enabled my youngest daughter, Jennifer, to join the Trust to work with the central team on these sporting offshoots. Over a two-year period she co-headed the rugby initiative and its regional relationship with schools, putting together programme copy for rugby matches and sponsorship letters, among many other tasks. Apart from meeting some of her sporting idols through this, I think that it also had a deep social impact on Jennifer. In setting the clubs up, Jennifer worked with some of the most demanding of students associated with the programme, many of whom had drug issues. Her role included helping them to write their CVs and to prepare for job interviews.

I was so impressed by xl that I decided to fund some of the central cost of the team that was responsible for running xl at Park Square East. My work on xl was acknowledged by HRH the Prince of Wales and I became a Patron of the Prince's Trust, something of which I am very proud.

I found the whole concept of helping people and making a difference to their lives a hugely rewarding experience. It was such a complete and refreshing change from the focus on meeting profit targets at Capita.

Working with this remarkable charity was fulfilling and surprising. It was a fantastic experience but, to be honest, it was also upsetting as I came to learn more about the dreadful lives some young people suffered. It made me quite angry. I had been so busy developing a career and building a business that I had never seen any of this side of life.

Getting involved with the Prince's Trust was, therefore, something of an education for me and I think it helped me to grow as a person. I had been very blinkered for a long time, always focused on the next set of financial results. Working with the Prince's Trust helped me to develop as a human being.

Of course, it was my business success that enabled me to get involved in the first place but the philosophy of The Prince's Trust, helping to give young people the chance to succeed, mirrored my own lifelong opinions and feelings

I was fortunate enough to meet the Prince on several occasions and one of my fondest memories was taking him to visit an xl club in the London Borough of Hackney, for him to see first-hand the impact of the programme. I think he is a very brave man. He does difficult things to help people, and he gives an awful lot of his time to every one of his charities.

Along with Charles Dunstone, I was invited to join the main Prince's Trust Council and became the member who led on xl. Another person who became a member at the same time was Fred Goodwin, the CEO of the Royal Bank of Scotland. This change also coincided with John Jarvis stepping down and Sir Bill Castell was appointed as chair of the enlarged organisation.

It was clearly an honour for me to be appointed by HRH into my new role but it thrust me headlong into competition for funding and managerial resources for xl against the much more established programmes that had been developed in other parts of The Trust. These included an enterprise project run by Lord Young, whereby loans were awarded to young people encouraging them to start businesses, and another major programme called Team. Team took long-term unemployed youngsters and set them to work on a project for twelve weeks, under the guidance of people who were employed to kick-start their confidence and aspirations to get a job. Both of these initiatives proved to be very successful and attracted considerable government funding, which became something of a drawback during a subsequent round of public expenditure cuts when they were among the first areas to have funding withdrawn.

To me there was a bigger point. In xl we had tapped into an area where there was clearly a need and the innovative nature of The Trust's work, starting new things, was something that the educational system found difficult to do. In some ways, I felt that The Trust was losing its edge by gravitating towards large, government agenda-led programmes. It was difficult for me to defend xl against this and I found myself taking an increasingly defensive position at Trust meetings. I wrote to the Prince, briefing him directly on the benefits of the xl network but, although x1 remained a major programme for The Trust, references to it rarely appeared in his speeches and mentions of xl were not prominent in fund-raising events that he held. I humbly felt that these were massive missed opportunities.

In 2004, Sir Tom (Shebbeare), who was a supporter of mine and of the xl network, stepped down as CEO and moved to a more central role based at St James's Palace to assist the Prince in his broader charity work. Martina (later Dame Martina) Milburn was appointed to replace him in May of that year, with the remit to review the overall direction of The Trust.

The inevitable occurred and the accountancy firm, Deloitte, was retained in October 2004 to analyse the strategic direction and operational capabilities of xl. This review was also to test the understanding of the role and nature of the relationships between advisers, schools and The Prince's Trust central, regional and national system.

At the time I felt that this report was used by a number of influential people around The Trust to curtail the development of the xl network. To me, what was needed was either for the programme to be franchised to an operator that could invest in its development, or for it to be outsourced, with the approval of The Prince's Trust, to a training provider, with The Trust responsible for monitoring quality. The fact that neither happened was very frustrating and demotivating.

Ironically, perhaps, had I established my Foundation at that point I would have made an offer to the Trust to take on responsibility for the programme. But as I was still Chairman of Capita at the time, I was not able to make such a move. Notwithstanding my views on its development, I find it immensely satisfying that the Prince's Trust xl network is still promoted by The Trust as one of its five major programmes, so our work on developing it has had a lasting legacy.

I think my one personal regret with The Trust was that I never had the opportunity to become its chairman. At the time that Sir Bill stood down in 2003, in the typical way that things happen in that world, I was sounded out by Sir Tom about whether I might like to take on the role. I know that I had supporters within The Trust executive team but there was a strongly developing relationship with the Royal Bank of Scotland and, with Fred Goodwin as its CEO, the Bank became the largest benefactor of The Trust's activities. There was a sense of inevitability when Fred was appointed Chairman and, in view of the need to curtail some of The Trust's activities in order to rein in the budget, this was probably the right move. All our board meetings were then held in the palatial surroundings of the bank's offices in Broadgate, on the top floor of the building. Our meetings were serviced by staff from the bank welcoming trustees and serving food to the standard of a high-calibre restaurant. It was most definitely something which I could never have matched at Capita's offices in Victoria Street. It was also more in keeping with the standards expected by HRH for his regular attendance at our meetings.

Fred was a challenging and demanding person to work with. He was obviously a very clever individual, but I was never convinced that he had the sort of empathy for The Trust's work with young people that I knew that I had, and that others who were involved with The Trust had. He saw his role more akin to a business process than a social cause. I recall sitting next to him at a Trust dinner held at the bank around the time that he was celebrating the bank's infamous acquisition of the ABN Amro Bank. He remarked to me: 'Yes, we got there in the end.' This subsequently proved to be a deal too far for Fred and led to the collapse of the bank.

I stood down from the council in 2006 after doing two terms. This decision, I feel, was driven by the issues surrounding the 'Labour Loan saga' (more of which later). While it was the right time for me to move on it represented, along with my decision to stand down from being Chairman of Capita, a huge change in my life.

I recall being asked by Fred if I could join him in his office after one of The Trust meetings, as he wanted to discuss something with me. It was akin to going to the headmaster's study at school as he told me in a perfectly logical, but no-nonsense way that he felt it was timely for me to leave the council. Other members had been serving on it for a similar period, but I was more outspoken about the direction of travel for The Trust than they had been. Maybe that was another factor.

I met and worked with some incredible people at The Trust and many have gone on to be CEOs of other charities and I would work very closely with two of these again through my activities post Capita, when I was appointed as the inaugural chair of Vinspired, the national volunteering charity. Terry Ryall, who was the Regional Director of the South East Region of The Trust, became our CEO at Vinspired and was inspirational to work with. Manny Amardi, whom I met when he was the Director of Fund Raising and Development at The Trust, joined me as trustee on the board of Vinspired. The three of us had seven ground-breaking years together, pioneering a change in young people's attitude to volunteering.

Much to my surprise, my involvement with work of the Prince of Wales was not over. In early 2007, I was invited to join a council that HRH formed to review all the charities that he had under his control.

While The Prince's Trust was the largest by far, there were a further twenty charities covering areas in which he took an interest. It was truly amazing to see this in diagrammatic form, a clear illustration of an entrepreneurial brain at work. It was even more incredible that he could create space for each of them in his already packed diary, attending events to assist with fund raising and promotion. Each of these charities had a CEO and a Chair along with a Board of Trustees.

We came together as a group initially under the auspices of Tom Shebbeare in his more central role at St James's Palace. The Group also included the wonderful Dame Julia Cleverdon who, amongst other roles, was Chief Executive of the charity Business in the Community and had been named as one of the '50 Most Influential Women in Britain' by *The Times*. Essentially, the task was to review the structure and to make recommendations for change.

If ever there was a 'hospital pass' in the charity world this was it! In business terms, the route was obvious, although it was not what HRH wanted to hear. It was clear that a number of the charities should be merged, and others phased out, because they had achieved their purpose. The problem was that each had a major donor, who had been persuaded, most probably by the Prince himself, to support the cause. To shut down or merge a charity was a tad difficult to explain to the sponsor without it having an impact on any ongoing relationship. Using my Capita brain, I could see the opportunity to centralise some of the back-office services, such as accounting, HR and payroll. This would save money, which could go into the frontline work of the various causes, but again required structures to be changed. A number of us also felt that many of these charities should be in one building, instead of being spread out all over London.

It was fascinating to be in a room with a mix of business and financial brains, working alongside those who had known the Prince in a personal capacity for many years. People from HRH's own team were involved, to take him through the recommendations, and Dame Julia took over the chair of the group when Sir Tom finally moved on to a new role.

The committee set out its recommendations in a letter and I am told that this letter had a range of comments written in the margin by the Prince himself in response, some of which were complementary while others were most definitely not!

The outcome was that some small changes were implemented, but not the ones involving shared back-office services, and the recommendation that all The Trust's charities should be moved into one building was blocked by The Prince's Trust, which ultimately moved away from Park Square East to a new building near Charing Cross Station, completing a merger with another trust as part of this move.

Through the Foundation, I would continue to be involved with The Trust, especially in projects connected with trying to break the cycle of criminal offending, listening to the views of young people who have served a prison sentence. The most vulnerable time for a prisoner is just after their release from custody. Young offenders who are not met by a family member or a youth worker may go straight out to buy drugs and alcohol, which results in reoffending. We looked at a project where mentors assisted young offenders throughout the custodial process and, vitally, continued doing so once they were released. The mentors provided assistance on basic issues in the court process, then on release they gave essential advice on housing, employment and the like.

The pilot went well and received a good response but I felt that this was not the direction in which to take the Foundation. I wanted to help prevent young people going to prison in the first place, and much of this depended on them receiving a good education. It did open my eyes to the harmful repercussions of having a criminal record in our country. Even the most basic of mistakes that leads to a custodial sentence means that you will have difficulty getting a job.

One of the amazing things that came out of this work for me was that I met Mark Johnson. Mark is an ex-offender and had become an adviser to HRH the Prince of Wales on the whole area of youth offending. He maintained that you needed to tackle the root causes of offending and to hear directly from young people about what had helped them stop reoffending. Mark had a great effect on me and we ended up working together to help him form a charity called User Voice, one our first projects when I started the Foundation in 2006, and a topic I will return to later.

Working with the Prince's Trust crystallised my idea of creating my own Foundation and shaped my thinking around the importance of a good education, which should be the right of every child.

It was around 2004 that the Academies Programme, which allowed private sponsors to get directly involved with improving educational standards, was launched by Prime Minister Tony Blair. One of the key people initially driving the introduction was Andrew Adonis, now Lord Adonis. He had worked as a journalist with *The Times* and had covered Capita's development. I got to know him quite well.

Andrew then moved to Number 10 to be Tony Blair's adviser on Education. Ultimately he was elevated to the House of Lords and became a Minister for Education and the key architect of the academies policy. Andrew was very direct when we met and said to me: 'We would love you to become one of the sponsors for the Academies Programme. I'd like to take you to visit one of the first schools. He knew my background, and something about my feelings on my own education.

There weren't many to see at that time, but I decided it was definitely something I wanted to do. Prompted by Andrew's support, that same year and while still on the Council of The Prince's Trust, I set up the Rodney Aldridge Charitable Trust (which now operates within the Aldridge Foundation) specifically to fund the sponsorship of a city academy. Becoming a sponsor meant making a contribution of £2 million towards the cost of the capital build of an academy.

To me this fitted well with the criteria I had set for my philanthropic plans, since I was to be directly involved and it would give me a first-hand opportunity to monitor improvement in performance. Capita was still thriving but I knew I wanted something else in my life and I became very enthused by the whole academy project.

The key decision was where I should become a sponsor. I needed to decide this. I did not want to be allocated a school by the Department of Education. I began first with a place that I knew well, my home City of Brighton. I approached Brighton and Hove City Council, with the help of Lord Steve Bassam, a former Leader of the Council, and offered to support a school in the city. Sponsoring an academy close to where I grew up seemed the most obvious step. There were early discussions about Falmer High School, which was not performing well and needed a substantial rebuild. Steve Bassam and I visited the school together and then I had a meeting with Leader of the Council, Councillor Ken Bodfish.

I thought everything was going well, but after a little time the council decided not to go ahead. I felt surprised and very let down by the whole episode. My strong sense was that David Hawker, the Director of Children Services was not a supporter of the school becoming an academy and influenced the councillors accordingly. The whole academy concept was a controversial piece of legislation, to be quite honest. The introduction of an academy made very direct statements, which some local authorities and some parents clearly found unpalatable. Effectively, Government was saying: 'Your school is underperforming, therefore you can't run it so we're going to find a sponsor to take over in your place.' Academies might be common nowadays but they weren't always welcomed initially.

I was still determined to find a school that I wanted to work with, rather than wait for the Department of Education to allocate me one, so I next turned to Blackburn with Darwen, a local authority in Lancashire, in the north-west of England, many miles from Brighton. I had no personal link with the area, but I had come to know the officers and councillors through Capita. We had a ground-breaking partnership involving a long-term contract outsourcing a wide range of back-office white collar services. As a part of this partnership, Capita had created over 300 new white-collar jobs and built a major new business centre in the town. It was a very challenging area socially and it was reported that large numbers of the local population survived on benefits.

The partnership we had set up with the local leaders established white-collar jobs as opposed to blue-collar ones which had historically been the norm. I had worked well on the project with the CEO, Phil Watson, and the Leader of the Council, Sir Bill Taylor. I phoned Phil and said: 'I have an idea which I think you will like, can we meet?' and I went up there to see them both. They were taken by the idea and identified a school that was struggling: Darwen Moreland High School, on the outskirts of the City. More to the point, they were open-minded about turning it into an academy because that triggered government funding that was otherwise not available to them.

I went to look around Darwen Moreland School. It was based out of the town and most definitely required considerable work. The school was not performing well and had had five head teachers in five years. The plan was to rebuild the school closer to the centre of Darwen and they showed me the area they were considering. In my mind's eye I can still see the assistant chief executive, Harry Catterall (who subsequently became the CEO when Phil retired) being thrown out of the car to point out exactly where the suggested new site was. It was raining and windy and it took a great deal of imagination to think of a brand new school being built there. It was an area where the council planned to knock down some of the old houses, which were in a bad state of repair, moving residents to a new development.

It was that windy visit that started the ball rolling for the application that my Trust made to the Department of Education to become the sponsor of Darwen Moreland School. This was supported by the Labour-led council and, in return for their brave decision, £46 million was received from the Department to build a new school, of which I had to contribute £2 million. This investment represented a lasting opportunity to transform the education that pupils received. To the great benefit of the people of Darwen, and most importantly its young people, the town would have a brand new school

Today, the most obvious difference between the old school and the new Darwen Aldridge Community Academy is the inspiring new building. What goes on inside that building is also significantly different and has become a template that is being used for new academies across the country. Academies are about fundamentally changing the way education is delivered. We recruited an exceptional Principal, Brendan Loughran, who has transformed the school and has changed the ethos of the organisation.

I'll talk much more later about my experiences with the academy at Darwen and how it led me to set up the Aldridge Foundation. The school looks wonderful today and it has done some suitably wonderful work, but we had a long and difficult road to travel before we could achieve my ambitions. In 2005 we made an application to the Department for the school to achieve academy status, which was approved, but we then ran into the planning issues that delayed everything for a number of months.

Although the school we were replacing was clearly struggling, our suggestion of replacing it with a brand new academy wasn't popular. Lots of local people had been to the school and in some areas it was well loved. There was also opposition to the proposed site and the need to demolish a large number of houses. The planning process ultimately dragged on for far too long and it required a public inquiry before planning approval was given.

Unfortunately, during this period the press turned on me and there were articles suggesting that establishing an academy meant there were going to be benefits flowing back to Capita. There was a suggestion that, because I was going to build a school there, Capita was going to win other contracts either locally or nationally. At the time, because of the controversial nature of the academy legislation, it seemed that a number of academy sponsors were finding themselves in the tricky waters of suspicion on all sorts of fronts.

Even though I was putting £2 million of my own money into the project, it was suggested that conveniently using my own company to build or service the school I could somehow make a 'profit' out of education.

The fact was that Capita could have provided services on virtually all aspects of the build but was involved in nothing connected with it. We had our own property services capability that could have designed and project managed the construction of the academy. We also had a recruitment company that could have handled the recruitment of staff, HR skills to deal with the transfer of staff and an outsourcing resource that could have provided back-office services. We did none of that.

The only thing that Capita *did* supply was the SIMS software to provide the support services to the academy, which was a miniscule involvement in relation to the £46-million project. In any case, the SIMS software was by far the market-leading system, being used by 23,000 schools in the country. All of this was made clear up front to the Department and to the press.

There was a stark difference between Brighton saying 'No' to me sponsoring an academy and Blackburn with Darwen Council saying 'Yes'. In Blackburn there was a leader and a chief executive who worked well together. They had majority Labour control where decisions could be made, whereas in Brighton the leadership proved to be quite weak. This disappointed me, because this was most certainty not the case when Lord Bassam was the leader and, going back even further, when I worked for the authority.

The critical thing about Blackburn with Darwen was that they accepted that they needed help. Allowing a sponsor to come in and run a school was seen by some councils as admitting that the local authority wasn't up to the job. I think Blackburn with Darwen were very bold to back me. I don't think we knew at the time that we would get £46 million to build the school, but it was a good illustration of how a politically strong council, which wants to do things to improve the lives of young people, can operate for the common good. I was very proud to be associated with Blackburn with Darwen, and I still am.

Brighton did change its mind four years later, eventually getting £24 million from the government to rebuild Falmer High School. By then the level of funding on offer had been reduced. So, thanks to their inactivity and prevarication, Brighton & Hove City Council had to manage the project with severely reduced funding and as I will explain later in the book, without my intervention through the Foundation, it is my opinion that they wouldn't have received even the £24 million. The key point that this illustrated to me is that politicians can get in the way of a young person receiving a top-class education and experiencing top-class facilities.

My experience with Capita was so valuable because I understood the way that a local authority worked, therefore I knew how to work with them in a partnership. At the end of the day, though, you've got to have somebody who shares your aims. I like the people of Blackburn with Darwen. They were straight and honest. They did what they said they were going to do and they stood by me. But before my move into the world of education was to develop much further there were some interesting developments in my business career.

13

CAPITA – SURVIVING AND THRIVING

One day the Capita story will be written in full. If one stops to think, this company was built around many people, whom Maggie Thatcher believed were incompetent, being transferred from the public sector. It shows that with the right vision, investment and belief, people respond and anything is then possible. The Capita story changed the lives of so many for the better, including most definitely mine and that of my family.

Only through writing this book do I realise just what an enormous impact these years have had on me as a person. In many ways the influences on me have been for the better but equally there are some things that don't make me feel proud about the individual that I became. Much of my motivation was driven by a fear of failure and a desire to win at all costs. Having wealth has an impact on the way that you think and act, meaning that you are living in your own world, not the real world. Sometimes this makes you feel very isolated. I recognise it has brought about an amazing transformation in my life, but I have never forgotten where I came from or the struggle that I had for many years to make ends meet.

On the family front, we would all agree that we have been fortunate to have had some wonderful experiences together, whether those be the places to which we have travelled or the homes in which we have lived. I am proud of the way that our children have remained grounded in their outlook throughout this and in the way that they now approach their own lives.

During this period, working under a Conservative administration, Capita changed out of all recognition from the company that floated in 1989. Many of the major contracts won and the acquisitions made during this era proved to be core to the development of the range of services that formed the business platform for the growth of Capita going forward. The key thing was that throughout this period we kept the innovative, entrepreneurial flair, strongly resisting a bureaucratic, big-company mentality, something that I hate so much.

Irrespective of that, my role changed through necessity. I moved away from what I enjoyed most: being close to people and creating a team spirit, to spending far more time externally – face-to-face with customers and with people in the City. We needed shareholders and analysts because, for a company of our size, this became a key role to get right. Another factor was intrusion from the Press, which intensified enormously. It was my belief that it was right for them to understand me both as the chairman of the business and what I stood for, as much as it was to focus upon the contract wins or the increasing profits that Capita was making.

At the point we became a fully listed company in August 1991, our profile increased and, with the results that we reported in that year, Capita joined the FTSE All Share Index, which included the top 800 companies on the stock market. We were firing on all cylinders, reporting a large number of significant, high-profile new contract wins. The group was then divided into two divisions covering outsourced services, where we ran things for others, and advisory services, where we gave advice to others, leading us to brand ourselves: 'Capita, the management services Group'.

However, with this growth came a big issue. It was obvious that we needed to make a similar investment in growing our senior management, particularly in the area of IT, which became of escalating importance in how services were to be transformed.

In one of the meetings that Paul and I had with a potential client, the person mentioned to us a guy called Paddy Doyle, by whom he had been impressed, and who was working at Hoskyns, a major IT company.

We made contact with Paddy to suggest meeting up – obviously to see if he might want to join us. This turned out to be a long and protracted courtship but the outcome was to prove to be one of the most significant appointments in our history.

As the name suggests, Paddy was of Irish descent and, although outwardly he had a laid-back style, he was a very clear, engaging thinker. You could understand why people wanted to work for him. He had been at Hoskyns for a number of years working closely with CEO Geoff Unwin, and felt a high degree of loyalty to the business.

Paul and I persisted with our approach, arranging for Paddy to meet all of the executive team at different times. Clearly, the growth that we had achieved and our plans to grow Capita were of interest to him, as was the share option scheme that we had in place. Gradually we came closer to a deal and I recall a dinner that he and I had at the La Cappanna restaurant in Cobham, Surrey. It was similar to the meeting I had with Paul three years before, with Paddy wanting to be convinced about the plans that Paul and I had outlined to him and to make sure that he and I could work together.

Ultimately he joined us in mid-1992. On almost his first day in the office at Tothill Street, Paddy retreated into one of the offices at the front of the building to look through the business plans for the business as a whole, but in particular those of Telecom Capita. He went through the terms of the long-term contracts that we had signed up to as well as the performance we had achieved to date. More importantly, he evaluated our liabilities for non-performance contained within these contracts. After two days he emerged only to say to Paul and me that we had major operational problems and in the way we were structured we would have serious financial difficulties.

Through our growth we had established sites all over the country with no strategy for consolidation. Equally in our major contracts in Berkshire and Oxfordshire we had signed up for a seven-year contract but with ten-year leases with ICL for the hardware. This basically meant that unless we won other new business along with winning the main contract in the rebid, we had a significant overhang on leasing costs, which technically were down to us.

We had also won a large number of deals in a relatively short time.

A number of these had come about in a slightly strange way. Paul and I were in the office at Tothill Street one day when the receptionist came in to see us saying that two gentlemen named Hawkins and Moretti had turned up in reception without an appointment, but were asking to see us both. It turned out that both men had literally just walked out from their current employer, Municipal Mutual Computing Ltd, a competitor of ours in IT outsourcing contracts. John Hawkins had been their sales and marketing director and Kevin had been his deputy. They had fallen out with MMC about bonus payments and wanted to know how we would feel about them joining us. The added attraction was that they came loaded with three deals they had been working on and they believed that they could bring to us. We listened and agreed a deal with them to start with us.

All three deals were won, including one with the Borough of Torfean, which led to us establishing a Wales & West Business Centre. John became the Sales and Marketing Director for Telecom Capita. He and Kevin most definitely came as a pair and were both at the aggressive end of selling, an approach that was more drastic than we had encountered before. The way that they ran a sales process, while being totally above board, was designed not only to win but to marginalise the competition, using pricing as a major tool. In some deals this resulted in contracts where financial and operational problems would emerge further down the line, when bonuses would have been paid to the sales team. It was the implications that this kind of arrangement had for the business that Paddy had spotted.

I think Paul and I really felt that Paddy was about to walk out and return to Hoskyns, where there was no doubt he would have been most welcome. Thankfully he did not, but he prompted a major change in direction over our bidding strategy and the contractual liabilities that we were prepared to take on. He also persuaded us that we needed to increase the IT capabilities that we had in our team to enable us to get the operational economies that were possible by merging some of our sites.

This resulted in two of his close colleagues from Hoskyns – Tim Johnson and Phil Braithwaite – joining us, and both went on to hold senior positions with Capita for many years. It also resulted in a further twenty or so people joining us from Hosykns over a considerable period. This shaped our recruitment strategy for many years, since what became clear to us was that, if you can persuade one senior person to join, others will follow.

Paddy was made a main Board director on 22 July 1994, taking over responsibility for the Outsourcing Division which combined both our IT and managed services businesses.

With the wins that we had achieved and the lead position that we had in the market, it was inevitable that we would attract attention from NALGO, the union that represented those employed in local government. We made a visit to Wirral Metropolitan Borough Council at the request of Ian Wood, the Director of Finance, whom I knew from my CIPFA days, to explore the options around outsourcing the authority's IT function. Very soon after this visit there was a major centre-page spread in *NALGO News* of January 1993 under the banner headline: 'The private face of Capita'. Above the headline was written:

What is Capita? That's a question a lot of people would like to know the answer to. Which is why *NALGO News* has done an in-depth investigation into the company. If you haven't heard of Capita yet it's likely you soon will – especially if you work in local government or health. Because Capita is the company targeting any compulsory competitive tendering going in your area- and this affects your job, your service conditions and your union.

John Jasper, in his role as MD of Telecom Capita, took the brunt of the attack but the article also made accusations about Paul Pindar and myself. It suggested that we had the habit of securing contracts from local authorities by giving one message about how we intended to conduct ourselves, and then doing something totally different. It claimed that we did not recognise trade unions, which was untrue as we were happy for staff to be members of trade unions but we would not negotiate with trade unions for pay bargaining purposes.

The article used emotive words such as 'duped', suggesting that we could not be trusted to manage sensitive and confidential information in a secure way and claiming that there was industry speculation that Capita was about to be taken over by IBM. This was a deliberate attempt to discredit us and, as NALGO saw it, to protect the jobs of their members. Ironically, it soon became apparent, as local authorities cut the cost of back-office services, that Capita was definitely a far better place for members of NALGO to work.

We took legal action, which was unusual for us, and our solicitors wrote to the General secretary of NALGO, pointing out that there were eighteen substantive inaccuracies in the article. It was important to do this because we had a number of deals that we had won but for which we had yet had not yet signed contracts and this article put a number of these in jeopardy.

At this stage of procurements, staff opinions were crucial and there was always a vote taken about which of the bidders staff were prepared to work for. We had never lost a staff ballot up to this point but clearly the NALGO claims could affect that. I recall being involved in another bid around that time and, when walking around the site, I saw a copy of the article pinned on a staff noticeboard under the NALGO section. Our lawyer issued a High Court Writ insisting that a retraction was issued in the next edition of *NALGO News* along with an apology in terms to be approved by us. We achieved this and it duly appeared, but of course the retraction and apology were nowhere near as prominent as the original article had been.

Nevertheless, some good did come out of it because I got to know NALGO's Assistant General Secretary, Keith Sonnet, very well. He soon realised that, with the onslaught of CCT, outsourcing was not going to go away. He recognised from my background and the involvement of my late father in the union world, that I was a person who had a great deal of sympathy for the rights of his members. I had been a member of NALGO in my local authority days, so I was a person he could work with and trust. Capita subsequently negotiated a ground-breaking deal over terms and conditions with NALGO, which merged with two other unions later in 1993 to become UNISON. I also got to know Dave Prentis, the General Secretary and we worked equally well together, sharing a speaking platform on a number of occasions. While UNISON members usually preferred to stop services being outsourced, when they were, the union often recognised Capita as the preferred bidder. Capita developed and agreed with UNISON one of the first national agreements struck by any outsourcing company. It was regarded as a good and fair employer.

Returning to Paddy Doyle, operationally one process that he bought to us from Hoskyns was the 'MOB forecasting method', which changed the way that we operated and managed the financial performance of the business. MOB stood for 'monthly operating board' and was a process that encouraged openness in the way that managers reported on progress against Budget. The most dangerous thing, particularly with a six-month reporting regime with the City, was to have a person or team that held back bad news, believing that things will work out all right. Invariably they don't.

The system that Paddy introduced became a standard throughout the business. It only allowed people to reflect in their financial numbers the things that had been achieved or sales that had been concluded. This showed up any shortfalls against budget in the discussions that took place with management teams each month. To support this approach, we majored on having a 'no blame' culture, whereby teams were encouraged to declare issues so that they could be addressed. This team culture meant that, if people were open, we had a chance to deal with problems before they became bigger issues. The MOB meetings with the management teams holding budget responsibilities were held every month and went on for two or three days, covering the entirety of the business.

With Paddy's appointment we now had in place three of the people, Paul, Paddy and myself, who would work together for the next twelve years to build Capita into a major force in the market. The fourth was to be Gordon Hurst, but it took a chain of events to bring about his arrival as finance director, more of which I will explain later.

14

SHAPING A NEW MARKET

J ust as our IT outsourcing business was growing, so were the plans that we had to offer managed service options to local authorities. This was to address the government-driven radical changes in local taxation arrangements. These affected more people than any other council function and the service, therefore, needed to be of the highest quality.

The base line was that we designed a solution whereby the contractual responsibility for collection levels and quality of service was guaranteed under contract at a cost lower than that being achieved by the in-house team. If we outperformed these service levels, we received a bonus but the local authority received a better service than specified, including higher collection rates. It was our job to invest in the new technology and to deal with peaks and troughs of workload demands. The solution that we offered used the same thinking that we had achieved in IT outsourcing, whereby staff involved in the services transferred to us, becoming Capita employees.

It felt convincing on a flipchart in our boardroom and the informal discussions that we had with senior people working in the front line of these services also gave support for the idea. So it was down to Rich Benton to go out and sell the concept to a client!

The first local authority to subcontract all the council's Poll Tax and its later replacement, Council Tax, as well as the Business Rates and Housing Benefits was East Cambridgeshire District Council. They signed a contract with us worth £3.5 million over a five-year period. It may seem a small amount but it represented another first for Capita, giving us a market lead position in another new area. All twenty-three revenue staff chose to transfer to us and then we delivered the contract from the same offices in Ely, giving us another business centre and a reference site for other prospective clients to visit.

We needed to find a person who wanted to be seen as a pioneer and in Richard Carr, the Assistant Chief Executive, we found such a person. Richard needed to get himself comfortable with us as a team and visited our IT centre at Berkshire. He also sat in on a presentation about the experience we had gained through operating the arrears-chasing service which by then had more than thirty clients.

Local government, my home market, is a wonderful market to operate in because once you have convinced one body, others will follow. It is important to find the individual that wants to be the leader, and in this case it was Richard Carr. We were good at finding such leaders and the key to success was that we took equally great care not to let them down.

In short order we were implementing twelve new contracts, giving us a dominant position in the market and resulting in a further 300 people becoming Capita employees.

Another contract was for Kent County Council, involving the outsourcing of its IBM mainframe and setting up a data centre at West Malling Business Park. The Chief Executive was Paul Sabin, whom John Jasper knew well. I had met Paul many years ago when he worked for Redditch New Town Development Corporation. Paul's Managing Director at the time was Bill Evans, a wonderful person to work for and who was the chair of one of the committees that I serviced in the secretariat. Bill became the President of CIPFA and my role was to look after Bill and his wife at the CIPFA Conference. The person of whom Bill was most proud was his 'high flying' deputy, Paul Sabin. It was Paul and his wife, Val, that Bill took with him to the conference and so, yet again, the CIPFA network had paid off.

Two other firsts which resulted in us shaping the emerging outsourcing market followed very rapidly. In the case of the London

Borough of Bromley, it was where we won a contract to manage the entire exchequer services function, covering revenues, benefits, payroll, pensions, creditors and income. This contract was three times larger than any previous white collar outsourcing arrangement, with 170 people transferring to us. The pioneer here was the Treasurer, David Bartlet, but, helpfully, the Chief Executive of Bromley was Nigel Palk who had been Deputy Treasurer at Crawley Urban District Council when I worked there.

Once the contract became operational, we found that it was more overstaffed than our bid model suggested. In keeping with our culture of taking action we decided to make a number of people redundant. I am not sure how we came to the decision on timing but the staff involved got notification of it on Christmas Eve. This was a stupid decision on our part, giving the unions the ammunition to question our methods of operating. It also had a bad impact on staff morale and in the relationship with the client. The decision was right but the timing of the action had been completely inappropriate.

The other deal was much smaller but in a way equally significant. It was with Mendip District Council. The CEO, Graham Jeffs, decided to outsource to us all sixty-four staff responsible for the services previously provided by the council's Finance Department as well as the IT services. This was another first for Capita and a sign that outsourcing was capable of stretching to entire departments of organisations.

Capita was now the number one provider in the market by some way. We had established the platform for growth both in the realms of winning new contracts and, in operating terms, integrating these contracts in the business centres that we now had in Berkshire, Oxfordshire, Bromley, Cambridge, Kent and Cardiff.

All was going well but there was no doubt it was creating a hostile environment with an 'us and them' culture. I recall a visit that I made to the offices of the London Borough of Newham to see the Chief Executive whom I had known for some years. He wanted to pick my brains on outsourcing of services. After signing in at reception, I was collected by his PA and as I walked through to his office, in the large outer area where 200-plus staff worked, on the wall was a sign in large letters saying: 'Beware of Capita, remember they are the enemy'. No wonder he insisted on paying for lunch, which was in a small Indian restaurant well away from the town centre.

What was occurring here was that Compulsory Competitive Tendering was effectively forcing in-house teams to see external bodies such as Capita as a threat to their very existence. We were portrayed as an organisation that would come in, adversely change terms and conditions, make redundancies and make profit from running public services.

As a result, consultancy-based organisations emerged, whose role it was to help the in-house team win contracts against external bodies. This reached a farcical situation, when adverts were being placed in journals such as *Local Government Chronicle* and *Public Finance* depicting party balloons and champagne corks popping, celebrating the winning of a contract by the in-house team.

This was not in the best interest of these teams as they may have 'won' a contract for the next five years but they would have no monies available to develop the service, having needed to cut costs to win the contract in the first place. The long-term prospects for their employees were weakened by this, there being no opportunities for development and the likelihood of the team winning other work being very remote.

So, in line with our innovative approach, we refused to bid against an in-house team because we felt that even if we won, the staff joining Capita would be hostile towards us. We developed a 'VCT option to CCT'. This meant that our solution was driven by an approach called Voluntary Competitive Tendering. In this way we would bid with the in-house team to win the contract as a partner and not a contractor. This was a less hostile approach and in many cases involved adopting a partnership approach with the local authority .To us was a 'no brainer' as we needed the staff to deliver the service but the staff needed investment in them to be able to develop, investment in technology to improve performance, and also investment office refurbishment to give them a decent place to work. As these services were considered to be back-office functions by the local authority, and non-core to the organisation, the office conditions that some teams worked in were appalling and added to the low morale that already existed.

In every contract our initial move was to redecorate the place, give it a lift with new furniture, new technology and an overall new vision. Staff knew that they were joining an ambitious organisation that had growth plans and that they were very much a part of this story going forward. Many of these places became reference sites for prospective customers to visit. Many of the staff were promoted into bigger roles and all knew how they were performing, as for the first time they had targets against which to measure this.

Another first in 1993 was a very large contract with the high profile London Borough of Westminster. The pioneer here was Peter Rogers (later Sir Peter), who subsequently became the CEO of the local authority. We had worked with Peter previously in the early days of CIPFA Computer Services and post our MBO at West Midland Travel, where we did some major pieces of work for them. The significance of the contract here was that it not only involved the entire outsourcing of Revenues and Benefits, but the authority allowed the services to be provided from one of our other business centres. This meant that in return for a lower cost of providing the service that we offered to the local authority, a large percentage of the staff involved would not be transferred to us but made redundant at the authority's cost.

This was a major change in the position taken by an authority and was a recognition that the level of inefficiency was higher than the 20 per cent reduction that we offered as part of our contract, particularly if economies of scale were used to offer multiple contracts from a single site rather than services being delivered from multi sites, as was the present position.

Another factor was that in London it was difficult to attract and keep good personnel. Many were temporary staff – again a service provided by Capita – but this meant that continuity in quality was more difficult, whereas outside of London, staff tended to be of a higher quality and stayed longer in the job, many of them being important second earners within their families. Of equal significance was that the level of salary paid was lower.

In April 1994 an article appeared in *Forbes*, the widely read and highly respected US magazine, saying: 'when it comes to reinventing government, Britain is some ways ahead of the US' followed by the headline: 'Let Rod do it'. The opening paragraph of the article said:

'Vice-President Albert Gore talks about making government more efficient. He might like to chat with London's Rod Aldridge...' It went on to speak about the contracts that we had in the public sector and the successes we had achieved in reducing costs and improving performance. It was very nice of *Forbes* to say it and it most definitely played well into our growing US shareholder base at the time.

During this period, we also made a number of acquisitions, some of which could be described as opportunistic and others strategic, but all made with the intention of extending the services that we offered to our clients, taking us even further away from our competitors.

One service that would come into the opportunistic category was of John Crilley Limited which took us into the murky world of debt collection. It took some explaining to the City that we were buying a bailiff company, particularly with the stories in the Press of wide-shouldered blokes turning up on domestic doorsteps and removing the TV set and sofa, the children in tears as these items were loaded on a van outside. The thinking behind our decision was that, since we had contracts to collect council tax and business rates, the next logical phase after chasing the debt was to follow up with a formal debt recovery service.

John Crilley had been established for over one hundred years, but I must admit that it was something of a different world to me when I visited their offices. They were tucked well out of the way in a backstreet with bars on the windows and the car parking within a well-protected compound. The entrance area was also not very welcoming as many 'customers' that turned up to pay were not happy to be there. It was most definitely not a site that we would take our investors to see on our 'City Days'.

We stressed the professional nature of the business, its utilisation of sophisticated IT systems and talked about it enabling us to offer an 'integrated management collection service'. Also key was the fact that John Crilley had 130 local authority clients, giving us access to this client base to sell an outsourced solution on revenue and benefits.

In 1995 Paul did a deal transferring the control of this business to Madagans, the largest bailiff in the market, taking 20.4 per cent in the enlarged business. Madagans had more than 220 clients to add to our already substantial portfolio. Over time, we bought out the rest of the 79.6 per cent stake of Madagans, with Capita then becoming the largest professional debt recovery company in the UK. This service became a key part of the integrated solution we offered to win the congestion charging contract for London and the TV license revenue collection contract with the BBC.

Another business we acquired was the International division of the Royal Institute of Public Administration. RIPA International was established in 1922. Over the previous thirty years it had developed a major worldwide programme of training courses and consultancy services for the public and private sectors overseas. Its consultants, many of whom were ex-civil servants, had worked in more than forty counties and trained more than 6,000 public servants from over sixty nations.

All of the customers were seeking to create similar structures to our civil service in their own countries, proving just how strong the UK brand is. There is a certain irony about this as Capita's outsourcing activities were designed to move away from these highly bureaucratic and inefficient structures. The courses were attended by people from places such as Estonia, Ghana, Kyrgyzstan, The Gambia and Vietnam. Courses lasted from two to fourteen weeks, delivered from RIPA's centre in London's Regent's Park.

On many occasions delegates would literally turn up with a suitcase full of cash to cover the course fee and their accommodation costs. Had we decided to take Capita down an international route, RIPA could have provided that opportunity, but for all the time that I was at Capita the line that we took was that there was no need to go outside the UK as there was plenty for us to do in our own country, with customers we knew well.

Our property services division that was started with J.E. Greatorex had grown in its own right under John Brameld's management and the division by then was well on its way to becoming the largest multi-disciplinary property consultancy in the UK. Estates Design and Management, an architectural business specialising in the health service, with over one hundred staff, was acquired in 1992. Beard Dove, providing a comprehensive range of management and construction related consultancy services through its 250 employees, became a part of the group in 1994.

The division was involved in some amazing projects across the public and private sectors. As well as building hospitals and prisons, I used to refer in our City presentation to the fact that we were involved with iconic projects, such as the retractable roof at Wimbledon and the building of the new Wembley Stadium.

The emerging story here was that, as a team, we were planning a much bigger play, whereby we could win long-term integrated contracts covering all back-office white collar services – IT, finance, HR, revenue and property services. This would give us a major advantage, as no other company in the market had this range of capabilities.

During this same period, we also started to build our software services division. This started in August 1993 with the acquisition (for £4 million) of West Wiltshire Software, the business that the local authority had built, and with which CIPFA Computer Services had the agreement when we had first started in business nine years previously.

West Wiltshire had developed this business to a point where it now had contracts with over one hundred local authorities, involving applications in the areas of council tax, non-domestic rates and housing benefits. However, it was considered by the District Auditor that it had become a legal risk to the local taxpayers should anything go wrong, as it was not the core responsibility of the local authority to provide such a service. It also required further capital investment to develop it. The authority was, therefore, required to dispose of the business.

As we already had a relationship with them, we were a natural partner rather than ICL, against whom they had competed for years. Part of this deal was that we were awarded a £3-million outsourcing contract to manage the computer facilities of the local authority for three years and all the staff involved transferred to us. We traded as Academy Information System rather than as Capita, as at the time we felt that this avoided people feeling that they had total reliance on Capita, although in local government terms this was increasingly beginning to be the case. Through two or three smaller acquisitions of companies providing other software packages around housing and income management, we rapidly became the second largest supplier of software to local government, with over 370 systems installed.

Another key early acquisition and one of the most significant ever made by us, was the Schools Information Management Systems (SIMS) in July 1994. SIMS was a business that which had been owned by Bedfordshire County Council prior to it being sold by the council to its management team. SIMS basically became the back office IT system for countless schools across the country, providing support on finance, personnel, curriculum and assessment issues. It was a very creative enterprise for a local authority to have done. At the time that the council sold the SIMS business to its management team John Tizard, who would coincidentally some 13 years later become a senior Capita Executive, was joint leader of the council.

I'll ask John to explain what happened:

In 1987 a group of entrepreneurial education officers, advisers and teachers had created a software platform to support many back office and assessment processes for schools and local education authorities. This became known as SIMS and became very well used across the country by schools and local authorities. There were issues about local authority staff developing and managing and financially benefiting from a local authority business – some parallels that Rod experiences at CIPFA.

Eventually, as SIMS became ever more successful, the District Auditor advised the County Council that we should not operate such a business – this would not be the case today when local authority companies are encouraged – and the council decided to allow the SIMS management team to buy the business whilst allowing Bedfordshire schools to have 'free' access to the SIMs systems forever. It was this new business not the County Council that would ultimately sell the company to Capita.

At the time of the acquisition, SIMS provided software to ninety-seven of the 119 Local Education Authorities (LEAs), representing 20,000 of approximately 26,000 schools in the country. It was the largest supplier of management software to schools and LEAs in the UK as well as being a major supplier of software to systems to post-16 colleges.

SIMS not only provided an impenetrable position in the software market because it was very difficult to displace it, as many found out who tried, but it also gave us our first foothold in the education market, which went on to become one of the Group's major markets.

However, this deal created an interesting problem involving the financing of the acquisition where the investment circular offered our shareholders the opportunity to subscribe to new shares in the Group. At around this time, with the growth that we were achieving, the share performance continued to be strong and our market capitalisation was growing, as was our position in the All-share Index. This led to a discussion generated by Hill Samuel, our Merchant Bank, about whether it was time to move away from our brokers, Credit Lyonnais Laing, to a larger firm in preparation for our future development.

Such a move is not an easy one. We had developed close relationships with the team at Laings, including the house analyst and the sales team who knew us well. We were regularly pitched at by virtually all the brokers in the 'Square Mile' for our brokerage as we were seen as a successful and desirable company with ambitious plans to grow.

After speaking to several Houses, the Board decided to take the advice of Hill Samuel and we appointed Cazenove & Co, who were the Queen's financial advisers and as 'blue blooded' as one could get. After the courtship the problems started virtually immediately. Paul and I expected to go through the learning curve of the team at Cazenove for them to understand about Capita, our markets and our plans but receptiveness of them to do so was off the pace we had expected.

Equally, we had gone from being a key client getting the 'A' Team attention at Laings to being the smaller 'new boys', who had to gain trust to warrant attention at Cazenove. Some of the meetings we had led us to believe at a very early stage that we had made a mistake. In City terms, by making the move we already had brought attention to ourselves, whereby questions were raised about our motives. There was a suggestion that we were planning to make a substantial fund raise and required the 'heavy hitting' of the client base that Cazenove enjoyed, whereby one was told through a simple call that shares were placed on trust in the full knowledge of the recipient that when another deal of a higher quality came along, they would be at the head of the queue.

There were also rumours in the market that there could be issues with us which Laings were not prepared to go along with. It was very possible that some of these rumours were started by those who were unsuccessful in winning our brokerage.

After several weeks our share price had weakened considerably at a time when our trading was going like 'gang busters'. Despite saying this to them, we got little support from the team at Cazenove, which resulted in tough exchanges with them by Paul and myself, something which is not normally experienced by the Queen's brokers.

Things came to a head when, on 21 June, Hill Samuel issued a circular to shareholders announcing the acquisition of SIMS Holdings for a total consideration of £10m. The circular contained a trading statement along with the reasons for wanting to acquire SIMS. The initial consideration of £6m was to be satisfied by the placement to institutional and other investors of 2.6m new shares in Capita at a discount to the market price. When we presented the deal to the sales force they were clearly not as excited by it is as we were. On the day that the shares were to be placed to raise the funds led by the same salesforce, I received a call from our link director at Cazenove, saying that they had difficulty in placing the shares at the price offered and had an unfulfilled position, meaning that the shares would have to be underwritten by Hill Samuel Bank. Clearly this was not good news and it would inevitably cause some concern, not only with Hill Samuel but it would cause questions to be asked within the 'City World' about what had caused this.

I well recall the conversation we had with the gentleman and it reminded me of the approach I adopted once when playing the grammar school at football: hit the person you are marking hard at the beginning of the game so that he understands that you mean business. Whatever motivated Paul he was of similar mind and the message was delivered to the gentleman in a way that he had probably never experienced before. The outcome was they found a home for the shares, probably to the 'friendly' clients that I referred to earlier, and the deal was completed on 21 June 1994 – but the damage to the relationship was irreparable as far as Paul and I were concerned.

As a result, I called a Special Group Board meeting on 11 July 1994 to discuss my concerns. Cazenove had become our broker on 29 April 1994 and at that time the share price was £2.30, thus capitalising the company at £120 million. On the day of the meeting the share price was £1.58, a fall of 45 per cent. We had daily calls from analysts trying to understand the position and asking if they had missed something! Existing shareholders were confused and receiving no comfort from Cazenove. Staff were getting concerned and journalists were beginning to believe that they had missed a story.

Against this backdrop we knew that when we reported our half-year results planned for 25 July they would show profits up 30 per cent and a forward order book up 30 per cent. I suggested two alternative courses of action to the Board. Either we saw things through with Cazenove or we secured a negotiated return to Credit Lyonnais Laing so that could build a platform for the results. It was my recommendation that we negotiated a managed return to Credit Lyonnais, particularly as they had made the first move, formally inviting us back. The option to seek another large broking house to take us on was briefly considered but rejected as it would inevitably be seen as though we were touting ourselves around the market. The Board supported the recommendation I had made, as did Hill Samuel Bank.

The meeting with Cazenove duly took place on 13 July and Paul and I told the director that we could no longer work with them. I was later informed by one of their employees that no other company had ever sacked them and they did not know how to react, as nothing was in their training to prepare them for such an unthinkable situation!

I recall Paul and me coming out of that meeting and standing on the corner of 100 Wood Street, where the offices of Hill Samuel are, with the realisation that at that precise point Capita did not have a broker. We made a call on the mobile to our contact at Credit Lyonnais, asking if we could come round to their offices at 5 Appold Street immediately to discuss the proposition of them returning to act as our broker.

To Credit Lyonnais this was a major coup, since they had won us back against the competition of the Queen's brokers, but to their credit they got straight to work broking our shares, which were clearly undervalued. We then experienced the reverse effect of the rumour mill that suggested that the analyst team at Cazenove had found something about the company they did not like, or that there was a fear we were going to miss a forecast. The only way to allay those fears was to deliver trading results in line with expectations, which we duly did. Ironically the shares that the team at Cazenove placed with 'friendly clients' at £1.73 proved to be an amazing bargain – I wonder if any of those Cazenove clients held onto their shares?

As the business grew we made several new appointments to the Group Board. One of these was to make a separate appointment as Finance Director, enabling Paul, who held that role, to focus on his role as Group Managing Director. With the help of head hunters the board ultimately interviewed a shortlist of three candidates, one of whom was Gordon Hurst, our Financial Controller. I had the highest regard for Gordon, but I felt that we could benefit from appointing a person from outside the Group to bring new experiences to us. The role of Finance Director is a key one and from the flotation until that point the post had been Paul's. So the individual assuming this role had to perform to the same high standards.

Another person on the shortlist was Simon Stock, who had worked for five years with Hanson PLC, latterly with the Chief Executive as part of a small head-office team and was currently the Group Finance Director of Electron House, an electronic component distributor. I was attracted by the possibility of him bringing to us the experiences of the Hanson model that had proved to be so successful in City terms. A similar view was held by our non-executives and my executive colleagues apart from Paul, who very clearly wanted Gordon.

It was announced to the City on 7 July 1995 that Simon had been appointed and he started with us at the beginning of September. Gordon similarly joined the board as our Commercial Director to look after the commercial terms of all our contracts and acquisitions. At the same time as these appointments John Brameld stepped down from the Board in anticipation of his retirement and Gordon also assumed a responsibility for the Property Services Division.

I, therefore, had a new executive team to bring together and this did not prove to be an easy job. Paul and Simon did not get on well from the outset. There was a complete personality clash which was very apparent to all, including the City analysts. Simon's style of operating was very different to Paul's and, while he was clearly a highly competent individual, his approach was far more formal. It became increasingly clear that I needed to resolve this situation as it was not going to work. The following June we reached a deal with Simon for him to leave and Gordon was duly appointed as Group Finance Director. I freely admit that I was wrong not to have appointed Gordon in the first place and have subsequently said this to him.

Thankfully, we now had in place the four key people that would take Capita forward for the next ten years of its growth: Paul, Paddy, Gordon and myself. I believe that we became a great team and I think that this was recognised by the City to be one of the best executive teams they had worked with. The previous November, Capita had been selected by *Forbes*, the leading US business magazine for its list of "The 100 Best Small Companies in the World."

We had the challenge of moving ourselves away from being predominately in the local government market place and having limited exposure in central government and health. While some of our other divisions had this mix, particularly in the property division, our core managed services business needed to reposition itself. To help with the specific task of opening up the central government market we employed (on a part-time basis) a person by the name of Alan Kemp, who at the time was also special adviser to Michael Heseltine in his role as President of the Board of Trade. Alan had also previously worked with Peter Levene, now Lord Levene of Portsoken, who had been a personal adviser to Michael Heseltine when he was Secretary of State for Defence, becoming a Permanent Secretary in his role as Chief of Defence Procurement and holding a number of posts in the Thatcher government. In 1992 he was appointed Adviser to the then PM, John Major with the brief to improve efficiency and effectiveness in the provision of government services.

Through Alan's introduction, we invited Peter to our offices in Tothill Street to explain how we had successfully externalised services in local government. Specifically, we took him through the outsourcing contracts that we had at both Berkshire and Oxfordshire. Rich Benton and I explained to him the procurement process used, the treatment of staff through the TUPE process, and the terms of our contracts. Peter was comforted by our achievements in local government, which gave him the confidence to push forward with a similar agenda with central government departments, knowing that a market existed in the private sector to bid for contracts. Alan subsequently left us and became full-time special adviser to Michael Heseltine in his new role of Deputy Prime Minister.

To deal with the change in the market that we could see coming we created a unit called the 'Big Ticket Sales Team', which was to prove to be one of Capita's greatest differentiators. We decided that certain opportunities were too large to be run by a divisional team and needed to be elevated to a Group level, as the executive group directors needed to be involved. Equally, if we were going to persuade customers to shape tenders for the integrated offering which played to our strength, this conversation needed to start before the procurement was advertised.

We decided to form a team that was capable of selling at this level. The people we recruited were individuals who had the confidence to have a conversation about an opportunity with the most senior person within an organisation. They would most probably had a 'consultant type' brain, meaning they'd have to be able to conceptualise both how the current service is run as well as seeing how it could be re-engineered. The person also needed to have the ability to run a team over a period, as these bids would take up to nine months and could involve ten or more people from within the business. They would need to have the capability to run a business or a contract but would have to concentrate on the winning end rather than the operational side of life.

Around this team we placed a process, which Paddy had a great deal of influence in designing, where winning was to be driven by our operational ability to deliver a contract at a sensible price and not by a mentality adopted by some competitors in the marketplace who would win by offering the cheapest solution. This process, which was termed the 'black hat' featured heavy qualification at the beginning of a bid, questioning our ability to win it, and continuing to ask that question throughout the process. This was necessary, as bidding was costly both in terms of direct cost of time but also in lost opportunities – cost of not focusing on other bids. This team drove our growth in the years ahead and the bid list became the focus of our presentation to the City in terms of what we won, what we were bidding for and equally what we had lost and why. This team went on to win one out of every two contracts for which it bid, way ahead of the industry norm which was one success out of five.

In 1995 the work of our customer services and administrative outsourcing began to outstrip IT outsourcing in revenue and sales orders. We began to move to contracts which featured a combination of both. This was testament both to the increasing confidence in the clients to outsource large elements of their services, and to our ability as market leader to influence their thinking to do so.

A good illustration of this was the joint venture (JV) we had with JHP Ltd. Better known as Pitman, this company specialised in organising tests for shorthand and typing candidates throughout the country, and had great experience in the field. The JV was formed to win a contract from the Government's Driving Standards Agency to run the new 'theory' part of the driving test, which was introduced in July 1996. DriveSafe was responsible for invigilating, collecting fees for and marking the written test. We provided this service throughout the UK from 140 test centres.

This venture brought to bear our call centre capability, which received two million calls a year from customers seeking to make appointments for tests. It was the largest contract that we had won to date and was significant because it involved the biggest change in road safety ever introduced. The CEO of the Agency, Bernard Hearden, had decided not to run it in-house but to outsource it. This was also significant because it established a trend in central government whereby 'greenfield opportunities' such as this would be delivered through an outsourcing model rather than in-house.

The first major opportunity we had in central government for a large integrated contract involving an entire operation was the outsourcing of the Teachers Pension Agency. This agency was responsible for the pension arrangements of 1.4 million teachers and ex-teachers in the UK. While we were not pension specialists, we did know how to transform a system of paper-based services. The Agency was responsible for collecting £3.6 billion and for numerous calculations involving final pension arrangements of teachers leaving the service and transfer values from one authority to another. Keith Evans, who had joined us from Anderson Consulting and was a member of the Big Ticket Sales, ran the project from the outset. The first task was to persuade the team at the Department of Education and the management team at the Agency to put the whole agency out to a bid and not to allow the implementation of a traditional IT contract that was designed to upgrade the technology without addressing the central need of re-engineering the service.

The agency was based in Darlington. The north east had historically not seen too much outsourcing to the private sector. Jobs were massively important and it was felt that the best way of protecting them was to keep services in-house, so it was very controversial and involved many discussions with the unions. The agency employed around 500 people and in our bid preparation we found that it was a heavily paper-driven agency. In fact, there were seven miles of paper files! One file for every teacher and ex-teacher employed in the country who had a right to a pension! There were shelves and shelves of files, the files packed in so tightly that it was impossible even to get your fingers between them. They had a system in the agency at the time whereby a bell sounded if a person could not find a file and all work stopped until it was found.

We had to make decisions about how we were going to transform it and make the service better while also taking costs out of it. It was a huge ask, but the chief executive, Denise Metcalf, who subsequently transferred to us after we won the contract, was open minded about transforming the service, given the freedom of operating in a non-bureaucratic style that came with Capita. Denise worked well with us and later she became a very senior individual in our business.

The local MP was Alan Milburn and I built a great working relationship with him. At the time of the General Election, there was a concern locally that there were going to be mass redundancies at the Agency. I gave Alan my word that this was not our strategy and Capita's plan was to build the Centre, creating more local jobs. I provided Alan with my mobile number and during the election campaign I agreed that if he had any issues or I had any news about the site we would speak. Alan Milburn went on to be a senior member of the Blair Government, becoming Secretary of State for Health. In my view, had Alan decided to remain in politics he could well have become leader of the Labour Party.

We successfully transformed the teachers' pensions service and it became an important flagship for us. The teachers' pensions contract was renewed in 2003 and Capita still has it to this day. We halved the cost to the government to £8.9 million a year, saving £20 million over the first seven years of the contract, while vastly improving the service.

We ultimately delivered six other contracts from the same business centre in Darlington, serving both the public and the private sector. While some staff who were not performing well left the organisation, overall the number of people employed in the centre grew from 500 to 650. The unions saw the new jobs coming and recognised that we were good employers, investing in the staff.

John Major's government then had a series of new initiatives they wanted to introduce, including the Department of Education & Employment's Pre-School Voucher System – known as the nursery vouchers scheme. The idea was that every child was entitled to a voucher for nursery education. Officials were persuaded that, rather than set it up as an in-house service, they should outsource it from the beginning. We won the contract to administer Phase 1 and had the responsibility for the processing of applications and the issue of vouchers. We also constructed and maintained the database covering eligible children and educational establishments. We were able to use SIMS to support the operation. This proved to be a very controversial policy, attracting a great deal of press coverage and time in parliament. Ultimately the second phase of it was not implemented.

The Major administration was quite weak at this time and in many ways took its foot off the accelerator for competitive tendering. The expectation had been that outsourcing would be extended right across government services, including white-collar services, and into wider areas of health and police. This didn't happen, although the impact of it was sufficient to have its own momentum stimulated by our presence in the market along with other competitors that began to emerge. It became the right thing to do. We would say: 'If it's not a core service to you, why are you running it?' We were the specialist. In a way, what we didn't want was an exploding market, with twenty or thirty contracts coming out at a time. That would have invited even more competition. Our key task was to broaden the thinking so that larger, longer-term contracts were offered, covering the range of services that only Capita had in the market place. We had a very prominent position and we wanted to keep it.

As a public company there was a need to report to shareholders on our performance every six months in addition to the AGM. We also ran very successful City 'away days', where we took analysts to see one of our sites so as to give a closer look at what we did and for them to meet other members of the senior team. This was my domain. It was important to package the story but that story needed to reflect what was actually happening in the business, and for there not to be a marked difference between it and the actual position, which is a dangerous strategy.

Any person considering floating a business on the stock market needs to understand the enormous amount of senior management time that it takes post flotation. Also, one should never underestimate the adverse impact of not making a City forecast, meaning that you have to issue a profits warning should such a situation arise. This never happened to me all the time I was responsible for Capita but we came close to it on several occasions, where drastic action was taken to avoid it.

In looking through the papers I have, I came across a classic Pindar confidential memo with numbered copies issued to the top twenty-four members of our staff, including the Group Board. Paul listed the likely consequences of not making our target, including collapse of share price, which he pointed out was more than a passing interest to all on the list! The actions were made clear that to support this line all the Group Directors must take a 10 per cent reduction in salaries with immediate effect. I can tell you we did make our City target, but it was this sort of team approach and taking immediate action that became a hallmark of how we ran the business.

Our reporting periods were in February for our year ended 31 December and in July for the half year to 30 June. Work would start on this reporting process a good month before then. An initial draft would be done on the statement covering the salient points around the financial results, the proposed dividend and then the developments in each of the divisions. A key section would be an update on the market and prospects for the future, including any senior management changes. This draft went through a dozen or more iterations before we signed it off, in many cases waiting for late news of contract wins. Very early on we also commissioned an independent report from Richard Holway, an industry analyst, enabling us to calibrate the size of our market, our position within it as a leader, and the range still available for growth. This showed a market of £3 billion, expected to rise to £6 billion by 2001. In City terms it was becoming difficult to bet against us, particularly as our win rate on contracts was so high. We would also speak of the competitive landscape and how we differentiated ourselves. The presentation would set out the key details of new contracts and give details of how we planned to both position and use the companies that we had acquired.

I insisted that we rehearse the presentation as a team a number of times over several days to get the timing right and ensure that our messages were clear. It was the general pattern that I set the scene and speak of developments in the market, Gordon would cover the financial performance, and Paul in his capacity as MD would outline the performance of the business.

As part of this preparation and to evidence my paranoia for preparation, I would prepare a Q & A pack of about sixty questions that we might be asked. In this, as well as covering the obvious, I would let my mind wander to think of more extreme issues that could come up. I remember on one occasion I needed to reassure a junior member of the team typing up my tape of such questions that there was nothing to be worried about and that the company was not going to fall off a cliff!

In the late afternoon the day before Results Day the house analyst would be 'taken inside' from a dealing sense so that he or she could read the statement and be prepared to brief the broker's salesforce and to publish a note with his or her views early the following day. This would confirm the profits and turnover forecast for the following and subsequent years.

The key thing here was to thoroughly prepare the analyst so that they could ensure the sales desk were fully prepared to 'broker the story' and could deal with any sensitive issues covered by the statement, perhaps involving underperformance in one of our divisions. They also needed to be able to understand the top five or six selling points as to why institutions should buy the shares.

On the morning of the results, the statement would be released to the Stock Exchange by 7 a.m. and by the time that we stood up to present the results the share price could have either been marked up considerably or even down substantially, dependent upon the initial reactions to our statement or to events of the day.

Before the formal presentation to the analysts, on several occasions I was asked to go for an interview with Bloomberg TV or with BBC News to discuss the results. This normally happened when we had a notable or controversial contract, but overall our results never garnered anywhere near the same level of interest as the performance of the banks or the retail sector until, that is, we became involved with implementing the London Congestion Charging Scheme!

When we arrived in the conference room, normally at our broker's offices, to present the results it was important to be in a confident frame of mind with a smile on one's face. Paul and I would regularly say to each other prior to starting the presentation: 'Remember, they have never created anything in their lives, whereas we have created a great business.' After the formal presentation we would then take any questions with nothing off limit. This would probably involve thirty or so questions being asked by analysts from the various houses, the answers being available to all in the room to use. Some were known supporters of the stock, whereas others were most definitely not. Near the end of my time with Capita, these results presentations were telecast to anyone who wished to see them, which changed the dynamics.

Once the analysts were briefed, they would go away and write up their interpretations of the results. Our PR advisers then had interviews lined up for us with key journalists at *The Times*, The *FT*, the *Daily Telegraph* and *The Guardian*. Some of these could be face to face, whereas others would be over the telephone, making it important to get the key points over to them: facts that you wanted them to print the following day or to publish online immediately. It was Shona Nichols' role and that of our PR company to ensure that any online material was accurate, and to ensure that it was corrected if wrong. In the early days, the coverage by *Investors Chronicle* was of particular importance, as we had a large following of small investors. It was particularly pleasing that Capita became a share held by the highest proportion of those who had a personal PEP (Personal Equity Plan) the forerunner of the ISA.

In the afternoon, Paul and Gordon would get calls from the analysts, wishing to have a private discussion about the numbers and their financial forecasts for Capita going forward. There would also most probably be further calls with the trade press such as *Public Finance* and *Local Government Chronicle* that I would deal with.

The following day, I always held my breath until I had seen how our results had been interpreted in the press, as this set the scene for the day and in my case, established how I felt about things. I must say that I never liked criticism of Capita and perhaps defended it too much. In particular, I was wound up by *Private Eye*'s description of us as 'Crapita', but after all these years I can now see the humorous side of it.

Paul and I then went into a series of one-to-one presentations to our key shareholders or those who wanted to hear our story. This would entail six one-hour back-to-back meetings in a day. These were held in the institution's offices and timing was an involving logistical exercise in getting to meetings on time. In the early days we did it by taxi, carrying the presentation packs for the day with us. Latterly we progressed to a chauffeur-driven car, enabling us both to relax more between meetings. This routine would go on for a week.

I likened these presentations to that of an actor giving a performance on stage: every performance had to be your best. It was helpful that you did these as a pair, since one person could speak while the other thought of other angles to cover.

These meetings could be with just one person but it was more common for there to be six or seven in the room, since Capita's shares could be held in several different funds managed by a single institution. Paul and I always agreed that it was better to be challenged in these meetings rather than to be allowed to move slavishly through our well-rehearsed presentation pack. It was very clear that some people in our audiences knew little or nothing about the company, and had equally done very little background research on Capita before seeing us. I was left with the view that there were not too many teams that Paul and I presented to that I would wish to invest my personal money with!

In the middle of the week, one of us would go to Scotland, covering Edinburgh and Glasgow in one day. Another feature that started in 1996 was the cultivation of a US shareholder list. In September of that year we acquired from the government the Recruitment and Assessment Agency. Amongst other things, we looked after the 'high flyers' graduate recruitment scheme. When this deal was announced I was in New York with my eldest daughter, Debby, watching the US Open tennis at Flushing Meadows. An analyst in the UK from Kleinwort Benson, who followed Capita, knew of my visit to the tennis and persuaded me to go into Kleinwort's offices in New York to meet the sales team to brief them on the Capita story and the acquisition we had made from Government which had featured in the national newspapers. After the tennis on the Tuesday, I turned up at their offices to meet with two of the senior sales guys, William Bristowe and Julian Plant. This meeting ended up with me giving a presentation to the entire sales force and was the beginning of a long association with them. City life in New York is actually a 'village' and over dinner I then also met William's younger brother, Tom, who worked at another broker, Schroders, and this again developed into a long-term relationship as Capita grew.

Obviously, following my presentation, the sales desk spoke to their clients about the Capita story and before I knew it this went a stage further and I found myself on a plane to Denver in Colorado to visit

Janus Capital, whom they believed might be interested in the stock. They were, and bought a small amount of shares at that stage, although they ultimately became a substantial shareholder in our company. All this activity was great but I was in New York to watch the tennis with Debby and I needed to placate her for my absence. This Kleinwort's duly sorted by inviting both of us to their box at Flushing Meadows, which was a great deal nearer the action on the court than our tickets allowed us to be!

American interest in Capita led to Paul and I doing a US roadshow twice a year for a week following the presentation to institutions in the UK. We did this for the next eight years. This entailed flying to New York on the Saturday in preparation and having time to experience this wonderful city. On the Monday and Tuesday we would have six one-to-one meetings each day around New York, then we would fly to Boston on the Tuesday evening, giving six presentations the following day there and catching a late flight to Chicago for the same regime on the Thursday. We then went onto San Francisco to present on the Friday and flew home to the UK overnight that evening. Coping with the time difference going from east to west across the US was a challenge. In the week the schedule meant that we probably did approximately thirty presentations to institutions, but we always returned home, shaking hands as we went our separate ways at Heathrow congratulating ourselves on a successful trip.

I do recall one of our receptionists in the office saying to me 'enjoy your holiday' as I left the building on the Friday night. I soon corrected her that it was most definitely not a holiday. However, I must admit that it was quite a buzz for me to present a company that I had started and felt so passionate about to American institutions. It felt surreal to be doing this in a place where just eight years previously, as a family we had cruised on the *QE2* past the Statue of Liberty for our first ever visit to New York. Today we have a flat here in 'the city that never sleeps'. I still recall making presentations on the Capita story in offices of fund managers, using a backcloth of Central Park, the skyscrapers of Manhattan or indeed that of The World Trade Center.

We found that shareholders in the USA were far better prepared for our meetings and asked far more intrusive questions. They loved the 'Capita story' because, although outsourcing had occurred in the US, it was mainly in the private sector. Many felt that the government services in the US needed to be tackled in the same manner as were doing in the UK, because they could see the inefficiencies in the services provided.

In between results, Paul and I were regularly asked to meet with institutions that were passing through London. I recall the experience of presenting the Capita story to a room full of Chinese institutions via a video link in London. I did my best but I must say that it was difficult to gauge at the time how successful I was in persuading them. I subsequently found out that a number of them actually bought shares.

I also did regular trips to give presentations to potential shareholders across Europe in Holland, Germany, Italy, Sweden and France. These trips were organised by brokers from other houses and it enabled me to spend time with their analyst to deal with any points that he or she had. Some of the most bizarre meetings were in Paris, where in hour-long meetings I was rarely offered even water to drink, and sometimes gave hour-long presentations at lunchtime while my audience ate a two-course meal, and I was offered nothing. However, it was fun winding them up in Paris about Margaret Thatcher's government and its sometimes confrontational stance towards the EU!

We also organised 'analyst days', where we took a group of analysts to see operations such as the Criminal Records Bureau in Liverpool, the Teachers' Pension Centre in Darlington, and our Life and Pension site in Gloucester. On one hilarious trip we took them to one of the centres where customers took the Theory Driving Test. When they got there we immediately sat them all down in the examination centre that was laid out like a school examination room, and presented them with an actual Theory Driving Test to take. One young analyst got rather panicky, as she thought that the lamentable results of her test would be sent to the DVLA, and she would lose her driving licence!

The period from 1991 to 1996 had a number of personal milestones that I recall with great pride and pleasure. In November 1993 I received a very unexpected letter from No. 10 saying that I had been awarded an OBE for my services to the computing industry.

One never knows how these things happen or who has nominated you but I can only think that it was as a result of the work that we had done involving the consortia of local authorities which had led to the creation of Capita and the outsourcing of IT services which we had led.

Of course, the announcement of the award was to be in the Queen's New Year's Honours List and until then it had to remain confidential. This is not easy, as you really do want to share the news with your immediate family. For us at the time there was an added complication in that Michael, my eldest son, was about to go on a cricket tour to Australia. We were going out there to support him, along with Jennifer and Robert but Debby, who was working, and my mother would not be travelling with us. The problem was that I did not want them to find out about the OBE from reading the announcement in the newspaper, so I told both of them the day before we left for Australia on 14 December.

Just ten days before the tour began Michael damaged his knee in a semi-final of a house football competition at Charterhouse. I was watching from the touchline and saw the incident and helped to carry him off the pitch. It looked as if he might miss the tour but he had a week of intensive physiotherapy and just made it.

The tour went very well for Michael and we all had a great time. The trip inspired us as a family with a lifelong love of Sydney, Melbourne and Perth. It was memorable to celebrate the announcement of my OBE at a New Year's party in Sydney Harbour accompanied by Michael's cricket team and with all the fireworks.

When I went to collect the award at Buckingham Palace in the January from HM The Queen, I had to face the delicate question of who to take to the ceremony, since only three guests are permitted. Aside from Jacqui, we had four children, so there'd be disappointment for some. We decided that Michael and Jennifer would go into the ceremony and we solved the problem of the family photo by having Debby as our driver, taking us into Buckingham Palace accompanied by Robert. They waited outside during the ceremony but were then able to have their photographs taken with us.

I had to face the difficult decision not to take my mother, who was so obviously very proud of my achievement. I still recall seeing her standing outside the gates of Buckingham Palace with my Aunt Joyce, waiting for us to come out. I had a photograph taken with Mum as we emerged. I had a real sense that I had made the wrong decision by not taking her and I admit that this upset me. Fortunately, several years later I had the opportunity to take her with me to a Garden Party at Buckingham Palace and was even able to introduce her to the Queen at the event. I vowed on the day that I would be back for another award so that I could right this wrong for my mother's sake. It took eighteen years, but at the age of ninety-six she was with me at the investiture to receive my knighthood in 2012.

The marriage of Debby to Tim Faircloth on 22 January 1994 was a very special day for all of us. For me it was particularly emotional to lead my daughter down the aisle. I recall those very special moments when everyone had left the house in Farnham, leaving just the two of us. At that time, and during the car journey, one says some very special private things that will always remain with you both. I have no doubt that she understood just how special she was to me and remains so today. It was a brilliant family celebration that we had at Frensham Ponds Hotel in Surrey.

In the previous summer (1994) Michael had left Charterhouse, having acquired three A Levels at A grade. He had an offer to go to Durham University if he got two A's and a B grade but the plan was that if he got three As he would take a gap year and apply to go to Cambridge University. I had visited both Durham and Cambridge with Michael the previous summer. In the case of Cambridge, a client of mine, Mike Fitzgerald, Vice Chancellor of Thames Valley University, insisted on hosting a day's visit for Michael to his college, which was St Catherine's and that day had very much influenced Michael's decision of wanting to go there.

The application to Cambridge University was, of course, all about Michael but Jacqui and I very much saw it as a 'family' task for him to be successful. We set out a plan, each of us taking responsibility for various things. The selection of the college to apply to was key. We had all read the 'Alternative Cambridge Prospectus', a document produced by students that had attended Cambridge, telling you the real inside story of all the colleges. It was very clear that coming from a public-school background some of the colleges would not even consider an application from him. It confirmed Michael's original decision of wanting to apply to St Catherine's, that was a smaller college but where the subject he wanted to study: PPP (Politics, Policy and Psychology) was prominent. He applied on the basis of his results and was granted an interview.

I set up a mock interview for him run by Alan Kemp, the Special adviser to Michael Heseltine, to discuss with Michael the finer issues around political and economic policy. We researched in some detail the people who would interview Michael which was helped by the fact that Annabelle Nyren, who worked with me at Capita, had attended the college.

Michael decided that it was important for him to look right on the day which is something I can relate to with my City presentations. I agreed to finance an entire new wardrobe for him. Michael has never been one to miss out on an opportunity and duly went to the right shops and covered all the angles possible to comply with the task. A hotel was booked for the night before, so he could get up fresh in the morning for the interview and not have any travel worries.

So he set off with our good wishes only for us to receive a call from him where he showed some signs of panic. He had found out on re-reading the letter that his interview was a day earlier than he thought and he had, therefore, missed his allotted time slot. Thankfully, they agreed to see him the following day but clearly he started off on the back foot rather than being on the front foot as planned. The interview appeared to go well from his feedback to us but we had to wait for the outcome.

When the letter with his interview result arrived at our house several weeks later, Michael was working in London and staying at our flat in Westminster. I had the task of carrying it up on the train for him to open. After opening it when he was alone in another room, he returned to me with that beaming smile on his face and I knew that he had been accepted. We simply hugged one another and I suspect both with tears in our eyes.

From my perspective, I would still put it as one of the most wonderful moments in my life. It proved that Jacqui and I were right to invest in his education but most importantly, he had maximised that opportunity to the full. He went off to Cambridge in September 1995 and it was the beginning of a great three-year adventure for both him and us as a family. He was made president of the May Ball Committee, which took place on 17 June. His graduation on 26 June 1998 at the Senate House was also very special. The incident of him being a day late for his interview was not forgotten, though, and was referred to during a lunch that we had with his tutor just last year at his college!

So things were going well both on a personal front as well as with Capita. However, on the political front the Conservative Government under John Major's premiership was running out of steam and one could see the emergence of a possible Labour administration under Blair and Brown. To the City this was a problem because it destabilised the CCT (Competitive Compulsory Tendering) regime that had driven all the outsourcing opportunities that had fuelled our growth.

As a company we needed to address these growing concerns over the envisaged change in political control since our share price began to show some weakness in the market. Internally, we had several presentations to our management meetings from those close to Labour, thinking about who the key people would be in a Blair Government and what the likely stance would be towards outsourcing and working with the private sector.

We also commissioned some research from the University of Strathclyde involving Professor Alan Alexander testing out how various areas of our business would fare under Labour.

Another person we met was Paul Corrigan, whose wife Hilary Armstrong was MP for North West Durham and likely to be in the cabinet if Blair was elected. I recall Richard Benton and I having a lunch with Paul and Hilary to explain how we operated, particularly with regard to staff terms and conditions and any potential redundancies. Paul was working at the London Borough of Islington at the time and fully understood the inefficiencies that existed in local government. Equally, he had experience of how the CCT approach had taken its toll with the unions and the Labour councillors alike.

John Tizard also joined us at around this time in a consultancy role and this proved to be a very key relationship, as John and I were destined to work on a number of critical issues that needed to be resolved to get the new government comfortable with working with the private sector.

Another vital player in this new world was Robert Hill, who some time previously had joined Capita as a management consultant straight from a role that he had at the Labour Party HQ. Robert subsequently left us to move to a role at the Audit Commission and in the Labour Government he went on to be Tony Blair's Political Secretary in No. 10.

I also knew Steve Bassam well, the former Leader of Brighton & Hove Council, through my work in Brighton and his role at the Local Authority Association. Steve was elevated to the House of Lords very early after the election and he became the Government's Chief Whip.

One of the key moves that happened was the formation of an organisation called the New Local Government Network (NLGN). This attracted both organisations that sold services to local government and CEOs, along with elected members from Local Government. The main instigator of this was Geoff Filkin, who had been Treasurer of Reading and the Secretary of the Association of District Councils. Capita became a founder member of the NLGN. This was very much my territory and important because unless we got this relationship right it would affect our ability to grow and win contracts.

The NLGN was the body that all the people mentioned above gravitated towards to rethink how a new Labour Government would work with local authorities, particularly with regard to the repeal of the legislation involving compulsory competitive tendering.

The thinking that emerged, driven by Filkin, Hill, Corrigan and others was to replace CCT by the concept of 'Best Value'. This required a local authority to prove that the services it was delivering were being delivered at the best value for the local community. Whilst there was not the mandatory element of CCT, this still very much put into play a discussion about how services could be delivered in a different way. With the momentum that Capita and others in the marketplace had started, the alternative way of delivering services automatically involved some form of outsourcing.

Geoff Filkin was subsequently invited by the new PM to enter the House of Lords to oversee this change in thinking and the legislation that it required. He went on to become a government minister, initially in the Department of Education and then the Home Office.

We were well plugged into current thinking and involved in shaping this around working with the private sector, but we were still very much an employer that was on 'the other side of the tracks'. We needed to change the way that we thought and acted with far more emphasis on partnership and engagement with the unions. This very much played to my strength gained from my upbringing and my beliefs about how you should treat people who worked for you.

I recall one of my presentations to the City at that time, where I had a picture of the door of No. 10 painted red and another with the door painted blue, essentially emphasising that there would be no difference to the opportunities for Capita if either party were to be elected. That turned out to be untrue because the opportunities for us under New Labour became even greater than ever.

15

CAPITA UNDER
NEW LABOUR

B y the end of 1996, Capita employed 4,500 people, had a turnover of
£173 million and was making profits of £26 million. Our market
value on the Stock Exchange had reached £1 billion.

The group was getting large and very diverse. As a Board we felt
that it would be timely to organise a roadshow so that Paul and I could
meet a number of the staff to explain the plans for Capita for '1997
and beyond'. We started this on 2 December in Brentford, moving
on to Oxford, Bedford, Basingstoke, Wakefield, Bristol, Glasgow,
London, Darlington, Coventry, Isle of Wight, Bromley and finishing in
Chelmsford on 15 February.

On 1 May 1997, 'New Labour,' led by Tony Blair, won a landslide
victory with a majority of 179 seats and formed the first Labour
Government for eighteen years. So the work that we had done with
the City preparing them for such a change and with key people who
would be a part of the new administration, was invaluable.

The new government's 'Best Value' policy replaced Compulsory
Competitive Tendering, requiring councils to provide efficient and
cost-effective services. The essence of this was that, over a five-
year period councils, had to review how and why they provided all
their services. Councils had to compare their performance with the
best and demonstrate they were competitive. Part of such a review
meant considering how outsourcing non-core back-office services to

239

companies like Capita could improve costs and efficiency. The other key point for us was that this approach presented the opportunity for a far more orderly market, which was ideal for us.

During 1996, prior to the General Election, we began the bidding process to win a contract with the London Borough of Lambeth. This involved assuming responsibility for the running of its revenues, housing benefits and frontline cashiering services. This area of work, particularly around housing benefits, had become a popular area to outsource, since it was causing a number of local authorities considerable problems with backlogs. Many inhabitants of the borough relied upon benefits being paid in a timely fashion. Capita, along with competitors such as CSL and ITNet, had become specialists in this area and was keen to bid for these contracts.

I recall that we took the winning of the Lambeth contract extra seriously because we had lost two contracts for other London local authorities to another competitor. I was directly involved with the bid team and even turned my own office over to them for the duration of the bid process, which took around six months.

In local government terms the London Borough of Lambeth had been through a very difficult time as a local authority. There was extreme resistance to change, political insecurity, and some very volatile behaviour. John Tizard recalls some of the difficulties at Lambeth:

> Lambeth Council had been through some very turbulent times and had led the campaign of not setting budgets in opposition to the cuts required by the Thatcher government. Lambeth faced many challenges as a borough and a council, but the political and officer leadership of the council was still struggling to address these when Capita took over the contract. The leadership was beginning to turn the council around and letting the Capita contract was seen as part of this process as, more significantly, was the appointment of Heather [later Dame Heather] Rabbatts as Chief Executive. This was not an easy environment in which to deliver and improve a critical service such as housing benefit administration.

When I met Heather, I believed I could work with her and I could relate to her mission to transform the authority. As the bid process developed, Heather felt that Capita was the right company to deliver the contract. Just to illustrate what it was like working there, Heather told me that she had to vary her travel to work on a daily basis, using four or five different routes because there had been threats made against her. There were plenty of dark hints about corruption, particularly concerning the misappropriation of public funds, where a number of people were keen to keep things just as they were.

Overall it was a fairly hostile kind of place both politically and because it was heavily unionised. Paradoxically, while Lambeth had all this extreme left-wing activity, it was also home to more judges, MPs, journalists and senior executives working in the City than almost anywhere else in London. It is also one of the most densely populated areas in the country with around 300,000 residents. Not all are affluent – 20 per cent of its citizens at the time were unemployed and 40 per cent of residents received housing benefits. It was a place where a lot of people had opinions and was therefore very high profile, just as our relationship with the council was destined to become. We walked into a very hostile situation.

The service we inherited was recognised locally as a failing service but we were at a period in the development of outsourcing where the private sector company was expected to turn it around overnight. We were selected to run the service in December 1997 in a contract worth £50 million over seven years and assumed operational responsibility early in the following year.

What became apparent was that Lambeth's service performance was way below the level they had admitted to when we and our competitors were bidding for the contract. They had allowed the service to decline to a critical level immediately pre-outsourcing, trusting that the contractor would sort out the problem. Large numbers of vital temporary staff who had maintained the service were laid off and overtime had been curtailed. As a consequence, we found that backlogs of applications stood at 100,000 rather than the 60,000 stated to us.

Even after many of the temporary staff had left, the number of people used to deliver the service in-house was greater than the number advised to all the bidders. This was significant because it meant that all our estimates of the cost of running the service had been based on a false assumption. This resulted in a larger number of staff transferring under TUPE than we expected, meaning that we had to downsize by making controversial redundancies and deal with disgruntled unions.

One of the more surprising discoveries was that we found out that staff had a novel way of clearing the backlog of complaints. We found sacks of unopened letters at the bottom of a lift shaft, a way of making sure that they were never registered as arriving! Staff who transferred to us could, therefore, discuss things with us thinking that everything was on track, while urgent requests for help went unanswered. The staff at the front-line cashier centre also had many stories about furious customers who took their anger out on them. One visitor even decided to pick up a chair and hurl it at a member of our staff before storming out – luckily there was a glass protection panel.

By this time, we were at a point with the contract where the incoming Labour Government became involved and we had calls from both the Department of the Environment, Transport and the Regions along with No. 10, wanting to understand more about what was going on. In a letter to the Minister of Local Government and the Regions, Hilary Armstrong (now Baroness Armstrong of Hill Top), and in a meeting with Beverley Hughes (now Baroness Hughes of Stretford), the then Local Government Minister, I set out the facts around the improvements in service that we had achieved, the investment that we had made and our plans going forward. It was definitely a time when there was an orchestrated attempt by MPs, local councillors, unions and the Press to discredit the private companies with a view to stopping further outsourcing of services.

We were all over both the national and trade press, probably for the first time, being accused of poor levels of service. It was then that the satirical magazine *Private Eye*, began poking fun at us, referring to us as 'Crapita'.

As you can imagine, I had regular meetings with Heather about the backlog situation and numerous operational changes were made in an attempt to address the issues, but the pressure from elected members and the Press escalated. As part of the transformation, we totally refurbished the offices (which were appalling), installed a new computer system and introduced a customer call centre. This was run from our centre in Coventry, where we could recruit a higher standard of operatives who were more likely to stay than was the case in Lambeth.

Thankfully, the other parts of the contract involving collection of Lambeth's council tax and business rates were going extremely well, with substantial increases in performance. In July 2001 we took the unprecedented decision to hand back our role in housing benefits, effectively returning it to an in-house run service. As you can well imagine this led to stories in the press about us being 'sacked' by the council, which reverberated in the City and had to be dealt with.

In actual practical terms, we continued to work with Lambeth to improve the benefit service through providing key support services to their staff, including IT and customer call centre services, all of which helped to clear the backlogs. The ironic thing is that Capita is still in that contract with Lambeth, including re-engaging with housing benefits at a later stage. The contract has been renewed and renewed since for more than twenty years, becoming one of Capita's longest-running relationships.

We learned so much from this contract, driving us to change our whole method of bidding, insisting on being thought of as a partner and not a contractor. In every bid we undertook a complete audit of the operations for which we were bidding, verifying the information given to us before pricing the contract and signing up to performance levels. This was a growing-up period for the industry itself.

The beginning of 1998 saw Rich Benton retire from the company after thirteen years with Capita. We had been on a long journey together since first meeting in the days we were within CIPFA. He had been part of our original team of four, who had led the management buyout of the business, and his leaving was for me a symbolic ending of an era.

Rich had made an incredible contribution to our development through his success in leading the winning of contracts, shaping not only us as an organisation but also the entire industry. He travelled many miles on business, always insisting on driving rather than going by train and thought nothing of travelling to two different parts of the country for sales visits during a single day before returning home in the evening. I always felt that a deciding factor for Rich in believing that this style of life needed to stop was the tragic death of one of our employees, Mark Goodman. Mark was a key member of Rich's team that developed our managed services business and he worked closely with Rich over a number of years. Mark travelled a great deal in his role and sadly died in a car accident on an icy road leaving home very early in the morning to get to a client visit in Bromley.

The big news on the sales front in 1998 was the winning of a £34 million contract with the BBC to set up and manage its new information service centre for viewers and listeners across the UK. This centre was to be located in Northern Ireland and it created one hundred new jobs. We already had over forty people in the province including those who were administering the Theory Driving Test and, of course, our first major client as CIPFA Computer Services, DENI was based there.

Creation of the information centre meant that viewers and listeners would be able to contact the BBC on all matters via one dedicated telephone number while also being able to access the service by fax, mail and e-mail. This also represented a partnership between us and the BBC, whereby a BBC customer operations team based in Television Centre was responsible for briefing the call centre staff in Belfast on forthcoming issues. This was a major break in tradition for a highly traditional organisation where departments did not normally speak to one another.

I went to Belfast on 10 May 1999 to open the centre at Blackstaff House with the BBC Chairman Sir Christopher Bland and the Secretary of State for Northern Ireland, Rt Hon. Dr Mo Mowlam MP. It was a wonderful moment meeting Mo for the first time and I saw first hand, as we walked around the centre meeting staff, just what an incredible talent she had for putting people at ease. Her style was deliciously informal and unpredictable, making her difficult for officials to handle. I had the chance over the lunch break to speak with her privately on a one-to-one basis about Capita's ability to transform services, and our frustration over this not being used by civil servants to reduce the cost of services run by central government. She had extreme views about changing this and agreed to raise this with the PM.

Running the BBC centre presented a wealth of stories that I used in presentations to the City or in speeches that I gave. There was a call that came in after a murder in *Eastenders*, when a member of the public contacted us to say that she knew who did the murder and gave us the address of her next door neighbour.

The one that made me laugh most was from a woman in Suffolk. Between programmes, when a presenter introduced what was to follow, the backdrop on the screen showed two or three large red hot-air balloons floating across the UK countryside. The Suffolk caller wanted to know when the balloons would be passing over her way, as she had been looking out for them in her garden for some time!

This contract was not only groundbreaking but marked the beginning of a relationship which would see us win other major contracts with the BBC, including the outsourcing of all of its HR function, again to be operated from a centre in Belfast and in 2002, one of our largest ever contracts: assuming the responsibility for the collection of the BBC TV Licensing revenue. Effectively it was the beginning of the transformation of the way that the BBC operated, much of which was driven by the review of its charter by the government. The charter renewal process drove a wider modernisation programme within the BBC, including a review of how programmes were commissioned, how the trading arms operated and in improving the effectiveness of TV licence collection.

It was also the year where we became a leading provider of integrated Human Resource services with over 1,200 HR professionals. Through acquisition and contract wins we were already major providers of services involving recruitment, training and development, payroll, pensions administration, outplacement and career change consultancy. We were responsible for the pay and pensions of over 3 million people, issuing 12 million pay slips annually, administering an annual pension spend of £4.3 billion and overall processing a £8.4-billion payroll per annum.

We began the discussion with several organisations about how a number of the services provided by an in-house HR function could be outsourced. This would reduce costs and increase efficiency of the service, leaving the HR director with a much smaller team to set and monitor policy. This was not popular with HR Directors, who saw this as an attack on their domain.

I will always remember an HR conference held in Amsterdam that I was invited to speak at, attended by over a hundred HR directors. In my session I floated the idea of outsourcing most of their functions to a specialist organisation such as Capita. I think it's fair to say that the idea received a very cold reception. I was joined at the event by Maggi Bell, who ran our HR Services division at that time, and we both commented on the hostile feeling that was in the room and the questions that followed our session. Despite this we were a popular pair to speak with over dinner and in the bar afterwards, with many delegates seeking one-to-one discussions with us the following day. I think that many present knew that the game was up and the world of the HR director was about to change.

In June of 1998 we won our largest integrated HR services contract, combining pay and pensions services for the Metropolitan Police's 43,000 police officers and civil staff as well as 30,000 pensioners, worth £29 million to us over seven years. In September, Westminster City Council became the first local authority in the country to outsource the entire personnel function for its 8,000 employees to Capita in a contract worth £34 million over five years, giving us a market leading position in outsourcing in another new market.

Entering 1999, the group had 6,700 staff, the majority of whom had transferred to us from the public sector. Our turnover had reached £327 million and of this 66 per cent came from the public sector, of which local government was still the largest proportion, at around 30 per cent. Outsourcing in the private sector was in its infancy but the group was well placed to increase its penetration here through the business relationships that we had established with over 300 substantial corporate clients, many through our property services businesses. The big move for us in the private sector was to occur a year later.

We won the first ever local authority multi-channel customer services call centre for Hertfordshire County Council, providing the public with a single gateway to council services and moving away from a 9 to 5 opening regime for services. The objective set by the client was for the centre to resolve 70 per cent of the calls at the point of enquiry, rather than referring them to an individual in a specific department. I worked well with Bill Ogley, the Chief Executive of the council, who was keen to promote our contract to other local authorities and also to senior figures in government. It therefore became a good reference site to take customers to.

Our solution involved creating a brand new call centre with new operatives recruited to work in it. To us it seemed easier to train a person about local government services than to attempt to retrain an existing local government office to act in a new customer-oriented fashion.

One real-life example of how we improved services was that of a person who wanted to arrange to get a wheelchair for their disabled daughter and had to make fourteen different calls to different parts of the authority to arrange it, whereas under the arrangement we operated just one call was needed.

In February my results statement for the year ended 31 December 1999 to shareholders included a reference to a strategic alliance between Capita and Microsoft. The intention was to develop a dedicated education internet portal which would co-ordinate and deliver all aspects of e-learning, e-assessment, e-commerce and e-services, obviously drawing on the enormous position that we had in education through our SIMS software. The attractive feature was the development of the systems to check pupils' performance online and monitor attendance.

It was at a time when the mention of Microsoft, and a separate alliance with Oracle, as well as anything with an 'e' prefix was jumped on with great excitement by the City and the Press. The share price reacted accordingly, running away with itself and rising by more than £2 to £13.55. Our visit to the States at that time, particularly to San Francisco with the Silicon Valley effect, required us to put some parameters around the story before we became thought of as a 'dot com stock'!

In June 1999, Derek Fowler, our Non-Executive Deputy Chairman, retired from the business after ten years on the board, having joined at around the time of our float on the USM. Derek had been an invaluable source of advice and support to the board and particularly to the executive team. Looking back, I would say that, for me, his retirement was a defining moment. It is not easy being the leader of any organisation and in that role you need a person that you can speak to openly. For me Derek was that person. I turned to him for help and advice which he gave to me in a straight, uncompromising way.

I never replaced that sort of relationship with any other NEDs (non-executive directors) that followed him onto our board. I now consider this an error on my part, and it would be my strong advice to others who find themselves in a similar managerial situation to identify such an individual to work closely with.

16

GAME-CHANGING CONTRACTS AND JOINING THE FTSE

The year 2000 was very big both personally and on a business front. In March of that year with our market capitalisation exceeding £4 billion, we were notified by the Stock Exchange that Capita, ranked at number eighty-three, had been elected to join the FTSE 100 Index, which contained the top 100 leading public companies.

We were always schooled by our advisers never to speak of this happening. Our job was to deliver the profits and the way that the market valued the shares would follow. I had consistently said that with the emergence of the business process outsourcing market, a company providing such services would eventually enter the FTSE and I very much wanted this to be Capita. It was an amazing performance for a company to achieve this from a standing start in just sixteen years, especially from the background that we had and our original flotation on the USM for £8 million! The next task was to stay in the Index, since one of the key advantages of being in it was that a number of the investment tracker funds had to hold your shares in their portfolio as a FTSE stock.

We had a family celebration at The Withies, a favourite local restaurant close to Charterhouse, and I received a number of very nice letters congratulating me on the achievement. One letter came from the very bank manager at Lloyds who gave me a hard time over the original loan that I needed to purchase my shares in the MBO. Another came from a very close colleague, Bill Capps, with whom I had worked while at the CIPFA secretariat. I also had a note from Paul Waller of 3i. But there was no word from Noel Hepworth or Philip Sellers, which I thought was a missed opportunity, since it was the Institute that had effectively started a company that was now in the FTSE.

In March 2000, Jacqui, Jennifer and I joined Robert in a cricket tour that went to Zimbabwe from Aldro School. It turned out to be an amazing experience with a group of fourteen twelve-year-olds travelling around the country playing local schools along with a party of twenty parents, which is where we first met Sue and Giles Schofield, whose son Harry was in the team and they have become close friends over the years. This trip was at a time when President Mugabe was bringing the country to its knees and his troops were everywhere in Harare. The trip was also special because Jennifer celebrated her twenty-first birthday on 1 April with a dinner in a local hotel in the capital with all the team and parents.

This was also the year when we made a significant move in building up our private sector presence through the completion of two acquisitions. The first of these was in April, when we acquired IRG PLC, a share registration business, for a consideration of £100 million. This opportunity came about through a chance introduction to Paul, and it was not an area that we had planned to go into.

However, through rebranding the business Capita IRG PLC, the business brought 1,200 new public company clients to the group. It considerably increased the brand awareness of Capita across the private sector, which we felt would help us to provide other outsourcing services to this client base. The deal was not initially well received by the City because it represented a new service in what was then considered a non-core market, the private sector. It therefore took time to convince the analysts about the move.

In October we also concluded the acquisition of Eastgate Group, one of the UK's largest independent providers of outsourcing services to the insurance industry. We had acquired a minority stake in the business in March 1999 so as to gain access the market where we could see that increased competition in the sector would provide opportunities for large scale outsourcing, driven by the need to reduce costs of the services provided. Eastgate provided services for 145 Lloyds syndicates and seventy insurers, dealing with over 5 million assistance calls and approaching 1 million household, motor and travel claims.

Through this deal we became the UK's largest third party insurance claims administrator and the largest provider of insurance helpline facilities in the UK, dealing with 20 million people throughout the country. Our decision proved to be a good move because the following year we were awarded our largest ever private sector contract to manage the core processing activities of Abbey National PLC's insurance business, in a contract worth £323 million.

On the major contracts front, 2000 also proved to be our most successful year to date. Wins included a £50 million agreement with the Department of Education for the introduction of the Individual Learning Accounts. However, the most notable was the announcement on 20 July 2000 that we had been awarded a ten-year partnership, worth £400 million, to set up and administer the Criminal Records Bureau. This was a new government agency to be launched in Spring 2002, and was designed to support safer recruitment to protect children and vulnerable adults from harm. Very soon after this in the October, Blackburn with Darwen Borough Council selected us as its preferred partner for what was to become a fifteen-year partnership intended to deliver transformation of services and promote regeneration throughout the Borough. It was the longest and most comprehensive to be agreed by a local authority, involving the transfer of 500 council staff. The contract was worth £215 million to Capita over a 15-year period.

All three of these contracts propelled Capita into the limelight. Before this we had grown by sitting below the radar without attracting attention other than that which we sought or organised. The leap in the profile and size of these contracts changed this dynamic and we became a news item for the press, requiring us to increase the in-house PR team. All three contracts were controversial, complex operations and all three brought operational challenges to us, problems not of our making that fuelled the Press coverage.

In central government through the Tony Blair years, Capita

continued to grow and prosper. Blair was good news for us because of the number of new policy initiatives his government sought to implement to drive the social change that they believed was necessary. We were seen by officials as a leading player, with a strong record in implementing and running such new 'greenfield site' government initiatives. The advantage of using the private sector to run these was speed of implementation, since resources were not readily available within the civil service. In my view, it was also their way of gaining access to private sector thinking without provoking the inevitable reaction from the unions to outsourcing.

The contract that we had with the Department of Education and Employment for Individual Learning Accounts (ILAs) was very much an illustration of how to involve a partner such as Capita in the implementation of a new initiative. Unfortunately, the initiative was to run into serious headwinds in the implementation stages, but it did lead to a complete rethink on how partnerships working between the public and private sectors should operate.

ILAs were designed to help people of all ages to overcome financial barriers to learning and to stimulate a culture of lifelong education. To achieve this, it was necessary to grow the number of learning providers and the subjects available for people to study.

During the first three months, nearly a half a million people opened an ILA. They most definitely caught the attention of the public but unfortunately they also caught the attention of those who saw it as a way of 'earning a fast buck' by defrauding the system.

Capita's role was to provide a membership service for individuals and learning providers to register for the scheme. We used a dedicated call centre and an administrative team at business centres we already had established in Coventry and Darlington. At a basic level a member of the public would register to open an account to confirm a desire to learn about a subject and would be connected to a learning provider, triggering the funding application that was needed to deliver this learning.

The IT system at the heart of this was our responsibility to design and run. As part of the scheme, Capita did not have the responsibility to accredit learning providers or for the quality of training they provided. This rested with the Department. With hindsight this meant that there were no quality controls on the learners and their courses. In the desire to encourage the development of a learning community, the accreditation of learning providers prior to gaining access to the system had been dropped by officials at the Department.

At this stage the style of operating between a private sector provider and a government department was more a contractor style relationship, whereas in local government this had moved on to be far more of a partnership. One treated a partner in a far different way than you would treat a contractor. In hindsight, as an experienced operator, we should have shouted louder and escalated our concerns to senior officials within the Department, since some of the changes made clearly weakened the integrity of the overall ILA Scheme.

We were first alerted to an issue when members of our HQ staff in our Victoria Office were approached by a team of people operating up and down Victoria Street representing a training provider encouraging passers-by to sign up for training on a course that the organisation was planning to provide. Clipboard in hand they were 'collecting' signatures and contact details in a sales orientated approach which was not the intention of the scheme. These concerns escalated and I still recall receiving a call late on a Friday from Peter Lauener of the Department, saying that we needed to meet urgently on the Monday as they had serious operational concerns about the integrity of the scheme Capita was operating, including the belief that the IT system had been hacked into. I had an event to attend that evening for the Prince's Trust at Windsor Castle, which was very special, but overall it was not a good weekend!

On the Monday Paddy and I visited the Department to meet Peter along with his boss Janice Shiner, who was the Director General of Skills. I imagined a scenario whereby a blame culture was to prevail from the outset but the approach adopted by Janice to the 'problem' that we both had enabled Paddy and I to respond in a solution-driven fashion, recognising the reputational risks to both organisations.

The scheme was initially suspended and then inevitably wound up by the Department after it was established with reasonable certainty that there had been significant amounts of fraudulent activity by a small number of training providers. This was the only course of action that the Department could take but, if allowed to continue, ILAs could well have stimulated great changes in peoples' approach to learning new skills, improving their employment opportunities and their quality of life. By the time the scheme was withdrawn, the ILA programme had surpassed the objectives set to attract learners, with some 2.6 million applicants against a target of 1 million. It also created a supply market of learning providers that had reached 8,000 by the time of closure.

The fallout from this required Janice and Peter to agree a termination of the agreement with us which I believe was negotiated in an open and constructive manner. As for me, I had the additional challenges of explaining it all to our shareholders and of dealing with the inevitable Press interest. The Department had to recover public monies that had been paid to fraudulent providers, which involved legal cases that went on for years after.

Another thing that this triggered, again led by Janice, was a suggestion that since the Department and Capita had some major relationships on a number of fronts both within central and local government, it was important for the key people in both organisations to better understand one another and the way that we operated. There followed a series of informal meetings involving our respective teams and hosted by Janice and me. The teams spent time together to develop a partnership style of operating.

Janice subsequently left the Department to go to New Zealand to lead the transformation of the education service there over a number of years. I have the highest regard for her style of operating and I have no doubt that if she had chosen to stay in the UK Civil Service she would have made a very successful permanent secretary of a government department. We kept in touch and when I formed the Foundation following my retirement from Capita, Janice was one of the first people I asked to become a Trustee. Her contribution has been enormous in this role both to me personally and to the family of academies. Peter Lauener went on to hold very senior positions within the department including heading the Education and Skills Funding Agency.

The work that Janice and I did, proved invaluable, as almost inevitably the publicity around the ILAs attracted the attention of the Public Accounts Committee (PAC), who wanted to understand what had happened. I can promise you that appearing before the Committee is an experience to be avoided because of the time involved in preparing for it and the style of challenge that it brings. In keeping with its normal style, the Committee wanted to interview separately David (later Sir David) Normington as Permanent Secretary of the Department and myself as Executive Chairman of Capita. This would have led to a confrontational style, forcing us to defend our respective organisations and the role that we had.

We did not want to be set against each other. There was also the bigger policy point, that if the modernisation of government services was to happen in the way that the Prime Minister wanted, the public and private sectors had to learn how to work together successfully. In David's world of fellow permanent secretaries, there was a risk in taking a decision whether or not to outsource services. This fear influenced the way that contracts were shaped, usually with the involvement of external consultants who had no on-going responsibilities for the project. This in turn drove the service provider to act in a certain way, causing them to question whether they wanted the hassle of bidding for large government contracts. Most definitely at that time our shareholders were strongly starting to put that view to us.

What David and I agreed was that we would go to the PAC together. We shared all the preparation of information produced by our respective teams to ensure that the NAO had full access to information and data and to ensure accuracy of facts for the hearing. This was an unprecedented approach and one that many officials around David, I am sure, felt uneasy about. David and I had a number of sessions in his office where we ensured that we both had all the background and information needed to answer fully any specific lines of questioning from MPs on the Committee. This preparation mirrored the approach that I had adopted in preparation for our City presentations of thinking the unthinkable.

I also had training for my appearance before the Committee from

LLM Communications, who at that time had as directors Ben Lucas, Neil Lawson and Jon Mendelsohn (now Lord Mendelsohn). They were a formidable team, each taking different approaches with me in their questioning style. Inevitable Neil and Jon were the direct aggressive sorts, aiming through their questions to prepare me for being demolished as a person from the private sector wringing profits out of public services. Ben was more concerned about questioning the policies around establishing ILAs and the procurement process leading to the selection of Capita. John Tizard attended the session with me to cover the investor/city angle of the preparation.

I also watched two or three very telling videos which are used for training purposes showing people being interviewed, which are both funny and serious, depending upon the role you are about to play.

One was of a senior army general who was responsible for procuring a large number of tanks at considerable cost to the public purse. The tanks were to be used in the desert, where in the extreme heat the vehicles' tyres melted, thus immobilising them. MPs questioned the general about how he came to the decision to select such tanks, demanding details of the contract that was in place with the supplier, since the tanks would now have to scrapped or used in non-desert theatres of war. It was very clear from the video that the individual was not prepared for such detailed attack.

Another video involved the CEO of an organisation being questioned by the Chair of the PAC with the camera face-on to him, showing the CEO's team sitting behind him. As the Chair asked a particularly direct question of the CEO, one of his team is seen to be shaking his head in disbelief and in disagreement with the answer given by his boss. This prompts the PAC Chair to suggest that he may wish to check his answer, as clearly his team responsible for the operation in question disagreed with him!

David Normington and I survived the attack from the Committee, whose chair at the time was the Rt Hon. Edward Leigh MP. I feel that this provided the opportunity to demonstrate that we wanted to be a serious partner to government. I was told later that when in the presence of a group of permanent secretaries, such an exercise was considered by them as an intellectual challenge, and that there was a club for those who had been through the process and even a tie to recognize such public service!

In November of that year I took a rather special break from Capita when Jacqui and I experienced an amazing, round the world golf trip in the company of none other than the legendary Peter Alliss. Although Jacqui, along with several others on the trip, did not play golf, the organisers laid on a very impressive programme of social events. It was an unusual holiday to say the least. I saw the trip advertised in the *Financial Times* one Saturday offering a golf trip lasting twenty-one days, where you went round the world playing golf on some incredible courses. The trip was organised by a company called PrivatAir who provided the large aircraft that was customised for around sixty people. A similar plane was used by clubs such as Manchester United to travel on their away legs in the European Cup games.

The party left from Stansted in November and we went to Bermuda, Las Vegas, to Pebble Beach in California, down to Hawaii, back up through Australia, into India and home via Dubai. In all we played twelve rounds of golf and had an awful lot of fun. There were about forty-five people on this private plane, including support staff. It's probably one of the best things I've ever done in my life. I recall on the final part of the trip over a matter of two days I played golf in Katmandu, where we were treated like royalty with "ball spotters" hiding up trees to ensure we didn't lose any golf balls. I also visited the Taj Mahal, and then flew over Everest on my way to dinner in Dubai!

In the end, much to my surprise and delight, I won the overall competition and was presented with a trophy by Peter Alliss at a final dinner held in the six-star, Burj Al Arab Hotel in Dubai, where we were staying. Winning was nice but the trip itself was the holiday of a lifetime. Golf has become an important part of my life. I have enjoyed playing in many different parts of the world, on many occasions with my sons Robert and Michael, and made many friends through the game.

I returned from the trip refreshed and straight back to the reality of business with Capita in full swing, implementing major new contracts and preparing for our next results statement for the year ended 31 December 2001, which we announced in February the following year.

One such major contract implementation that was underway was for the Criminal Records Bureau. This was a major initiative for Labour, designed to support safer recruitment to protect children and vulnerable adults from harm. The Chief Executive of the Criminal Records Bureau was Bernard Herdan, whom we had worked with previously at the Driving Standards Agency to set up the Theory Driving Test.

Capita's role was to design and build the Agency's IT and administrative infrastructure. On 1 March I was in Liverpool at the centre in Shannon Court to welcome The Home Secretary, David Blunket, on a visit to mark the official opening of the building and the launch of the Disclosure service for Registered Bodies. It was the client's choice that the service was to be based in Liverpool, a decision driven by the opportunity to recruit staff from the area's community of long-term unemployed.

The Home Secretary was very complimentary about the staff that he met and we had a good conversation over lunch. It was the first time that I had encountered his faithful dog that sat under the table while we ate. It was unfortunate that when things went off course with the implementation, civil servant protection around him precluded me seeing him to discuss it.

The Agency had to be ready for Spring 2002 and we had the contract for ten years. It was a large and complex job, involving a development team of over sixty software engineers and 9,000 days of software development, with over fifty weeks of training to prepare 330 staff and the staff of forty-three local police forces for their role. There were lots of 'moving parts', which when put under a real stress test could go wrong, which was indeed to prove the case. It was our expectation that following the launch we would carry out over 3 million Disclosure checks in the first year. This represented a threefold increase in the number of organisations requesting sensitive information on job applicants and volunteers seeking positions of trust.

The legislation required part of the process to be handled by the police, which involved the checking of criminal records which was thought, at the time, to be inappropriate for the private sector to do. So the CRB had police involvement from the forty-three forces spread around the country, civil service teams that verified and collected information, along with the Capita staff, who essentially dealt with the beginning of the process involving applications and the end of it: covering printing of disclosure.

In the building were both civil servants and Capita staff. For this to work all three parties needed to work together but the issue which became increasingly apparent was that this was difficult to achieve. The key point was that Capita was not the CRB which, when issues emerged, was not the line taken by the Press and MPs, sometimes encouraged by the Home Office as the client. It always struck me as odd when I visited the building, that civil service staff could visit our floors but we were not permitted to enter theirs without a special pass, something which did not encourage partnership working. So there was still an element of control and mistrust.

A side effect of this contract was that it took Capita from being a boring City success story into a company which attracted great, and often very negative, media reports as backlogs and delays emerged. Within the contract that we signed up to, Service Levels were set, and if we did not reach these we were fined, which again was reported by the Press and mentioned in an answer to parliamentary questions.

Two things happened to change the dynamic of this contract for us. One was administrative and the other tragic.

On the administrative front, shortly before the launch, the Home Office decided to allow paper-based applications rather than the expected 70 to 85 per cent of the people who would be expected to apply by telephone to a call centre, while others would apply online. We had quoted on this basis, which was not an unreasonable expectation since Tony Blair was calling for more government services to benefit from 'e-government'.

This decision triggered an overwhelming preference by the public for paper applications. In the event 80 per cent of applications were paper driven, which swamped the centre and massively affected the front end process. We needed to completely rethink how we handled this. Additionally, a large number of the forms had to be returned for correction and/or additional information, which compounded the backlog situation.

The second factor was prompted by a terrible event. On Sunday 4 August 2002 two little girls disappeared in Soham. On 17 August their bodies were found and a school caretaker, Ian Huntley, and his girlfriend Maxine Carr (a teaching assistant at the girls' primary school) were arrested for the murders. There was, naturally, overwhelming public outrage.

This very sad event put the CRB front and centre in the press. Estelle Morris (now Baroness Morris of Yardley), the Minister for Schools, announced on 21 August that all teachers would be vetted by the CRB before the schools reopened in September. This involved a lot of teachers and a lot of applications! It also meant that a school could not open without the checks being completed. This decision was never discussed with Capita and it is my belief it was also not cleared by the Home Office. This meant that the system had to be radically altered because it required the prioritisation of teacher applications when it had been designed to put all applications through the same process based on the date the application was received.

The press went directly for us and I even experienced journalists waiting for me outside my flat in London, asking if I was considering resigning as a result of Capita's failure to deal with backlogs. This inevitably spilled over into the City and caused a number of analysts to question both our ability to run large contracts and to work with government. There were also concerns over how this would affect the financial returns on the contract.

These all seemed to me to be secondary to the tragic events that had unfolded in Soham, but I felt it was my job to put the record straight in the press. So I arranged an interview with the *Financial Times*. Two journalists that I had worked with before, Jim Kelly and Andrea Felsted, were to put Capita's side of the story. In the article published on 6 September, I confirmed our role with the agency, making it clear that the CRB was not an exclusively private sector operation. I also relayed the implications of the decision to allow paper applications, and confirmed our performance to date. Above all it was necessary to state on record that the Minister had not consulted us about her decision to say that all teachers would be vetted over the next two weeks before schools reopened, but that we were doing all that we could do to accommodate this.

We still had an issue with the City with the fallout. So we took a group of analysts to Liverpool to visit the centre, helping them to understand the scale of the operation when they published their notes about the problems that we were having along with the solutions to address it.

The Permanent Secretary of the Home Office at the time was John (now Sir John) Gieve. He was a very traditional civil servant who saw his job as protecting his Minister. Paul and I dealt with him in meetings we had about the CRB operation, explaining our plans for the team to handle the backlogs. David Blunkett (now Lord Blunkett) was Home Secretary but the Minister responsible was Charles Falconer (now Lord Falconer of Thoroton). By the time that we met the Minister, relationships were very frosty, as the briefing he had received held us very firmly responsible for the failure of the operation.

There was clearly a need to look at the total operation to work out how to resolve the issues, and this is what eventually happened. Our contract was revised to reflect the greater reliance on paper processes and the plan that we had to deal with this. When the criticism was at its highest, we were actually blocked from meeting the Home Secretary and the only briefing that he was receiving about our performance was from the civil service team. In the end I got a private briefing note to him via another source who knew him well.

Following this experience, John Tizard and I recognized that the approach of central government to contracting and outsourcing, especially the relationship between the government department and the company, could be significantly improved. We set about developing a partnership model with a partnership board composed of senior client and contractor personnel. This board would oversee performance but not negate nor dilute the important contract management role of the client, resolve differences and above all ensure dialogue rather than confrontation. We also proposed measures for greater transparency and accountability of contractor and client, open book accounting and profit sharing and ensuring market terms and conditions for staff.

This approach, which was to some extent adopted by much of government, built on the pioneering work that Capita had already done with its local government partners.

There is no doubt that the instant and constant scrutiny that ministers are under through their accountability to the House makes it very difficult to achieve an open relationship. The added challenge of a review by a select committee or the Public Accounts Committee compound this problem. There is also the role of the National Audit Office (NAO) to contend with, who, after all the attention following Soham had subsided, came along eighteen months later to undertake a review of the CRB's performance. They published a report in February 2004, which again raised the issue in the press. Sir John Bourne was the Director General of the NAO and someone I got on with extremely well. We used to meet regularly to discuss the emergence of the outsourcing industry as a partner to government, and how this could be more effectively managed as had happened with the MOD and its suppliers.

This ultimately become a key feature of the Group that I chaired within the CBI, as there was little doubt that both the government and the BPO (Business Process Outsourcing) sector needed each other but the rules of engagement were wrong for an open and successful long-term relationship.

Another big breakthrough for Capita came in the local government arena, with Blackburn with Darwen Council. This was a Labour authority in the north west of England, where Barbara Castle had been the MP for thirty-odd years – you couldn't get more 'Labour Left' than that. It had recently broken away from Lancashire County Council and become a new authority. The officers were led by Phil Watson the CEO and the councillors, whose Leader was Sir Bill Taylor. They were visionary and open-minded.

Their prime purpose was to attract jobs into Blackburn and Darwen. It was a very industrialised and rundown part of the country. Mills had closed and manufacturing was struggling. What they were looking for was a partner who would run a whole range of their back-office business such as IT, revenues and benefits, council tax collection, human resource administration, school support services along with property and highways management, highway consultancy and a number of other services. More significantly they wanted 500 white-collar jobs of quality created and local people employed in these posts. In addition, they had diversity targets and insisted on local supply. They also sought a purpose built business centre in Blackburn. That is something we were able to provide in the deal and I'm happy to say it proudly stands there on Barbara Castle Way.

It was a fifteen-year contract from July 2001, so it was quite radical with all the savings it generated going back into front-line services. A great deal of our success there was about forging good relationships. The bid was brilliantly led by Tony Lubman, a member of our Big Ticket Sales Team and we spent a lot of time with our new partners working on shaping our future together. They trusted us and the outcome has been amazing. It gave them a profile that they were seeking, which led them to them being named Council of the Year at the annual awards event in 2002, organised by *Local Government Chronicle* and they were rated as 'excellent' by the Audit Commission.

This is what attracted me personally to working with them and it is what led me to return to the area many years later when I wanted to become the sponsor of an academy. They worked out what they wanted and how to get it, which was not through talking but by taking action.

At the time I opened the newly built £5-million Regional Business Centre with Sir Bill Taylor on 7 May 2004, we had delivered 700 new white-collar jobs that the council estimated would return an estimated £250 million to the local community over the following ten years. It was also the first new building in the area for thirty years!

The authority got a lot of kudos from it and we got a business centre in the North West, presenting an amazing opportunity for people to gain jobs and changing for the better many lives of local families. Over the years we took many other local authorities, government departments and private sector organisations to see this modern, vibrant and high performing Centre.

My colleague John Tizard who worked on this partnership with me points out:

This was the first and one of the few times in my experience that local government staff helped to encourage a council to outsource. The local Unison branch voted for the transfer. They were very keen on this outsourcing in spite of union policy. It opened up a whole way of a new of local government contracting with the private sector working and was another example of Capita and Rod shaping a market.

The period leading up to Christmas 2001 was to prove to be one of the most historic for Capita. On Thursday 20 December, I had a working lunch in my dairy with the Editor-in Chief of *The Guardian*, Alan Rusbridger, along with members of his editorial team to cover issues on outsourcing and the engagement of the private sector in the delivery of public services. The idea was for me to update them on progress and to deal with any questions about the industry or Capita. We had worked hard at our relationship with *The Guardian* who had taken a less than positive stance towards the outsourcing of public services.

Some of the journalists attending were generalists, covering the public sector from local government through to central government including health or even the role of voluntary organisations. Others were specialists, covering employment issues or legal issues emerging mainly from difficult contracts that had been let. They would also report stories circulating in the City around companies involved in delivering public services, including financial performance and even the level of remuneration paid to senior executives.

Capita was the market-leading company in the provision of outsourced services and as its Chairman I saw it as my responsibility to meet with a range of journalist to explain more about what we did and our approach. I was particularly keen to explain our stance towards staff that transferred to us. This was, therefore, definitely a meeting where I needed to be well briefed and, as they always did, Shona Nichols, our Director of Communications, and her team made sure that this was the case.

We had been bidding for more than a year on two of the largest contracts that the company had ever sought to win. Both were extremely high profile and one most definitely courted great controversy in the press. Both were bound to come up in the conversation over lunch. One of these potential contracts was with the BBC to administer the collection of TV Licensing revenues. We would become responsible for the task to issue and collect payment from 23.5 million TV Licences a year and revenues in excess of £2.1 billion. The bid had been run by one of our top Big Ticket sales people, Neil Wallington and Paul had also been actively involved with the senior team at the BBC. It was clear that they were close to making a decision.

Late on the previous day we got a call asking Paul and I to go over to Broadcasting House the following morning to see John Smith, the Director of Finance, and Zarin Patel, the Head of Revenue Management, the decision makers. We arrived at the BBC and were shown into an empty room to await our fate. The emergence of John and Zarin with smiles on their faces soon told us that we were the chosen company to deliver the contract.

That was good news but we had been also bidding at the same time for the dubious pleasure of running the proposed introduction of the Congestion Charging Scheme for Transport for London (TfL). We knew that we were down to the last two here and were against Serco. We were aware of this because, unusually, the decision had been taken by TfL to run with two bidders in the process for both to do more work on developing the specification for the computer system that would sit at the heart of the scheme.

To put this opportunity into context, a transport management scheme of this scale and type had never been implemented anywhere in the world. It had been bitterly criticised in the press, including *The Guardian*, and was seen as extraordinarily controversial, as was the London Mayor, Ken Livingstone, who announced its introduction when elected.

Again, this decision was close and the team had gone to the stage of having an exchange with the client over contract issues, even agreeing the terms of a draft press release should we be successful. This had become a regular strategy adopted on contracts procurement which would see the statement consigned to the waste bin in seconds if you were unsuccessful. On this occasion it was most definitely not the case.

When Paul and I came out of the BBC meeting we were called by Richard Betts, another member of the Big Ticket sales team to say he had heard from the TfL team that we were to be nominated as the preferred bidder in a statement to be issued the following day. These two wins would result in Capita announcing to the Stock Exchange and to our shareholders over the coming days the winning of £730 million of new work which would add nearly £100m a year to our turnover. The news would both cement our status as a FTSE 100 Company and change the profile of Capita. Above all, it would propel us from the City pages of newspapers such as *The Guardian* to become front page news.

So, as I made my way over from Broadcasting House to meet the editor and his team, I knew that Capita had been successful with both bids, but it as it was commercially sensitive information. I was unable to share this news with them until it was released to the Stock Exchange. Nevertheless, the Rod Aldridge that entered the room that day for the lunch was particularly buoyant about answering any questions on the future of Capita and that of outsourcing!

When I went back to the office in Victoria Street after the lunch, celebrations were in full swing with lots of high-fives and hugs going on. We bid as a team and celebrated as a team. The intensity of bidding for contracts that involve large numbers of people working as a team over long periods brings extreme pressure to win. This was most definitely a day to remember. Celebrations of the wins started in the office and then overflowed to the local pub. It was not a time to remind ourselves that we had to deliver what we had bid for, although I suspect that this had already dawned on the operations team as they celebrated.

The first part of 2002 was dominated by the need to get both situations to contract position. In the case of BBC TV Licensing, I was able to announce with our results on 20 February that on 7 February we had signed the contract with the BBC for a ten-year deal to run the service. This meant that 1,500 people involved with customer service and field operations would transfer from Consignia, who currently ran the service, to Capita on 1 July of that year. To aid the transformation the main contact centre in Bristol had relocated to more modern offices.

We also opened a second centre in Darwen at a place called India Mill, which was a start-up centre for new businesses, to deliver aspects of the TV Licences contract. We were able to take two floors here, which not only helped local employment but enabled us to deliver on our undertaking to Blackburn with Darwen to create more white-collar jobs in the town.

In March of that year we announced the signing of the contract with Transport for London, to administer the proposed congestion charging scheme in London which was to go live on 17 February the following year. This was worth £280 million over the first five years.

One of the most exciting prospects in winning the contract was the fact that more than thirty-five major cities in the UK had expressed an interest in the scheme and would clearly be watching the London experience to judge its efficiency in reducing congestion and improving the quality of life for inhabitants. We therefore saw a whole new market opening up for us to become a leader in the transport management sector. This did not happen and to date the London Scheme remains the only scheme in the UK.

Our teams under the project management of Simon Pilling, one of the executive directors, continued working on establishing the scheme alongside PriceWaterhouse Coopers (PWC), who continued to advise the client in agreeing the specification of the scheme to be used. Another unique feature of this project was that PWC was similarly incentivised to ensure that the scheme started on the agreed date. This was key because rather than there being any temptation to rack up fees as a consultant, PWC were working to a success fee model, aligning them more with us as a delivery partner. The system required 450 man-years of implementation resource within an eleven-month window, between signing the contract and the introduction of the scheme.

This Congestion Charge preparation work went on throughout 2002 but it became increasingly clear that I was right about the reputational risks around this for Capita. The heavy opposition to the scheme by the media and some politicians, particularly in the Conservative Party, propelled us from the business section of the national newspapers to the front pages and even to the main stories on BBC and Sky. The editor of the *Evening Standard* took it on herself to try to stop the Congestion Charge and to focus on Capita as a way of doing so.

Also in that year I had an intriguing meeting at Victoria Street at the request of Sir David Ormand, a former Permanent Secretary at the Home Office from 1997 to 2000. He was putting together an event in which CEOs from the private sector were given the opportunity to meet informally with a number permanent secretaries. The meeting was ostensibly for him to test out my views on engaging with government, but it turned out that he was testing out my suitability to join such a group.

I obviously passed, as I was invited to Chevening in Kent, the official home of the Foreign Secretary, a month later for a two-day stay. The attendees from the civil service in addition to David Ormand (who hosted the event) were: Sir Richard Wilson, Head of the Civil Service at the time; David Normington, the Permanent Secretary of the Department of Education; John Gieve, Permanent Secretary of the Home Office; Sue (now Dame Sue) Street, who subsequently became Permanent Secretary of the Department of Culture and Sport; Peter (now Sir Peter) Gershon, who was the first CEO of the Office of Government Commerce and later was appointed to advise on Government Efficiency; and Ian Blair (later Sir Ian Blair, now Lord Blair of Boughton), the then Deputy Commissioner of the Metropolitan Police Force.

Attending from the private sector were: Richard Christou, the CEO of Fujitsu; Dianne (now Dame Dianne) Thompson, the CEO of Camelot (who ran the National Lottery); Val Gooding, the CEO of Bupa; Stephen Green (who at the time was the Group Chairman of HSBC and who went on to become Lord Green, serving in the Conservative Government as Minister of State for Trade and Investment) along with myself as the Chairman of Capita.

It turned out to be a fascinating but demanding event for me which I thoroughly prepared for, as I usually do. It effectively gave me personal time with a number of our key clients and added greatly to the mutual understanding of our respective organisations. The event combined external speakers such as Alistair Campbell, who was the

Press Adviser to Tony Blair, with group sessions where we discussed the lessons learned from working with Government and the role of civil servants in protecting their Minister.

However, for me the most enlightening were two one-to-one, ninety-minute sessions that I had separately with John Gieve and David Normington, particularly since at the time I was still involved with the issues around the implementation of the CRB and the fallout concerning Individual Learning Accounts. I learnt a great deal from these discussions and my future business relationship with all those attending was very different. We understood one another far better. Sir David was a very special person to work with, and he subsequently become the first UK Security and Intelligence Coordinator responsible to the Prime Minister for the professional health of the intelligence community, national counter-terrorism strategy and 'homeland security'.

Returning to the Congestion Charging Scheme, it had really begun when Ken Livingstone was elected as London Mayor in 2000. He announced the introduction of a 'Congestion Charge' of £5 for all vehicles entering the centre of London. It was widely seen as an extraordinarily controversial idea: nothing similar had ever been carried out in a major city before.

The *Evening Standard* was bitterly critical and pilloried the idea in what seemed like every edition. I had watched this with increasing interest as it was now on our 'suspect' list for future bid opportunities. During our 'black hats' bid qualification process, we tested out at each stage whether we were in or out of a bid. In this way we controlled the use of our precious resources, focusing them on the bids we felt were right for us and we would win – there was no point in coming second! I recall saying from the outset that for me the scheme represented high risk and I wanted to be reassured about our technical ability to deliver it.

There was massive public feeling against imposing a charge for something that had been free forever. I felt there was a good chance that London motorists would rebel against it, flatly refusing to pay, and that the Capital would grind to a halt as a result. I told my team that it was not worth the risk and that our shareholders would not thank us if it went wrong, since it would affect our ability to win other contracts. I really didn't think we should do it.

However, as things developed the team got more and more confident about the technology and our ability to deliver the scheme. I was eventually persuaded that, apart from installing the 700 cameras, when you broke down the process there was nothing in the contract that we hadn't done before. We had dealt comfortably with complex computer systems, including with the CRB, which was now beginning to perform well. We needed a call centre to deal with registration and payments, but call centres were an area where we had bags of experience within the Group, including the business of processing payments from the public.

When it was analysed in this way, reduced to its component parts, I began to feel that the risk was more containable. The final comfort to me was the style of contract that the team was negotiating. Effectively, it was designed for us to be prepared to lose the profit we were expecting, but there was a floor in the contract to cover our base line infrastructure and running costs, regardless of operational issues – even if the scheme should fail totally because of public outrage and opposition.

It was fascinating to watch the politics unfold, particularly those surrounding the Mayor himself. One key thing that he did (although I am not convinced he realised how key it actually was in operational terms) was that he refused to move the date for the start of the scheme, despite being lobbied by all concerned, including No. 10, to do so. This meant that we had publicly known deadlines, which helped enormously with key decisions that we needed internally and also with our sub-contractor partners. The substantial incentives for PWC as consultants were also linked to that date and so were aligned.

The second thing that TfL did very well was to set the policy for the scheme and its operational parameters early and not to chop and change them, which would have necessitated changing the IT system.

Lastly, Ken Livingstone himself, consistently and regularly said it seemed that the introduction of the scheme was going to be a failure.

Perversely therefore, the only way was up for us because a poor level of expectation had been set with the press, politicians and with the public. This is an odd psychology that should not be tried too often. But it worked.

People will be surprised to learn that the Mayor never met with me or Paul or with any of our team. He never visited the centre in Coventry to see the troops in the build-up to the start. This even remained true after our successful beginning and despite my request for him to do so. This strategy was adopted to protect the Mayor and to distance him from one of the most controversial traffic management schemes ever introduced anywhere in the world. It also very clearly put down a marker that the running of the scheme was firmly with us, Capita, and not with him or with TfL who merely set the policy. The message was very clear: if the scheme is a disaster pin the blame on Capita.

The political interest in our progress was handled by Bob Kiley, an American who had been appointed by the Mayor to be the Commissioner of Transport for London amid massive criticism concerning his terms and conditions. The client at TfL, was Peter (now Sir Peter) Hendy, the Director of Surface Transport, with whom we had a good relationship.

At one stage, when the Mayor was being scrutinized by the GLA (Greater London Authority), TfL decided to post the entire contract that we had signed online, without giving us any warning. It may have been part of their philosophy to show openness in this way, but they showed no appreciation of commercial sensitivity and the possible impact it might have on us. It gave the Press plenty to write about and handed our competitors complete information on our commercial approach to bidding and contractual negotiations. It also set out the service levels that we had signed up to and the penalties for poor performance against these standards.

Helpfully, it also made it clear that we would be paid in full for the cost of developing the system, irrespective of any decision that might be made about whether the scheme was to continue. In this way our capital investment of £50m was protected. The contract also guaranteed us a minimum payment each month, underwriting our fixed costs in delivering the scheme. For those who troubled to read the contract, it was very clear that our team had done a great job in protecting the downside interest of the shareholders. The upside would come in minimising the penalties and maximising the performance to generate the profits built into our model. It all sounds very easy as I write it but operationally there was much to be done to achieve that position.

Simon Pilling and the team did a brilliant job but I think that they would agree there were many times when things were not going so well, particularly at the nerve centre in Coventry. We had to recruit 300 new staff while simultaneously running a training programme. We needed to recruit temporary staff to help us through crunch peak times in the set-up process. There was an associated risk to this, and therefore the vetting process of applicants needed to be very thorough, but one subsequent event led us to refine this further.

The attack on us by the *Evening Standard* continued relentlessly and then on one day a centre page spread appeared in an issue with the headline of something like: 'Fiasco at Congestion Charging Centre', questioning whether we would be able to start on the envisaged date. It turned out that one of the temporary people that we had taken on was, in fact, a freelance reporter for the *Evening Standard* who had been inside the centre for five weeks. The team had been impressed by her performance, as she seemed very interested in what she was doing and kept asking intelligent questions. They were even considering offering her a full time role!

Throughout 2002 and as we moved towards the start date of Monday 17 February 2003, the pressure for the implementation team intensified. For my part, the important thing to do was to work at managing the Press and to try to contain the more extreme stories about our perceived failures, led mainly by the *Evening Standard* and *The Guardian*. I appeared on the front page of the February 2003 edition of *Management Today* along with the heading 'Our Lives in His Hands – Meet the Boss of Britain's Most Unpopular Company'.

From the city perspective, and by that I mean our shareholders and the analyst world, there was a great deal of nervousness about the technology and the whole implementation process. We had regular updates with them and I recall one event where we gave a major presentation of the software solution and its connectivity to the cameras. I believe we even took some interested parties to the major central Hub that we had in London, where all the technology came together.

Many of our shareholders questioned our decision to go ahead with this contract, particularly after our experiences with the Criminal Records Bureau. There was the feeling that there was much more 'low hanging fruit' for us to bid for in the backwaters of local government, and that we were wrong to take the risk with our reputation. One way or another, the outcome would be transformational to the company!

Another good feature of the procurement process was that the decision to run with two contractors before making a final selection meant that the functional computer specification was 'frozen' early, giving the development teams the opportunity to conclude the system on time. This in turn meant that we had a good run at testing out the system. We did so for I believe for three months before we went live, which obviously reduced the risk of failure immensely.

In December 2002 Jacqui and I went to see Robert play for a Charterhouse touring side in Cape Town, South Africa. At only 15 years old, he was three years younger than his team mates but had taken 35 wickets in the previous season with his off-spin bowling and was a useful batsman. In his first game against Groot Drakenstein on 9 December, he scored his maiden half century. It was wonderful to be there and experience the whole trip with him.

As 'C-day' approached, another factor was that the results day for our year ended 31 December 2002, one week after the start of the scheme. It was not possible to change the date of our results to be before the seventeenth, because a date had been announced to the City and to move it would cause all manner of opportunities for concern, suggesting that we wanted to get bad news on the scheme out to the market.

From a practical standpoint, the audit of our accounts could not be completed any faster. Capita was already one of the fastest year-end reporters of its results – something that we took pride in as an indication of the efficient way that we ran the company. So we were faced by the prospect of our results day being massively influenced by the success or failure of the start of the congestion charging scheme. I recall that I did an interview with *The Sunday Times* which was to be published in the issue the day before the scheme started. In this I claimed, with genuine belief but some trepidation, that Capita was ready for the big day. However, I had everything crossed when I was saying it!

One thing that was never disclosed to the press was a meeting that Paul and I had with Bob Kiley earlier that week. We were called over to the offices of TfL, just across from Capita in Victoria Street for a one-to-one update on our progress. Bearing in mind that this was the biggest traffic management scheme ever attempted it would not have been unreasonable to expect a degree of team spirit to demonstrate a shared commitment for its success.

Not on your life!

Instead, after a short update from us, we were exposed to a tirade of what I can only describe as abuse. Without any sign of emotion on his face, Mr Kiley said: 'If you f**k this up I will bury you. I will see you never get another contract in this city. I will personally see that Capita's reputation is ruined.'

I think it fair to say that I was aghast. I can recall saying something along the lines that this was not a very helpful approach for him to be taking at such a critical time. I assured him that we were fully aware of the risks to us and that, while we would remain in the UK whatever happened, in the fullness of time he would doubtless return to live in New York, leaving it all behind him. We both walked out of his office feeling like naughty schoolboys who had just been told off by the headmaster. We did not relay this conversation to Simon Pilling, or indeed to any of our teams.

There was certainly a lot of tension in the build-up to the day that the congestion charge went live. There was media coverage from all over the world, with 200 journalists attending the hourly bulletins from the Mayor, describing progress during the day. Over breakfast in my flat I watched BBC coverage and it was a pathetic illustration of the media's hunger for disaster news. They had a reporter perched at the edge of the congestion zone with a camera crew ready to record what they hoped would be scenes of chaos as motorists screeched to a halt to avoid entering the zone, causing massive traffic jams.

I walked to the office from my flat, going down Whitehall and joining Victoria Street. It was early but there would normally be queues of traffic building up. Not today, it was quiet. I thought to myself: 'It's working! It really is working!'

I knew there was nothing the *Evening Standard* would have liked more than to have run a front-page story about chaos and failure, but apart from a few minor glitches, the launch of the Congestion Charge was a complete and utter success. The *Evening Standard* never acknowledged our success in delivering the scheme on time, on budget and to specification. They did, however, feature our financial results when they were reported to the City the following week, and these showed strong growth. Naturally, they linked our increase in profits to the money that we were making from implementing the scheme. When we were given an extra £38 million to the contract for the extension of the Congestion Charging Zone, based on Transport for London's satisfaction of the service we had given, the *Evening Standard* ran a front-page story on 23 February 2005 headed: 'Big rip-off'.

It is worth recording that the congestion charge achieved its sole objective to reduce congestion in central London. Congestion was reduced by 40 per cent, exceeding the target of 25 to 30 per cent. Traffic in the Zone was reduced by 16 per cent, exceeding the target set of 10 to 15 per cent, and traffic crossing into the zone was down by 20 per cent. It is also fair to point out that over time these reductions were not sustained, as motorists began to accept the charge as a cost of travel, or in the case of those running businesses, passed the charge onto customers.

Capita, as the operational engine of the TfL scheme, handled 15,000 items of mail each week. We handled 70,000 customer telephone calls per week with the website dealing with 120 million hits per week, peaking at 250,000 hits per hour.

In the first fifteen months of operation over 500,000 Penalty Charge Notices (PCNs) were issued for non-payment of the charge. As the software was refined to include on the PCN a photograph not only of the number plate but of the driver, there was a significant reduction in the number of drivers who denied being at the wheel. We even had some who attempted to 'alter' the number plate by taping out some of the letters or numbers, which of course was an illegal act. In addition to the 700 cameras within the zone there were also around thirty mobile patrol vans equipped with cameras designed to be placed strategically so as to catch motorists who believed they had found a way of not paying.

At the outset within the zone there were over 9,000 pay point terminals in various retail outlets such as shops and kiosks. Four hundred petrol stations offered the ability to pay the charge as well as forty Post Offices, plus you could pay via the call centre at Coventry or online. The dynamic of the payment method used by people changed once we designed the option to pay via SMS texting.

Big talking points were the ability of the embassies to claim diplomatic immunity and not pay the massive bills that they ran up. One embarrassing situation for us was the need to chase the inhabitants of No. 10 for the charges associated with their private cars!

In a later speech to the London Business school, Ken Livingstone said that: 'Capita's contract was delivered on time, to budget and to specification. How many times have you heard of such a major IT project going so well? I cannot think of another example in Britain or Europe that betters this ... Capita pulled together a quality team and they did deliver – and we can now all see the benefits.'

Paul and I saw Bob Kiley at a subsequent dinner event in the City. He, of course, greeted us with a warm handshake and smile, introducing us to his guests as the great company that successfully delivered the Congestion Charge. He seemed to have forgotten the threat made to us but I definitely had not!

The Congestion Charge was an operational triumph for us. Now everyone wanted to know how we'd done it. I was asked to write a paper for the Prime Minister, setting out the lessons learned about why the implementation of the congestion scheme was a success whereas we had experienced problems with the Criminal Records Bureau start-up, particularly as both had large IT components.

I would like to put on record the great job that Simon Pilling, Paddy Doyle and the operational team did in completing this massive logistical task in the face of some of the most aggressive attempts by many to destabilise the introduction of the scheme. I will long remember the conversations that Simon and I had on his car phone virtually every day to get an operational update in the start-up phase of the scheme as he journeyed home from Coventry. Shona Nichols also did an amazing job on our PR in dealing with the enormous press interest in us during this period, particularly as it came so soon after the CRB issues.

There is no doubt that the risks of failure were enormous and I do wonder what would happen if the scheme were to be introduced now instead of then, with the emergence of the massive influence of social media. I remain convinced that a well organised social media attack could have supported a protest campaign of non-payment. This would have increased the need to issue PCNs at a level that would have clogged up the debt recovery process, very quickly bringing the scheme to its knees, and us with it!

Another significant feature emerging for us around that time was the extraordinary rate at which the percentage of business in the private sector was increasing. When we first started most of our revenue came from local government, then central government and education played a prominent role. By 2004, our business was virtually 50/50 public and private. This move to the private sector was started by our property services division. It was further boosted by the acquisitions of IRG, the share registration business, and Eastgate, which opened up the insurance market for us.

What was beginning to emerge was a new market involving Life & Pensions. Third-party administration as well as competitive and economic pressures on those in the sector saw some of the biggest players announcing sizeable losses and heavy redundancies.

What was required was a fundamental review of the processes themselves, which played into the hands of the outsourcing-led solution that Capita was able to offer. It was estimated that the addressable market in the UK was around £9 billion. In the summer of 2002, we were awarded a ten-year contract worth £160 million, to administer Lincoln Financial group's UK portfolio of around 900,000 Life and Pensions policies for half a million customers. Through the deal we also acquired Lincoln's infrastructure and staff based in Cheltenham which transferred to us providing us with a firm platform from which we could grow our business in this sector.

On 10 April 2003, Capita was named as the winner of 'The Royal Bank of Scotland Sunday Times Business Award'. This award recognised the contribution made by British business to the UK economy through the creation of wealth and employment. I was presented with the award by Stelios (now Sir Stelios) Haji-Ioannou, of Easyjet fame, at an event held at the Grosvenor House. It was not only a recognition of the progress that we had made as a company but an indication of the role being played by outsourcers in the UK. We also won that year, for the third year running, the 'Management Today's most Admired Support Services Company'. So it was quite a year for Awards!

The growth continued and in 2004, Capita Insurance Services became the largest employer of claim handlers in the UK through being selected to administer all the miners' personal injury liability claims on behalf of Department of Trade and Industry. These injuries were caused by working underground in the British Coal Mines, and the contract saw the processing of claims relating to chronic obstructive pulmonary diseases and a condition called 'vibration white finger'. These claims involved 1,250 employees, largely based in Sheffield, transferring to us in a contract worth £125 million over three years. I visited the centre to meet the staff and to understand more about the cases we were involved with. Sadly, many of the claims were tragic stories involving family claims for a deceased person, who had suffered years of poor health.

The operational impact that we were able to make in these private sector deals was material. The level of inefficiencies that existed in the back office was greater than in the local government contracts and increased competition was a wake-up call to them.

At the time, what attracted us to the private sector was the size of the deals available and the decision-making process which was much faster. Equally, if the contract went off course there was less appetite for attributing blame (something which was a feature of the public sector market) and more focus on fixing the problem. The main disadvantage was, however, that in a private sector procurement the client could very easily decide to stop it or to implement it in-house themselves. In the public sector once a procurement process had started it would rarely be stopped, so there would always be an outcome even if that outcome was not favourable to us.

We were quickly able to demonstrate to analysts and to our shareholders that the Capita model was just as relevant to the private sector as it had been to the public sector for twenty years. The key point here was that this gave us the option to move across many different markets when deciding where to bid, dependent upon where the best bid opportunities were and the best conditions under which to do business prevailed. In other words, if the political world in the public sector became challenging, we could very easily switch our focus to, say, life and pensions, without taking a hit to our top line growth or profitability.

Looking back for me personally this also began to change the dynamics of the business and my relevance to it. I most definitely felt more comfortable dealing with public sector clients, whereas in the private sector organisations we dealt with I had to work harder at building the relationships that were needed.

I recall sitting down with our marketing team putting together a list of clients to approach in the financial services market, covering banks, life and pensions and insurance. I knew virtually none of the CEOs and while I had met some through my dealings with the CBI, the letters that we drafted were essentially 'cold-calling' efforts, or else a reliance was placed on knowing one or two of their NEDs.

The composition of our Big Ticket sales list began to change and I found that my role became one of having to 'argue the corner' for local government opportunities to remain on our bid list. My take on this was that no matter how other markets developed, the public sector, and in particular local government, would always be the bedrock of our business. The organisations that constitute these bodies spend a great deal of money and the networks that exist are a powerful force in doing business. What's more, unlike in the private sector, a public body cannot go bust or be the subject of a takeover bid!

That said, the way that public sector business was conducted began to change. The Gershon Efficiency Review, undertaken by Peter

Gershon, set the agenda for effective organisational change and service transformation across the public sector. Private sector involvement was now accepted as integral in achieving the stringent targets that the Review set of efficiency gains of 2.5 per cent per annum to deliver savings of at least £6.5 billion by 2007/8.

I had met Peter at the Chevening event and along with John Tizard we had an input into his thinking concerning the review. Within the civil service there was resistance to change and most definitely to embracing opportunities for the transformation of services. Peter and his team spent time with us understanding more about our approach so that when presenting his proposals to permanent secretaries at their regular Wednesday gatherings he could state with confidence that savings along the lines he suggested were certainly possible.

Perhaps the most frustrating thing to me was the lack of the will to embrace the opportunity to bring together services that were replicated and duplicated across government. This was how Capita operated but to do so we needed to win individual contracts with associated bid costs before being able to assimilate these within one of our business centres. Even with encouragement from the Head of the Civil Service, Sir Gus O'Donnell (now Lord O'Donnell), who in a letter to all his fellow permanent secretaries encouraged them to embrace shared services, the initiative never really got off the ground.

Under the Labour Government the unions undoubtedly had a stronger say in the conditions that applied, particularly regarding the treatment of the workforce. A great deal of the attention was on blue collar contracts. Contractors here had to deal with a price-driven selection, and where services had to be delivered on site, there were fewer opportunities to achieve economies of scale from centralising services the way we had done with white collar services. This led to an attack on terms and conditions as a way of addressing the problem.

Unions began to increase across the outsourcing space. The unions were pressing for legislation to ensure that when services were taken over by another company that workers transferred under TUPE and any subsequent recruits enjoyed similar terms of service and pay.

There was a suggestion that a 'two tier' workforce was beginning to emerge, with contractors using outsourcing contracts as way of making redundant highly paid employees, so they could be replaced by lower paid individuals.

In practical terms there was a need to review the workforce that you took over and this necessitated redundancies, some people being surplus to requirements while others might not be performing at an acceptable level. One of the most telling statistics was staff sickness records. It was important to differentiate between absenteeism for genuine medical reasons and malingering. Those in the latter category were known by their colleagues, engendering low morale, something that needed to be addressed.

What the unions were attempting to do was to slow down this process by suggesting that the moves were purely driven by reducing costs. In our case at Capita, we made a virtue of valuing the people who delivered our services. We required them to be positive towards us and so we were unlikely to use such a purely mercenary tactic. My colleague, John Tizard, did a great job working on these issues with No. 10 to get a workable solution.

The unions also maintained that only public sector workers could adhere to the public service ethos that was so necessary to run these services. The line that we took was that Capita very much believed in the public service ethos and placed an emphasis on the quality and efficiency of service. We regularly said that the public service ethos was alive and well at Capita.

Competition was growing in this period so there were probably twenty major public sector companies of different kinds and size in this area, covering white-collar and blue-collar services. Many of these companies looked to Capita as the largest to take a lead and, by implication, to myself as the recognised face of this debate.

There was some pressure to set up a trade body or something similar so that we all had a joint voice. I invited the chief executives of our major competitors to attend an evening event that I hosted to discuss this. There was a real sense that something should happen, but we felt a trade association was probably not the answer. Such a body could become quite cumbersome, we would have had to set up all the infrastructure and there was a risk of us being seen to be motivated by self interest. John Tizard and I were very closely supported in this initiative by Kevin Beeston, who was the chief executive of Serco (one of our largest rivals) and another Serco executive, called Gary Sturgess, who ran the Serco Institute.

Between us we decided that the best answer was to try to persuade the CBI to treat the public services agenda as a greater priority. Up until to then the CBI had previously argued that public services, as funded by the state, were often an inefficient use of taxes. Kevin and I, along with Gary and John, had a very productive meeting with Digby Jones (later Sir Digby Jones, now Lord Jones of Birmingham), the then Director General of the CBI, and convinced him that it was timely for them to become more active in lobbying government about modernising the delivery of public services. As a result of this, the CBI Public Services Strategy Board was established along with a small, separate secretariat within the organisation led by John Williams who did a tremendous job in representing us. About twelve companies joined the Board with the work financed through a relatively small additional premium to the CBI membership fee. I became the Chair of the Board for the first three years of its existence with Kevin as my deputy. We worked very closely with Digby's deputy at the time, John Cridland, who eventually succeeded him. My feeling is that this Board did a lot to support the government reform agenda and to shape the industry. In particular, it promoted ethical and quality outsourcing and challenged rogue contractors. We promoted better procurement and contract management, developing a partnership approach of working rather than a hostile CCT style. For Ministers and senior civil servants who often did not want to have a conversation with an individual company, but who talked continuously to the CBI, it presented a platform for a dialogue about modernising public services. We also did much to build positive relations with the trade unions and with user groups representing consumers of public services.

It was clear that my executive team at Capita did not want me to take on this role for the fear that I would give away the competitive edge that Capita had. Not only would I never have done that, but I could also see the bigger picture. If the industry did not correctly handle the sometimes thorny subject of outsourcing, the flow of outsourcing opportunities would dry up. We needed to make the case, perversely, for encouraging more competition in the market to give clients more options.

The Strategy Board was launched at the CBI conference in Birmingham in November 2002. We gave an interview to the *FT* ahead of the event and the session itself went very well, with the Rt Hon. Alan Milburn MP sharing a platform with Digby Jones and myself.

I had been very well prepared by the communication team at the CBI and agreed to meet with the press to give my take on why the industry needed a voice. It was going well until I was then asked to speak to a reporter from BBC Radio's the *World at One*, supposedly about the formation of the Board. Within ten seconds of meeting me and recording the interview she seized on the chance to tackle me about the backlogs at the Criminal Records Bureau, claiming that we were responsible for this what was I, as the Chairman of Capita, planning to do about it?

I made it clear to her that this launch was not about Capita but about the outsourcing industry. This did not satisfy her and she continued her line of attack on me, holding the microphone in front of my face to try to provoke me into making an inappropriate remark, which would become the headline for her news piece. This went on for some time and I can understand why there have been some infamous interviews, particularly on TV, where the interviewee simply walks off the set. This was never an advisable thing to do as it simply creates the kind of headline that the interviewer wants, so I resisted this but I warned her that I was going to terminate the interview.

This unpleasantness perfectly illustrated the need for the CBI Group, and I actually received a number of calls and emails from individuals congratulating me on how I handled a very difficult interview.

It was a very intense time. What was happening was that the industry was becoming more prominent and increasingly controversial as more and more things were being moved out of the public sector into the private sector. There were companies that had problems and difficulties, and if you were inclined to look at it in a less positive way you could construct the argument that companies were making money out of the public sector services but not delivering the change that they signed up for. On top of that, the remuneration packages of these top executives attracted increasing press coverage.

Leading up to the General Election – the re-election of Blair for the second term – the papers started publicising all the details of the chief executives and revealing where they lived and what they earned. As an industry it was very difficult to fight back. If an individual company had a problem, they had to sort it out in the full glare of adverse publicity while being taken to the cleaners in the papers. So the idea with this Board was to provide a more balanced view. The CBI could speak up for us and demand the production of evidence, particularly when we denied mistreating staff or providing poor services.

I believed that if we were not careful, what was happening would lead to the market stalling and outsourcing could become less attractive prospect than reverting to the in-house option.

We had to fight back and point out the great things that the industry had achieved. We had regular meetings with ministers where we could present our case, along with conferences where we presented the facts about the industry's achievements and capabilities. In my view we changed the way the outsourcing industry was perceived. At least we got it onto a level playing field. We published the facts about how we treated our staff, giving case studies around TUPE transfers, including information on improvements in performance. We also produced a report outlining the opportunities for improving quality and increasing efficiency through a shared services model. The report contained fifteen case studies illustrating what had been achieved through working in joint ventures with the private sector, including two from Capita.

John Tizard, who later was seconded to the CBI to act as Secretary to the Board explains:

There was, understandably, concern from the unions that Capita and companies like us would be undermining terms and conditions, especially when they recruited new employees, creating a two-tier work force. They wanted legislation and the progressive, responsible companies such as Capita recognised these concerns and wanted to find a solution. They did not want to win contracts by 'lowest price, poorest employment terms and conditions' bids. We worked through the CBI with the TUC and public sector unions, the government, including No 10 and the Treasury, to design and introduce a statutory Best Value Two-Tier Code to ensure that new recruits would be employed on terms no less favorable than those who had transferred originally to the contracted work under TUPE. This was a good example of pragmatic partnership between trade unions and outsourcing companies.

March 2004 saw us celebrate the twentieth anniversary of Capita's formation within the Chartered Institute of Public Finance and Accountancy. In a letter sent to staff thanking them for their support and dedication, I also said that I never believed in 1984 that I would eventually be part of a 23,000-strong organisation generating revenues of over £1.25 billion turnover, servicing 20,000 clients and operating across 240 sites. What a journey! Later that year, on 18 June, we re-entered the FTSE 100 Index, replacing GKN, the global engineering group, and stayed there until after I left and the company stalled in 2016. That was painful for me to watch from a distance.

2004 was also significant for two contract wins that I worked on with the bid team and that were to prove not only important to Capita but also to me after I left the company in 2006. The first was a contract won by our Strategic Education team to support the delivery of National Strategies in relation to Primary and Key Stage 3, on behalf of the Department of Education. Its work assisted Local Education Authorities to raise standards in learning. The team that transferred to us from the previous provider, CfBT, contained a large number of people who went on to help with the implementation of the Academies Programme.

The other contract was with our 'Urban Vision' joint venture with Salford City Council, where we would be assisting regenerating the City across property, engineering, highways and associated support services. This bid was run by Richard Marchant and won by our property services division, and it represented the beginning of a relationship with Salford that is still going, twelve years on. This relationship led to my introduction by the CEO John Willis to The Lowry, an exciting new theatre and gallery complex they had developed in Salford Quays. Although I didn't know it at the time, I was to become chairman of The Lowry.

For our property services business, which started all those years ago with the acquisition of JE Greatorex, it was also a highly significant year because it saw the acquisition of the Symonds Group, which propelled Capita Symonds into being the seventh largest multidisciplinary consultancy in the UK, with over 3,000 staff in forty offices.

On 15 March 2005, as we approached our twenty-first year, we had a dinner attended by over 150 people at the Dorchester Hotel to mark 'our coming of age'. I was joined as a speaker on the night by Charles Dunstone, the CEO of the Carphone Warehouse, who was on his way of building a massive business which would reshape the telecommunications market. I did comment in introducing him that in the year of our formation in 1984 the first mobile phone had just been launched, weighing three quarters of a kilo and measuring more than a house brick!

I also made specific references in my speech, welcoming John Scotford, a former President of CIPFA and my first Chairman of CIPFA Computer Services. Noel Hepworth, the director at the time of the MBO, who had taken a dim view of our plans all those years ago, also attended. I referred to the difficult time between us but stressed that I never lost my professional respect for him. If CIPFA had played this better, it could have taken credit for having had the forethought to create the beginnings of a FTSE 100 company from within the public sector. I was also delighted that my eldest son Michael was with me on that night as one of the guests.

Although I continued to work well during this period, on reflection building Capita had become an obsession with me. I felt for some time that Jacqui and I had been growing apart, perhaps compounded by my focus on work. This led me to think even more deeply about my life goals and ultimately to my feeling that Jacqui and I should go our separate ways. This was an extremely difficult decision because I knew the enormous impact that this would have on our children. My sense was that while Jacqui and I had come a long way together and enjoyed many precious family moments, it was the right decision. I eventually moved out of the house in Farnham in August 2004.

Carol McGoldrick joined Capita on 3 December 2003 from Liverpool City Council were she had been working on Liverpool Direct, the joint venture that the council had with BT. She had the responsibility of leading the transformation of back office services to take them into the front line provision of Liverpool Direct ultimately involving 250 staff. Carol was approached by our Big Ticket Sales Team for her to bring that experience to the bids that Capita had underway. Carol and I first met in March 2004 when I became involved with a review of Capita's Hertfordshire call centre contract. Carol had been asked to review its performance. She subsequently was part of the team that worked on the Birmingham City bid which we were successful in winning – it proved to be the largest contract won in local government in our history, worth £424 million over a ten-year period. As Executive Chairman I was part of the bid team, attending meetings with the Chief Executive of the authority and members of his executive team as well as meeting key elected members. Through my working relationship with Carol over a period of time our friendship developed and we found great happiness in each other's company. She eventually became the new lady in my life and we had been together for some time when Carol left Capita at the end of 2005 to pursue her studies at KLC School of Design in Chelsea Harbour, fulfilling her ambition to become an interior designer. We both had a love of travelling and decided that it was time for me to take a sabbatical, something that is common in the academic world but was unheard of in corporate circles. The team around me supported me in this decision, so Carol and I took time off to travel to South Africa, Australia, Fiji, USA and New Zealand. It was the equivalent to my 'gap three months'!

On reflection, I still feel that, while this should become a common feature of corporate life, it was effectively the beginning of the end to my career at Capita, both from my own standpoint and that of others within the company. For some time I had been dealing with questions from the City about what my plans were for the future. In their eyes, the retirement of the founder was a risk which increasingly prompted questions at meetings with our shareholders.

My time away from Capita was split over two periods but whenever I returned I felt an increasing need to reintroduce myself to my immediate colleagues. I recall on the second occasion Lynn Chidwick actually organised a drinks party at a local hotel to 'celebrate' my return. I sensed that they were beginning to question my commitment to the business. After all, I had created a culture which mirrored my own 'all-in or all-out' approach.

In fact, 2005 was to turn out to be my last full year at Capita. By this time an independent report from OVUM estimated the potential UK BPO market valued at £94.8 billion. The total outsourced was estimated at £4.4 billion. Across all of our eight markets Capita was rated No 1 with 26.7 per cent of the market. However, the market began to attract more competition with names such as Siemens, Fujitsu, IBM, Accenture, CSC and BT becoming involved.

Above: With my family after collecting my OBE at Buckingham Palace in January 2004. From left to right: Debby, Michael, Jacqui, Jennifer and Robert.

Below: A family celebration of my knighthood with my children. From left to right: Robert, Jennifer, Debby and Michael.

At Buckingham Palace for the investiture of my knighthood on 14 February 2012, with my wife Carol, my mother and my son, Robert.

Left: My debut on the West End stage in a performance of *Les Misérables* at the Queen's Theatre, 12 October 2011.

Below: Celebrating Chelsea winning the FA Cup by beating Manchester United 1–0 in the first game played at the new Wembley Stadium, 19 May 2007. From left to right: Michael, Debby, my son-in-law, Tim, and Jennifer.

With my son, Michael, on the day my mother celebrated her 100th birthday; she is holding the congratulatory message from HM The Queen.

Above: My mother at the celebration of her 100th birthday with Katherine Jenkins, who performed for her and the guests at the party.

Left: A picture of me ('Poppy') with Carol and granddaughter Annie Rose Doris Lavender, aged fifteen months, with her parents Jennifer and James, at our house in Marbella, Spain.

Above: Darren Bennett and Lilia Kopylova, stars of *Strictly Come Dancing* who performed at my sixtieth birthday party.

Right: Me with the wonderful Lulu, who sang at my sixtieth birthday celebrations.

Above: From left to right: Gary Barlow, Howard Donald and Mark Owen of Take That with Carol and me before performing at my seventieth birthday celebrations.

Below: Sir Tom Jones and Alexandra Burke with Carol and me before performing at my sixty-fifth birthday celebrations at the Lowry.

Carol and me (Poppy) with grandchildren Florence and Atticus at our house in Spain.

17

THE LABOUR LOAN – FIVE DAYS THAT CHANGED MY LIFE

As early as 2004 it became inevitable in my mind that I would leave Capita at some point in the near future. I was in my late fifties and I had achieved far more with the company than I would ever have thought possible. But I also began to wonder for the first time in many years: 'What's next?' I was getting to the stage where I was beginning to feel that there was more to life for me outside of Capita.

I was going through the final stages of the divorce proceedings with Jacqui and I was concerned about the effect that was having on our children.

I also had a growing sense of unease about my role within the business which, quite rightly, was becoming more externally based working with the City, meeting existing clients and working on new bid situations. The size of the business grew so much that I was drawn into areas that took me further and further away from the people within the organisation.

I was enjoying my role as the Chair of the CBI's Strategy Board because it gave me a national profile and a route to work with government ministers and senior civil servants. It was clear to me that the outsourcing industry was at a crossroads. It needed to say more about its achievements and illustrate its ability to tackle the inefficiencies that existed unchallenged in public bodies.

The industry also needed more companies to challenge the competitive positioning of the big boys such as Capita, Serco, EDS and IBM. Without this competitive challenge my view was that the opportunities in central government would remain in-house, and events have proved my forecast accurate. Many of the smaller companies resisted growth, either through lack of ambition of the management or a fear for the impact that growth would have on them. So many were happy to remain specialist niche players, benefiting from sub-contractor roles with the top end of the market.

As early as August 2004 Paul, Paddy, Gordon and I had begun the discussion about succession as we got more and more questions from both the analysts and shareholders about my future plans. We were equally aware that Paul was being approached on a regular basis by headhunters for other larger roles. So on both fronts it was an issue that the team needed to plan for in our usual open way.

Following one of our meetings Paddy circulated a paper he called an 'Aunt Sally' which summarised our discussion and was intended to act as a thought provoker to help us get our minds around a structure that we could live with going forward. In his paper he linked this to a suggestion that we needed to make significant changes to the Executive Board if we were going to develop other senior players within the business.

The paper started from the premise that I might move to non-executive Chairman in July 2005 with reduced hours, giving me the scope to develop my other pursuits, mainly my philanthropic work as an academy sponsor. At the same time, it was planned to promote two or three of the existing executive board directors to the Group Board, with two having the title of Co-Group Managing Directors, giving the opportunity for them to shadow Paul. In June 2006 the paper suggested the appointment of a new Chief Operating Officer (COO) from one of these two people.

In January 2007 we modelled a theoretical date when Paul would announce he would leave in June that year, with the new COO taking over as Chief Executive. With the June 2007 results statement I would then announce leaving at the end of 2007, at which time I would be sixty years old. As for Paddy, he would move to a non-executive role in January 2007 and Gordon would 'call his future' any time after June 2007. We had the strong feeling that succession should come from within the business so as to protect the culture that we had worked hard to create.

But the plan did not quite work out. History confirms my openness in sharing my intention to step down with my colleagues. As other events unfolded, however, I only made it through to July 2006 and not to the end of 2007.

Of the members of the Executive Board, Simon Pilling was made Joint Operations Director in August 2006 with Paddy assuming a similar role. However, Simon left on 20 January 2007 because of a disagreement with Paul about the direction of the business. Paddy moved to a non-executive role in March 2010, ultimately retiring in March 2012. Paul stepped down as CEO in February 2014. Gordon Hurst remained as Group Finance Director until his retirement in February 2015. All of the original members of the Executive Board, therefore, had left the company apart from Maggi Bell, who had been promoted to the Group Board in August 2008 as Business Development Director responsible for the Big Ticket sales operation. She retired from this role in 2016.

All the other Executive Board members at that juncture left the company at differing times for various reasons but in my view, the key one was that they had reached the limit of their capability and capacity to deal with the growth that Capita was still experiencing.

In hindsight, deciding to promote from within was the wrong decision and the time had come to recruit a person into the business, perhaps as Chief Operating Officer, to introduce new thinking and allow time for the individual to become acclimatised to the business.

Towards the end of 2005 I had decided that rather than moving to the non-executive Chairman role we had discussed, the time would be right for me to retire from Capita completely the following year. It was a big decision but I was quite comfortable that it was the right one.

At around that time there had been increasing criticism of other executive chairmen who had moved to become non-executive chairmen of the same company, with shareholders and the press claiming that they could not be considered to be as truly independent as the other

NEDs on the Board. Ahead of making this big decision, I actually went to see three individuals I had known for some time who had been through this process themselves to learn more about their experiences and views.

That was the background to how I was feeling when I began to be seriously courted by the Labour Party. It is important to differentiate between the party itself and those who held ministerial roles in the Labour Government. The HQ machine was run by a general secretary along with a team of supporters who dealt with the regional network, keeping a clear eye on local and national elections.

There was also a heavy focus placed on fund raising and for Labour a high proportion of this still came from the unions. This was no different from the Conservatives' money-raising strategies, except that 'successful business leaders' instead of Unions were the ones who made major contributions to the party. The experience that I subsequently had points to why there is a serious need to continue the work that has been done on reviewing and changing the way that political parties in the UK are funded.

My political views are something I have never expressed publicly, even when pressed by journalists. Internally, in meetings with Paul, Paddy and Gordon there was regular banter, particularly with Paul, about my leanings towards the Labour Party and my socialist views. It was always very clear to them where I stood, as it was equally clear that Paul was not a Labour supporter and more capitalist in his leanings.

In political terms I was very much a 'centre ground' supporter, which was the territory claimed by Tony Blair in positioning the Labour Government. I was most definitely not a supporter either of the hard left or of the far right extremes of politics. Therefore, in Blair I saw a moderniser holding a position that I could support, particularly concerning his plans for public service reform and his stance on the importance of education. He was also prepared to take on the unions to drive through the changes he saw as important, even though a considerable amount of funding for the party came from that direction. I became a member of the Labour Party on the day of the 2005 general election.

THE LABOUR LOAN THAT CHANGED MY LIFE

Some people may have believed that I was a passionate Conservative supporter, particularly after Capita's early successes under Margaret Thatcher when we were dubbed 'Thatcher's child'. Yet if they knew anything about me and my deep affection for my dad, who served proudly for many years as a trade union branch secretary, they would know I was a Labour man from background and upbringing. The truth is that throughout my whole career, and most definitely my twenty-two years in charge of Capita, I have worked very closely and successfully with senior politicians from both Conservative and Labour Parties, nationally and at local level, without ever openly supporting either of them or them asking me to do so.

I had built up many good relationships with senior people in the Labour Government and so, as the CEO of the largest and most dominant operator in the outsourcing sector, it was no surprise when I was seen as a person whose views should be sought. As early as April 2000 I had been asked to submit a paper to the No. 10 Policy Unit to feed radical ideas into the development of the government's long-term strategic thinking relating to the transformation of public services and the customer experience of them.

After the success of the Congestion Charging Scheme, I was asked to write a short paper for No. 10, setting out the reasons why I believed the implementation had been such a success and why the Criminal Records Bureau had initially run into high-profile problems. This I did, as it seemed to me it could become a template to be used for future projects.

I was asked to go to No. 10 to meet some of Tony Blair's closest advisers and discuss my report. It was not the first time I had been to Downing Street because for well over a decade one of my most important functions as Chief Executive had been to make sure that everyone around government understood the benefits of outsourcing, and that they knew the ethos and values that Capita had, particularly towards staff and our method of operating with clients. The team at No. 10 was at the heart of this and it was important to have a relationship with the PM's key advisers such as Andrew Adonis, Robert Hill and Sally Morgan (now Baroness Morgan of Huyton) along with the senior civil servants, including the Cabinet Secretary as head of the civil service.

To Capita, in a business sense, it did not matter which party was in power, only that whoever was in government continued to outsource the services that were the foundation of our business.

To confirm how it works in the real world, the contracts that Capita and other companies bid for in the public sector were subject to EEC procurement regulations. This meant that the whole procedure was deeply process orientated, with civil servants and their appointed team of external management consultants from the large firms running the show. The chosen operator would emerge from this process which will have taken into account price, suitability to deliver and the acceptance of contractual conditions set by the client. The recommendation for the successful operator in the bid would then go to the appropriate permanent secretary and on to a minister for final sign-off.

In this world there is no way that any personal commitment of the chairman of a bidding company to any political party is relevant to the final decision. To ensure that no such favouritism is shown in central government bids, the National Audit Office monitors things from an independent standpoint, and MPs on both the select committee relevant to the department concerned as well as the Public Accounts Committee have the power to investigate any suspicions.

MPs, of course, can also ask questions in the House and Freedom of Information requests can be made by anyone about virtually anything. Sitting alongside this is the press and social media's insatiable appetite for a news story. The idea that Blair or anyone else close to him, could have called up someone in one of the government departments and said: 'Rod's a good bloke. He is one of us. Give him the contract will you?" is absurd.

Similarly, I have to say that if you are in difficulty with a contract there is no way that any political allegiance helps you with the client. I have ample evidence for this in the case of the Criminal Records Bureau as at no time during the troubled start of the agency did the Minister responsible come anywhere near us to support me as CEO just because I was a supporter of the Labour Government!

Sadly, in today's cynical society, people in Britain will never believe, rightly or wrongly, that political allegiance has no influence on the awarding of contracts. That is why I hold my hand up to the mistake I made in lending money to the Labour Party. It was also around this time when the 'cash for questions' incidents occurred, drawing into the debate the role of PR lobbying companies with MPs. There has always been a question over who receives honours, and in particular those who are elevated to the House of Lords.

For this very reason, I was always absolutely clear that as CEO of a company that benefited from government contracts, I would never make a donation to any political party. It was just never going to happen. That didn't stop the Labour Party inviting me to events and some of them were fund-raising dinners.

On reflection, this was when I may have first stepped over the line, since a number of these events caught the eye of the press. The people attending were named in press articles and some pieces even included the seating plan for the event. I always paid for attendance myself to make it clear that I was attending in a personal capacity and not on behalf of Capita, and the company always knew of my intention to attend.

It should be noted that the Conservative Party held similarly high profile fund-raising dinners attended by many of the great and good from industry. In the early days, I even had invitations from them to go to their events as well, and did attend several drinks receptions, including one about e-business on 6 November 2000 with William Haig and Michael Portillo.

I attended these events, as many of my counterparts did, partly because they were a good way of meeting ministers to explain the benefits of outsourcing and the services Capita could offer. However it was usually clear from the body language of many ministers that they were attending under sufferance, most probably under a 'three line whip' from the party.

In a personal capacity, I also attended small dinner parties, some organised by the Labour HQ team and others hosted by private individuals, to learn more about the government's approach to areas that interested me, such as education, public service reform and unemployment. I even took part in a plenary session at the party conference in my capacity as Chair of the CBI Strategy Board on a panel stressing the benefits of outsourcing and the role of the industry that I represented. It was a way of answering the extreme feelings that some members of the Labour Party had towards the private sector and our supposed mistreatment of staff.

Capita also attended the Conservative Party conferences, but not the Liberal Party conference which was most probably a mistake since they would go on to form the coalition government with the Conservatives. I personally nursed a hatred of attending these events. To me they were places used to foster disloyalty as much as loyalty to a cause or a person. There were also too many people there who never listened to anyone else's point of view, and were only concerned with their own opinions.

At one major Labour Party fund-raising dinner that I attended in March 2001 I met Gordon Brown, along with several other ministers and was introduced to Lord Levy. I knew he was extremely close to Blair and his role was to raise funds for the Labour Party. I agreed to his request to meet for lunch.

When we met, it was apparent that Michael Levy had done his homework on me. He knew just about every fact about my life and career that had ever been printed. I am not naïve. I knew I was being targeted. He had worked out my own personal politics from press interviews that mentioned my father's union activities Although I recall he did struggle with the definition of a 'sheet metal worker' when I proudly told him that was what my father did. I was also well known to the general secretary of the day and no doubt Michael would have had a briefing on me before we met.

They clearly hoped I would change my mind about making a donation to the party, but neither Lord Levy nor anyone else asked me to go back on my word. And so I continued to accept the invitations to events as it enhanced my understanding of the current thinking around transforming public services. I have often wondered since if choosing to do so was a mistake, as I was being openly drawn into a well constructed and selected inner circle.

Some of the invitations were not to fund-raisers at external venues, or to receptions at Downing Street, but to Lord Levy's home where Jacqui, and subsequently Carol, accompanied me. These visits were hosted by Michael and his wife Gilda, with typically around twelve people invited for a supper. At some point over pre-supper drinks Tony Blair would arrive with his wife, Cherie. This obviously felt very special, yet these were extremely informal occasions.

Unlike other events Blair attended, here he was far more relaxed. This was a chance to hear his views on a wide range of national and international topics. It was also an opportunity to have a few minutes' private one-to-one conversation with the Prime Minister.

I was invited to attend three of these dinners over a period of three years, and one involved a cross-party discussion on the proposed City Academies Programme, where I was well on the way to becoming a sponsor. One of the first sponsors that I met through these dinners was Sir Clive Bourne, who was the sponsor of an academy in Hackney where he was born and lived. This was to become known as the Mossbourne Community Academy, named after his father Moss Bourne, and its first Principal was Sir Michael Wilshaw, who went on to become the Head of Ofsted.

The team at Capita always knew of these invitations and I was briefed accordingly about points that they wanted me to stress to the PM. I included my attendance at all such events in my reports to the Group Board.

I had been a big supporter of Blair and found him to be a charismatic leader whose views I could support, apart from his later decision of going to war. I don't think these evenings were just for our benefit. The Prime Minister spent his time constantly surrounded by advisers and civil servants and I think it was genuinely valuable for him to have frank discussions with people outside politics, where he could take the pulse of new policy initiatives.

At these dinners I always took the opportunity at some point in the evening to reiterate that I could not donate to a political party for as long as I was with Capita. I suppose that statement implied that if ever I left Capita I would be willing to think about it.

It just so happened that I had started to think it might be time to move on. I thought it was nearing the time when the best thing for the company would be for me to announce my intention to retire and give the shareholders time to get used to the idea. I even drafted a potential statement confirming that but pulled back from sharing it with the Board it at the last moment.

Michael Levy was also an ambassador for the academy movement and so I had previously worked with him and with Andrew Adonis when I became one of the first sponsors of the Academies Programme. In a sense, this was supporting a Labour Government-led initiative to change education for the better in the UK. To become a sponsor meant providing £2 million of funding towards the capital cost of building the academy, and this played into the hands of the network of Labour supporters that Levy had developed, many of whom also made political donations to the party.

The Academies Programme was also an outward demonstration of New Labour in action, openly soliciting donations to be used for the benefit of the community. Had the academy policy been led by a Conservative Government nobody would have thought anything about Tory donors, many of whom would have been business leaders, becoming beacon supporters of such a scheme. The difference here was that the private funding for this big change in education policy came from cause-related donations rather than politically-led donations, even though the initial sponsors were mainly Labour supporters.

The experience I had of working in both the public and private sectors at a senior level was an unusual combination for one individual to have and therefore of real value in thinking through the structuring of public policy changes. Equally, the work that I had done in the voluntary sector, called the 'Third Sector' at the time, with my appointment as Chair of V, the volunteering charity, and now as an academy sponsor through my own Foundation, increased my ability to work in any of the three sectors or to hold a post which related to all three.

My thoughts were, therefore, on how best to use these skills after leaving Capita. I began discussing this with a whole range of people, including civil servants and politicians, usually in meetings that had been arranged to discuss public sector reform.

I had several meetings with Lord Levy over lunches and talked about a range of different subjects, including his role as the PM's Ambassador to the Middle East, my role as the chair of the CBI on public service reform, along with my position as chair of V, as he was President of Community Service Volunteers (CSV) and therefore interested in my thoughts on the sector. We also had spirited discussions over football, as he was a long-time season ticket holder at Arsenal, as I was at Chelsea. In July 2004 Jacqui and I were also invited by Gilda, Michael's wife, to his sixtieth birthday event at No. 1 Horseguards, attending along with 300 other guests.

At one of these meetings in late September 2005 I was told by Lord Levy that the Labour Party had serious cash flow issues. Apparently it was even getting to the stage that they would soon be unable to pay salaries. They knew I would never give a donation, but asked if I would consider making them a short-term loan. It was confirmed to be the case that if this was made on a commercial basis there was no requirement for it to be reported or registered, other than in the party's accounts.

I was then referred to Peter Watt, who at the time was Deputy to Matt Carter, the General Secretary of the Labour Party. Peter confirmed that they could not pay forthcoming salaries and bills. The party was up to its limit on borrowings and the Co-operative Bank was not prepared to extend their overdraft facility.

I decided after much soul searching that I would lend them the money. It was at this point that I crossed the line from my corporate world into the political world. I've thought about why I did it a great deal ever since. I admit that, at that time, I was emotionally charged by my divorce and the added prospect of leaving Capita. A big part of the decision to go ahead with the loan was also driven by thoughts of my father who, had he lived, would have been in his ninetieth year. As a union rep, the party obviously meant a lot to him and he had dedicated himself to ensuring that people received a fair return for their hard work. I felt that if I could help out the party at a time of crisis, as the son of a sheet metal worker, I certainly wanted to do so.

After various conversations with Peter Watt, I received a letter from Matt Carter on 4 October 2005 setting out the terms for the loan of £1 million to be made by two advances of £500,000. The interest on the loan was at a rate of 6.5 per cent, equivalent to Bank of England base rate plus 2 per cent, and repayable in October 2006. I made the first payment of £500,000 in October 2005, just before Carol and I left for a holiday in South Africa and Mauritius. I followed this with the second payment of a similar amount in December 2005.

It was later alleged that this was a secret arrangement between me and Labour, but that is frankly ludicrous. It was documented on headed Labour Party notepaper and sent to me at the Capita offices in Victoria Street. I mentioned it to my accountants, as the interest would need to be declared to HMRC on my Annual Tax Return and to my bank manager at Lloyds, to whom I recall saying: 'I expect to be having this back!' To be clear, Lloyds were not the bankers to Capita, who continued to be Barclays. I say this because one newspaper article even suggested that I had used company funds to make the loan – what a world we live in! I knew that the transaction would appear in the Labour Party's annual accounts, and I remember asking Peter Watt the date that these accounts would be published. Hardly the actions of anyone hoping to keep the affair under wraps!

However, I did keep it from my colleagues at Capita because, as far as I was concerned, it was a private arrangement between me and the Labour Party. I was using my own money. I also knew that when the Labour Party published its annual accounts and the loan was disclosed I would be out of Capita, since I had already made the decision to retire in the summer. I would no longer be the Executive Chairman of Capita at that point.

Of course, that's not the way it turned out! The key question that I failed to ask at the time, and I am deeply disappointed in myself for not doing so, was: 'Am I the only one lending money to the Party?' As it transpired, a similar approach had been made to other individuals, in some cases involving larger sums than my own million. Had I asked that question and been told the extent of the loans being asked for, I know that I would have refused to be involved, simply because I would have definitely have questioned the party's ability to repay loans of this magnitude, judging by its financial position.

At some point in early 2006, I became aware of stories in the press about two or three people who were going through the formal approval process with the Lords Appointment Commission, chaired by Lord Stephenson, to be elevated to the House of Lords. As part of this process it was revealed that they had made loans to the Labour

Party and their applications had been blocked because these loans had not been declared.

I was stunned. This was the first time I knew that I hadn't been the only one to lend the party money. Suddenly I was no longer the guy who had helped to save the day when the party was facing difficulty in paying salaries. I was part of something much bigger and more orchestrated.

As the story unfolded, the basic allegations were that, since political donations had to be declared to parliament, Lord Levy had arranged for certain people to lend money to the party instead. In some cases, it seems there was an implicit understanding that these loans would eventually be converted into donations. It became known in the press as the 'Loans For Peerage scandal'. I must make it clear that at no point was I ever offered a title as an incentive to provide the loan, nor did I ask for anything in return for my loan apart from its repayment. I was quite clear; it was a loan, *not* a donation.

The media began to focus on the story and started to investigate how many other people had lent money to the party. Articles appeared daily, although no reference was made to me, and I could sense that, politically, this was gaining a head of steam. Within the party itself and from the Conservative opposition it was seen as a way to get at Tony Blair, who was on the ropes at this time.

Carol and I were at the cinema on the Sunday evening of 19 March and I received a text from Michael Levy asking me to call him that evening no matter what time I got home. I must say that I lost interest in the film from that point onwards. When I called Michael at his home at around 11.15 p.m. he told me that the National Executive Committee had requested, and was to be given on the following day, a list of the people who had made loans to the Labour Party. This list included my name. He informed me that No. 10 had decided to publish the list in advance of the NEC meeting to avoid the information leaking to the media from that source. He was obviously very annoyed about this and apologised to me as he had already done to all the others, but this move was caused by No. 10 wanting to get ahead of this and make its own statement to usurp the National Executive's plans.

I was livid, to put it mildly. I knew I was about to be catapulted into a media circus when I had done absolutely nothing wrong. I did not know it at the time but in just four days I was going to stand down as Executive Chairman of the company that I had taken twenty-two years to create.

DAY 1, MONDAY 20 MARCH.

On Monday morning when I was walking to the office, by chance I bumped into Hilary Armstrong, who was then the government chief whip, along with her husband Paul Corrigan, who was an adviser to No. 10 on health matters. I knew them both well on a personal level and Paul had done some work for us at Capita prior to the first Labour election win. I recall that I made some garbled comment about checking if they were around later in the day as I would like to call them about an event likely to happen that afternoon. I have never asked Hilary but do not believe that, even as a member of the Cabinet, she knew of the announcement at that moment.

I continued to walk to the office in Victoria Street, past Parliament Square, thinking through how I was going to handle this with my colleagues, knowing full well that the matter was serious.

This was to prove to be the worst week of my working life.

When I got in I called both Shona Nichols, who was responsible for our PR, and Jonathan Hawker, who specialised in dealing with the more challenging issues that we had around some of our contracts, such as the CRB and Congestion Charging – so he was most definitely the man for the job here!

I asked to see both of them in my office immediately. I told them of the impending announcement concerning the list of those who had lent money to the Labour Party and that I was on it. The immediate reaction was shock, but Shona seemed placated by the confirmation from me that I had not been nominated to join the House of Lords, and was not tainted by the claims being made in the press of 'loans for peerages'.

Shona and Jonathan immediately then went into 'defence mode', discussing the risks of the story to Capita. We agreed that they should discuss this with Financial Dynamics, our External PR advisers, and we should regroup after that.

I then called Paul on his mobile because I knew he was at a presentation that we were making for a private sector sales situation involving Volkswagen. He was measured, clearly not totally surprised, but equally very angry that I had chosen not to discuss it with him before making the loan. We agreed to speak later in the day.

Shona, Jonathan and I had a meeting involving Andrew Lorenz of Financial Dynamics later that morning to form an agreed initial position statement prior to the announcement which was scheduled at midday.

The battle lines were clearly drawn as, not unreasonably, Shona recommended that I should appoint my own PR adviser to act for me, to help make it clear that the loan was my own personal decision and had nothing to do with Capita. She recommended that I should speak to Gordon Tempest-Hay of Blue Rubicon, who we had worked with before and with whom we had good relations. This proved to be one of the best pieces of advice I had because Gordon did a brilliant job for me. He was calm, clear and decisive throughout.

The news broke and all hell broke loose. It immediately spilled over onto the political pitch and the government and the Conservative opposition lined up against each other, with, it felt like, me and other lenders on the list becoming the political football.

Next I called to speak with Paul Corrigan as I had promised, and while he and others close to me expressed profound sympathy, effectively the shutters came down. I felt completely isolated.

I had warned my immediate family, including my mother, to expect bad publicity but had reassured them that I had done nothing illegal! My face appeared on every newscast for the BBC, ITV, Channel 4, Sky News and even CBS News. Capita issued a statement saying that it was my personal decision to lend money and it had not been discussed with the company. Gordon Tempest-Hay handled the immediate requests for interviews from BBC News, ITV News, Channel 4 News, Channel 5 News, World at One, News 24, Radio 4 Today, BBC Scotland, BBC Hard Talk and the Dimbleby programme. We rejected all requests for an interview and basically went to ground that day to see how the story developed.

The news happened on the very day, believe it or not, that Jacqui and

I were at Heathrow Airport to see my youngest son, Robert, depart for his gap year. That is an emotional occasion for any parent. I remember seeing my own face on the BBC News, just as he was going through passport control. That was not a great moment in my life. The whole thing was pretty tough and was bound to get worse.

DAY 2, TUESDAY 21 MARCH

On the Tuesday the newspapers were full of the story and my face, along with that of others who had lent money, appeared on the front of the *Daily Telegraph* under the headline: 'The 12 who bankrolled Blair'. I was also portrayed in the piece as the 'most controversial name' on the list simply because of the prominence that Capita had in working with central government. All of the national newspapers carried the story but it was my smiling face alone that appeared on the front of *The Financial Times* under the heading: 'Labour Party's financing – Aldridge loaned £1 million'. Gordon Tempest Hay again had requests for me to go on BBC TV, Channel 4 and Sky to 'put my side of the story' but we rejected all approaches.

I had a meeting at the Home Office first thing in my role as the nominated Chair of V to discuss the progress that had been made in setting up the charity. I was determined to go to the meeting, despite the storm clouds that were gathering, in order to show the team, mainly consisting of civil servants, that it was 'business as usual' for me. In their world there must have been many occasions when they had to weather a political storm around their minister or issues in the department itself. There was a degree of sympathy for me but I am sure in the back of all their minds the question was: 'How long would I remain as Chair of V?'

When the meeting was over, I was on the way back to the office when I took a call on my mobile from Carol who told me that the cinema area of the house we had recently bought in Spain had been flooded due to torrential rain the previous night. In a way this brought a sense of reality to what was going on around me. The fact that I was even remotely concerned about that at that time demonstrated the importance of Spain in our plans after my retirement from Capita.

Once I had arrived back at Victoria Street I couldn't get in because of all the press people outside, so I had to enter via the back door. There was a sense of deep shock in the building, along with a cold uncomfortable feeling on our normally 'warm and positive' floor, with even Lynn clearly nervous.

Paul's office was next to mine. His door was closed and I could see that he was on the phone. I waited until his call was finished and went in to have a conversation with him. He was clearly very angry, informing me that my action had put at risk the Birmingham City Council contract we had recently won and he had just spoken to the Leader of Birmingham to reassure him that it was my personal decision to loan the money to the 'f****ing Labour lot' and that he knew nothing about it. He suggested that he and I should speak later rather than now. I decided it was best to leave the office and go home. I recall meeting my close colleague John Tizard on the way out, and finding that he was equally shocked at the announcement by No. 10.

As I reflect on this terrible period, I remember that I increasingly felt that this may have been the moment that people had been waiting for, the thing that would bring my departure to a head. It's not easy when you're the founder and you've been there for twenty-two years. You're not impregnable, but it's not likely somebody is going to come in the door and fire you.

When I arrived home I suggested to Carol that we moved out of our London flat for a couple of nights because there were media people all over the place. So we took a room at the Soho House Hotel, hoping that things would blow over.

Paul and I spoke later that morning and he suggested that he came over to the hotel to have lunch with me. This he duly did, walking past the pile of *FTs* in the hallway with my smiling face prominent on the front page as we went into the restaurant. It was clear he had had a conversation with both the Non-Executive Directors as well as with Paddy and Gordon. He was no longer angry, but having worked with him for fifteen years I recognised the charm offensive for what it was and the underlying clarity of thinking that was emerging.

He suggested that I should come over to the office to meet with himself, Paddy, Gordon and Shona later that afternoon. This I did but from the tone of the meeting it was clear that there was little sympathy for my position. I spoke of the need not to overreact to this and that things would blow over. After all, the claims of favouritism affecting contracts were obviously ridiculous and all those in the industry would recognise this as such, as would our clients.

I listened to them talking about the concerns that had been expressed by some clients about my now declared political allegiance to Labour, and how our Big Ticket bid team was concerned about the reaction to the coverage from a number of the prospects that we were bidding on.

It felt like an unreal situation where people were waiting to see how we reacted rather than seeing the situation for what it was: an escalation of the political battle between Blair and Brown. I can recall even good old Gordon Hurst shaking his head, saying that it was a crying shame and asking: 'Why did you do it, mate? They are not worth it,' with several expletives added to his sentence! We agreed to regroup the following morning to give me time to reflect on things and, I assumed, to allow Paul to take further soundings.

What then began to emerge was a wave of emails expressing support for me. These came from members of staff, from current clients and even from competitors who stressed the need not to overreact. These messages, of which there were many hundreds, were collected together by Lynn and eventually found their way into a printed book for me to keep.

That evening Carol and I had dinner with my son, Michael, and his then girlfriend (now his wife), Georgia. I have always valued Michael's input and with Georgia being a reporter for both BBC and Sky, her judgment was particularly relevant in these circumstances. Over dinner we decided that I should stand up for what I had done as it was a personal decision and I had been well within my rights to make it. We should allow the storm to pass before making any final decisions. However, Michael said that there was a growing wish within the family that I should retire from Capita and do some of the things I wanted to do, particularly with regard to education. It was therefore felt that I should use this opportunity to set a date for this to happen.

THE LABOUR LOAN THAT CHANGED MY LIFE

DAY 3, WEDNESDAY 22 MARCH

The next morning the real reason behind the 'rushed' decision to publish the names began to appear in the press. Apart from an attempt to turn the political spotlight on the Tories, who had refused to name those who had lent them around £20 million in the run-up to the General Election, it seemed that Labour's National Executive wanted to seize back control of party fund-raising.

A meeting to discuss this was held on 21 March and had been attended by the Prime Minister, the Deputy Prime Minister, John Prescott and Gordon Brown, to discuss a report prepared by Jack Dromey (the party's elected treasurer) on the origin of the loans. It was Dromey who had reported to the press the previous week that in his role of treasurer he had not been told about the loans, and the Chair, Sir Jeremy Beecham (now Lord Beecham), claimed the same.

The Home Secretary, Charles Clarke, fuelled the debate between the government and party chiefs by reportedly claiming that there were: 'serious questions about Jack Dromey's capacity as Labour Treasurer if he did not know about the loans.'

I find it difficult to believe that the person in charge of finances for the Labour Party, or indeed any organisation, would not be aware of £14.9 million of funds that appeared in the party's bank account! This was a material sum and it must have featured in any financial reports prepared for the Executive, particularly around election time, when without it the party would be bankrupt. So this was a political game of which I had unwittingly become a part.

Back in my world, I went into the office that morning direct from the hotel, with added resolve to see this through. The same group of close colleagues assembled in Paul's room, a domain that he always used since it is where he feels most comfortable. I opened the meeting by stating the tactics that I had thought through with my family the previous evening, about not overreacting. However, I could immediately judge by the body language in the room that things had moved around me and it was definitely now a game of them against me. We were no longer a team.

I think the non-executives had already been primed by Paul. Basically, it was stressed to me in the meeting that there was a sense that this wasn't great news for the company and that it was time for me to go and do whatever I wanted to do. I fought against that initially, believing I was in a strong enough position to win their support, but when something like this happens, you are never the same as before and the point comes when you have to work out whether you can get through it or not. My instinct was that it had reached a point of no going back. I wanted to go to do other things, so the discussion now had to be about how to achieve the best outcome.

The meeting finished without an agreed position, but the direction of travel had been set. I went into my office and shut the door to reflect on it all. I had a conversation with Gordon Tempest-Hay to discuss tactics and then followed this with calls to the three NEDs. All three were of a similar view that I should go, so as to limit the damage to the company. My strong sense, particularly in the case of Martina King, was that the 'party line' had been pushed on her by Paul. The other two, Peter Cawdron and Eric Walters, would never stand up to Paul to fight my corner.

I needed to take independent legal HR advice on my position from my lawyers, Withers, who were already dealing with my divorce. I needed to be clear about where I stood under the terms of my contract.

So I sat in my room on my own composing the statement that I would make. I was clear that I was not prepared to resign, equally I was advised that it was not a sackable offence, and neither Capita nor I would want to go to court over a constructive dismissal claim. So I had to find a more elegant solution.

At no point over these four days did any of the executive board colleagues come anywhere near me, which was a further indication of the hardening of the position around me and a lack of courage on their part to express a view to my face.

What we agreed for the statement issued was that I had taken the decision to stand down as Executive Chairman with immediate effect and to become Non-Executive Chairman, meaning that technically I was not involved in any executive decisions about the business and therefore became another NED on the Board. Simultaneously the statement announced that I would retire as Non-Executive Chairman and leave the company at the end of July, timed so that I could front our next presentation to the City on 23 July, reporting our results to 30 June 2006.

The comment from me in the statement said:

> At present, the Group's reputation is being questioned because of my personal decision to lend money to the Labour Party. As I have made clear, this was entirely my own decision as an individual, made in good faith as a long-standing supporter of the party. There have been suggestions that this loan has resulted in the Group being awarded government contracts. This is entirely spurious. Whilst anyone who is associated with the public procurement process would understand that this view has no credibility, I do not want this misconception to continue, as I remain passionate about the Group's wellbeing.

In the evening I went with Jennifer, Robert and Michael to watch Chelsea play in an FA Cup sixth round match against Newcastle. While we were watching the game I got a call on my mobile from David Hill, the PM's political adviser, asking why I saw the need to resign over such an issue, which was merely a political scrap. These people are truly amazing, living in a Westminster bubble of their own. I told him that it was too late, the damage had been done and it would be announced to the City in the morning.

Thankfully, Chelsea won!

DAY 4, THURSDAY 23 MARCH

An announcement to the city was made first thing, confirming my decision to stand down as Executive Chairman and become Non-Executive Chairman until my retirement. It was also widely reported in the media. My mobile was overloaded by messages, many of them emotional expressions of sadness from people within the business that I had worked with for years, and even from some who had left the business.

It was a tremendously difficult decision for me. For twenty-two years I had loved every day at work and I had always imagined a fond farewell from colleagues and investors, all of whom had done well out of Capita. I was genuinely upset that a single lapse of judgment on my part had deprived me of the perfect end to a perfect career. I had to accept that I had made the wrong choice when I made that loan. The consensus of my colleagues, our shareholders and the Press was that my swift resignation had been the right choice.

I had agreed to speak at a lunch that day on public service reform and I was determined to go on with life as normal as much as I could. So I went to the event and the organisers were both relieved and pleased. Relieved that I had turned up and pleased because they had pulled off a coup with me being so newsworthy! I was pleased that I went as former permanent secretary Sir Richard Mottram, who is infamous for his liberal use of expletives in tough situations, was also at the lunch. He was able to back up the points that I made over both procurement and the politics around the matter.

On my way back to the flat my driver took me around Trafalgar Square, where there were several placard boards on stalls selling the *Evening Standard*, and the words emblazoned there were: 'C-Charging Boss Resigns over Labour Loan.' I thought that you had to commit a murder to achieve such notoriety but the *Evening Standard* had finally got the story they wanted.

AFTER DAY 5 24 MARCH

On the Friday, *The Times* attempted to bring Gordon Brown into the loans issue by declaring that I had been made Chair of his flagship project youth community service scheme for young people just weeks after making the loan in October. The timing was correct but there was most definitely never any connection between the two. I did not meet Brown until he succeeded Tony Blair as PM. Brown continued to maintain that he had nothing to do with party affairs.

Also on that day, Carol's mother and father came to stay with us from Liverpool, as did my mother, in preparation for Mothering Sunday. We planned to go out for a meal that evening to Ken Lo's Memories of China, a favourite restaurant of ours. While sitting in the lounge the side door bell to my flat rang. This was very unusual as there was a concierge who screened visitors, allowing those who were welcome to come up to the penthouse by lift. It turned out to be a reporter, who had got through this system by making her own way to the penthouse, seeking an interview with me. She even continued asking questions through the intercom system as I politely told her to leave immediately. We ended up going straight down to the basement by lift, where our driver was waiting to take us to the restaurant to avoid other journalists that were in the road outside the flat.

The weekend papers were clear that I had done the right thing in my decisive action to stand down. Robert Cole of *The Times* wrote a piece headed: 'Aldridge has done the honorable thing' along with a cartoon depicting my head being held in my arms with the word 'decapita'. In the piece he commented on my decision to act decisively rather than following the politicians' normal route of hanging on as long as possible before going.

On 27 March I received a call on my mobile from the PM's office asking whether I would mind the PM contacting me directly, to which I agreed. Tony Blair called me the following day. He recalled our previous meetings and said that he was very sorry for the week that I had had. He apologised for the fact that he had not spoken to me personally before the matter blew up in the press. During the call I told him that I had been summoned before a select committee. He didn't comment about that and indeed it never happened because the subsequent Metropolitan Police enquiry made this impossible. I explained that this situation had caused me to step down from Capita, the company I had built up over twenty-two years, and how badly I felt about this happening. I felt sympathy in his response, but it was time for him to move on to the next crisis he had to deal with, and so the call ended.

I took two weeks off, meaning that for the first time since I started the company I missed a Group Board meeting of Capita. I was angry, very angry, but I kept my nerve and kept my own counsel. I didn't do anything unadvisedly press-wise. I wanted to get through the AGM to be held on 25 April and the results that were due to come out on 20 July.

THE AFTERMATH

The days that followed were pretty horrendous. Every journalist in the country seemed to want me to say if the Prime Minister was involved, and it seemed at least half of the country's newsgatherers wanted me to comment. Papers and news channels rushed to choose me as a target for their investigations. Gordon Tempest-Hay dealt with this for me and we retained the rule of making one statement and not adding anything further to it. This turned out to be a masterstroke, as by commenting I would simply give journalists more to comment on.

I felt angry with myself and with people in the Labour Party, and at No. 10, who I felt had handled things badly. I was angry with Paul and some of my colleagues because I felt they could have been more supportive. But mostly I was angry with myself. I could not believe that I had never asked if I was the only person making a loan. If I had known there were twelve of us, if I had known the loans added up to nearly £15 million, it would have been quite clear that the Labour Party's 'cash flow problems' were a lot more severe than Lord Levy or Peter Watt were making out. If only I had asked. But I hadn't.

The atmosphere in the office at Victoria Street showed no signs of recovering. People were walking around, heads down, avoiding eye contact with me. After several weeks I had had enough of this so I asked Lynn to arrange for all the executive directors along with Paddy, Gordon and Paul to a meeting in the boardroom first thing on the following morning. I had scripted at home what I wanted to say, as I knew it was an emotional time and words do not always flow as well at such a time.

I started by apologising for my actions. I confirmed that I had been thinking about leaving for some time and had even drafted a statement to that effect. I explained the background to my decision and that I had discussed it with no one. I was equally promised nothing in return. I explained about the timing of the announcement by No. 10 and how I first heard about it. My decision to stand down immediately as Executive Chairman was taken to protect the reputation of Capita, particularly because of the suggestion that we won contracts because of the loan. I recognised the enormous work it had required by a number of people to limit the damage.

And I then said that I had found it deeply distressing to have been treated in this way by many of the people around this table. I could only compare how I would have reacted to a close colleague that had gone through such an experience, whatever the rights or wrongs. I said that it would have been inconceivable for me not to have made contact with them on a personal basis, no matter what the individual had done.

I ended by setting out my plans for the future, confirming that I had no intention of retiring. I went on to say:

> Nothing can change what has happened but I ask that we draw a line under it and move on. I know that you will continue to be successful and that Capita will continue to go from strength to strength. As a shareholder and the founder of the business I want nothing else. I leave with a sense of a job well done, of many happy memories and Capita very firmly in my heart. I intend to have a leaving do in September because I have had so much support from within the business about my leaving and I want to say goodbye to Capita in the right way.

This had impact. Many heads were down, and people were unable to look me in the eye. Maggi was in tears. Throughout my speech I did not even look at Paul. Following my words, one by one, four of the five executive directors came to see me in my office, expressing their personal views to me. What this confirmed to me was that I should have called us together sooner. At the AGM on 25 April, I was able to say that under my guidance, since the flotation in 1989 the shares in Capita had increased 127-fold, meaning that £10,000 invested at the float would be worth £1.27 million today.

There were other unpleasant consequences that I subsequently had to face. In April, I received a letter from John Yates, Deputy Assistant Commissioner of the Metropolitan Police, asking to interview me as part of their inquiry into allegations regarding the loans and honours.

Clearly I needed to appoint a lawyer at my personal expense to represent me. I went to Christopher Murray of Kingsley Napley, who was superb. He helped me draft a statement about the whole affair and this was submitted to the Metropolitan Police ahead of my interview, which took place in May at the offices of Kingsley Napley and with my lawyer present. I sat in front of the Metropolitan Police officers and simply read the statement word for word. Under instructions from Christopher, when the police asked me questions, I simply didn't reply. When you see people being interviewed by police officers in TV dramas and refusing to say anything, it all looks so easy, but it is actually really difficult to give no response at all when someone is firing questions at you.

It was a thoroughly unpleasant experience. I thought: 'Why am I going through all this?' They obviously had no evidence that I had done anything wrong as I most definitely had not and it was equally obvious from the body language of the officers that this was their conclusion as well. The senior police officer concluded the meeting with an attempt at humour, thanking me for overseeing his pension through the contract that Capita had with the Metropolitan Police!

As is always the way with these things, when the police investigation cleared all parties, including Lord Levy, of any wrongdoing, the news did not get quite the same publicity as the original story. To be fair, it was not such a big deal for me either, as I had always known I had done nothing wrong. There is nothing illegal about an individual making a loan to a political party. I should add that the loan was repaid in full with interest as agreed, but over a longer period than originally expected.

During this very stressful and challenging period in my life, a wonderful family event took place. On 10 June my eldest son, Michael, married Georgia. The wedding was in France in the Gers region, the area famous for foie gras. The ceremony was in the cathedral in the centre of Lectoure and the reception was at the chateau home of Georgia's mother Saint Mere. It was a glorious setting and a memorable event spread over three days of celebrations. Robert flew home from his gap year travels in Australia to be an usher, only to return to Sydney after the event was over.

Returning to the realities of life in London, the July board meeting proved to be the last I would ever chair for Capita. On the agenda was confirmation of record results to announce the following week and a record level for our Big Ticket sales list. I concluded the meeting with one plea, two observations and one regret.

My one plea was that we should consider seeking a purchaser of the company, merging the business with a global operator. Early exploratory conversations had been held with EDS (Electronic Data Systems). I had long seen Capita's future as the European arm of a worldwide business. It was my view that it would be difficult to keep the level of growth going that shareholders were expecting. Under no circumstances did I want Capita to fail or to see the fallout of a profits warning. Equally, I always felt that Paul would leave within a two-year period and it would be difficult to replace him.

My two observations were that the NEDs needed to be more challenging to the executive team, and that more value needed to be placed on the development of the market: a role that I had played, particularly for the last four years. This had not been fully appreciated but needed to be recognised as there was nobody in the executive team equipped to do it and without it, outsourcing would stall.

My one regret was that it had ended like this for me. While nobody can take away my record of achievement, I told them that I left Capita feeling completely empty.

My last report to shareholders was on 20 July 2006, which updated analysts on the first half of the year. It was a very emotional occasion for me and I was glad to have the support on the day of Carol and my four children: Debby, Michael, Jennifer and Robert, who were in the audience.

In the statement I said that:

This will be the thirty-fifth and final time that I have presented results to shareholders as I intend to retire from the Group on 31 July. Under my chairmanship, Capita has grown from a start-up in 1984 to a FTSE 100 company today and has shaped the BPO marketplace in the UK. During the seventeen years as a public company shareholders have enjoyed a total shareholder return of 165 times, equating to a 35 per cent per annum compound growth.

I concluded by saying:

> I am proud of what we have achieved together. Our revenues have grown from £300,000 to £1.4 billion. The market capitalisation has grown from £8 million at the time of the float in 1987 to £3 billion. Our employees grew from one, me, to 26,000 and our clients grew from four to 25,000 today. I leave the business in the best possible financial and operational health, with many happy memories and above all a sense of a job well done.

I received a vote of thanks and a round of applause from the audience. I understand that in the world of the City this was a very unusual occurrence, virtually unheard of. It meant a great deal to me.

On Saturday 22 July in *The Times*'s TEMPUS column there was a piece that I am enormously proud of. It was headed: 'Runaway winner that made a virtue of being boring'. Patrick Hosking wrote:

> The shares (in Capita) have grown from an adjusted 3½p placing price in 1989 to close of play yesterday at 517p. Anyone investing £1,000 at the float in 1989 and reinvesting all dividends would now be sitting on a £165,000 nest egg. That return outperforms any other FTSE 100 Company ... From a tiddler with a market value of just £8.1 million, Capita has grown to a £3-billion company that dwarfs it rivals.

The article concluded by saying:

> Tempus first alighted on the company in February 1992 when it advised investors to steer clear on two accounts. First, Neil Kinnock might be elected and second, Labour would be less enthusiastic than the Tories on outsourcing. Wrong on both counts!

The honest truth of the matter is that I made a mistake. I have a perfect right to lend my own money if I want to. Everybody knew my politics and that I was more Labour than Conservative but I made an emotional decision, which had the potential to be misinterpreted. The loan was not illegal, but it put the company I started and loved in an awkward position by exposing Capita to false accusations of currying favour. Emotionally I was in complete turmoil. I had found myself in the middle of a political game, which I could never win. The politics were pretty shitty and not something I ever want to get involved in again. My mistake lost me something that I deserved: the chance to leave the company that I had started in the way I wanted to leave, with my head high. That thought is not very nice to live with.

A lot of people gave me massive support, but I just wasn't in the position to want to fight it. I thought, 'Well I'll move on with my life,' because I was at the point where I thought I should do that anyway. I didn't enjoy the publicity, and I certainly wasn't proud of it. I am not happy that my mistake was public, but it happened. It was an honest mistake and I dealt with it as honestly and as well as I could.

It was a difficult time and I felt the pressure. If I had been emotionally unstable then I think it could have caused depression and even a nervous breakdown. But I had incredible support from Carol and my children. They were amazing. It was bloody unpleasant for all of us, with the press even going to Charterhouse where Robert was at school. But we got through it.

I don't think many founders of a business handle their departure correctly. And at some point somebody is going to tell you to go. A lot of people stay on in a senior position as an ineffective figurehead for too long, and I think you're either doing the job or you're not. My departure could have been a lot worse, and at least this crisis brought things to a head.

I'm including this chapter in my book as a warning for any other senior business executive who may think about getting involved with the political world. I suggest that you should think twice about it and then think again. The cultures and values of these two worlds are totally different and incompatible. The political world is totally short-term and the players all know that at some time that they will lose either their power or their post, or both.

If you enter their world as a non-political person, you need to be aware that under the rules of their game, *anything goes*, as I found out. Information can be weaponised at any time without regards to its impact on the individual. Certainly a person that makes a donation will forever leave themselves open to challenge and be a target for the press. My strong recommendation is to keep well away from it, at least until a more sensible method of funding political parties is in place.

To put my comments into context and as an illustration of how easily politicians forget, I was contacted on my mobile by Peter Mandelson (now Lord Mandelson) ahead of the 2010 general election. At the time I was staying in our New York flat. Peter opened the conversation by saying that he recognised that I had had: 'a little difficulty over the loan to the party in the past' but nevertheless went on to ask if I was now in a better position to make a donation towards the party's general election costs. Unbelievable!!

There is an epilogue to the Levy saga which puts everything into the right context. It's something that I have never mentioned before, but it reminds me that, as bad as that period was, it may actually have been a blessing, indeed it is just possible that it saved my life.

Paul and I were due to be in the States to meet shareholders in New York in the week beginning 10 September 2001. One of our shareholders who we met regularly on previous trips had offices in the World Trade Center. It is, therefore, entirely possible that Paul and I could have been in the Tower that morning of Tuesday 11 September when the tragic events that changed the world forever unfolded.

It was only a dinner invitation from Lord Levy to meet Tony Blair on 12 September that prompted Paul and me to change our travel plans. Whilst, understandably, that meeting with the Prime Minister was postponed, so often we make decisions that seem almost insignificant, yet have major consequences. Had we chosen to go to New York, who knows what might have happened?

18

THE FOUNDATION – A NEW BEGINNING

On Monday 31 July, my final day at Capita, I arranged to meet my son, Michael, for a drink in Covent Garden immediately after leaving the offices in Victoria Street for the last time. I felt completely numb and disorientated. I recall what I said to Michael as he gave me a hug and ordered a pint for me. 'It's all over for me now, son,' were my words.

How wrong can you be? What I didn't know on that day was that the greatest achievements in my life were yet to happen.

It was the wrong way to leave Capita, but the right time to do so. In the month leading up to my departure I was sidelined from any operational activity and decided to focus on two things. Firstly I made sure that I visited a number of our sites around the country to thank people for all that they were doing for Capita, and for the support that they had given me through the time that we had worked together. I reiterated to them how great a company I felt Capita was, and how very proud I was of our achievements. This was not an easy task, as I remained very emotionally drained and upset.

The second thing that I focused on was what I was going to do next, particularly ideas concerning the creation of my Foundation. I had some work done during this time regarding fancy names for the Foundation, which inevitably included some words with a Latin derivation. In the end I said: 'This work is about me and my family, so why not recognise it as such and keep things simple?' So the 'Aldridge Foundation' it was.

Carol and I had a month away in our house in Spain but at the beginning of September. The Aldridge Foundation then opened its doors for business. I deliberately kept it very low-key to start with. I had made more than enough appearances in the press recently.

We began life in very cramped, leased accommodation in Tavistock Street, Covent Garden, London, just a couple of streets away from Maiden Lane, where Rich, Mike, Roger and I had planned to start Capita all those years before. There was hardly enough room to swing a cat. Still, we didn't have a cat and at first we didn't need much space. The Aldridge Foundation might have sounded rather grand but there was just myself, Sally Ritchie who joined me from Capita, and a PA.

The moment I left they cut Sally's role, and several other external roles I had, including Capita's membership of the CBI and our seat on the Public Services Strategy Board. Ironically, it was Paul himself who, I'm told, several years later made a call to John Cridland, the Director General of the CBI, asking for Capita to reinstate its membership!

So my own influence was swiftly jettisoned internally, externally with customers and with the City. I suppose that was the reaction you could expect from my successors in charge and I accepted it without comment. I never made any public remarks about it. I wanted to concentrate on throwing myself into a new world with the Foundation. I had left the job of running a hugely successful business employing more than 30,000 people on more than fifty sites around the country to start work on a new empire that could fit in one room. Well actually, we had two rooms, and we had a handy corridor, which we made into a boardroom by putting a table in it. I found myself enthused by the new, hands-on approach I had to adopt. I was happy and I had a new outlet for my energy, which remained undimmed.

Sally Ritchie did a lot of important initial preparation work involving the meetings that I had, including helping with speech writing. She was extremely able and hard working and could turn her talents to anything. She also had a great deal to do with the developments planned for the academy in Blackburn with Darwen.

THE FOUNDATION – A NEW BEGINNING

In the beginning, this was the Foundation's only project, along with the preparation work around the establishment of the new charity, Vinspired, that I was to chair. It was interesting how quickly our telephones started to ring with requests to become involved once people knew what we were doing.

I had numerous calls from headhunters, and still do. I also had a large number of private equity firms wanting me to join them to build another Capita. Why ever would they think I'd want to do that again? Even supposing I did, why would I want to do it for them? In any case, I did not want to compete with Capita, although it was difficult to find a business that did not touch it in some way, since Capita's tentacles were everywhere.

I met with a number of the private equity houses because I did miss the cut and thrust of business, but frankly it was not a world that I ever took to. In the end, to balance out my charitable work, I did get involved with two deals. The first was with Advent and its purchase from Lloyds Plc of its share registration business, which subsequently became Equiniti. I was involved until the business floated on the market in 2016. The other was with Ontario Teacher's Pension Fund and its purchase of Acorn Education, a special education needs and fostering business. Neither of these deals was as fulfilling for me as building Capita.

Of course, the painstaking business of creating the sort of Foundation that I believed would make a difference was far from easy. There was no obvious route map. I made mistakes and I later regretted putting money into a few projects but it was a learning process. For sure, I never lost the drive and passion for what I wanted to achieve. I held onto my two central planks of wanting to work with young people in demanding communities and maintaining a focus on education.

How did it feel in this early period without the trappings and lifestyle of being at the top of a large and successful business? That is a question lots of people asked me and there are two answers.

At a work level, I missed working with the highly talented people in Capita. With the team culture I promoted when I was there, anything was possible.

At an emotional level, I felt very angry throughout this period. It rankled that I had been vilified and forced to change my life, but it was right that I controlled my anger. I issued one statement to the press about my leaving, but never added to it. Gordon Tempest-Hay, the CEO of Blue Rubicon, did an amazing job for me over this period, fending off press enquiries. I refrained from giving TV interviews or making verbal or written statements, despite the constant requests, which I still get now when issues involving the outsourcing industry crop up, the most recent being the failure of Carillion. Two publishers approached me for 'tell-all', scurrilous articles, even suggesting a book. I could see it would have made a great story, but it was not the right story, and most definitely not the one I was then ready to tell.

It was a very troubled period but for some time I had known what I was going to do. I had set up the Charitable Trust in 2004 to become an academy sponsor. The work that we had started with the Darwen Aldridge Community Academy (DACA) came with me and was our first project. I was very happy to start the Foundation in a small way, without the trappings of a large organisation. I have always been a person who 'makes things happen', and quite soon they did.

All my life I have had a tendency to try to take on too many things. Sometimes this creates conflicts both in how you spend your time and in how others view your decisions. At one extreme there is a danger of slipping into the wrong work/life balance, which can be particularly difficult when it comes to accommodating all-important family commitments. Although I must say that my youngest son maintains that at Charterhouse I achieved legendary status because, as a father, I missed very few matches that Michael, Robert or Jennifer played in whether those were on a Saturday or during the week. During the week I would be in office early in the morning, go to the match and then return to the office for meetings in the evening. I have no regrets about doing this as this precious time passes very quickly.

There is a limit to how long you can go on in that way, because in the end there is always a compromise, and I think that had happened with me in Capita. There were times when it became hard to balance my role as chairman with my charity work and the work that I did with the CBI network. My colleagues never valued my work with the CBI as highly as I did.

THE FOUNDATION – A NEW BEGINNING

Carol and I were very happy together, as indeed we still are! We had two or three month-long trips away from the UK during my final year at Capita, which gave me a great feeling of freedom and escape.

Certainly I never wanted to be on holiday forever and the idea of spending my life lying on a beach horrified me. It still does. Similarly, while I love golf, the idea of playing two or three times a week is equally horrifying. Deep down I am happy to admit that I enjoy working, but I need to believe in what I am doing, and I like to throw myself into it 100 per cent. Work to me is not a chore, but a mental stimulus.

Carol was amazingly supportive of me during the traumatic period surrounding my departure from Capita. We had become very close by then and without her guidance and support over this very difficult time, I am not entirely sure where things could have ended up with regard to my wellbeing. I had the added strength from my 'Liverpool family', as I called them, with Carol's father and mother, Frank and Sylvia, along with the whole family and our wide circle of friends being incredibly supportive of me. The tremendous strain had an effect on my confidence for a time but in the end I realised that no one can take away my track record of success and achievements.

I had one event to get through before finally moving on from Capita, and that was a dinner, which my former colleagues wanted to arrange for me at the Grosvenor House Hotel on 29 September. We had deliberately agreed to delay the timing of this dinner until September to allow the 'dust to settle' after my departure. It proved to be a highly emotional evening and it was great that Mike and Rich were able to attend. Paul Pindar presented me with a book containing copies of the many hundreds of emails and letters that I had received from staff, customers and competitors wishing me well. They also had a replica made for me of the award that we received from *The Sunday Times* as 'Company of the Year'.

I look back at my speech on that evening and can recall my temporary PA at the Foundation saying to me, as she typed various drafts, of it: 'This company obviously meant a lot to you didn't it?' That was an understatement. In re-reading the speech for this book, I believe that it captured this feeling very well. I concluded by saying:

Tonight is a very special and emotional occasion for me because it is the last time that I will ever have the opportunity to speak to you as a group. I wish you well in your careers and I wish you continued success with the company. Capita is a great company and is the envy of everyone in the sector. I would go so far as to say that it's the envy of many who work in corporate life. Treat it well. Keep winning. I hate losing anything! I have no doubt that you will continue to produce good results, but I do ask that you also keep the passion for the business high on your agenda as well. For the past twenty-two years I have very much been the face of that passion and I have lived and loved every moment. The history of Capita, when it is written, will tell a great story of success. I am now a part of that history. You are the future now but I will always be your founder. I will always be the first managing director, your first chief executive and your first executive chairman. To many Rod Aldridge and Capita will always be synonymous and I'm proud of that association. Rod Aldridge may now be out of Capita doing other things with his life but there will always, always be a real love for Capita in the life of Rod Aldridge.

In November 2005, nine months before I retired from Capita, I was approached to become the chair of a new charity. It sprang from the work of the Russell Commission established in May 2004 by the then Home Secretary, David Blunkett, and Gordon Brown, the Chancellor of Exchequer, to develop a new national framework for youth action and engagement. The chair of the Russell Commission was Ian Russell, a person that I knew well. In the early days at Capita we had tried unsuccessfully to persuade Ian to join us as our Finance Director. He had gone on to have a great career with Scottish Power. Ian reported to the Chancellor in March 2005, following a wide-ranging consultation with over 6,000 young people, the voluntary sector, business and the media.

The headline recommendation was to create a new charity to take the lead in delivering the new framework. It was felt that such a major change could not be led by the civil service, nor by an existing Third Sector organisation.

The government allocated £50 million over a three-year period to support the implementation of the Commission's recommendations. This was an unusual act by government since it was giving this level of funding to a brand new body over which it had no direct control. A further unusual feature was the declared aim to attract a further £50 million from the private sector, which the government would then match pound for pound. The potential £150 million funding made gave this a high profile and provided a major opportunity to drive change in the sector through a project focused directly on young people.

They wanted somebody to chair the group responsible for creating this new charity. It was Gordon Brown's baby and he would come forward with major policy ideas when eventually he succeeded Tony Blair as Prime Minister. I was interviewed for the role by the headhunters and officials from the Home Office but, more relevantly, by a selection of the young people who had been associated with the report. I desperately tried not to come over as too formal, but more as a cool, laid-back person they could envisage working with young people. I think I even came to the interview with an open-necked shirt rather than wearing my customary tie! It must have worked, because I was offered the job and my appointment was announced on 5 December 2005, with the intention of my taking up the role in spring 2006.

This duly happened in March 2006. The timing was not great as it coincided with the publicity around the 'Labour loan' saga, prompting *The Sunday Times* to run an article trying to link my appointment with the loan. I have no doubt that there were a number of conversations held within No. 11 about dropping me from the project.

There was a popular theory that the furore over the loan stemmed from differences between Gordon Brown and Tony Blair and, as Gordon set out to distance himself from the loans issue, I was concerned that the appointment was going to be stopped. I believe that there was a lot of lobbying in support of me from different people, including the great Digby Jones, who was then Director General of the CBI.

Gordon Brown never spoke to me at that time. However, the moment he got into No. 10 I had a call asking me to go and see him.

We sat outside in the rose garden at the back of the house and he said he couldn't be in touch before then because it 'didn't feel right'. It confirmed to me the strange world of a politician! Don't go near something that's toxic, as it might rub off on you, no matter what it is!

'Vinspired' became the nation's leading youth volunteering charity, responsible for revolutionising volunteering in sixteen- to twenty-four year-olds, inspiring and engaging one million new young volunteers. The aspect of 'matched funding' from private sector bodies enabled us to attract a number of large companies to sponsor programmes which we delivered, although it effectively enabled them to design a programme to fit their key interests. The seven founders that were announced at the time were were Sky, T-Mobile, ITV, KPMG, MTV, Tesco and the Hunter Foundation.

The first thing I did was to appoint our chief executive and I made a great choice in Terry Ryall. She proved to be an incredible CEO and a remarkable person to work with. Together, we were a great team. The inaugural board of trustees I recruited with the help of the Youth Advisory Board included Manny Amadi, whom Terry and I had worked with at the Prince's Trust. Other trustees were Justin Davis Smith, Deputy CEO of Volunteering England, Fiona Dawe, the CEO of YouthNet UK, Dame Tanni Grey Thompson, then Britain's most successful Paralympic athlete, Larissa Joy of Weber Shadwick the PR Company, Oona King (now Baroness King of Bow), former MP for Bethnal Green & Bow, Trevor (now Sir Trevor) Pears, Director of the Pears Foundation, along with four members from the Youth Advisory Board.

Terry built a great senior leadership team around her and there was always a buzz in the offices at Dean Bradley House in Horseferry Road on the many occasions that I went there. Building a new organisation is never easy, but it presents a wonderful opportunity to stamp your mark, and most definitely Terry did just that. The official launch of the charity took place at the Vue Cinema in Leicester Square on 8 May 2006 in front of a theatre audience of 200 people. We themed it like a film premier, calling it "Russell Commission – The Sequel." The charity was unveiled as 'V' but we later changed it to 'Vinspired'. However, the letter 'V' inspired a number of very useful themes such as 'Vnice to meet you' on a business card or 'Vuseful' in briefing notes or 'Vgood news' on press releases.

I recall in the early days several 'high-powered' breakfasts hosted at No. 10 by Gordon Brown to encourage the CEOs of large corporates such as Adidas, Red Bull, Sony, GlaxoSmithKline, Lloyds TSB, Sainsbury's, The Body Shop, Nintendo, Bank of America, ASDA, and Nationwide Building Society to make a financial contribution to the matched funding programme. Whenever the PM was due to make a statement to the House, the team at No 10 was on the phone pressing for the names of new sponsors that he could include in his speech.

The role provided me with the opportunity of having a number of one-to-one meetings with the Prime Minister at No. 10. I recall one meeting on 9 February 2009, when it was announced on the TV at No 10 that Scolari had been sacked as Chelsea's manager. This gave us the opportunity to discuss football, particularly the PM's passion for Scottish football and his team, Raith Rovers. I would definitely say that he had a sincere wish to change the lives of young people for the better, particularly those from the most challenged communities. He saw 'community engagement through volunteering' as a key mechanism, and the work of V was very important to him.

What was different about this charity was how it engaged with young people in the way that it operated. For the first time it was possible for sixteen-year-olds to have a say in a charity representing their interests, as opposed to 'grown ups' completely running the show. This particular aspect was attractive to me but also inspired changes in the governance in other bodies.

This work left me with a very clear view of the Third Sector as one that I felt needed radical change. There were clearly too many organisations doing the same things for the same groups of people. Many were too small to be effective or sustainable. The Prince's Trust, Community Service Volunteers (CSV) and Barnardo's dominated the sector, but were rigid in their approach and I felt they had lost the innovation that led them to be so prominent.

The arrival of a new charity, formed as a result of a government-led funding initiative, was viewed as being highly suspicious in the sector and many tried to head us off before we got started. However, in the end they realised that we had both the mandate from government and the all-important funding to deliver the change in youth volunteering. I recall Terry and I going to an event attended by all the great and the good from the charity world, only for the Minister to mention the work of Vinspired six times in his opening address. I think that this gave the clear message to the audience that we were the main game in town.

The seven years I had working with Terry, her team and the trustees, was a great experience. There is no doubt in my mind that we led a massive change not only in what young people thought about volunteering, but how the Third Sector organisations approached this area of work. Essentially, V was a start-up company but it changed so much in a relatively short time.

By the time I stepped down as Chair, Vinspired had over 200 corporate partners who helped us meet our target of raising the £50 million matched funding from the private sector, which led to a massive increase in volunteering opportunities for young people. These new partners included the FA Premier League, Vodaphone, HSBC, Barclays Bank, J P Morgan, BAA and Channel 4. This was an impressive list of supporters by any measure and indicated the importance of the cause.

The Aldridge Foundation played its part in the matched funding programme in 2008 when we made a contribution of £200,000 to jointly fund the Young Speakers' Programme alongside V. This was delivered through an organisation called 'We Are What We Do' which started in 2004 as an East London charity called Community Links. They aimed to inspire people to use their everyday behaviour to make a positive difference to the world around them and had a growing online community. We went on to work with them and they caught the imagination of the press and TV, when they produced a book where young people described fifty 'game changers' who would make the most difference to the community. The publication was named after the most popular suggestion of 'Teach Your Granny To Text' which came from Sally Ritchie's daughter, Erica. Just think of the impact of that!

The aim of the Young Speakers programme was to create 400

volunteering opportunities from a diverse range of young people. They attended training in public speaking and creative campaigning methods, and received support to gain skills, knowledge and confidence to go into their communities as social activists and public speakers.

The programme was a great success and we eventually trained and supported 450 young people, mainly women aged sixteen to eighteen, from diverse schools and colleges in four cluster areas: London, the Midlands, the North West and the South West. The Young Speakers engaged in a variety of activities along with campaign groups, including delivering presentations and workshops in their own school and in other schools. In the case of the North West, it was our own academy students at Darwen Aldridge Community Academy (DACA) who led the initiative. Overall our programme involved more than 52,000 children being trained to have the confidence speak in public.

If one looked at a cross section of the young people Vinspired had interacted with, a report confirmed that we had reached 25,000 homeless young people, 25,000 young people in care, 32,000 with lone parents, 332,000 people on low incomes and 44,950 young offenders. But the key thing to me was that the independent evaluation showed that 99 per cent of young people who engaged felt more confident as a result of volunteering and 90 per cent felt that they had a better opportunity of finding employment. Almost half had gone on to further education or to get a job. An independent report on our work showed that in our first five years, when the major government investment was made, Vinspired delivered a social return on the investment equivalent to at least £6 for every £1 spent. That was a very pleasing statistic and vindicated the decision to set up an individual and independent body. There is no way that such a good return would have been achieved had the money gone directly into the voluntary sector.

The interactive website that we created (*vinspired.com*) became a national standard, enabling volunteering opportunities to be registered, linking these with young people. In its first year of operation it was used by over 200,000 young people to volunteer on projects and by more than 4,400 charities to advertise opportunities.

We held a major annual celebratory event to recognize the

successes of a large number of young people who had taken part in the programmes delivered as a result of our funding. These were wonderful, uplifting, well-organised events, hosted by Terry, who was a great communicator of our cause, using her charming Irish brogue to enormous advantage.

I find it fascinating to learn something new, and have found that my experiences since leaving Capita have changed me enormously. At Capita I had the confidence and ability to make things happen, but I didn't actually have to do all of the 'heavy lifting' involved in the implementation. Building something is what drives me, so after leaving Capita I had the urge to 'get my hands dirty' with a new project, and in the process discovered that I have even more confidence than I would have imagined. I enjoy new challenges. If I'm not tried I'm not tested. But it's not always easy. I think one of my most important qualities is my self-belief and stubborn determination, which is what carried me through into this new phase of my life. It was the same determination that had driven the management buyout all those years before. I was just a bit older. I certainly wasn't ready to disappear from the scene as many would have expected.

I was soon to learn that nothing moves swiftly when it comes to establishing academies, and persistence is supremely important. In 2006, about a year before I left Capita, I read that Brighton and Hove Council had appointed a sponsor to the Falmer High School to become an academy. This was Jon Aisbitt, a guy whom I knew and had met at several events in London. I must admit, I was quite upset by this because it was my home town, where I had tried to get involved several years earlier, before going to Darwen.

However, on 23 January 2008, I received a telephone call from Rowena Mattacks, the wife of my cousin, Keith, saying that according to *The Argus* Jon Aisbitt had given up on the Falmer High School project because of the lack of progress! I immediately rang Vanessa Brown, a Conservative councillor and Chair of the Children Services Committee. I knew Vanessa from my childhood days. Her brother, Christopher, was one of the three male dancers at our same dance school and my parents were great friends with hers. I said to Vanessa:

'If you're up for it, I would like to become the sponsor at Falmer and I am prepared to get involved right away.'

Fortunately, the Minister of Education at the time was Lord Andrew Adonis and he was very supportive of me becoming the sponsor. He'd also had enough of the council and told me: 'They have taken me down the aisle once too often.' He said I was the only sponsor that he would consider as he reopened the discussions. We were able to reach an agreement quite quickly with the Department, and that became the next academy we worked on.

I made the call to Vanessa on a Tuesday and on the Thursday I was in a meeting with the then Chief Executive, Alan McCarthy, and his team. This was something else to throw myself into but I learned that embarking on such a project in my own town was difficult. In Blackburn with Darwen, a long way from home, everything was much less emotional. In Brighton, where lots of people knew me, I felt anxious. The stakes were higher and failure was inconceivable. Press coverage very quickly ramped up and my mother, an avid reader of the local paper (*The Argus*), regularly asked me: 'Rodney why are you doing this? Let them get on with it!'

When I finally went to revisit the school, I found that it had deteriorated even further since my visit in 2004 and was in the most appalling state. It had panes of window glass missing, large sections of peeling paint, weeds growing on roofs and classrooms in disrepair. It was disgraceful that kids were in this shocking environment. I recall being shown around the school by an individual (who I won't name – he doesn't work for us any more), who said: 'I don't know why you are coming here. They don't need you as they will only end up as hairdressers or labourers or on the dole.' With anger, I realised that all those years ago, the same could have been said about me by my teachers!

Unsurprisingly, the lamentable condition of the buildings was heavily linked with the school's poor academic results. Those in charge had to do something and obviously they had already decided that they wanted to have an academy as a way of addressing the funding issues for rebuilding work. The two outstanding features that the school did have were amazing playing fields and a wonderful view across the Downs. It was very close to the new home for Brighton and Hove Albion at the newly constructed AMEX stadium. This had taken 18 years to get through the local authority planning process! For me it was definitely a case of being in the right place at the right time and I was determined to make a difference. It was time that the students and community had a voice.

I had spent some time getting the local politicians on side and the next move was to meet the existing governing body and the teaching staff of Falmer High. Irrespective of what I have said about the condition of the school and the poor reputation it had, there was still a great love for Falmer from parents who were ex-pupils. While I naively thought that I would be welcomed as a sponsor, I actually faced a great deal of hostility to the plans from the community, the staff and the local unions, attracting the attention of the local press.

In one of my first visits to the school, one of the senior leadership team explained to me that, based on the background of the students and their level of academic understanding, the results achieved were actually very good. I listened intently to an explanation attempting to present the shocking statistic of eight out of ten students leaving school aged sixteen without five A–C grades in GCSE (including English and Maths) as 'acceptable performance'! From my first meeting with the teaching staff it was clear that many were stressed and some had been there far too long. Change was necessary, and I had learned from my Capita days that in such circumstances honesty was the best approach.

Meanwhile, the road to success in Blackburn with Darwen was still a long and troubled one. We had a design for the new building and we were ready to go, but there was still the fraught matter of planning permission. In the end the matter went all the way to an appeal and the High Court. During 2007 we ended up giving evidence to a public inquiry at a time when the atmosphere was very hostile against us, and particularly against me as the sponsor.

The inquiry was held in a hotel in Darwen over a three-day period. Our newly appointed Principal designate for the Academy, Brendan Loughran, spent the first nine months of his time with us, not in a school but preparing for the inquiry. I was questioned in public and, thanks to the unfortunate timing, I was also grilled about the 'loan to Labour' business, implying that I was trying to sponsor a school as some kind of penance!

There was an attempt to discredit me as being a suitable person to sponsor an academy and it was suggested that, since Capita was a large local employer, I was set to make huge financial returns from my sponsorship. There was a certain irony about this, as I was about to make a personal £2-million contribution towards the building of the academy. Our opponents did not have a QC on their team, as we did, and their case was run by an individual who was a strong campaigner against the academy. His name was Simon Huggall and he was ultimately elected as a councillor. I will always remember as I left the room after giving evidence for an hour, Mr Huggall came over to me and said how much he wanted my involvement in the town and what a great company I had built in Capita!

This opposition was irritating and very frustrating, delaying us for almost two years. Eventually we won the appeal hands down, and then forged ahead. We gave a clear message to the people of Darwen that we were there to stay and had no intention of throwing in the towel, as several other sponsors had done in other towns because of the hostility they faced. The Anti Academy Alliance was spreading rumours and gossip about us, turning up at public meetings and running campaigns against us. Having been chairman of Capita, I was frequently targeted. It sometimes put me in a difficult position being both a sponsor and the chairman of a company that had a substantial business relationship with the council, and it is probably another reason why I should have left the company earlier. I was beginning to do things, which, while you could argue that they were good things, some would say might be compromising Capita's position, even though there were no financial or political benefits to the company from my involvement as an academy sponsor. Public opposition was not nice but in Blackburn with Darwen, I had the strong support of the council. I don't think I would have succeeded without that.

The school in Darwen first opened as an academy in September 2008 but it was in the old building in what was termed the 'predecessor school'. The name over the door was changed from 'Darwen Moreland' to 'Darwen Aldridge Community Academy'. This was more than four years after I had first approached the council. Initially Brendan Loughran had to manage the opening of the academy in the existing school we were replacing, while we were building the new one. We eventually moved to the site of the new £48-million school in September 2010. So something which started in 2004 opened six years later.

Once I became involved in the bid I remained committed to the project, and I made that point to the inquiry. Effectively, I used the situation against the critics, particularly as the educational performance in the existing school was so far below standard. Much of this was down to poor leadership.

I was angry about the delays engineered by a handful of local people determined to stop the academy by using the planning process to appeal against decisions that had been approved by the local councilors. They were denying the rights of local children to receive an outstanding education. I thought, 'You're just plain wrong,' and so I kept going. Once you're in a public process you have to keep going if you feel you're right, whatever the opposition. I'm a stubborn kind of guy. One of the key traits of being a successful entrepreneur is determination, and I certainly don't like the idea of giving up on something I believe in.

Once we had a design and an indication from the Department that the funding would be available, the next stage was to select a contractor to build it. It was a complex site and the design mirrored this, with an incredible educational space along with a new sports hall and artificial surfaces for sport. The only thing that the site lacked was sports fields with natural grass surfaces.

My job then was to chair the monthly meeting that was held to check on progress. We had a group to work with Brendan in structuring the curriculum and designing and equipping the classrooms. That was an eye-opener for me to the world of interior design, with no previous experience to draw on. It was only when the site was cleared of houses and sundry buildings that you could begin to envisage the finished school's appearance. There was a further delay, however, when it was discovered that we had Japanese Knotweed. This had to be eradicated because, if it got into the concrete foundations it would, over time, cause untold damage. The treatment to kill off the knotweed needed three months to do its work.

As the building began to take shape it was breathtaking to see it grow. Brendan used this stage as an opportunity to involve the students in regular visits to the site. Our excellent contractors, Kirkland and Whittaker, played their part by offering apprenticeship-style opportunities to the older students.

At this time, the sponsor had the right to select a specialism for the academy to follow. I decided to go for entrepreneurship, because I wanted students to be in a position not to wait for a job, but to have the desire to create a job, through starting a business. That didn't mean I expected every pupil would one day start a business, I just believed our school would open up their young minds to such possibilities.

On one visit to the school, one of the boys asked me where I had parked my helicopter! He had watched *The Apprentice* and thought we all flew around the country like Lord Sugar. I got to know Steven Birch when he was just twelve. What struck me was his motivation for becoming an entrepreneur. He told me that his granddad had an engineering business but it got into difficulty and the bank closed the business down. Steven said that he intended to buy the business back from the bank because he felt that his grandfather had been badly treated. Having met him at various times, notably when he left DACA to go onto university, I would not want to be the bank manager that he eventually negotiates with, but I would definitely back him to make a go of his business.

Returning to Lord Sugar, he is most definitely not my favourite person, and I have constantly had to explain to parents that if their son or daughter wants to follow an entrepreneurial route, aspiring to be like *The Apprentice* contestants is unnecessary. During my time none of those egotistical types would get a job at Capita. In my book, being self centred and obnoxious does not make you a person who can work with a team and command respect, as many of them seem to think. These awful character traits are demonstrated weekly on *The Apprentice*, and were mirrored by Donald Trump in the show's

American equivalent as well as in his personal behaviour as President of the United States.

I have also had to make clear to parents that the programme *Dragons' Den* is not real life. Anyone who wishes to start a business needs to be encouraged, because it is not easy, as I know. Such entrepreneurs should never be criticised or humiliated.

I will not forgive Lord Sugar for the way that he treated a student from DACA. We arranged, through one of my contacts at the BBC, for twelve girls from Darwen to visit the BBC to speak to a senior female executive about women in business. To travel to London from Darwen requires a big commitment, and the intention was to demonstrate to the girls attending that anything was possible for them. One of the keenly enterprising girls who was waiting in the reception at the BBC recognised Lord Sugar, who had arrived for a meeting. She was very excited about this and summoned the confidence to approach him to ask for a photograph with her. He was direct and rude in his refusal. While that reaction can perhaps be understandable if you are famous and frequently approached, sadly the impact on her was shattering.

To try to repair things, I wrote to Lord Sugar and suggested that he should visit DACA to see what we are doing on entrepreneurship and to explain to the student why he acted in the way that he had. I did not even receive a reply. However, I have vowed to mention his actions in every speech that I make on entrepreneurship, because I believe that you do not need to treat people so appallingly to be deemed a successful business person.

In fact, we are keen to ensure that our pupils see that an entrepreneur is not just a super-rich tycoon. We want them to know that the person running their corner shop is an entrepreneur as well as a shop assistant, and that the individual who fixes their family car is an entrepreneur as well as a mechanic.

We majored on the entrepreneurial attributes such as team working, determination, risk taking and passion, so as to drive the thinking of both students and staff. These were very much the attributes that helped me build Capita and to develop as a person. To implement this, we designed into the building structure a series of entrepreneurial pods, which would allow students and the community to run a business. These were housed on an entrepreneurial bridge at the very front of the building, in full view of everyone who passed the Academy.

The problem that we faced was that the money for the structure of this assembly was not in the funding envelope from the Department. In stepped Blackburn with Darwen, and they helped us find a source of money to which we could apply for the funding. We made a successful bid to the LGI European Fund for £836,673 to build the Entrepreneurship Centre, including the Entrepreneurial Bridge, which housed eleven business pods. These provided workspace for young entrepreneurs and community social enterprises. I always said that I could have started Capita in one of these! This whole concept was branded as 'Darwen Creates'. To unlock this funding was most definitely a great example of entrepreneurial thinking and the power of acting as a team.

Another first was the introduction of a Sixth Form. Previously, students had left school at sixteen, with some going to the local college and none going on to university.

All this was about to change and it was one of the challenges that I had set myself. A key part of staffing was, of course, the TUPE process for staff moving from the employment of Blackburn with Darwen to the employment of the Trust established for the Darwen Aldridge Community Academy, or DACA as it became known. The issue it was necessary to address after the transfer was: 'How many of the teaching staff would stay and how many were to leave, based around competency and the budget that we had to run the school?' We kept the staff regularly updated and I did a number of presentations setting out the Foundation's vision for the school.

We had to set up a new governing body and, for the first year, I chaired this, proving to myself what a difficult role this is. One or two of the governors on the previous governing body seemed keen to join the new body. One was Bob Simpson, who proved to be a wonderful supporter of our work. Along with this we persuaded two or three people with educational experience to join, one who had a national role in education. A local businessman joined and we recruited a staff governor and a parent governor. The legislation around governance had been written with the intent of the sponsor having control of the governing body should a vote ever occur.

All things considered, sponsorship is most definitely not easy and brings with it huge responsibilities. The time commitment for meetings of the main monthly group and various sub-groups was not inconsiderable. This whole sponsorship experience is definitely not for the faint hearted and takes a lot of energy. I stuck with it, and Sally Ritchie played a major role in making things happen on time.

DACA was my first big experience of the Foundation's work and I am still very proud of what we achieved. It is a massive improvement on what was there before and will provide life-changing opportunities for generations ahead.

There were many reasons behind my decision to establish The Aldridge Foundation, but the central motive was to bring about social change for young people through the education they receive. It also provided a structure around me to determine where I donated money. I had the time to be able to get involved in projects, rather than simply providing the funding. My time working with The Prince's Trust most definitely opened my mind in so many different ways, particularly concerning education. For that I will always be grateful.

I met a number of people through The Prince's Trust who made an enormous impact on me, none more so than Mark Johnson. Mark is a very charismatic individual with a colourful background. He is an ex-offender who has written a remarkable, award-winning book called *Wasted* which charts his own experiences on the wrong side of the law. Having been through The Prince's Trust programme himself, he established his own small enterprise in Dorset, employing ex-offenders in a tree surgery business. He became an adviser to the Trust, endorsed by the Prince of Wales.

He shared his experiences about some of the hard times released prisoners go through when they try to find work, and the handicapping effect of an ever-present criminal record. Mark wanted to work supporting ex-prisoners to get back into society. When we met we got on so well that I was happy to help him, and gave him a desk at the Foundation so he could come and work in our offices. This inevitably involved many other ex-offenders joining him, so at some times we had maybe ten people with criminal records working on a project in the building. By then we had much more space than the original two-room set-up in Tavistock Street, having moved to larger offices at Buckingham Street.

Mark's point of view was that, rather than simply locking criminals away, you should try to understand the causes of their criminality. He was very articulate and very persuasive. I always said of Mark, to his face, that he is one of the few people that I have met who has the ability to make himself central to everything about which you are thinking. I became involved to the extent that I could have gone down the route of helping people in prison but, after a great deal of consideration, I resisted it because, frankly, I found the problem so depressing. My role in life was to stop young people going to prison.

You were given a startling reality check when you walked with Mark around the area of the Strand or cut through Villiers Street to get to the Tube. Mark would say: 'I used to sleep in that doorway,' or when passing Pret a Manger: 'This is where we came to get sandwiches at the end of the day, when they were out of date.'

I went with Mark to Feltham Young Offenders Prison just outside London, and I will never forget the shattering experience, my first visit to a prison. Mark was there to meet prisoners to answer their questions, explaining about how to go straight once they were released. The deal was that they had to read his book as a sort of homework project. I sat in with one young lad, no older than my youngest son, who was inside for a series of burglaries. He had a girlfriend and baby outside, waiting for his release.

Not only had this chap, let's call him Tony, read the book, but he had numerous yellow post-it notes on various pages, where he wanted to ask Mark questions. It turned out that he had been excluded from school, was dyslexic and his father was also incarcerated. The intensity of Tony's questioning indicated to me that he was serious about going straight, but I wondered how he would cope with the pressures of the outside world without reoffending and finding himself back in prison like so many recidivists.

While I was there the prison staff demonstrated two things to me about what it felt like to be on drugs, and the impact that this could have on you. Both involved putting on a set of glasses to look through, simulating what it felt like to be under the influence of drugs. The first exercise that they asked me to perform was to take hold of a ball and to roll it towards a set of skittles. This I duly did, missing by a mile. My sense of distance and direction had gone. It then got more serious, as they gave me a plastic knife and formed a circle around me. The head guard then told me to attempt to stab the person opposite me. Although I could identify the person I thought was opposite to me, I ended up 'stabbing' the person two to his left. Thus I understood how an innocent bystander can become a victim just by being in the wrong place at the wrong time.

This visit upset me so much that I cancelled everything I had planned for later that day. I couldn't handle what I saw, but I believed in the message that Mark was trying to put across. I think Mark is an incredible man, even though he can be very demanding to work with. He is equally very persuasive about getting pro bono support, which I admire, plus as I found out personally, he's good at raising funds!

In April 2008, as part of his plan to start his own charity, The Foundation funded a seminar, which was Mark's brainchild. It was held at a hotel just outside Birmingham, and aimed to examine why 75 per cent of young offenders reoffend within two years of release. What was different about this event was that it was designed to give a platform to current and former offenders. The thirty-five delegates had clocked up 200 years of incarceration between them.

It was run and organised entirely by offenders. Although me and my team were there, we did not take part in the discussions, which helped to increase the openness within the group. Interestingly, they were predominantly people who had already made a decision to change their lives. Many had taken degrees, and several had two degrees or even a masters, but as I remember it, few had been able to secure a job.

Again, this was a real eye-opener for me. The seminar included people on a methadone programme (designed to control a heroin addiction), tagged offenders and a serving offender released on temporary licence to attend the event. The crimes they had committed varied from gang related, violence and drug-related offences to armed robberies and even more serious crimes, which carry life sentences.

The report of the seminar was called 'User Voice of the Criminal Justice System.' We published the report and it received wide press coverage. I was even interviewed on the *Today* programme on Radio 4. It was 'User Voice' that Mark was to go on to take as the name for his charity. A central point of the findings was that it is the 'User Voice' which can express the reasons for the failure of the system that costs so much public money, but because they are never asked they do not have a voice.

This experience deeply influenced my thinking relating to how students are dealt with in the academies that we sponsor. There were some concerning statistics in the report to show how much impact education has on people's lives, such as exclusion from school. In the general population, some 3 per cent have been excluded. In prison it is 30 per cent. There were similar figures around numeracy and literacy. So many prisoners had problems that started in their schooldays.

From my visits, I found out that many people learn to read in prison, which is too late to stop the damage that is done to young lives. This put into context the work that I did with The Prince's Trust on the xl programme, and the enormous responsibility of being an academy sponsor.

I spoke with the then Cabinet Secretary, Sir Gus O'Donnell, about my work in prisons. He agreed to meet the team to listen to their points. To me this was testament to how open-minded Gus was about the transformation of public services. Mark and the team were very nervous about presenting to the Cabinet Office, and I encouraged them to rehearse what they were going to say, which they did in our offices.

And I remember walking down Villiers Street, the very same road that Mark had slept rough in, with his team of fifteen ex-prisoners on our way to Whitehall, to present the findings of the report. Gus had assembled his senior team of policy advisers on reoffending and our team presented the case to them very well, not holding back on formality! They explained exactly what it was like to be in prison and how prison authorities were then working, and why their methods were not going to stop reoffending! It was a very striking performance. They got Mark's message across very well and I felt that much of what he said was absolutely right. Reoffending is a huge problem and Mark brought a great deal of good sense to this difficult subject. I am pleased to have helped him to get his message across.

I learnt through this experience that 66 per cent of the people who go into prison have no job, 75 per cent have no job to go to when they come out and 30 per cent have nowhere to live on release. It is therefore not rocket science to see why they reoffend.

In 2009 with seed funding from The Foundation for three years, plus the transfer of the talented Daniel Hutt from our staff to be his number two, Mark established User Voice as a new charity that would allow him to realise his greater vision. He was determined to allow users of the criminal justice system across the country to have an input into how their own futures can be changed, and to show how young people at risk of offending can be prevented from entering a downward spiral.

It was a fairly low-key start-up but User Voice went on to create a unique model of Prison Councils, leading to a democratic, issue-focused process for constructive dialogue between prison staff and their charges. User Voice now employs over 300 people, and is a highly successful social enterprise with a head office and five regional offices.

I have long had an instinct for backing people and that is still with me. Mark has done a great deal of good work and helped to create a lot of opportunities for ex-prisoners. He has gone from offender, to local entrepreneur, to nationally respected adviser and reformer. I was attracted to Mark for a variety of reasons. He was open and honest about what he had been through and passionate and determined about what he believed in. He was fighting what he saw as injustice. I learned a lot about what it was like to go through rebuilding a life after passing through the prison system.

In the 2015 Queen's Birthday Honours list, Mark was awarded an MBE, which is an amazing statement of how highly he is regarded. In the speech I was asked to make at the gathering to celebrate his award I said that the award represented the next phase of his story and achievements. I concluded by saying that that he now had an added responsibly to continue with his journey and that he now owes this to others. He has done just that and now has a regular column in *The Guardian* in which he continues to promote the cause.

For my sixtieth birthday celebrations I held an event at the Dorchester Hotel in London. Following all that happened concerning my departure from Capita, for me it was a way to combine a celebration with the broadcast of a clear message that I had no intention of disappearing from the scene.

I thought hard about how to mark this landmark and in my speech I confirmed my decision that with matched funding from The Prince's Trust, I would have a special edition of Mark Johnson's book *Wasted* produced and we would fund the placing of twelve copies into the libraries of all 136 prisons and young person's institutions in the UK. The impact of this was incredible. Mark received dozens of letters every week from prisoners who had read about his own transition and who were inspired by it.

For the event itself, we had the legendary Lulu to perform after dinner. She was wonderful! Also, as a big fan of BBC's *Strictly Come Dancing* I arranged for Darren Bennett and Lilia Kopylova to give a dance demonstration for us.

What nobody other than Carol knew, was that I had spoken with Lilia about her partnering me for a dance routine. This would be hugely embarrassing for me if it turned out to be a disaster, so I took it very seriously. I met up to practise with Lilia on four occasions before the night of our performance. I had chosen the Tina Turner song 'Simply The Best' to dance to. It was incredible to experience Lilia choreographing a routine simply by listening to the music and basing it around my dancing capabilities.

Although I had danced before, Lilia bore in mind that it was a very long time ago, and she was very kind to me, but I was left with no doubt about why she had won *Strictly* with England cricketer Darren Gough. She was an amazing teacher.

During the time that we had together practising I spoke to her about the power of dance that I had experienced as a young man and how I thought that dance had a place in developing the students that we had within our academies. It became clear that she and her husband, Darren, felt the same. They already had a large dance school in Sheffield called City Limits, working in association with Darren's father and his brother Dale. We agreed to meet up to discuss this after the event at the Dorchester.

To dance with Lilia was an amazing experience. I am not sure if I scored one of Len Goodman's 'Sevens!' or Craig Revel-Horwood's 'Darling, it was terrible!' and three measly points, but to me it did not matter. In a very small way, at sixty I had experienced again what I had felt like dancing in front of a crowd at the age of twelve. What a great night!

Subsequently there was plenty of activity on the Foundation front. Meeting Darren and Lilia had given me the idea of introducing dance into our academies, and the three of us met to discuss this at the Foundation's offices, in Buckingham Street just off The Strand.

Darren and Lilia felt that introducing more dancing into schools would help with a lot of social issues, about the ways boys and girls treat each other, and with discipline. With my own childhood experience of dance, I recognised all that. So I agreed that The Foundation would fund the start-up for the programme and we committed to work together on producing a teaching product for schools to encourage young people to dance.

We named it 'Essentially Dance' and it began as a small working group that I chaired. We had representatives from professional ballroom and Latin and American dancing through Darren and Lilia. They are professional dance teachers, as is Darren's brother Dale, who was also involved along with another dance teacher, Lorraine Drolet. We also had a physical education teacher, Sue Cooper. The thinking was based around successful projects that had taken place in Croydon run by Lorraine, and by Sue through the Rawmarsh School sport partnership.

The concept of Essentially Dance was that we trained teachers to deliver to pupils in school the basics of cha cha cha, waltz, quick-step and jive. From the experiences of Dale, Sue and Lorraine, this type of dance had motivated many disengaged children to participate in an activity not normally offered in the curriculum. Also, the nation's enthusiasm for dance had been boosted by the Saturday night viewing figures of *Strictly*. Carol and I got to know the late Sir Bruce Forsyth and we were fortunate enough to be invited by him to see the show on several occasions, which was a wonderful experience. Bruce truly was a national treasure!

The resource was designed by the team in our offices and it was great fun listening to them writing down the steps through the closed doors to our boardroom. There would be calls of 'one-two-three, one-two-three' and 'forward, side, together, back' interspersed with shouts of laughter, plus other interludes involving loud discussions and disagreements. What they prepared was a dance programme that complied with key stage one to five of the national curriculum.

The package included three booklets and DVDs covering beginners, intermediate and advanced, with step-by-step demonstrations from Darren and Lilia. Each resource included three separate training days for two teachers per school. The basic concept was that you taught teachers to teach. You put a professional dancer into a school who then taught the teacher (probably the music or PE teacher) how to teach dance and provided them with scripts and videos outlining the details.

This training was delivered by Dale and Lorraine in a cluster of schools, with primary and secondary staff all dancing together. I am told that it proved to be immense fun and was most definitely a great success judging by the take-up. We piloted the programme in twenty-nine schools around the country, based around Blackburn with Darwen, Salford, Rawmarsh, Bromley and Brighton. This resulted in Darren and Lilia visiting each area, demonstrating the programme and wowing teachers and youngsters alike with their performances.

I was at the events held in the Darwen Aldridge Community Academy, Brighton Aldridge Community Academy and in the Studio at The Lowry. It was truly amazing to see the impact that Darren and Lilia had and their huge popularity. It was equally special to see the kids participating.

The pilot we produced was evaluated by Roehampton University and the results were phenomenal. It found that the Essentially Dance programme had the potential to be educationally beneficial, proving that there was a crossover between dance and academic learning. It also provided students with new learning opportunities, motivating pupils to become involved with dance and stimulating an appetite for wider physical activity. The Rt Hon. Ed Balls, who was Secretary of State for Education at the time, wrote a foreword to the report. Of course, Ed was to appear in the 2016 series of *Strictly*, experiencing the benefits of dance.

The feedback from staff was equally positive, indicating that it helped to build a more effective relationship with students that flowed over into the classroom. The challenge was to keep the quality of the delivery, which meant that further training would be required. Overall, it was deemed that the programme improved children's fitness, engagement in physical activity, social skills and classroom behaviour, with many students experiencing a boost to self-esteem.

Essentially Dance was formally launched at an event at the Festival Hall in the Southbank in front of an audience of parents, dance teachers and the Press, from whom we received rave reviews.

Unfortunately, the national dancing associations found it difficult to come to terms with Essentially Dance because, in their eyes, the programme was being delivered by non-professionally trained people, that is schoolteachers, rather than through dance schools. This seemed to me to be incredibly short-sighted. Through the programme we were stimulating more young people to dance, and it was inevitable that many would find their way to local dance schools to develop their talent.

We promoted it widely at conferences and events around the country with great success. One event I will always remember was an evening held in the banqueting suite at Stamford Bridge, the home of Chelsea Football Club. It was designed to celebrate the success of the Academies Programme, with the various academy sponsors taking tables. The evening included demonstrations from students of two academies and one was ours. In front of over 200 people I witnessed a demonstration of Latin American dance undertaken by twelve students – six boys and six girls – from Darwen Aldridge Community Academy. None had danced before going on the Essentially Dance programme. What made it even more impressive was that none previously would have had the confidence to attempt this before we got involved with the school. For many of them it was probably their first visit to London.

We later estimated that more than 100,000 children from all over the UK went through the programme. It was great: a case of The Foundation acting like an ideas farm. Its growth was not helped by the Conservative Government's decision to scrap the funding for the sports partnerships that existed across the country. These partnerships provided a focal point for the development of sport in local schools, including the scheduling of fixtures for matches. With the demise of this facility which essentially was the 'glue in the system', much rested on individual schools taking the lead by asking already over-committed teachers to do even more. In the case of Essentially Dance it also took away our ability to market the programme to clusters of schools, forcing us to sell it to schools individually.

Learning from my experiences at The Prince's Trust and the xl project, I realised the programme had also reached a point where the Foundation had done its job in funding the pilot and effectively the start-up. We reached an agreement that the marketing and selling of the programme, along with the support around training, would be provided via the team at City Limits.

As a result of my involvement with Essentially Dance, I was delighted to be asked in August 2009 by then Secretary for Health, the Rt Hon. Alan Johnson, to chair a 'Dance Champions Working Group' aimed at encouraging 100,000 more adults to regularly engage in dancing. It was part of a wider government target to get two million more people of all ages active by 2012 in the lead-up to the London Olympics, part of 'improving the fitness of the nation'.

My working group included the *Strictly* judge, Arlene Phillips, the TV and radio presenter Lisa Snowden, Darren and Lilia, choreographer Wayne McGregor, Mark Foster, the Olympic swimmer, and Angela Rippon. Meeting Angela Rippon for the first time was an experience I will never forget! She was one tough, focused lady. Although I must admit I had to smile when I remembered her infamous appearance on the *Morecambe and Wise Show,* when she appeared at a desk reading the news only for the desk to part and for her to step forward, kicking her legs high into the air!

I can recall a bizarre moment when charing a meeting in the Foundation boardroom. I was looking across the table to Arlene and Angela with Lisa one side of me and Darren the other and thinking, 'What the Hell am I doing here among all these experts from the world of dance?'

We held a Dance Summit attended by over a hundred people. As a 'new boy' to this, it demonstrated to me just how introverted this industry is; how full it is of people wanting to promote their own agenda rather than looking at the bigger picture. That is astounding given that the interest in dance nationwide could not have been higher with the success of *Strictly*.

I spoke at the event, outlining the broader intention of the group and the opportunity for dance to play a major part in shaping the way forward. I was able to give feedback on the new *dancechampions.org* directory, which was a free website that creates a meeting place for dance providers and the public. In spite of my feelings about the dance industry, we managed, through Angela's firm chairing of the day, to agree a range of ways to make dance more accessible. These included working with large employers to offer dance classes in offices during lunch breaks and before and after working hours. There were also calls for a government campaign to inform the public of the benefits of dance and to tackle the perception that dance is only for those who already have perfect bodies. There's a relief!

My experiences with dance have meant that we now feature performing arts in all our academies. I continue to be involved with the programme that The Lowry leads on for the North West of England. I don't dance very often myself any more, though I am always one of the first on the floor when there's dancing going on at a party.

I love watching the competitors on *Strictly Come Dancing*. I wasn't anywhere near that standard, but with the benefit of hindsight I am convinced that I gave it up too soon. I think I could have had more of a life around dance.

Essentially Dance was one of the more successful, new and different things that we tried in the early days with the Foundation. Another example of this was a pilot project called 'Your Life is Your Business' that we funded in 2009, working with DACA, a national charity called Youth at Risk and Blackburn with Darwen Local Authority. This was a personal development programme aimed at young people lacking opportunity and motivation, facing an uncertain future. It was designed to develop their entrepreneurial capability to help them become self-employed. It focused on the terrible term used by government of NEETs, meaning: young people who were Not in Education, Employment or Training. Sadly this still applies to many in our country.

We engaged a hundred young people across Blackburn with Darwen in an intensive coaching programme. Following this, we were delighted to find that 49 per cent of participants either returned to full-time education or sought to pursue a business venture. One of the great benefits of the project was that through it I met Beki Martin, Business Development Director of 'Youth at Risk'. When we advertised at the Foundation in 2013 for a Deputy Director, Beki applied and we appointed her. Overall, however, this project demonstrated that the Foundation should not go down the route of funding a series of such projects.

As a Foundation, we didn't want to become a 'think tank', issuing thought-provoking reports, since these have a limited shelf life. I wanted to be involved in 'real things' that changed lives in an ongoing, sustainable way. This led us almost naturally to becoming a Foundation that would build a family of academies working in challenging areas and using all our experiences to date, gained in working with young people, to encourage an enterprising outlook to life. As part of this journey, Sally Ritchie and I met with Michael Gove on 11 June 2005 when he was opposition spokesman for education to brief him on our work in Brighton and in Darwen. Michael went on to become Secretary of State for Education at the time when we were building our family of academies.

It was put to me once that such a structure effectively gives us a 'University for Life' in each of our communities for them to lead the transformation themselves in an enterprising fashion. We now have a plan to develop the Foundation into a charity that has a family of academies encouraging students to be enterprising and entrepreneurial in their outlook. It just took a while to get there.

This was a very happy time in my personal life. On 14 May 2008 I proposed to Carol when we were in Florence. I was delighted when she accepted but the very next month we were shattered by the discovery that she had a tumour in her tongue. We had decided to get married in December. On 8 July, the day after Robert's twenty-first birthday, Carol was admitted to University College London Hospital for a major 17-hour operation to remove the tumour. This was followed by a course of chemotherapy and radiotherapy. She also had speech therapy for more than a year. Meanwhile, still determined that the wedding would go ahead, I visited Spencer House in London as a possible venue while Carol was still in hospital. We decided to book it for our wedding. Happily Carol made a full recovery but it was a very difficult time for her and I have complete admiration for her courage in the way that she dealt with the physical challenges that she endured.

My son Robert had left Oxford Brookes University as he was not enjoying his course and had prepared a brief persuading me that he should go to follow his dream of studying for a golf degree at the American Golf Academy in Arizona. It was a very brave move on his part, as it involved him moving to a place that he did not know and with people that he had never met. My sense from the calls that we received was that he was missing the family but had made a number of new friends and was doing well on the course. Carol and I visited Arizona three times to see him and it was always difficult leaving him to fly home. We used the time that Robert was based in the USA to experience America's biggest sporting event, the Super Bowl. On 7 February 2010 Michael, Robert and I met in Florida to go to the Met Life Stadium to see New Orleans Saints play Indianapolis Colts. The Saints won 31-17 and the game had a viewing audience of 106 million people, making it the most-watched Super Bowl to that date. We had an amazing day together, being picked up for the game and returned to our hotel in a stretch limo!

There was a very happy end to the year when, on 5 December, Carol and I were married at Spencer House. My best man was Ken Maynard. We had met Ken and his wife Anna, along with their sons Sam, Alex and Tom on holiday in Mauritius in 2005. We had a celebratory dinner at the Dorchester the following night with entertainment from the

THE FOUNDATION – A NEW BEGINNING

Sugar Babes! Our honeymoon was over Christmas in South Africa and Mauritius.

There were more celebrations in 2009. Debby and Tim had their fortieth birthday party at their farm in Tavistock with a large gathering of family and friends. It was also the day of the FA Cup Final when Chelsea beat Everton 2–1. I managed to go to this and to get to the party by chartering a private plane to fly us from London to Plymouth – what a special day!

In November, Carol, Michael, Georgia and I went to New York to complete the purchase of a flat in the West Village. This has brought enormous fun and pleasure to us all as a family with many happy memories from the city that never sleeps..

December saw Robert graduate from the Golf Academy of America. I went to see the graduation ceremony along with Jacqui. It was wonderful to hear about how well he had done and to see that his determination to follow his dream had proved to be the right decision. He had turned into a very special golfer which he proved to me when we played the famous Whisper Rock golf course together on his last day in Arizona before flying home to the UK.

19

THE LOWRY – MY THEATRE OF DREAMS

Just as the Foundation started in September 2006, I was approached to become the chairman of The Lowry, the iconic and hugely impressive performing and visual arts venue in Salford that I had visited when I was chairman of Capita. At the time we had won a major contract with Salford City Council and the CEO, John Willis, was always talking about the Lowry. He took me on a tour of the place that would end up playing a major part in my life. On the visit I met the extremely impressive chief executive, Julia Fawcett, who was just amazing in her enthusiasm for the place and her plans to develop it.

I certainly liked what I saw but I was later surprised to receive a call asking if I might want to apply for the role of chairman. My initial reaction was to decline because I didn't feel I had enough experience of working in the arts. I remember thinking, 'I'm not sure that's me at all.' It was Carol who persuaded me to reconsider. We had a great many interests in the North West, regularly visiting Carol's family and friends in Liverpool plus, of course, we had the academy in Darwen and plans for other schools in the area.

Upon further investigation I realised just what a great story was behind The Lowry, and what an impressive organisation it had become. I liked what they did. They had a learning and engagement programme through which they worked closely with young people in the community who were going through difficult times in their lives. So I decided to let the headhunters put my name forward.

I recall going for my interview with Julia and two of the trustees. When I arrived at the place it was on a day when there were performances simultaneously in both the Lyric and the Quays theatres. The place was buzzing with people and I thought to myself, 'I really want this role.'

In November 2006, while away in South Africa, I heard to my delight that I had been offered the position. The Lowry is a place where I always feel happy. It is a vibrant and positive space. The original brave decision taken by Salford City Council to build The Lowry was a massive gamble, but it has paid off handsomely. At the time it was being built, pictures show that the area was otherwise deserted. Not many years ago the space where MediaCity now proudly stands as the northern home of the BBC, was previously The Lowry's staff car park!

It was the whole regeneration story that first 'hooked' me when I was shown around the area by John Willis. As part of the preparation for my interview as chairman I looked back at the history of Salford Quays. It is fascinating and says much about the The Lowry's symbolic importance to the city.

Salford's docks suffered a terrible decline at the end of the 1960s. The glory days were over and the worsening economic conditions, precipitated by the oil crisis of 1973 and subsequent industrial unrest, hastened the decline. By the late 1970s, job losses in the north of England were alarming and when Salford docks closed forever in 1982, unemployment in the North West soared above 30 per cent in some places. Unlike Liverpool or London, the docks did not even have good warehouse buildings that could be renovated. They were rotting wooden grain stores.

The City Council decided that it had to act. In late 1983 it acquired the majority of the docks from the Manchester Ship Canal Company for £1.5 million, then engaged with the private sector in an early form of public/private partnership to find a solution and investment.

The first mention of the Salford Quays Centre For Performing Arts was in 1988, the initial vision being for the creation of a cinema and hotel on the site. On 22 February 1996, support was received from the National Lottery for the project. Other funding came from The Millennium Commission and The Heritage Lottery Fund, along with European Regional Development Fund, English Partnerships and Salford City Council. The £106-million project started in 1997 and The Lowry opened on 28 April 2000.

Along with John Willis, two city councillors, Councillor Bill Hinds and Councillor David Lancaster, have been involved as trustees from the outset, as have Jane Frost and Adrian Vinken. All were very helpful to me when I first took on the role as Chair. The person who received some of the greatest accolades was Felicity Goody, who had been the first Chair of The Lowry, holding the project together. Felicity also recruited Julia Fawcett, who became the CEO in June 2002.

The Lowry is rooted in the City of Salford, the eighth most deprived city in the Uk with 25.3 per cent of children living in poverty. To me, The Lowry is a physical manifestation of how entrepreneurial local government at its best, can deliver. I fear that, had this been in my own city of Brighton, the area would never have been developed with such a determined vision. A good illustration of my point is that in Brighton we still wonder at the remnants of the West Pier that closed in 1975. Major sections of the pier collapsed in 2002 and there were two fires in March and May 2003, meaning that very little is left of the original 1866 structure. The only reminder of the wonderful times that I had as a child on the West Pier, memories that will be shared with countless others, are the remnants of the infrastructure that protrude out of the sea!

When I started working with The Lowry I knew I had an awful lot to learn. People who chair these kinds of organisations tend to be great art lovers, passionate followers of opera or ballet. I am more of a generalist in that I enjoy a broad range of things.

I knew I couldn't really compete at that 'expert' level. I was appointed to bring something different to the role. My business experience with Capita was relevant, as was the fact that I was based in London. Part of my job was to lift the profile of the North West, promote the region in London, and publicize the important cultural role that The Lowry plays. It shocked me how difficult it is to get members of the establishment, most of whom are firmly London-based, to go up to the North West to see first-hand what we have. We needed a plan to change this and I was a part of that plan.

The real attraction of the role for me was that I would experience a new world and new experiences. You're never too old to learn about new things. I have also always been attracted to the North West, having had such good experiences of working there. What I like about the people is that they have distinct likes and dislikes. They talk in a straightforward and direct manner, unlike the approach sometimes adopted by 'soft southerners'.

I approached the situation from the point of view of asking: 'How can this industry be better run?' It struck me immediately that there was scope for change in the business model for running a theatre. Some of the back-office services needed to be more efficient and effective. Many would rightly say that the box office forms a front-line service that one would want to protect by running it in-house, yet organising it in a more centralized way was an obvious way to increase its efficiency. We needed to use modern technology, to reflect our customers' changing buying patterns. A seat not sold is like a vacant hotel room: revenue lost forever.

The Lowry had so many things going for it and it still excites me to be involved with it today. From the outset I realised that Julia Fawcett's enthusiasm for the organisation, perhaps driven by the fact that she was born locally in Ordsall, has enabled her to build a very talented team that has developed over the years. She is one of the most accomplished CEOs I have worked with. The speed that the team, through her leadership, responds to issues or challenges is impressive and mirrors the culture that I developed in Capita. Julia's approach is 'solution driven' rather than 'problem led'.

Much of this approach and financial discipline stems from the fact that only 5 per cent of The Lowry's funding comes from the public purse. This is well below the average 40 per cent for regularly funded arts and cultural institutions. We have to generate 95 per cent of our income from ticket sales, other theatre-related sales, commercial activities or funds raised for educational projects. This disparity was helpful, however, when the national funding we received was cut, for that cash crisis came as a rude shock to other arts outfits.

Some of the strategy I was involved in developing has brought financial benefits. The commercial operations run by Tony Smith are very important to us. These cover catering, conferences and events, and things like wedding and the graduation ceremonies for students from Salford University as well as our retail outlets. I worked particularly closely with the fundraising team, Gwen Oakden and Rhiannon McKay-Smith who do a great job in raising funds for the Lowry's work. Our booking office used to cost £150,000 a year to run. However, in 2005 we established 'Quaytickets' as a venue-based primary ticket agency, capable of offering an outsourced solution to clients over a complete range of booking office services covering ticketing, as well dispatch and marketing through e-marketing, social media and Facebook sales. This service also includes a forty-seat contact centre that has the capacity to handle over 320,000 calls a year, at a standard Capita would expect to deliver to its clients.

Quaytickets is run by Rachel Miller along with a team of 120 employees. As well as looking after our own operating needs, Quaytickets now runs services for fifty clients throughout the UK across leisure, sport, entertainment and theatre. The clients include, believe it or not, Brighton and Hove Albion Football Club! The business now delivers ticketing for thirteen West End theatres, including recently winning the rights to do all the booking for Nimax Theatres' production of *Harry Potter and the Cursed Child*.

Today, Quaytickets makes an operating profit of £550,000, meaning that we have improved the monies available to run The Lowry activities by £700,000. So, a business that was costing us money to run, is now making a very significant contribution towards our overall running costs. My skill is to identify better ways to do things but to successfully implement major changes in any organisation you need a receptive and talented team, and at The Lowry we most definitely have this. I found that our Financial Director, Jon Brabbin, is all over the numbers and runs a very tight ship. His private sector experience is again unusual in the industry, but the forecasting and control over budgets again mirrors what I had in Capita.

Another feature that attracted me to The Lowry is that it is one of the largest performance and visual art centres in the UK. It houses the world's largest public collection of paintings and drawings by the famous artist L.S. Lowry. There are over 400 works in the collection, fifty-seven of which are oil paintings. This means that we have a very active gallery space, which enables Michael Simpson, the Director of Visual Arts and Engagement, to stage a number of exhibitions, enabling us to juxtapose the work of L.S. Lowry with that of other great artists.

Many people that I speak to about being the Chairman of The Lowry initially assume that The Lowry is simply an art gallery. It is wonderful to be able to shock them by saying that in fact The Lowry also has two theatres, the Lyric – the largest stage outside of London – and the Quays, plus a Studio for smaller productions. During a typical year we present approaching 1,000 performances of over 360 different shows to an audience of 550,000 people. On many occasions there are three different productions going on alongside a very active gallery space, with approaching 900,000 visitors to the building each year.

One of the duties of The Lowry, set from the outset as part of its charter, was to push the boundaries of presenting an eclectic mix of theatrical art forms from around the world. It was important not to do this to the extent that the local community could feel marginalized. The idea was more to help develop the interests of local people by offering a wide range of different forms of entertainment. Analysis of the audience base shows that we have definitely achieved this. Around a quarter of The Lowry's shows are either world or UK premieres and of an international calibre: shows only made available to audiences in the North West because of The Lowry.

An exciting part of this, I believe, is the Studio, which is the home to an extended family of up-and-coming theatre makers and companies from the North West and beyond. My family has donated a sum of money to support the development of this work over the next ten years. The objectives here are to develop the wider local artistic community. Furthering people's artistic ambitions fits well with our objectives as a family, particularly as the Studio encourages risk taking and innovation in its work.

The thing that struck me most when I first became involved, however, and that continues to be the big attraction for me, is The Lowry's Learning and Engagement programme, now run by Lynsey

O'Sullivan. Unlike most artistic organisations, many of which operate similar schemes, The Lowry puts this programme front and centre in our strategy of involvement with the local community. The work focuses on young people – some of the hardest-to-reach young people and families in Salford.

What really excites me is that we use the arts as a vehicle for social change, helping young people to develop creativity both personally and professionally. This helps them to better understand and interpret the world around them, developing skills that increase their employment options. It amazes me when I am told that we have approaching 36,000 participants on our programmes every year.

I have seen first-hand that, for many people, The Lowry is a safe haven. It is a good illustration of what can be achieved through delivering social change in a space that people enjoy coming to and that they trust. The same cannot be said of some services provided by the conventional public sector organisations. This, therefore, chimes very much with the approach to public service reform that I promoted both through the CBI and Capita. It is also fits completely with the aspirations that I set for my own Foundation.

The impact from this programme is amazing to see, and never more so than in the showcase of dance and verse that Carol and I recently attended. Staged by young people with challenging lives, there was not a dry eye in the house as each performer openly expressed the pressures that they face every single day as young carers, or young parents looking after small children. Some had been excluded from school, but through their engagement with The Lowry they had found what was almost an alternative form of education. One illustration of this was a verbatim play about a year in the life of three young carers. This embarked on a five-week tour of 27 venues culminating in a performance at the House of Lords in front of 200 people. I was there to witness the telling impact of the messages they delivered.

Dance, of course, is another of my personal passion and connects well with the work with which I am associated in Brighton with 'South East Dance'. The Lowry houses the North West Centre for Advanced Training in Dance (CAT). This provides important access routes into dance education and training. Every year we offer fifty-two Music and

Dance Scheme grants, allowing young people of all backgrounds the opportunity to progress into full-time training. As trustees, it has been reported to us that CAT students are now feeding through into full-time training at recognised conservatoires and dance schools, such as The Northern School of Contemporary Dance, Laban in London and some are also securing places with the National Youth Dance Company.

Something else that sets us apart are the 350 'Lowry Volunteers' who greet me with smiles on their faces every time I visit The Lowry. They are front of house in the organisation, meeting and greeting visitors, taking tickets, selling programmes, assisting disabled visitors and much, much more. The group is very diverse, made up of people from all different backgrounds and ages. The youngest volunteer is seventeen and the oldest is ninety! We were all very proud that in 2015 The Lowry Volunteers were awarded the Queens's Award for Voluntary Service, which is the official MBE for voluntary groups. To me, this group (dressed in red) epitomizes the community spirit of The Lowry.

A very telling independent report by consultants New Economy and entitled *Beyond the Arts* was published on 27 November 2013. This revealed that The Lowry has had an unmatched economic and cultural impact on Greater Manchester and the UK, delivering outstanding value for public money. The study showed that The Lowry had been the cornerstone of the £1.4 billion regeneration of Salford Quays. It has seen the former docks regenerated into one of Greater Manchester's strongest-growing areas in terms of employment and households. Every £1 of public money invested in The Lowry has a return of £16.27, far higher than other public sector organisations. The statistic that really excites me is that there are now more people employed in MediaCity than when the Quays was a working dock! Amazingly, my youngest son, Robert, remembers that studying Salford Quays was part of his course work for GCSE geography.

What struck me when the BBC came to MediaCity was that so many of the workforce did not come from the local area, but were 'shipped up from London'. This needed to change if the community was to feel as connected with the BBC, and now ITV and other technology related companies in the Quays, as they do with The Lowry. There is clearly also the need for a large technical resource to support these organisations. To create this workforce the partnership between The Lowry, Salford University and my Foundation supported the development of the UTC which helps to feed the supply chain with the enterprising, skilled talent that all of these companies need if they are to flourish.

MediaCity UTC is, therefore, the bridge allowing 14- to 19-year-olds to benefit from local employment opportunities and to forge careers in the creative and digital industries. This will provide a massive lift in an area that is challenged by significant deprivation, unemployment and social problems. MediaCity UTC opened in September 2015 and has started very well. The building is amazing, with phenomenal teaching spaces and two studios, in one of which students can stage a production in the round for an audience of 300 people. There are also entrepreneurial pods for students to use to start businesses.

When I first took up my role at The Lowry, there had been calls for an exhibition of Lowry's work to take place in London and I set it as one of my personal goals to make this happen. I met Carol Anne Lowry to discuss the feasibility of such a plan. Carol was not related to L.S. Lowry but first met him at the age of thirteen. She wanted to be an artist and her mother had suggested that she should write to him for advice. She came to regard him as her mentor and they remained close for two decades. When he died in 1976, L.S. Lowry bequeathed his entire estate to her, not telling her in advance of her extraordinary inheritance. This was an enormous pressure and responsibility for her and I sensed a degree of frustration in her that an exhibition had not been organised before.

One of the many attributes that I could relate to in L.S. Lowry was that he was anti-establishment. He holds the record for the most honours declined. The last showing of his works by a public institution in London was in 1976, just months before his death. Being an 'action-oriented-route-one' person I thought that a new exhibition of his wonderful paintings would be quickly achievable. This proved not to be the case – it took five years. The reasons that it took so long were that these things are planned years ahead and that, unbelievably, there was a need to persuade those in authority that L.S. Lowry was worthy of such an exhibition. Michael Simpson and I first met with Nick (now Sir Nicholas) Serota of Tate Britain in 2008 and it took until 2013 to secure the exhibition.

We were helped along the way by many interested parties. The exhibition *Lowry and the Painting of Modern Life* ran at the Tate Britain from 26 June to 20 October 2013. We were told it was the second most popular ticketed exhibition in the Tate's history after Damien Hirst at Tate Modern.

I will always remember the evening that, as representatives of The Lowry, we had to entertain guests. To see the splendour of his paintings, large and small, on show all in one place, allowing one to appreciate the range of his work, was truly breathtaking. It was a real privilege as Chair to welcome our guests and to set out our plans for the collection going forward, including the possibility of an exhibition in China. Michael Simpson and the curator of the Lowry collection at The Lowry, Claire Stewart, did a wonderful job and I have no doubt that, quite rightly, it was one of the highlights of their careers.

The Lowry remains a very important part of my life. and I will always be grateful to the many great people of the organisation, and in particular to the trustees for their immense contribution and assistance to me in my role as Chair. I have always valued especially the opinions of the excellent chief executive Julia Fawcett and her former deputy, Stephen Crocker, and I turn to them both now to explain a little about my life with The Lowry.

Julia Fawcett says:

The first time I met Sir Rod he was working with Capita when they were hoping to broker a partnership with Salford Council. He was ultimately successful, and I was impressed by how decent and down to earth he seemed. Something I have seen over the years is how Rod wears his accomplishments really lightly, and he always underestimates the impact that his achievements and his reputation have on other people. He definitely made an impact on me.

At first there was no intention to have any involvement with him. But somehow we got to understand the motivations we had in common. Initially that was around our business model, which frequently involves helping the less well-off members of society. I could see immediately how much he approved of our work. I also quickly learned that it really winds him up that the establishment often undervalues young people from less privileged backgrounds. He didn't know that much about The Lowry at that point, but it was clear he 'got' it. Somehow in the space of an hour or so we kind of just 'clicked'.

Soon afterwards, unexpectedly and for tragic reasons, we were looking for a new Chair. Traditionally, organisations like ours would go for someone with an established interest in the arts and Sir Rod didn't have that. At that time he was self-declared not interested, but all the same he kind of understood us. I knew he would understand aspects of our programme like 'learning in engagement' so we approached him.

He said: 'Yes.' That was the starting point. The values we shared with Sir Rod were all important. In all the years since then that has never changed. It was great timing for him and for us. It was serendipity. I meet lots of people, but I knew he was the right person for us. Thereafter, once he was appointed, the way I have seen him work has been staggering. He really quickly focused and I believe The Lowry helped him with that.

Just today a candidate that I was meeting for interviews was saying how impressed he was with Rod's investment in The Lowry. He asked about Rod's motivation and I said, 'You've got to remember with Rod, he is the son of a sheet metal worker and when he talks about what drives him, it is always failing his 11-plus!'

So when you talk to people like me in my organisation, who have got to know him over the years, he is always on our side. He shares our values. He really fights your corner, even if it is not a popular fight. A lot of trustees and chairs in the arts world think it is a glamorous job and they are there for the nice bits, like getting the chance to shake hands with the Queen. But what has really impressed me over ten years or more is that we've had some tricky moments and Rod has been more than there by my side. He really knows how to roll up his sleeves and get stuck in and that's unusual. He does stuff that other people won't touch because they think it's too difficult or complex to get involved with.

The downside of all that, though perhaps it's not really a downside but a challenge, is that he's never satisfied! So if we do something amazing you don't always get that moment to celebrate, because in Rod's mind it doesn't count because it's done now. What's next? Tomorrow quickly takes over in importance from today. But after working with Rod for ten years the thing that completely staggers me is that he doesn't understand his own power and his own impact. I don't think he has any concept of it. I don't think he 'gets' it. That is the thing that I find the most endearing. You see many people with power don't wear their power anything like as lightly as Rod does. I think that's a really endearing quality. It makes people feel incredibly loyal to him. He is also incredibly loyal in return.

The way Rod talks to young people is very impressive. He connects with them as he tells his story and he can become very emotional when he listens to some of the young people's stories. There is something about supporting the underdog that really does drive him. It's great to see the way he works with other trustees and to see the way he plays to their strengths and draws them in. His persistence opens so many doors. It is a foolish mistake to underestimate him. I've seen it happen, and you can see Rod quietly note that someone feels they have the measure of him and then, usually in language that is very clear and simple, he will pull the rug from under them and cut to the crux of the argument. He is a powerful communicator, but I do think he underestimates his skills.

He is very competitive. He has to win. I don't think he thinks 'if only' for himself. I've heard him articulate over many, many years that he thinks he was lucky. He often says that there were many talented people around him who didn't have the luck. He feels the system didn't help people like that and the system should be different. It's not about how it could have been different for him, but about how it can be different for others.

There have been so many marvellous moments with Sir Rod. We have got a bunch of 350 volunteers who won the Queen's Award. It's the equivalent of an MBE for voluntary groups. Our voluntary workforce won and Rod stood them a champagne celebration. It was such a lovely touch because as an organisation we couldn't have done that, and he didn't have to do that. They didn't expect it. He knows when to come in at those key moments and make a difference in people's lives.

When he was having his sixtieth birthday, he invited a number of us, trustees and staff, to go down to his party, a big flash do at the Dorchester. It was lovely and then the lights went down and the spotlight came up and all of a sudden up stepped Sir Rod and a member of the *Strictly Come Dancing* cast and he did this dance routine. I didn't know he had been a top young ballroom dancer. It was almost him taking the mickey out of himself and putting himself on. I think he'd had some secret lessons. It was such an unexpected thing for someone like him to do. He is a shy man in a way.

When he had his sixty-fifth party at The Lowry he had booked an artist and he wouldn't tell us who it was. He didn't want to spoil the fun. We had a game that went on for weeks and weeks for us to guess. None of us got it. It was Sir Tom Jones. He had a twinkle in his eye, and it was great to see the humorous side of him.

His taxi etiquette often gets a laugh. In London you pay for the cab outside the car. In the North West you don't. Usually the car doors are locked so you can't run off without paying. He couldn't quite get over it. He once got quickly out of a Manchester cab and the taxi driver wasn't happy. Carol told him: 'He thinks you're going to do a runner.' He's great fun.

Sometimes it is a bugger to get that human side out. It is there but he can seem very reserved. He is very inspirational.

Thank you Julia, you're beginning to embarrass me!

And now I turn to Stephen Crocker, who has now left The Lowry to become Chief Executive of the Theatre Royal at Norwich. Stephen says:

Rod drives the regeneration project brilliantly from the top right down to grass roots community level. Rod has had a phenomenal effect as chairman.

We exist in Salford which is one of the most deprived areas of the country. There are major pockets of worklessness and social deprivation is a massive issue. Rod talks a lot about social mobility and that's exactly what we're trying to engineer here. We work with lots of young groups, such as young carers. The youngest of them is just four years old. Rod is very passionate about social mobility. He is an amazing leader.

Rod's mantra is, 'If old solutions are not working, look for new solutions.' The Lowry helps many, many people from all kinds of difficult and troubled backgrounds. One of the greatest problems for young carers is that often no-one knows they exist. Rod is determined for them to have a voice that is heard. We work with local authority agencies to help deliver creative engagement, which produces a massive outcome. We work with children with complex needs like autism. Organisations like The Lowry can go deeper than social services by using creative approaches and that very much comes from Rod.

We find people with raw talent who need the channels and the pathways to succeed. The Lowry is a centre for advanced training and dance. We have students who go right to the top, to the Royal Ballet School or to America to train. That's through a partnership with the department of education, and again there are some similarities with Rod's work.

We try to look after children who are NEET, or at risk of falling out of school and college. How can we, The Lowry, intervene? Rod is leading the way as we try to encourage young people back in to some form of training or life improvement.

We have a huge range of skills and opportunities under this roof and we try to provide opportunities for challenged young people. We have helped so many. Rod encourages us to take that risk. His Foundation invested so we could bring in support. Now it is funded by other bodies but Rod kicked it off. Rod's challenge to us all the time is How do you do it bigger? How do you do it better? He really inspires us all the time.

I have been here since 2008 and now I am going to Norwich Theatres. I was the first appointment Rod was involved in so I have always been grateful. Rod thrives on being pat of the team. He is an amazing person for joining up the dots. We need his freshness of thought.

I know Rod feels hugely protective as chairman as being a custodian of that spirit of The Lowry. He lives it out through his interaction with us and I can tell you it's brilliant the way he tunes back into that. It's really great. It's Rod's spirit that drives us on into being part of it all. Hopefully he will spend another ten years with us.

When he first came Rod said: 'We've got to raise money for building.' He did that. He raised £5 million and he put his hand in his own pocket. Rod led the meeting that led Tate Britain into taking a look at Lowry again. They had all sorts of reasons why they shouldn't stage an exhibition, but Rod pushed it through.

I do think Rod identifies with Lowry, the great artist who gives us our name. They are both highly talented individuals who faced many setbacks yet emerged full of determination to go their own way to great success.

Well, Julia and Stephen, that is very emotional stuff! It seems as though you know me very well, which is worrying. I obviously need to sharpen up my act to keep you on your toes!

I chose to hold my sixty-fifth birthday celebration at The Lowry simply because the place means so much to me but I also wanted some of my 'southern' friends to experience its magic. We used the Compass Room for the dinner, from where guests could see the full panoramic view of MediaCity lit up. One guest even compared it to like being in Dubai, but then perhaps that was after too much champagne. However, turning a derelict piece of land and waterway into brand new city does hold some similarity to what has been achieved in Dubai with vast expanses of desert! We turned the Quays Theatre into a nightclub for the evening and I had Sir Tom Jones perform at the event along with Alexandra Burke, who won *X Factor* in 2008 but more recently performed amazingly well in *Strictly*. A wonderful evening in a wonderful venue.

The Lowry will always be a special place to me. I called it my 'theatre of dreams' in my speech that evening. While the same term of endearment is also used about Old Trafford, the home of Manchester United which can be seen from The Lowry, as a Chelsea supporter I do not see the association. In writing my story, I wanted The Lowry to have a chapter to itself as, without a doubt, my connection with it has been a wonderful experience and continues to be so today.

We all have a lot for which to thank L.S. Lowry.

20

BUILDING OUR FAMILY OF ACADEMIES

In 2009 I appointed Honor Wilson-Fletcher to become the first Chief Executive of the Foundation and together we began the developments which shaped the Foundation's direction of travel for the next seven years. Our plan was to develop our role as a sponsor of academies by adding to the two that we already had in Darwen and Brighton.

The process of sponsoring an existing school is long, both in terms of getting local and national agreements and then either building a replacement school or refurbishing the existing accommodation. This process can take two years. It would take as much time to sponsor a brand new school, but that has the added advantage of starting afresh with no preconceived local baggage.

Honor and I both realised that building a family of schools and academies would take a great deal of work. It was an immature industry at that time as choices of schools were limited and there remained strong opposition to the policy of academies. We most definitely needed to work with a local authority on any bid in a partnership arrangement. This was not wholly encouraged by the Department of Education, as in many cases the local education authority was seen as the body that had failed to provide students with a good education. It was necessary, therefore, to take care in selecting both the authority and the area in which we chose to work.

Becoming a sponsor is not a short-term commitment. In one sense, it is a responsibility that can go on forever. A student's education affects their entire life and the lives of their families. Becoming a sponsor also requires resources, financial investment and a very thick skin!

My belief is that a good education gives students skills and qualifications, as well as instilling confidence, preparing young people for the challenges of life. Everyone has the right to expect an exciting, engaging and relevant education. Sadly, they don't always get it and in today's world, if you are not educationally equipped doors are very quickly closed to you. Your options for a fulfilling life are immediately restricted.

'It is not where you come from that matters, it is where you want to get to that counts.' That's one of my core beliefs. The deal with Aldridge students is that if you work hard we will help you to move forward in the way that you choose and to be work ready. At the Foundation we decided from the outset that we would work in the most challenging of communities where there were high levels of unemployment and related social issues. This was most definitely the case with our first two schools in Darwen and Brighton. The quality of education had been poor. I was not prepared to accept this and I set out to change it.

What was not apparent at that time was the resistance to change that we encountered. I was shocked at how easy it was for those working in education to cling onto methods that had clearly failed. In the commercial world if you provide a poor service you go out of business but in education, because there were no alternatives until the Academies Programme came along, many schools could continue to underperform and children would simply be badly educated. This was changing but to move a teacher out of a school takes a long time. They are massively protected by the unions and the system around them. The difference between a business and education is that education is life-changing and a student only gets one chance at it.

We set out a vision for every student and this remains our goal today. We wanted them to be exceptionally successful, surpassing their initial personal academic expectations and previous levels of attainment. It was important for them to be capable, independent and entrepreneurial. We wanted them to be proud of their school.

We spoke of respect for teachers and other students and we

wanted them to feel safe and happy. It was very obvious that for some pupils the school was the haven that they did not have at home. It was important to give them the confidence and social skills taken for granted by those from more affluent areas. I was keen for students to have a social conscience and feel a responsibility for their community. From my Chairmanship of Vinspired I knew the power of volunteering and of having a sense of belonging to a group or community. We also spoke of having a healthier lifestyle through being physically active, of respecting their bodies and minds.

Our aim was to provide students with an education where they would develop a passion for learning as well as acquiring an enterprising and entrepreneurial mindset, enabling them to take responsibility for their own futures and for their neighbourhoods. The attributes we promoted had developed in me over time but in essence they were creativity, determination, problem solving, risk taking, teamwork and passion. These did not come out of the blue nor were they a 'light bulb moment' for me. They were the attributes that drove the development of Capita and changed my life. This did not mean that we expected everyone to start a business, although some inevitably would. What we did believe was that, no matter what our students went on to do, they would have the drive to be successful and would stand out in a positive way from the crowd.

It was with these objectives and this vision at the Foundation that we set off to build our family of schools and colleges. It was a very exciting and demanding time but richly rewarding and life-changing for our students and all of us associated with this journey.

In late 2009, we had a call from Vanessa Miner of the Office of the Schools Commissioner to sound us out about meeting with the Royal Borough of Kensington & Chelsea (RBKC) to discuss an academy planned in North Kensington. Vanessa set up a meeting for Sally Ritchie and I with Sir Merrick Cockell, the Leader of the Council and the late Baroness Shireen Ritchie. It seemed to go well but they were also in discussion with other potential sponsors. A local authority could not sponsor an academy but the Royal Borough was very keen to be an active co-sponsor.

It appealed to them that we were not one of the 'large' sponsors and that this academy would, therefore, mean a great deal to us. They were also attracted to our entrepreneurial thinking. We liked the idea of starting a brand new school where we could set the ethos from the outset, even if the opening was five years away.

I knew the CEO of RBKC, Derek (now Sir Derek) Myers, from my Capita days and I have always had a very high regard for the authority. (I actually applied for the job of Deputy Treasurer many, many years ago whilst I was at CIPFA.) We had a second meeting and were effectively interviewed for the role over a buffet lunch. I believe that Sir Merrick then met with the Conservative Leader of Brighton, Mary Mears, to get her take on what we were like to work with. As a result, we were selected to be the Lead Sponsor for a brand new Academy in North Kensington for eleven to eighteen-year-olds, with the specialism being Entrepreneurship supported by a secondary specialism of Expressive Arts.

RBKC had already co-sponsored another academy in Lots Road, Chelsea with the London Diocesan Board for Schools. The Chelsea Academy was about to open in September 2010 and the development had gone well. What impressed me a great deal about the council was that they were very clear in why they wanted to open an academy in North Kensington: they wanted every student to have a school they could walk to. At that time a large number were attending schools outside of the borough as there were not sufficient places in Kensington.

In February 2010 it became clear that the educational performance of Portslade Community College required rescuing. This was the school that I had attended although, to be precise, my school was actually the sixth-form college that was attached to the school. I expressed to John Barradell (now Town Clerk of the City of London Corporation), CEO of Brighton and Hove Council, and council leader Mary Mears a strong interest in becoming the sponsor of the academy. I knew there could be some strong resistance to this as I was already the sponsor of the only other academy that the city had, at Falmer. I was, however, insistent because of the personal importance of it to me and in the end I think it was this that won through.

We submitted an application to the Department with the Foundation as the lead sponsor and the council as co-sponsor. It was at around this time, however, that Michael Gove, Secretary of State for Education, decided to rein in the funding for academies under the "Building Schools for the Future" (BSF) programme. Some applications were too late to get funding and were rejected. Ours was on the cusp but had a great deal of support from the Department officials and it helped that I had spoken to Michael Gove about it. He was aware of our work as a sponsor and of the importance of Portslade to me from the meeting that Sally and I had had with him several years before.

The deal with Brighton & Hove Council was that if I could unlock the funding they would continue with the application. The team at the Foundation worked hard to find a workable solution with the Department officials and we achieved this by offering to be the lead pilot to develop a speedier procurement process. This obviously had to be signed off by the Secretary of State. I recall taking several calls from Michael Gove on my mobile to agree the finer details while I was on holiday in Spain.

In September 2010, the Darwen Aldridge Community Academy (DACA) opened in its amazing new £48-million building, marking the culmination of five years' work. This presented our Principal, Brendan Loughran, with the opportunity to put into action our carefully thought out plans. DACA will always have pride of place for me because it was the first academy that I sponsored and it represents the manifestation of the work we planned sitting around the Boardroom table in Capita's offices with a polystyrene model in front of us!

Brighton Aldridge Community Academy (BACA) opened on 1 September 2010 in the grounds of the old school, Falmer High, and became our second academy. Only the first phase of the building work was complete and it would be another year before the full transformation of Falmer High was complete.

In October, despite the scrapping of the BSF Programme, we negotiated a commitment for £12.7 million to renovate the existing school building at Portslade Community School, including the construction of a new Sixth Form on the site. Solely through the Foundation's efforts and taking into account the £28 million for BACA, it meant we had unlocked £40 million of public funding for the city to enhance the educational facilities for students who previously had to put up with very poor accommodation. I am convinced that without our determination the buildings would still be the same today.

In January 2011, Honor was asked to visit the Isle of Portland off Weymouth to hear about the proposed 'all-through academy', involving children from nursery through to secondary education. An application had been made but little progress had been achieved. I subsequently went to Bournemouth University to meet the principals of all the schools who wanted the academy, accompanied by Professor Stephen Heppell, who is based at the university. Stephen had a worldwide reputation as the proponent of the project-based learning concept. He also had a close affinity with the island and had led the previous unsuccessful application.

The project attracted us because we had found that many of the issues pupils faced came from the transition from primary to secondary education. To a young person it was a large step to go from the top of one to the bottom of the other. The proposal in Portland was to follow a 'stage not age' philosophy, meaning that students moved when they were ready to progress, regardless of age.

The Isle of Portland desperately needed inward investment and job creation. The coming of the Olympics in 2012 was heralded as the salvation of the Island since it was to be the site for the Olympic and Paralympic sailing regatta and ultimately the home of the Weymouth & Portland National Sailing Academy. Unfortunately, while the events leading up to Olympics did have an impact, this soon dissipated after the games were over.

March saw us confirmed as sponsor of the new academy in North Kensington. Work then began on the submission we had to make to the Department of Education in support of the funding we required.

On 11 April 2011 Darwen Aldridge Community Academy, although it was already up and running, was officially opened by HRH Prince William and Kate Middleton. It was the couple's last official engagement before their marriage. The opening attracted enormous attention in the town. Many wondered how we managed to pull off this amazing coup but, most importantly for the students, it was a marker that this sort of innovation does happen in Darwen. His Royal

Highness and Kate took a great interest in the academy, spending a long time with the students on the tour that we arranged for them. It was also a big day for us as a family and all were there to celebrate with me, including my granddaughter Florence who was only two months old at the time.

In August 2011 we reached agreement over the funding for the academy in Kensington. The capital grant for the build was in line with the expected level of £17.6 million and the Royal Borough agreed to top this up with a further £10.4, giving a total of £28 million. The council had decided to completely rebuild the leisure centre and baths that were on the site, which had been there for years, at a further cost of £29 million (it's rumoured that Prince William and Prince Harry learnt to swim there) so the total investment in the community amounted to £57 million. This would lead to the regeneration of the entire area.

The project had first been discussed in 2009, and we still had another five years work ahead of us to open it in September 2014. We had monthly project meetings that I chaired with the support of our project manager, Rama Venchard, the team from the Foundation, Merrick and Emma Will from the Royal Borough, and, once appointed, with David Benson as the Principal elect. This was onerous but it was an incredible experience. We continued to encounter strong resistance from the local residents, but the overall benefits to the community were huge. I urged residents to think positively about the project and its benefits.

In September 2011, Brighton Aldridge Community Academy moved into its award-winning new £24-million building. It was amazing, with the facilities that matched any independent school. We now needed to match the educational performance expected of an independent school, which was to prove a long road, requiring considerable changes. The chair of governors at this time was Peter Kyle, whom I had met through Hilary Armstrong when he was PPS to her in government. Peter did a great job for us and went on to be elected MP for Hove in the May 2015 general election.

In the same remarkable month, the former Portslade College opened as Portslade Aldridge Community Academy in its existing buildings. So I had achieved something very special to be sponsor of a school I attended in an area where I was born. The capital project began on the new Sixth-Form Centre and the refurbishment of the old school would take a further eighteen months.

I made a nostalgic visit to the Sixth-Form Centre in Chalky Road that was to be closed as part of the rebuild. Sadly, very little had changed in nearly fifty years. The classrooms where we were taught by Martin, Bennett and Broadbent were still there, including the science laboratory used by Mr Cheesman. The room where I took my O Levels was still there, reminding me of my exam fears. It was also the room where Mr Parkinson smashed a technical drawing board over Miller's head.

They even found all the registers that were used to take down class attendance, which, I am pleased to say, proved that I did turn up virtually every day. These records proved useful to Mike Harding, who set up an Alumni group for our year. There were also boxes of photographs still in what was then the headmaster's room. A number of these featured me and my schoolmates in form photographs and sporting teams for football, cricket, basketball and athletics. I rescued them, as that sort of memorabilia would no doubt have been lost forever when the building was closed. The most noticeable things to have gone were the ghastly air-raid shelters where new boys were traditionally beaten up. I wish that we could have refurbished this site and I still have a hankering to do so. It is currently being used as a temporary home for Kings School, a Free School, until a new site is developed for them in central Hove.

To drive some of the radical transformation in attitude and ethos in the early days of the academies, we developed a programme called 'opening eyes'. This was designed to offer our students challenging and very ambitious experiences, many of which were overseas. The aim was to put students, and the adults with them, into tough but rewarding situations, giving them a chance to be surprised by their own skill and capacity.

We found that a large number of students rarely travel outside their immediate environment let alone experience air travel. I was told of one twelve-year-old student in Brighton who had never travelled to Brighton seafront to view the sea! We have had some amazing experiences from this programme. Honor Wilson-Fletcher led a BACA/ PACA trip to India, which was a life-changing experience for them all, including Honor. Students based in Brighton went to New York and it had a similar effect. While working in food kitchens they learnt that in the States benefits are short term and not a way of life as they can be in the UK.

Students in DACA now do a regular trip to Uganda in Africa. They call it 'Afadaca' and have made several visits to local schools, keeping in touch through social media. Even the cricket tour that was organised to South Africa was an 'open eyes' programme, since the players visited the townships to understand more about the life and the conditions of local children. Typically, we find that students return with a greater confidence, a greater sense of opportunity and ambition, and a heightened social conscience.

I raised money for this programme as part of my sixty-fifth birthday celebrations, and believe wholeheartedly in it, but it requires regular fund-raising to cover the trips, as this enrichment is not seen as being part of the funding received from Government to run the schools. My intention is to put in place a relationship with several schools in Africa so that both students and teachers can benefit from working there. As a family we have a great love of Africa and my son, Michael, is now the CEO of 'Sunbird', a management services company based in Nairobi and operating throughout East Africa.

While everything was forging ahead with the Foundation and our family of academies, there were significant personal landmarks to celebrate in 2011. February was very special for me because on 16 February my first grandchild, Florence Willow, arrived, the daughter of my eldest son Michael and his wife Georgia. It was an amazingly emotional experience to meet her for the first time and really drew the family even closer together.

Later in the year, came a 'first time' that was totally different. On 12 October, I did something completely off the scale in terms of being outside of my comfort zone. I made my debut on the West End stage!

Several months before I had been at a charity event for The Roundhouse in Camden Town, an organisation that runs amazing programmes for disadvantaged children. One of the prizes in the auction that night was the opportunity to be in the cast of *Les Misérables*. I have been to see it many times and I love the music. So I bid for the opportunity and won it! Even if I had thought about foregoing my prize, I was not allowed that luxury and the follow up from the Cameron Mackintosh organisation was very thorough.

I was asked to go along to the Queens Theatre to meet some of the production team. I recall getting to the stage door and nearly turning back before I was whisked in to meet them. I was asked to sing along to a number of the songs so that they could 'assess' my singing voice. This felt incredibly intimidating to me but I assume that I passed the audition as I was then allocated three songs to learn. These were, 'At the end of the day', 'Master of the House' and 'One day more'.

They then invited me back to a rehearsal with the cast so that I got to know people. It was also to acclimatise myself to the set and in particular learn how to get off the revolving stage backwards in the dark, without falling over and becoming a heap on the floor traveling around helplessly in a circle! They were all incredibly kind to me, a date was fixed for my 'performance' and I was sent away to get word perfect.

I arrived again at the stage door on the appointed evening and was duly met and shown into make-up and costumes. Needless to say I played the part of the 'old man', so I was dressed accordingly. As I was taken to the waiting area I could hear Alfie Boe going through his exercises to warm his voice up for the role of 'Jean Valjean' that he plays so brilliantly. I was introduced to him in his dressing room, which was very special, and then every single member of the cast came up to me saying, 'Break a leg' in true theatrical tradition. It was an amazing evening, made very special by the cast, who set me up for a surprise at the end of the evening when Alfie Boe called me forward to take a special bow. The audience, apart from my twenty guests, must have wondered: 'Who is he?'

2012 was a year of awards. We were named by the British Council for School Environments as Academy Sponsor of the Year and in November I had the honour of being selected by *EducationInvestor* magazine as the person who had made the 'Most outstanding contribution as an individual to education'. What people in the audience that night did not know was that same day I had received a letter from the Cabinet Office informing me that the Prime Minister was minded to recommend to Her Majesty the Queen that I should receive a knighthood. I was in a meeting at our offices in Buckingham Street and my PA Elizabeth Anderson sent a note into the meeting saying that my wife Carol needed to speak to me urgently. When I called, Carol could hardly contain herself with excitement. She had opened the envelope by mistake, so she said! What an amazing and emotional day.

In fact, 2012 proved to be a particularly special year for a number of reasons. One of the most emotional days of my life was 14 February 2012, the date of my investiture at Buckingham Palace. Most importantly, this time, unlike with my OBE, my mother was there to see this honour bestowed on me. She was ninety-six years old but she was determined to be there. The only thing that she kept saying to me was: 'I wonder what your dear old dad would have said?'

The staff at the Palace were incredibly helpful, making sure that she was well looked after. I was also joined by my wife, Carol, and my youngest son, Robert. The family were out of the country on a trip to Canada with their mother which had been arranged almost a year earlier. Following discussions between them, Robert was designated to fly home for a couple of days to represent all of them. My investiture was undertaken by HRH The Prince of Wales. This was very special to me in view of my involvement with The Prince's Trust and the council of his charities.

As I entered the great room, so many thoughts flashed through my mind. I thought a great deal of my father and what my parents had done for me. I thought how lucky I was to have such a great family and wife, and all that they meant to me. Above all I thought about my home town, thinking to myself, it's been a long journey, but yes this can happen to a boy from Portslade. After being knighted by His Royal Highness, I was very touched for him to congratulate me on my work with young people, my academies and his Trust.

On 24 April, I received a letter from the Vice Chancellor of the Manchester Metropolitan University, Professor John Brooks, inviting me to accept an Honorary Degree of Doctor of Business Administration

(DBA). Each year the university conferred awards on those who have made contributions to public life. The letter said that the invitation was: 'in recognition of distinguished achievements in the field of business and your outstanding commitment to supporting young people reach their potential through the work of the Aldridge Foundation.'

The ceremony was on Tuesday 17 July at the Bridgewater Concert Hall in Manchester. The honorary award was conferred at the ceremony at which students from the Institute of Education received their awards. This was, therefore, relevant to the work of the Foundation as many of those receiving awards would go on to teach in primary or secondary institutions, perhaps with some even finding their ways to one of our academies.

It was made even more special by the fact that the University Chancellor was Dianne Thompson (later Dame Dianne), the Group CEO of Camelot, whom I had met at the Chevening event all those years ago. I felt greatly privileged to be asked to address the students 'fully robed' on such a special day.

Earlier in the year, on 16 March, 2012, I had received an email from the London 2012 Olympic Team congratulating me for making it through the selection process to become an Olympic Torchbearer. I was nominated by Lloyds TSB for the charitable work I do across the UK through the Foundation. I felt that it was a fantastic honour both to the Foundation and to me personally. I would be one of only 8,000 people to carry the London 2012 Olympic Flame, and play a historic role in the Olympic Torch Relay. I had become a part of the London 2012 team!

I read from the information sent to me that for each Olympic Games a new Olympic Flame is captured in a historic ceremony in Greece. The Flame arrived in the UK on 18 May in Cornwall on British Airways Flight BA2012. It would travel 8,000 miles around the UK, starting in Land's End.

The slot allocated to me was in the London Borough of Lewisham on Monday 23 July: Day 66 of the Olympic Torch journey with Day 70 being the Opening Ceremony on Friday 27 July. I was Torchbearer Number 5 of 187 torchbearers who carried the flame 60 kilometres that day on the leg from Lewisham to Wandsworth.

On the same day the torch was carried by Andy Murray, who carried it onto the Centre Court, having received it from Sue Barker. He then passed it onto Venus Williams with Tim Henman being the final Torchbearer of the day, carrying the Flame into the stage at Tooting Beck Common, where he lit the celebration cauldron.

The organisation around the relay was unbelievable and an enormous logistical exercise. Carol and I arrived at the meeting point by car a little late because of a mix-up in our transport arrangements.

When I got to the meeting point the atmosphere in the Trinity Laban Conservatoire was absolutely amazing. I was placed next to Doreen Lawrence, whose son Stephen was murdered in 1993. I only had the opportunity to speak with her briefly but I gathered from this why she was such an effective campaigner. It was fitting that the route for the torch relay should go past the Stephen Lawrence Centre that Doreen helped to establish. Shortly after this event she was elevated to the House of Lords to continue her work there. We were told to enjoy the moment and not to run too fast, as this was a 'once in a lifetime experience'.

My leg was programmed for 07.43, from Deptford Church Street to Brook Mill Road, some 390 yards. My name was posted on the lamppost and trees along the route to enable family and friends to be in the correct place. As I was dropped off from the coach, I was given an Olympic torch with a gas canister inside it for the flame to be transferred to me. I got to the point where all my family were waiting to cheer me on, including my granddaughter Florence. We had time for family photographs. We were warned in the briefing to expect to be very popular and that we'd have many people flocking around us, wanting to be photographed and to touch the torch, which proved to be true.

I could then see the previous runner coming towards me and as he arrived we simply touched torches, meaning that the Olympic flame came to me.

Running was a magical feeling because I knew at that moment I was the only person in the world holding the Olympic flame. I was a guardian of a symbol that universally represents friendship, respect and excellence around the world. For those short minutes the eyes of the nation were on me. A good friend sent me a text later in the day after seeing my run on TV, and said that the smile on my face said everything.

I tried to run as slowly as possible to soak in the atmosphere of the cheering, not for me but through happiness and pride that the Olympics had come to London. It was very special and I could see out of the corner of my eye my youngest son Robert running the leg with me and he gave me a hug as I got back on the bus, having handed the torch on to Doreen Lawrence.

It was a magical day. Carol and I drove back into London to go to the office just off the Strand to show the Torch to the team at the Foundation. As I got out of the car, still dressed in my white tracksuit, workman on a nearby building site saw me carrying the Torch and all downed tools and came onto the street, wanting a picture with the Torch.

The Torch now has pride of place in my sporting memorabilia. It is triangular, intended to represent the years 1908, 1948 and 2012; the three years when London hosted the Games. Each of the 8,000 Torches produced had 8,000 holes punched through it; one for each Torchbearer – how special is that!

To me, the London Olympics in summer of 2012 was as great a success as 1966 when England won the World Cup. I have never felt so proud of our country. We showed the whole world just what we are capable of doing when we unite behind a single cause. Carol and I were fortunate to visit the Olympic Stadium for a number of events . We were always struck by the ease of getting there on the underground and the warmth of the welcome received from the team of volunteers. The most special time, however was on Sunday 5 August when we were fortunate to be in the stadium with Michael and Georgia to witness Usain Bolt win the final of the 100 metres – the atmosphere was electric!

The following year I had the privilege of having lunch with Lord Coe, along with six of our students, representing our academies, which gave us the opportunity to hear more about the Olympics and to congratulate him personally on what he had achieved. It was a great day for the students and he was incredibly generous in the way he dealt with them. One of our students who attended, Stephen Ferroni, was from BACA. He is a very good athlete, having represented the County and South East running distances from 800 metres to 5,000 metres. Lord Coe was particularly interested in Stephen's development and took the time to give him advice. Stephen has subsequently gone on to represent England.

In February 2012 the Foundation decided to take on the lead sponsorship of the Isle of Portland project with Dorset County Council as the co-sponsor. The site that we had identified for the academy was an old MOD building that had been built to last. It shared the site with a hotel, a theatre and a swimming pool. However, prior to the building becoming an academy, it needed complete renovation. Funding was the issue because, in the offer agreed with the Department, only £9 million had been allocated for the project. After a further review of the building it was obvious that this would not be sufficient and it was difficult to see where the £17 million now needed would come from.

The team at the Foundation was determined to find a way and I asked my son Michael (who at the time was leading on setting up the Aldridge Family Office) to put his mind to structuring the finances in a way that a commercial operator would, by putting some debt into the model. Michael came up with an ingenious idea, which basically meant the debt would come from the government, as it is the cheapest form of debt available and would be repaid over a period of years. This really caused a stir at the Department, and it was immediately referred to HM Treasury, which involved Michael explaining this to the team from No. 11. We were even requested to go to No. 10 to speak to the team there. I eventually received a call from the Minister of State for Education, Lord Hill, who said: 'You have the money.' It came without using Michael's initiative, as officials could see that bureaucracy would scupper the deal!

Another form of school – the 'Studio School' – had emerged. These were much smaller in size, catering for fewer pupils and designed to give students aged fourteen to nineteen skills in the workplace environment as well as traditional academic and vocational study courses. The original thinking came from the Young Foundation and I recall some years ago going to the launch of the concept and the announcement of four or five pilots across the country, mainly in the type of communities that we focused on.

In DACA there was a feeling from the team there, led by Brendan Loughran, that this type of offer would be appealing to students in the area and be a good alternative to what DACA offered. The decision was taken that we should submit an application to the Department to become a sponsor of a Studio School for 300 pupils to be based in Darwen. It was to specialise in Business Administration covering finance, law, digital creative media and marketing. In July we received notification from the Department that our application was successful and so we were in planning mode again for a September opening the following year.

While away on holiday in South Africa I read a newspaper report about a University Technical College (UTC) that had opened, involving the JCB Group. The concept of a UTC intrigued me, as the colleges offer fourteen to nineteen-year-olds technically orientated courses of study, combining the National Curriculum with technical and vocational elements. They have to specialise in subjects that require technical and modern equipment, but they also teach business skills and the use of information and communications technology (ICT). They also enable students to have a closer and earlier relationship with local employers for whom they could ultimately work.

The whole programme was sponsored by the Baker Dearing Trust, set up by Lord Kenneth Baker, whom I had known in my Capita days when he was part of the Thatcher Government. I contacted Honor and said I thought we should look into being involved, then expressed our interest to Lord Adonis (also a Director of Baker Dearing). I also discussed this idea with Julia Fawcett at the Lowry, as I thought it would be a great idea to link this with MediaCity and The Lowry. Andrew Adonis felt that it would be a good idea to replicate the Brit School that had been so successful in London.

Honor, Julia and I went to see the Principal of the Brit School, Nick Williams (now Sir Nick), and were very impressed. We left South London intent on pursuing an application. This was the start of a great deal of work, engaging first with the team at Baker Dearing Trust. However, much of our activity, led by Julia and myself, had to be directed locally, as we needed university and local authority support. Because the lead sponsor had to be a university, it was important to bring the University of Salford on board. They liked our concept and we decided to go for a specialism of creative and digital skills as well as the development of an entrepreneurial mind set among students.

We also needed to ensure that we had the City of Salford on our side, especially as they had a declared dislike of some of the new educational policies of the Conservative Government. A number of students would inevitably come from Salford schools, but not all, as the new UTC would provide opportunities for students across Greater Manchester. I met the Mayor, Ian Stewart, and we found common ground over the intent of the UTC, particularly as he had a keen interest in skills for young people. He became a great supporter of our application, as did a large number of local employers, including the BBC and ITV.

Julia and I presented the concept of the UTC to the trustees of The Lowry to confirm the Lowry's involvement and their support was unanimous. Since the plan was to build in Media City it was necessary to speak with Peel Holdings (who owned all of that land) to find a space for the UTC. John Whittaker, the Chairman of the Peel Group, was very positive about the idea. I have enormous respect for what he has achieved in Media City and he saw the impact that the UTC would have on the quays and especially the benefits to the local community.

So we had support and, after a great deal of work, the application was submitted, in competition with a number of others. We knew that many would be unsuccessful. It was, therefore, necessary to lobby to gain support for our bid and this included lobbying the local MP Hazel Blears. In July 2012 we were delighted to receive the news that approval was given by the Department of Education for the University of Salford, The Lowry and the Aldridge Foundation to be co-sponsors of a university technical college specialising in creative and digital skills in Salford's MediaCity. Then the real work began.

I have always loved cricket, but sadly much of the competitive sport in schools has fallen away. We had been discussing the idea of setting up a Cricket Academy in Brighton for BACA and PACA students, initially directed towards the Sixth Form. The idea was that you could study in the morning and then have top class tuition to improve your cricket skills in the afternoon.

This was a model that Darwen Aldridge Community Academy had pioneered so successfully, with a Cricket Academy in partnership with Lancashire County Cricket Club; a Netball Academy with Manchester Thunder; a Golf Academy with specialist coaching in partnership with Darwen Golf Club; and a Football Academy in partnership with Chorley Football Club. It was the Football Academy that first came to my attention. One student told me that his journey to Darwen each day was long and arduous, requiring him to leave home at 7 a.m., illustrating to me how highly regarded the Football Academy was. The team beat several public schools in the area and in one of the regional cup competitions the final was between DACA 'A' team and DACA 'B' team!

At BACA, after discussions with Sussex County Cricket Club, it was agreed that the coaching for our proposed academy could take place at the County Ground in Hove in their indoor school. We had a great deal of help with this from Zac Toumazi, the CEO of Sussex County Cricket Club, and from Jim May who was the Chairman. Jim was also a governor at BACA and subsequently became Chair of the governing body in 2018. In September 2012 the Foundation was able to announce the launch of the Aldridge Cricket Academy for students attending Portslade Aldridge Community Academy and Brighton Aldridge Community Academy, working in association with Sussex County Cricket Club. This was to prove a great move, as we attracted students to attend it from all over the county, some making lengthy and difficult journeys.

The stories that emerged from this proved it to be one of the best things we had done, and it received great coverage in the local newspapers. We had appointed a top coach in Alexia Walker, who at the time was the cricket coach for Brighton College and wanted to get back into the state system of education. Alexia had played for England, as well as representing Sussex more than 120 times. At the same time, I had also dealt with Simon Funnell at Sussex CCC about our plans and I persuaded him to join us as our Director of Sport in a shared appointment between BACA and PACA. This initiative also acted as a trigger for us to form other sporting academies involving football, digital media, and dance, something very close to my heart.

In September 2012 the Isle of Portland Aldridge Community Academy (IPACA) opened, operating across five sites and encompassing nursery, primary and secondary education. The idea was eventually to move into two sites. One had already been built at Osprey Quay and the other was at Maritime House, the MOD building that needed to be refurbished.

A planning application had been submitted to the local council for approval and signs emerged almost immediately that we had a problem. There were concerns in the local press about the site chosen for the academy, mainly around the transport routes. It was equally clear that a relatively small number of people were out to stop it completely. At the time of indicating our wish to become a sponsor we had a number of difficult public meetings.

The island is in many ways a strange place to operate. Scenically, it has so much going for it, with the most incredible coast giving breathtaking views. However, I became aware of the divides that occurred even on such a small island. For example, the north talked about the south of the island as though it was a completely different place. The indisputable point was that the education was poor and that the academy was an opportunity to address this. Many people had no personal interest in improving education, and put their own agenda above the greater good.

Despite the officers of the council recommending approval of the planning proposal, the planning committee, made up of elected councillors, turned it down. An appeal against the decision was lodged by the Department meant that the planning decision would be decided by an independent public inquiry. This was to delay the start of the work on the new academy by nearly a year.

At around the same time, Honor was approached by the CEO of Lewes District Council, Jenny Rowlands (whom I knew through working on BACA and a community project that we funded when she worked for Brighton & Hove City Council) to see if the Foundation was prepared to look at making an application for a UTC to be built in Newhaven.

Previously Newhaven was synonymous with ferry trips to France, and its trade had been badly affected by the Channel Tunnel. We felt that a brand new UTC building, a new opportunity for fourteen- to nineteen-year-old students, could lead the much-needed regeneration for the area. The suggested specialism was marine engineering with a strong emphasis on maths and science. We had discussions with University of Brighton, who were prepared to be the necessary academic partner. Veolia, the water, waste and energy company based nearby, were keen to back the community and became our Employer Sponsor.

After meetings of the four parties we agreed to submit an application to the Department. By chance, we also found an ideal site for the UTC through a local connection. The building was right by the railway station, and was a historic Grade II listed marine and carpenters' workshop on the quays. It had been vacant for years and required a massive amount of work to turn into a UTC building.

In November 2012, the Foundation was delighted to be awarded the title of Academy Provider of the Year by *EducationInvestor* Awards. It was quite an accolade! The judging panel included representatives from the Department of Education as well as senior figures from the world of education and business. From where we had come as a Foundation to win this against several more established chains was a testimony to the different approach that we had taken, particularly concerning entrepreneurship.

The date 9 February 2013 was very special. This was when my grandson was born to Michael and Georgia. His name is Atticus Jack, which is a wonderful, very powerful name. My father and granddad Aldridge would be so pleased, as I was, since it means that the Aldridge family name goes on for another generation. Quite a responsibility, young man! He is turning out to be very active person, exhibiting many of the characteristic of his father at a young age. His footballing skills look to be encouraging and he is already a supporter of Chelsea Football Club, wearing the Chelsea shirt when he plays.

A few weeks later, in March 2013, Sir Merrick Cockell and I, dressed in yellow hi-vis jackets and hard hats, performed the official sod-cutting ceremony to mark start of the building work for Kensington Aldridge Academy (KAA). Even on that special day we had to run the gauntlet of local residents who were still protesting about the academy's construction. We completed the exercise under police protection, but this did not detract from our subsequent tour of the site which, after the clearance of existing buildings and trees, impressed us by its sheer size. The academy construction was running concurrently with the new leisure centre building, with its eight-lane swimming pool.

Our idea was to engage with local people over the development, and our appointment of a Community Engagement Coordinator, with the role of keeping the local community updated on progress and dealing with any issues, proved to be a great move, defusing the situation enormously. I also chaired a number of partnership meetings with local organisations during the building phase.

We had begun the search for a Principal Designate for the academy and from a strong list of applications, Sir Merrick, Councillor Emma Will and I interviewed three short-listed candidates. I was delighted to make the call to David Benson that afternoon and recall my opening remark: 'I believe that I am speaking to the new Principal of KAA.' He accepted the role in March 2013 and the academy would not open until September 2014, so we had a long time to work with David on architect design and operating policies to make the opening happen as planned.

I can recall sitting with David in our board room at Piccadilly, designing the school uniform and badge as well as deciding on the school motto of *Intrepidus*, which was to prove so important to the school's strong beliefs. Following the tragic fire, the students identified with the motto, using it to unite them in a time of great adversity.   Led by the Foundation, and in particular Sally Lawson-Ritchie and Elizabeth Anderson, we put together a very special partnership arrangement of four educational partners, who would support the development of our curriculum. These included Godolphin and Latymer School; The Royal Academy of Dance (RAD); and The London Academy of Music and Dramatic Art (LAMDA), a world-class drama school whose tuition in 'public speaking' would be particularly helpful for students. The final partner was Charterhouse, where I had a close and long association because three of my children were educated there. The plan here was to develop opportunities for KAA and Charterhouse students to collaborate in various ways including the study of drama, music, art and sport.

In March 2013 we were delighted to get the news giving us approval to open a University Technical College in Newhaven, specialising in marine engineering. Our second UTC was under way.

In September of that year, after receiving approval for funding from the Department, Darwen Aldridge Enterprise Studio opened in a temporary space within the Darwen Aldridge Community Academy. Its ultimate home would be in a building in Police Street that required refurbishment, although it had historic memories for the town, as it was the home used by the inmates of the old Workhouse. Opening in DACA had mixed blessings, because although it enabled us to open on time it affected the Studio School's ability to set its own branding and ethos, which was not helpful in the start-up of a new school. Its first principal was Ruth Bradbury, who had joined as Finance Director of DACA when it first became an academy. The Chair of governors was Terry Boynes, whom I worked closely with at Capita for many years.

The exam results of the summer of 2013, saw our first Aldridge student being awarded a place at Oxford University. Her name is Khushna Sulaman-Butt and she embarked on her course in fine art at Ruskin College. I believe that because she has a special talent she would have made her way successfully whatever happened, but she would not have been able to put a top university on her CV without the work of the team at the academy, and in particular Brendan Loughran and the head of creative arts, Louise Klinck. It is difficult to appreciate that when we became a sponsor there was no Sixth Form for students. It was proof of what can be done with focus and hard work. Remember the name Khushna Sulaman-Butt, as I am convinced that she will be a highly sought-after artist one day.

On 23 January 2014, the building of the Kensington Aldridge Academy had reached its highest point and a 'topping out' ceremony was held. Sir Merrick and I once again donned our yellow hi-vis to lay the commemorative stone. Our guests could not fail to be impressed by what they saw in their tour of the building. It was incredibly clever how the architects had managed to pack so much into such a restricted site.

22 February was a major family event, being the day of the marriage of my youngest daughter Jennifer to James Lavender. James is a qualified chartered engineer and works as a Fire Engineer providing safety advice to clients within the construction industry. He is also a Freeman of the livery company, the Worshipful Company of Firefighters and so it was very appropriate that the wedding took place in the City of London; a city they hold close to their hearts. The service was actually held in the wonderful cathedral church of St Paul's, a historic place to get married. My journey to the church with Jennifer was a very private time that we had together on such a special day travelling through the streets in one of the original old London Taxis. Our walk down the aisle at St Paul's together was equally special. The wedding reception took place at the Royal Horseguards Hotel with guests travelling to it by a private boat under bright blue skies from Blackfriars to the Embankment at Westminster. It was a perfect day for a perfect couple.

In May 2014, two individuals, Mark Smith and Tom Fogden, approached Honor about using two desks in the Foundation to work up an idea for a 'Code College'. They had managed to get £100,000 funding from Gamesys, the Foundation's neighbours in Piccadilly. The pair had met in 2003 when they were inaugural beneficiaries of the Teach First programme. This has been an incredibly successful programme, encouraging newly qualified young graduates to go into teaching, rather than going to work in the City or in industry.

We were soon to learn that Mark and Tom were both very talented and clever operators, meaning this in a very positive way! They were in fact working inside our organisation, sizing us up as a potential partner in their venture. That venture would become a reality over the next fifteen months, coming from nowhere to beat off more established providers to deliver the vision that they had developed. Personally, the association also took me into the world of digital education, since I ended up chairing the Board for the Code College when the Foundation Trustees agreed to us becoming a founding partner in the venture.

The Principal of IPACA, Alison Appleyard, and John Tizard, the Chair of Governors, came to me to talk about an available building which was ideal for the Sixth Form that we wanted, in order to give students, for the first time, the opportunity to study A Levels on the island. This was an old police station called Victoria Building that was easily adaptable for teaching purposes.

Unfortunately, the academy had no money to purchase it and, with the building work going on at Maritime House, the Department was unlikely to fund it. The solution that I put forward to them as a goodwill gesture was that we would buy the building through our family office Aldridge Wealth and then establish a lease for the academy to pay a market rent for the building. This is what we did and IPACA was able to announce to an Open Evening that it could offer sixth form education for the first time. The new Sixth-Form Campus opened in Victoria Building in September 2014.

In the same eventful month for the island, the Public Inquiry granted planning permission for the Isle of Portland building in Southwell Business Park. This needless delay cost over a year and saw the costs of the project escalate. From an education standpoint it meant that we had to go on teaching across five sites rather than the two that were planned. This also caused an escalation in costs and prevented the effective introduction of the planned educational transformation. This was to prove a fateful outcome to the project, ultimately involving us withdrawing as sponsor. I will return to this later.

Also that month, the Darwen Aldridge Enterprise Studio (DAES) opened in its heritage building after a £4.1 million restoration. An amazing space had been created, full of natural light through of the clever use of a glass roof linking the two parts of the building. This move gave DAES the opportunity to build its own identity.

September was an incredibly busy month as it also saw the Kensington Aldridge Academy open in its £28-million building with some style. The plan was to open the brand new school with a one-year intake. We had held several open sessions in a local primary school to explain to parents about the academy and the plans that we had for it.

Principal David Benson fronted the session and Councillor Emma Will and I also contributed.

The sessions were all very positive, with David doing a great job. We spoke about entrepreneurship and how businesses could be run from office pods in the academy, giving the students first-hand experience. There was a slight intake of breath from the prospective students when David explained that the academy's working day would be slightly longer than usual, but some of this was because of the enrichment programme, consisting of various clubs included those for cooking, chess, table tennis, boxing, coding and street dance, as well as football and basketball.

David obviously did a good job, as we were five times over-subscribed for the first year's intake. I subsequently became a governor of KAA as did Sir Merrick Cockell and Councillor Emma Will, and we recruited a strong governing body. I was delighted that Janice Shiner had agreed to my request that she become the first Chair of governors. KAA went from strength to strength with the next year's intake being similarly over-subscribed.

The idea of a Code College, the vision of Mark Smith and Tom Fogden, began to gather increased momentum and increased support both from the Department for Business, Innovation and Skills (BIS) and No. 10. The initial submission from the team to BIS was in September 2014. This was rapidly followed by a breakfast arranged at No. 10 which I co-hosted with Dan Korski, the Deputy Head of the PM's Policy Unit. Senior executives from the large IT companies were invited, including Google, IBM, Bank of America and Deloitte. The idea of the breakfast was essentially a 'call to arms', pointing out the shortage of skills and how we intended to help fill that gap.

It was estimated that the UK will need to fill 766,000 new digital jobs by 2020 and train almost 2.3 million people to meet the demand for digital skills. It was strange that with this demand, few young people were studying IT in schools and colleges. In the previous year fewer than 4,000 students studied computing at A Level in England. This was why No. 10 was supportive of our initiative.

Several countries were way ahead of the UK in training people for these roles, so it was time for UK industry to address the issue by supporting the idea of a National College, both financially and by offering employment to graduates through an apprenticeship scheme. The meeting went well and we gained a lot of supporters. The founding partners of the college were: Bank of America Merrill Lynch, Deloitte Digital, Gamseys, IBM, King and my Foundation. On 9 December, No. 10 announced that it would be supporting a National College of Digital Skills, and naming us as their preferred provider.

For a number of years in Darwen, we had been discussing the possibility of Darwen Vale High School joining us and becoming an academy. When I first wanted to become the sponsor of a school, Terry Boynes, Capita's Business Director of our centre in Blackburn with Darwen, had taken me to look at Darwen Vale, a very imposing former grammar school. One of its attractions was that it was central, close to Ewood Park, the home of Blackburn Rovers. Nothing came of it and Vale subsequently went through a substantial build programme through a PFI-type arrangement whereby a contractor did the work and the school repaid the money over a number of years. During the rebuild, the school decamped to the site of the Darwen Moreland High School, the original home of DACA.

Darwen is a very close community and rivalry built up between DACA and Darwen Vale. As DACA developed and began to perform well on both academic and sporting fronts, the rivalry manifested itself in the way that, despite DACA having a flourishing Sixth Form while Vale had no such option, few students from Vale ever came to DACA. Many Vale students went out of the town by bus each day to complete their sixth-form studies.

Brendan and I agreed that we should meet with the Principal and Chair of Vale to see if we could find some common ground. My point was that with the amount of capital investment put into both schools, surely the government was entitled to believe that it should receive maximum benefit from this investment. They had a specialism in engineering and creative arts, while ours were in entrepreneurship and sport. There could be savings also in back office services as well as the ability to offer cover in teaching staff.

To me, the solution was obvious but the meeting did not go well. There was plenty of positive discussion and mutual respect expressed, but I was left with the clear impression that nothing would be settled. Subsequently, however, the Vale has experienced financial difficulties, and a falling role has made recruiting teaching staff difficult for the Principal, Fiona Jack.

It also had a poor Ofsted Inspection, prompting discussions about it becoming an academy and the need to find a sponsor. The Foundation was obviously very interested but, just as in Brighton, there were claims that it was not right to have two schools with the same sponsor. This required us to lobby both the Department and locally. This involved discussion with local MP Jake Berry, along with Will Straw, the Labour Party parliamentary candidate. The debate went on for some time, including discussions with Shadow Education Minister Tristram Hunt but ultimately Lord Nash, the Minister came down on the side of the Foundation. It was announced that we would become the sponsor and in December 2014 Darwen Vale School became an Aldridge Academy.

In January 2015, HRH The Duchess of Cambridge officially opened the Kensington Aldridge Academy. This was a very proud moment for us all. I have a wonderful picture of her sitting down at a table with students joining in a reading lesson in the library. She has a wonderful way with children and is equally able to put adults, including myself, at ease. After a presentation from students in the theatre, my granddaughter, Florence, presented the Duchess with a bouquet, which was a special family moment. When she arrived by car and I stepped forward to welcome her she immediately recalled her visit to the opening of DACA, and said how much her and the Prince had enjoyed it.

February 2015 was a first for the Aldridge Cricket Academy as a group of twenty-four players, along with coach Alexia Walker, went on tour to Cape Town in South Africa. A great deal of effort had gone into fund-raising for the trip and we had a very successful dinner the previous October. One of the highlights for me was that the tour party had helped serve food to the guests. All the team received 'silver service' training and they performed their duties very professionally.

For many of the party it was the first time that they had been out of the country. We had intentionally arranged the itinerary so that they would experience all aspects of African life. As well as visiting places such as the Cape of Good Hope, they also went to Robin Island where Nelson Mandela was imprisoned for eighteen of the twenty-seven years he served behind bars. They visited one of the townships, including going to an old people's home, which had an enormous impact on them, making them appreciate their circumstances in Brighton! I had experienced this sort of visit on a cricket tour when my son, Robert was in Cape Town with his Charterhouse team. My lasting memory was the pride that people felt for their homes, no matter how basic. It was both revealing and humbling.

The team was scheduled to play eight matches against some very tough opposition, several of which were private schools. We fielded a 1st XI and a 2nd XI at all venues. The other tremendous thing was that Alexia, our coach, had three girls in our squad, one of whom was already in the Sussex women's team!

Carol and I decided to go to South Africa for a holiday to catch games at three of the venues. We love Cape Town, along with Stellenbosch and Franschhoek, where we had spent our honeymoon. At the first game we attended, when we saw a squad practicing, Carol commented how well drilled they looked, and from my experiences of the Charterhouse tour, I knew how seriously they take their sport. As we got closer and recognised some of the players we realised that it was our squad we were looking at!

They went on to win six out of eight games played, beating one team along the way that had never lost to a touring side before. In my book the 1st XI should have won all their games, however they lost a very tight game in the last match. There was great excitement back at base in Brighton and Portslade as the results were tweeted live!

One of the team supporting Alexia was the one and only John Spencer. As a boy, on many occasions I had watched John bowl for Sussex. He went on to have a very successful academic career with Brighton College, becoming Deputy Headmaster. As well as assisting with coaching the team, it also turned out that he was a keen photographer and we have many happy memories of the tour from John's shots. He even presented me with a much prized album of the tour.

It was tremendous to spend time with the team to learn more about their personal plans and aspirations. I could not help but reflect on how well they presented themselves both on and off the field of play. They were a credit to the academies and to themselves. I am sure the tour is an experience that none of them will forget. I know that Carol and I will remember the trip with great pride.

When the team returned to England they went on to have a great summer, winning games against some very strong opposition. This included beating a number of public schools, such as Brighton College, Ardingly College and Charterhouse. The victory at Charterhouse was a particularly poignant one for me as it was where my two sons, Michael and Robert, played their cricket. I saw Robert take many wickets with his spin bowling, along with some swashbuckling innings with the bat, clearing the boundary ropes on many occasions. Aldridge Cricket Academy (ACA) beat Charterhouse on Green, the hallowed square where the great Peter May once played his cricket before going on to captain England.

By September 2015, I had been working on a plan to build an indoor cricket school at BACA for about 18 months. No other school in Brighton or in the county had such a facility and it would give us another USP for our academy. I had a great deal of help with this from David Brooks who was the former CEO of Sussex County Cricket Club along with Simon Funnel, our Director of Sports, and Alexia Walker, the Director of Cricket.

We opened discussions with Sussex Women's Cricket about making it their home, as they had no fixed ground and they were enthusiastic about accepting. We were also aware that Portslade Cricket Club, the club I played for briefly as a young man, were ambitious about moving up into the Premier League, but did not have the ground to match the big leagues requirements. So we spoke with Portslade's chairman Andy Glover and they jumped at the idea of our ground becoming the home for Portslade CC to play its first team matches. How amazing is that?

So far so good, but it then took me six months to get the governing bodies of both academies on board to support the idea. In the meantime, Dave Brooks and Simon submitted several applications to bodies such as Sport England, as we needed to raise building funds. We drew a blank: nothing could be started until the funding was in place.

We discussed holding fund-raising dinners and approaching affluent individuals, of which there are many in Brighton and Hove. I could see this going on for years and so I made a proposition to BACA that if they were to make a contribution from the money they generated from letting out the sporting facilities they had, I would make a sizeable donation. Having got over that hurdle we were still short of our target, which involved raising £1.8 million.

One needs a stroke of good fortune in such circumstances and it came in the form of a charity day at Arundel Castle to support the wonderful work done by Jonny Barclay, former captain of Sussex and manager of England. Jonny is Director of Cricket and Coaching for the Arundel Cricket Foundation. Here he is able to give young people from all parts of the country the chance to broaden their education and enhance their lives through cricket and coaching. Some of them are disabled or partially sighted and most are from inner-city areas.

The charity day involved four teams playing in a limited-over competition. BACA entered a team, as did Lansdowne Partners, whose captain was Peter Davies, whom I had known well in my Capita days. On the day Peter met our coach Alexia, spending some time learning about our vision for BACA in the communities that the academies served. He also spoke to several members of the team and was impressed by what we were trying to do. He was equally impressed by the team and the way that they played the game. ACA actually won the competition, beating Peter's team in the final.

Several days later, I decided to go to see Peter about our indoor school project. When we met I set out my plans. He said: 'How much are you short?' I told him the amount and he immediately said: 'Count me in,' but challenged me to make sure that the impact of the centre was felt as widely as possible in the county. To support greater involvement, Peter also put in place the funding to support a county-wide coaching programme for women and girls. I was shocked by his enormous generosity.

In October 2015 we were able to announce the construction of a £1.8-million Cricket School and Pavilion to be built at Brighton Aldridge Community Academy for the use of academy students, other clubs and the community.

In February 2015 BIS announced that the team supported by the Foundation had been successful in its application to open the National College for Digital Skills, which was to open in Haringey in September 2016. We were one of five colleges announced but the only one not to involve an existing college.

In March 2015 Sudell Primary School in Darwen, for pupils aged from four to eleven, joined the Aldridge North West Trust, thus becoming an Aldridge school. Discussion on this had gone on for some time and we were actually approached first in autumn 2014 when they asked us to sponsor the school. We were happy to do so as over 90 per cent of the students went on to DACA and this would bring about a smoother transfer, enabling more effective planning by the teaching staff.

When I visited Sudell, I came away believing that we could make a real difference. Most definitely the Principal, Kathryn Coiffait, the leadership team that I met and the chair of governors saw it as a chance for a new beginning. This now meant that in Darwen we had two secondary schools including a Sixth Form, a studio school and a primary school, which to me was very exciting. It gave us the opportunity for the first time to plan the curriculum, giving students the option of choosing their route.

In April I had the honour to be invited to become a Founding Freeman of the Guild of Entrepreneurs in recognition of my contribution to the growth of entrepreneurship in the UK. In a ceremony in the City of London on 15 April I was welcomed into the Guild by the Guild's Master, the late Sir Paul Judge. On 23 June I was asked to speak at the inaugural dinner of the guild held at the Mansion House. The Guild intends to become a livery company and is made up of people who have invested their own money and time in setting up and running successful businesses.

September 2015 saw our two UTCs open their doors for business. MediaCity University Technical College in Salford opened in an unbelievable building space containing two fully equipped studios, the largest seating an audience of 200. The teaching spaces were equally as impressive as was the entrepreneurship centre where there were four office pods for start-up businesses.

Thanks to the work of Anne Casey, the principal, we had attracted more than sufficient numbers of students both at the fourteen-year-old intake and at aged sixteen as well, opening in a strong financial position. I heard an amazing story from one student's grandfather, who had followed the development of the UTC and watched its construction. He said to himself: 'My granddaughter must come here.' The only problem was that his granddaughter lived in Kent with her family. As a family they took the decision that she should move to Salford and stay with her grandparents because the offer was too good to miss! UTC was formally opened on 2 April 2016 by Lord Tony Hall, Director General of the BBC.

Harbourside University Technical College in Newhaven opened, but in temporary buildings next to the main building, which was still under construction. This is never an easy decision but the sponsors and Chair of Governors took the view that it was better to open than defer for a year. It is sad but true that in the politics that existed in Brighton, delay would be seen as failure and its eventual opening would be subject to question. I am delighted that my son-in-law, James Lavender, who is a qualified engineer, was selected to become a governor.

Also in September 2015 Darwen Aldridge Community Academy was named as one of eleven schools from eleven countries across Europe, which won the Entrepreneurial School of the Year Award. DACA was the UK winner and it was international recognition for the work of Brendan Loughran and his team. The celebration took place in Strasbourg on 15 October in the presence of Members of the European Parliament.

21

TRANSFORMATION AND CHANGE

In January 2016, Honor Wilson-Fletcher stepped down as CEO of the Foundation to take up a role as the CEO of The British Exploring Society. Her contribution over six-and-a-half years had been enormous. We had worked together very well as a team and had achieved more than we could have imagined. When Honor joined the Foundation it was a small education charity supporting one school and a number of associated projects. In our time together we had grown it to become a national academy sponsor with a dedicated team of academic partners. Beki Martin, our Deputy CEO took over as Interim Chief Executive of the Foundation and was later appointed CEO.

More change was necessary. As it stood, each academy was an independent trust connected to the Foundation via a licensing arrangement. There remained a great deal of affection for the Foundation, but there was increasing confusion over lines of responsibility. We were not maximising the opportunity to centralise back-office services, saving money to be spent on front-line teaching and learning. Two of our academies also had bad exam results in the summer and we received a clear message from the National Commissioner of Schools, Sir David Carter, that our structure needed to change. So we began the process of forming a multi-academy trust (MAT). This was a structure encouraged by the Department and it resulted in a single legal entity being established providing a collaborative approach to improve and maintain high educational standards across all of our schools.

This was a big moment. The infrastructure that we created as a foundation was handed over to another related body, Aldridge Education, to run the family of academies and colleges. Within this structure at the time we planned four regional clusters in the North West, South West, South East and London. This gave the Foundation more freedom to develop innovative ways to help our academies on their journey of transformation.

It was this role of bringing innovative thinking that had attracted me to become a sponsor, but by necessity the major focus had been on the process of transformation, most of the time under the scrutiny of the Department, Ofsted and local media. The revised structure gave Beki Martin and me the opportunity to focus on repositioning the Foundation and building on the infrastructure of academies and colleges that we had created over the past ten years. In my role as chair, I have been massively supported by our Board of Trustees. I would like to thank Rich Benton, with whom, of course, I started Capita; Brent Thomas, who is now also the Chair of Aldridge Education; James Sporle, whom I first met when he was at Cambridge University studying with my son, Michael; Tom Ilube, who was associated with me many years ago as a governor at DACA and now also chairs the governing body of Ada College; and, of course, my daughter Jennifer Lavender and my wife, Carol. We have achieved a great deal together that will change young lives for the better.

31 May 2016 saw the birth of my granddaughter Annie Rose Doris Lavender to my youngest daughter, Jennifer, and her husband, James. By a coincidence hers is the same birth date as that of my eldest daughter, Debby and of my best friend Mike Harding! Annie is a pure bundle of joy and I have no doubt that Jennifer and James will be great parents. It is wonderful to see Jennifer so happy and settled working in a nursery. I am convinced that one day she will own and run her own nursery.

After dropping out from studying for a degree at the University of West of England when she was just twenty-two, Jennifer now took to studying while working full time, through her pregnancy and then the arrival of Annie. This was an amazing achievement as the degree required her to work at home in the evenings as well as attending university. Both Jacqui and I were at the ceremony earlier this year when Jennifer graduated from Kingston University with a BA (Hons) in Early Years Learning.

My mother reached the age of 100 on 16 June 2016 – an amazing achievement. On the day of her birthday we had a reception for her in the place where she lived in Harwood Court in Hove so that she could celebrate with all of her friends and show off her card from Her Majesty the Queen. On the Saturday, Carol and I held a celebration for her at our home with 100 family and friends – including Annie, her great-granddaughter, who was only nineteen days old. We had arranged for Katherine Jenkins, my mother's favourite singer, to perform for her. This was very special as Katherine was going on to perform at the Queen's birthday ninetieth birthday celebration that evening at the Royal Albert Hall.

June saw the completion of our indoor cricket centre at the Brighton Aldridge Community Academy. Jon Ward from the Aldridge Education team masterminded the construction project and did a great job. The centre was truly breathtaking both inside and out, with facilities that were world class. It also provided a wonderful 'front end' to the academy as people drove up to visit the school or walked past it on their way to watch the 'Seagulls' play at the Amex, no more than fifteen minutes away.

The Sir Rod Aldridge Cricket Centre was opened on 30 June 2016 by Charlotte Edwards CBE, the former England Cricket Captain. I wanted Charlotte to do this because I am a great admirer of what she achieved with women's cricket. Charlotte gave a coaching session to our teams in the centre during the day and was joined by Suzie Bates, the Captain of New Zealand. The inaugural game to be played to commemorate the opening was against Gordonstoun School. In a hard-fought contest sadly shortened by bad weather, ACA came out on top. The Gordonstoun Shield they presented to us now has pride of place in the new clubhouse. With his deep interest in cricket, my youngest son, Robert, became involved with the Centre, joining its Management Committee, now chaired by David Bowden, a past President of Sussex CCC.

After a long search process, Chris Tweedale joined us as the CEO of Aldridge Education Multi-Academy Trust (MAT) in October. Chris had previously held distinguished positions in education, with the Department, the Welsh Assembly and latterly with CfBT, another schools trust. The challenges of moving academies into the MAT were considerable. The real advantage of this was that through the local clusters it was possible to achieve shared support and shared services.

This presented us with a problem over the Isle of Portland Aldridge Community Academy as we had no other schools in the south west. It was also clear, following another set of poor academic results in the summer, that massive change was necessary along with considerable educational and financial support. Many of the issues had been caused by the unnecessary delay in obtaining planning permission, which had resulted in the capital cost of the project escalating. Most crucially, it had stopped us implementing the transformation plans that we had to reduce costs and to improve the effectiveness of teaching and learning. We could not fund this from the MAT structure without jeopardising our other academies and the Department felt unable to give us a grant to cover the work. We were, therefore, put in a very difficult position by the Regional Schools Commissioner and the Department. This gave the trustees little option but to make the reluctant decision to step aside as the sponsor. It was not an easy decision after the five years of work that we had put into the project but through our efforts, the infrastructure now existed to change the education received by young people on the island, something that was desperately needed.

So, going forward, the Aldridge Education MAT would have three regional clusters in the north west, south east and London with a team charged with the responsibility of doubling the overall number of academies that we support.

In November 2015, the Autumn Statement to Parliament by the Chancellor announced five new colleges involving the high speed rail, nuclear, on-shore oil and gas, creative and cultural industries as well as, of course, the National College for Digital Skills. These were the first new incorporated further education colleges in England for 23 years and our successful bid was the only one that would be delivered by a new institution. This was an amazing achievement and testament to the determination of Mark Smith and Tom Fogden to win through.

Over the period of the bid we had built up enormous support from the industry for the new college and this must have weighed in our favour. The stated mission of the College was to work with industry to design and deliver an institution that provided the education and support necessary for students to progress into highly skilled, computer-related roles. The aim was for 50 per cent of the students to be women and the curriculum was to be designed with the future in mind. We were essentially shaping a new industry. Mark and Tom were also determined to use digital skills as a tool for social mobility to help young people gain access to exciting, fast paced and well paid jobs with bright prospects and without the need to take on £50,000 of university-related debt.

The new college opened in Haringey in September 2016 with fifty-eight students in temporary accommodation in Broad Lane, converting a former Job Centre into a modern, spacious learning environment. Its new £31-million home for 2,500 students is to be built nearby, opening in early 2020. The Chief Executive of Haringey, Nick Walkley, his Deputy, Zina Etheridge, and the Director of Regeneration, Planning and Development, Lyn Garner, had all been incredibly supportive of the initiative from the outset. The College fitted perfectly with the council's plans for regeneration of the area, reinforcing Haringey's growing reputation for education, skills and training as well as complementing the boom in tech, manufacturing research and industry in the local area.

So much can be achieved by working in positive partnership, just as we have done with the Royal Borough of Kensington and Chelsea over the academy in North Kensington and the approach now being adopted by Haringey. I sensed that the relationship would to lead to other opportunities for the Foundation and this has proved to be the case.

Association with the college was particularly exciting for the Foundation in that it involved us in leading-edge thinking around digital education. It was agreed that, ultimately, there would be a 'hub and spoke' arrangement, where we would open similar colleges over time within our other clusters in the North West and South East.

Some time previously we had moved away from calling it Code College since, apart from the fact that an individual claimed he had registered the name and was trading under it, we did not feel it was a strong enough representation of what we were about. Mark and Tom came up with the idea of naming it the 'Ada College'. This was after Augustus Ada King-Noel, Countess of Lovelace, the nineteenth-century mathematical and computer pioneer, who was essentially the first 'computer programmer'. She worked on the Charles Babbage mechanical computer, called the 'Analytical Engine'.

I was fortunate to be able to persuade Baroness Martha Lane Fox to be our patron. This fitted well with her charity that she had launched in 2012 called Go ON UK, focused on making the UK the world's most digitally skilled nation. I must admit that I had always been a fan of Martha and I thought that her televised address for the annual Richard Dimbleby Lecture was quite brilliant. On 13 December 2015 we had a 'soft' launch of Ada College in an event hosted by IBM, one of our supporters, at its London HQ. Martha spoke at this very persuasively about Ada and the need to encourage more women to enter the profession. From our research it showed that women earn just 18 per cent of undergraduate degrees awarded for computer science in the UK and the US. Thirty years ago this was 37 per cent.

We still had to surmount another rather important hurdle, which was securing funding for the project. This was complicated because there was to be split funding, with funds of around £13.4 million coming from BIS as part of the national colleges initiative, and the balance to come from the Greater London Authority (GLA).

Two things added to the complication of getting approval from the GLA. The first was that a national review was going on concerning further education colleges, which would lead to some closures at a time when we were proposing to open a new one. The other was a timing issue, as Boris Johnson was coming to the end of his tenure as Mayor of London, meaning that if we did not conclude this it could be affected by the rapidly approaching Mayoral Election.

For us, delay was not an option if we were to open on time. This entailed the team of Tom, Mark and myself going before a full meeting of the London Economic Action Partnership (LEAP) chaired by the

Mayor to present our case for Ada to the members, many of whom were affected by college closures in their boroughs. It was fascinating dealing with the team of officers at the GLA and I must say the detailed preparation that they put into both testing out our case for Ada and the preparing the way for the meeting was as impressive as I have ever experienced in my time working with local government. The outcome of the meeting we presented to was that members failed to make a decision but referred it to a smaller group, also chaired by Boris, to make the decision. So on 18 March, on Boris Johnson's last day in office, agreement to the £18.2 million from the GLA and the LEAP was announced, meaning that signing this was his last act in office!

On 11 October 2016, in celebration of Ada Lovelace Day, Ada College was officially launched by Robert Halfon MP, Minister of State for Education and Jukes Pipe, Deputy Mayor for Planning, Regeneration and Skills. As planned, once the College was open, I would step down as the inaugural chair of Ada and hand over the chairmanship to Tom Ilube, whom I have known for over twelve years, initially through our membership of the Worshipful Company of Information Technologists. Tom was closely involved with The Foundation's first academy in Darwen and today is a Trustee of the Foundation. He has done some great work in Africa, being the Founder of the African Gifted Foundation which has recently launched the African Science Academy in Ghana, the first all-girl science and maths academy. I am staying as a Governor of Ada under Tom's Chairmanship and I am confident that the College will continue to thrive.

At the event held at IBM for the launch of Ada on 13 December 2015, Zina Etheridge, now CEO of Haringey, mentioned that her team at the council had been in conversation about one of their schools, Northumberland Park Community School. Zina wondered if we would like to meet the Principal, Monica Duncan, to discuss the possibility of it converting to an academy and joining the Aldridge Education MAT. Northumberland Park is a mixed secondary school with a specialism in the arts and located very close to Tottenham Hotspur Football Ground in White Hart Lane.

We met with Monica Duncan and her Chair of Governors, Malcolm Weston. Malcolm works for BT and was very interested in our work with Ada College. Quite rightly, they wanted to ensure that they made the right decision and set about the task in a very comprehensive way, visiting all our academies in the North West, as well as going to see MediaCity UTC. At each place they spent time with the respective principals to find out more about their school and what it was like to 'work with Aldridge'.

Northumberland Park was a large school and the accommodation had been the subject of various extensions over the years. The plan was to knock down the existing building and to rebuild the school on a new site as part of the redevelopment of the area planned by the Haringey Council. This would give the school the opportunity to reposition itself and one of the attractions in joining a MAT was that it would help the transformation.

Jon Ward and I were invited to go to the school to have a tour of the buildings and to have lunch with around twenty students, so that they could find out more about us and we could ask them what their thoughts were about the school. For Jon and I this proved to be a very informative session and we were impressed by the passionate way that they described their school. Most definitely the motto of 'motivate, aspire and transform' came over from the students who had ambitious plans for their futures.

I also arranged to meet the Leader of the Council, Councillor Claire Kober, whom I had met briefly over the application for funding of Ada College with the London Enterprise Partnership. Claire is also the Chair of London Councils, which brings together each of the capital's thirty-three boroughs to lobby for fairer funding for London. We had a discussion about the redevelopment and how some of the plans that the Foundation had for developing enterprise zones for start-up businesses could play into this.

All of the Foundation team that visited the school and met with different members of staff came back enthused about working with them and felt that the entrepreneurial attributes along with the 'Creates model' we had developed would resonate well with the students. The encouragement for students to start businesses would fit well alongside the collective corporate wish to see regeneration of the area through the creation of jobs and skills.

The process of becoming an academy is always long, but I am pleased to say that in early January the governing body gave its approval to Northumberland Park Community School applying for academy status. Although it was to take until the following April to get the final approval, Northumberland Park joined our MAT in September 2017 and is now newly opened as Duke's Aldridge Academy.

On 8 November 2017 we held an event at Spencer House to mark the tenth anniversary of the Foundation. Spencer House is, of course, very special to Carol and me as it was where we got married and had our wedding reception. It is a wonderful setting, tucked away in Pall Mall. I invited a number of people who had helped us along the way to build the family of academies and colleges that we now have. My youngest daughter Jennifer, who is a Trustee of the Foundation, was there along with James, her husband. Michael and his wife Georgia came, but unfortunately Robert and Debby were away.

I had the idea of exhibiting the amazing piece of art that Khushna (Saluman-Butt) had painted for her degree work at Oxford. This worked well and looked completely at home with the other art around the house. I also asked the choir from KAA to perform for our guests as they moved around the house. They did a great job and I hope that it will be something that they will remember for some time. The star of the show was Liam Dargen, a former student of DACA who enthralled the audience with the story of his perceptions of the journey that he had been on at DACA.

Beki Martin did a great job hosting the evening and explaining the plans that we had for the Foundation going forward. Sir David Carter, the National Schools Commissioner, did me the personal honour of speaking, commenting on the improvements that we had achieved working in some of the most disadvantaged communities. It was all very special and by the time I got to speak my emotions were running high. As well as thanking people, particularly our trustees, I returned to the theme of our ambition to prove that it is not where you come from that matters, but where you want to get to that counts.

Believe it or not, on the day of the celebration while in our Principals' Forum, Katie Scott, our Principal at Portslade Aldridge Community

School, got the call that Ofsted intended to visit the following day for a full inspection. Katie did not attend the celebration event, returning to Portslade to prepare for the visit. The inspection went well and on the Friday we were informed that the academy had been judged 'Good' in all categories, with some bordering on 'Outstanding'. On the last two inspections, in 2012 and 2014, the academy had been classified as 'Requiring improvement'. This was tremendous news and the icing on the cake for the week of celebrations. This was down to some tremendous work by Katie and her team along with Andy Weymouth, Aldridge Education's Director of Education.

We were still glowing with this success, only for Dylan Davis the Principal at BACA to receive a similar call from Ofsted two weeks later. This inspection was vital to us because the previous two inspections had also resulted in 'Requiring improvement' judgements. Again, great work had been done in preparation for a likely inspection and in the summer BACA had improved its examination results by 21 per cent. We had also had the opening of the new indoor cricket school and so the facilities that students had were exceptional. We held our breath as Day One of the inspection appeared to go well and so we went into Day Two hoping for the best. On Wednesday 7 December we got the news we all wanted to hear: the inspectors had given the Academy a 'Good' judgment.

We had to hold onto this news over Christmas for the inspectors' report to be ratified by Ofsted but when the school returned after the Christmas holidays, we were able to announce the outcome.

It is a fitting end to the chapter to say that the two schools converted into academies in my city by the Foundation had now been adjudged 'Good', which justifies the decision, taken seven years ago, to turn them into academies under the Foundation's sponsorship.

I am very proud of what we have achieved, and of all the people associated with the Foundation. We have so much to show for all our efforts. The structure now in place, with a family of academies and colleges, is a great basis for Aldridge Education to build on in the next phase of our development.

Not bad for a person who was originally only going to sponsor one academy!

22

REFLECTIONS AND FUTURE PLANS

Having reached the age of seventy, I feel incredibly lucky still to be involved with such a wide range of projects, all of which I am passionate about and allow me to work with some incredibly talented people. My thoughts continue to be focused more on what I want to achieve in the future rather than clinging on to what I have done in the past.

Through the work of my Foundation I have learned a great deal over the past twelve years. I recognise the social issues that so many people living in challenging communities face day in and day out. This has confirmed to me the importance of a good education but that is not simply about knowledge and good exam grades. For young people to have fulfilling lives, more attention must be devoted to developing skills that will enable them to work with others, communicate effectively and apply themselves to be creative in solving problems. These skills are increasingly more highly sought after by employers than academic grades, yet our education system frowns upon recognising this, believing such skills cannot be taught or are a waste of time.

Developing these skills in young people will have a major impact on addressing the damaging social mobility issues in our country. More importantly, they will set students up for the workplace of the future. It is obvious that more young people want to start their own businesses rather than following more traditional routes into employment which is good news since many jobs of today will no longer exist in tomorrow's work place.

I have also learned a great deal about myself. I am increasingly low on patience and have a real issue with those that block progress. I hate unnecessary bureaucracy. I am very much a proactive and cause-related individual, particularly where I see injustice or unfairness. In such circumstances, I am unable simply to walk away. I take it on myself to change things for the better. I am most definitely a team player but have exacting standards for myself and expect others I work with to take a similar approach. Much of what I have achieved has been through getting the best out of others which in turn has stimulated my own development. I demand loyalty to be given and to be received. Over the years, I feel I have become increasingly creative and innovative. I am prepared to challenge conventional thinking and to push the boundaries of what is possible, trusting in my belief that I can bring about real and sustained change.

That was what attracted me to become an academy sponsor – I felt that I could make a difference. The work of my Foundation has most definitely achieved that but I have found the pace of change too slow. In education there is incremental change rather than radical reform. Teaching and teachers may not be changing fast enough but their pupils certainly are, mainly through exposure to technology and social media. To young people life is not about slavishly learning facts – it is more about how they apply them, as mere information is now freely available from numerous sources. The need is now to stimulate the mind and let it go rather than to confine and frustrate it within a rigid educational framework.

I have sympathy for teachers as they have to cope with so many changes thrust upon them by successive governments. Yet a student only has one shot at getting his or her education right and it is clear that, for many, the traditional model of teaching and learning is not working. Employability is a major factor in achieving a fulfilling life, as is a belief in the family unit and having a community spirit. The idea that young people lack enterprising skills is a commonly held view among potential employers, who see a gap between what they need, and what is available to them, even at degree level. However, I believe it is time for employers to stop complaining and to get more involved within schools to help change this. Increasingly, apprenticeships will be the way forward, where young people can learn on the job and still have the opportunity to acquire academic qualifications

At Aldridge, we have the goal that by the age of twenty-five, all students will have experienced an outstanding and enjoyable education and be able to sustain a lifestyle of their choice. They will be independent, thriving economically and making a positive contribution in their communities. By twenty-five they should have gone through higher education or an apprenticeship and be on the way to developing a career. The emphasis is on working rather than relying on the social security benefit system, which might have been what they were used to at home.

I was shocked to read in an article some years ago that around 18,000 people in Blackburn with Darwen, which is 30 per cent of the local population, were on benefits for an average of fifteen years of their lives. Potentially, in the past a student could have left Darwen Aldridge Community Academy at sixteen and still have been dependent upon social benefits at the age of thirty-one, most probably with a family of their own by then. Our work with young people in Darwen has undoubtedly ensured that this statistic will be dramatically reduced in the future.

A good education gives you choices. This should be a right of every individual, but has historically been denied to so many particularly in the challenging communities with which the Foundation has chosen to work. I recall reading a speech given by Michael Gove in 2009 as Secretary of State for Education in which he spoke of the education system denying children from poor families the right to their intellectual inheritance. He said that, of the 75,000 children on free school meals each year (one in eight of all pupils), four out of ten fail to even get a single C grade GCSE. Only 189 of these 75,000 go on to get three A's at A Level, compared with the 175 'three A' pupils produced by just one school, Eton College. He confirmed that independent schools, which educate just 7 per cent of pupils, produce more pupils who get three A's at A level than all of the comprehensive schools put together.

I was attracted to become the sponsor of an academy because I thought that position was unacceptable. I felt that the original concept of the Academies Programme championed by the then Prime Minister, Tony Blair, and Lord Andrew Adonis provided the opportunity to address this underperformance which clearly existed in the schools that I attended as a youngster. Since its inception, however, the policy on academies under successive administrations has lurched forward, allowing the explosion of Free Schools, many of which it is accepted could fail. It has also brought about the experimentation of Studio Schools and University Technical Colleges (UTCs). There are many good things about UTCs, especially in the way that they involve local employers, but asking students to move from their school to a UTC at the age of fourteen has proved to be a real challenge as we have found with the two UTCs we have in MediaCity, Salford and in Newhaven, near Lewes in Sussex. The financial pressures brought about by the lack of student numbers and insufficient time being given to enable a new concept to be embedded into the system has led to a number of UTC closures. The UTC movement has been seen as a direct threat by schools anxious to protect their own numbers to sustain revenues, and as an opportunity to transfer – or, put more directly, to 'dump' – more challenging students. It has not been seen as a way of providing a more appropriate education for pupils who wish to have a career in the specialism offered.

I believe a number of these new policy issues will be questioned in years ahead. In political haste, some changes have been embarked upon without any real piloting of the concept. They have attracted huge sums of public money with teams of civil servants involved in order to fulfil the promises made by ministers. This is particularly true in the case of Free Schools in buying up property in order for the quota of schools to be opened to be achieved. Much of the thinking around Free Schools is based purely on a belief that competition and choice in education will solve everything. It is this rather than addressing the underlying issues of underperformance that will drive change irrespective of the disruption that this may cause locally.

Until the Conservative Government lost its working majority at the last general election, along with the undeliverable declared intent of every school becoming an academy which was hastily withdrawn, the PM, Theresa May, was set to embark on the re-introduction of grammar schools. That is definitely not the sort of change needed, a view supported by the former Chief Inspector of Ofsted, Sir Michael Wilshaw, and the recent decision by the government to provide £50 million of funding for existing grammar schools to create new places has brought heavy criticism, particularly when schools up and down the country are so short of cash.

I can assure the PM that, from bitter personal experience, those on the cusp of this experiment would have been scarred for the rest of their lives. To avoid this happening was precisely why I became an academy sponsor. The desire to recreate grammar schools was not based on a belief that it would bring about change for the good of the many but simply to address the wishes of the few many of whom are based in the Conservative heartlands.

As a sponsor I did not set out to be critical of independent schools. Why would I? After all, I chose to educate my own children that way. I set out to prove that with the best teaching and access to excellent facilities, there was no reason why the top notch education that my children received could not be replicated in the state system. The major issue is the difference between the level of funding made available in the state and independent sectors. In independent schools, as well as top level teaching there is a rich menu of extra-curricular activities, including sport and the arts. In the state system, with increasing pressure on funding through government cuts, schools struggle to provide even a basic level of education.

To help address this funding gap, state schools need to be run more efficiently. As well as keeping the percentage of the overall budget spent on teaching staff in check, the cost of back-office services such as finance, HR, and IT support must be reduced to make more funding available for front-line teaching. A shared services structure would avoid massive duplication and make huge savings. However, just as I found at Capita with the initial outsourcing deals, there is resistance to this from local management. School Principals and local governing bodies assume it is their role to protect what they have, falsely believing that this gives them greater control.

In the state system our academies are non-selective and open to all by right based on where a student lives. In the independent sector, including grammar schools, in many cases good exam results for the school are achieved through selection – sometimes also assisted by excluding students who are not performing well enough rather than helping them to achieve their full potential.

I set out with the strong belief that excluding students from school is very much a last resort. Finding the cause of a problem and dealing with it is more important than just making it someone else's problem. The most telling illustration of this was a student who came to us at Darwen Aldridge having been excluded for a range of reasons from every other school in Blackburn with Darwen. With us, and under Brendan Loughran's guidance, he went on to get nine straight A* GCSEs, achieved three As at A Level and was offered a place at Cambridge University!

My views on exclusion were reinforced after working with Mark Johnson of User Voice, examining the causes of why so many young people excluded from school can end up with a prison record. This work showed the direct correlation between the issues prevalent in the challenging communities where the Foundation works, and those affecting individuals who go on to offend. This really disturbed me and as a new academy sponsor gave me many sleepless nights. I felt my role was to stop this happening as the statistics are damming. Nationally, only 2 per cent of the population has been excluded from school, whereas in prison 49 per cent of male prisoners have been excluded at some time. With numeracy, it is not widely reported for obvious reasons, but 23 per cent of the UK adult population has only the standard expected from an 11-year-old – in prison it is 65 per cent. With reading ability, 21 per cent of adults in the country have the standard expected by an eleven-year-old, where as in prison it is 48 per cent. Clearly, there are numeracy and literacy issues to be addressed and exclusion is not an answer.

This does not mean we have been soft on discipline. In all of our schools the newly appointed leadership teams faced outright abusive language at the outset from some students. This was unacceptable and has changed dramatically. Ofsted inspectors now regularly comment on the calm atmosphere in the academies and the pride that students have, citing this as one of the reasons for the improvement in educational performance. Some of this change has come about through self-regulation by the students. They appreciate the investment that has been made and the opportunities that it brings for them.

A big part of the early change in culture came from making an immediate statement that things are going to be different. One such approach was the introduction of a new school uniform, which the students helped to design. This immediately generated a sense of pride – students knew they were representing their school when out in the community. We faced a great deal of flak from parents over the cost of the uniform but, with careful buying, we got this down to a reasonable sum.

It takes time to change perceptions about a school. Parents may have attended the same schools and not have good memories of their school days. In the area around Brighton Aldridge Community Academy, 49 per cent of adults have no qualifications, indicating that they have been completely let down by the education system. Hence, when they visit the school with their children there is great trepidation because it brings back unhappy memories.

Attendance needs to be monitored closely. Parents can now be sent a text message if 'little Johnny' has not appeared at school that day. I took it for granted that I attended school every day, and my mother saw it as her responsibility to instil that discipline in me. Today, that is not always the attitude our teachers have to deal with. In many of our academies teachers have gone to homes to collect students and bring them to school, sometimes suffering abuse from the parent or guardian for doing so. One parent in Brighton actually took her son on holiday to Devon without permission after he had taken only one of the two papers required for English language GCSE, meaning that he would fail. We even made arrangements with the Local Education Authority for the student to take the paper where he was, but the parent refused. I wonder how that young man will feel later in his life about his mother's actions?

Like me before I became a sponsor, most people have no idea that this sort of thing happens, but such stories do help to explain why transformation takes so long. Anyone who is approached by the

Department to become a sponsor needs to be aware of this and when I am asked to give a talk by the Department as part of my ambassadorial role as a patron to the Academies Programme, I refuse simply to give the good news stories, but balance them out with some of the starker experiences. The transformation of an existing school cannot happen overnight. While it comes with different issues, starting a new Free School where you can set standards right from the start and recruit the kind of teachers you want has more appeal to some sponsors than taking on the more difficult task of transforming an existing school with a poor track record.

The most critical appointment is that of the principal. The number of candidates to choose from is limited. Some teachers do not want the additional responsibilities of being a head, which are considerable, and lack the skills required to extend themselves beyond their training as a teacher. This is one of the big barriers to the extension of the Academies Programme. In the case of a multi-academy trust, my view is that in the near future the CEO will be a 'business'-orientated person, rather than following the tradition of appointing someone with a teaching background.

I believe when recruiting very senior people it is essential to get to know them as a person to ensure that there is a cultural fit and they fully sign up to the vision of the organisation. I have been surprised in the education world where reliance appears to be put on a single days interviewing to appoint. At least in the business world one can come to an early agreement if things are not working. In education to remove a Principal is a long process and the reputational risk to the school of doing so takes several years to get over. Nevertheless, if things are not working it would be wrong not to address it. I have been surprised on a number of occasions how teachers who we have 'moved on' are appointed into senior roles with neighbouring schools locally, sometimes without a reference being sought, or even into national roles. In one bizarre incident to illustrate this point, we parted company with a very senior teacher for under-performance issues only for him to be appointed by the local university to work on a 'high flyers' programme they offer to newly trained teachers, coaching them to become high-performing teachers.

REFLECTIONS AND FUTURE PLANS

One of the recruitment frustrations is the difficulty of attracting high-calibre teachers to difficult schools. Many prefer to teach in the leafy suburbs. This is particularly true of maths teachers. There is a national shortage which means the teaching received by some young people in the important subject of maths is not good enough. With resources continually being squeezed by Government, a top level resource in maths or English must now be used across a group of closely related schools rather than expecting every school to attract such a person. This is beginning to happen within Aldridge Education, our Multi-academy Trust.

The progression of a student from primary to secondary school can also cause issues. Even at my age I can remember what it felt like to go from the top of a small primary school to be at the bottom of a large and intimidating secondary school. In my view, insufficient attention is given to smooth this transfer. Some of this is due to the reluctance of primaries to partner with secondary schools. The reverse is also true. There appears to be a barrier between the two that can take a massive effort to overcome. It should be a natural for there to be taster sessions held on subjects such as ICT or sport so that a student gets used to being in the new environment before arriving in September. It is also very apparent that we need to start earlier as much of the gap between disadvantaged children and those from more advantaged/ affluent family situations is present by the age of five.

We find that the effects of this and the long summer breaks result in some transferring students falling behind up to the equivalent of two academic years in key subjects such as English and maths. This immediately puts added stress on the young student and on the system as the shortfall has to be addressed. This is why we are so keen on having primary feeders to our schools, either directly connected or in close partnership arrangements. Unbelievably, even in this new world of academisation, with regional school commissioners in place charged with the responsibility of assisting with feeder arrangements, it is not easy to construct such a model as local resistance to it remains strong.

The approach most teachers follow to address underachievement on transfer is intensive work on English and maths when a student starts in year 7. Pressure on resources means that this soon drops to a more formulaic approach where deficiencies are reported, but not necessarily effectively addressed. So as a student approaches year 11 with GCSEs in view there is a knee-jerk reaction to intervene with programmes designed to get the student through an examination at least with an acceptable level of grade. Sometimes this works, but often it is too late.

Technology must also play an even greater part in education in the classroom than it does now particularly as we need to come to terms with the fact that more needs to be done with fewer resources. Technology could help to ease workloads, help monitor progress, and introduce young people to new skills and experiences. This will also help students to learn at a pace that suits the individual and bring flexibility into the system to accommodate those who, for example, are talented at sport and need to train at certain times. In our sporting academies we have introduced a curriculum where students can learn in the morning and develop their sporting talents in the afternoon. All this will need teachers to respond differently with learning designed to fit the needs of the student rather than being designed around the needs of the teacher.

It could well mean longer working hours for both teaching staff and students. Carol and I visited a Charter School in New York, where students are encouraged to call their tutor on the mobile out of hours should they have a problem with their homework. Teachers are paid a higher salary to accommodate this but the message is clear – we are here as a team to achieve the best outcomes for you.

One of the major differences in my own children's education is that they worked far longer hours and most certainly did not stop at 3.30 p.m. Prep, as it was called in a public school, was set for the evenings and there was school on a Saturday morning before taking part in sports matches. State schools must ultimately stay open longer during the day and be used more in the holiday period. We already give many children their breakfast in the morning, so a supper would also enable them to complete their homework before going home, or to take part in after-school clubs or sports.

I am dismayed by the lack of competitive sport in schools these days. In some large part, this goes back October 2010 when Michael Gove and the coalition government decided to scrap the role played by the local school sports partnerships which had quietly achieved success in getting students to be more physically active during school hours. No longer is there a structure in place to encourage sporting competition through arranging fixtures and it is now left to an individual enthusiastic teacher keen on sport in a school to contact their counterpart in a neighbouring school to arrange matches.

I miss the programme that all my children had throughout their education for each term. The 'pink list', as it was called at Charterhouse, gave a parent the chance to plan their weekend around regular visits either to attend matches at the school or to travel for away games against other public schools. Success of the 1st XI in football or cricket against local rivals brings a certain buzz to the school. I also believe that those students actively involved in sport have a different stimulus that helps them cope better with the pressure of learning.

In Brighton, particularly with cricket, as a state school we have been forced to look to the independent sector for matches because of the lack of an infrastructure locally. My central point is that competition is healthy – it brings an edge that replicates what students can expect in the outside world.

Many of the students do not have a natural role model to follow and most definitely most do not have a natural network to open doors for them if they wish to follow a particular career. To me, work experience is vital as is training for interviews and creating an interesting CV. We are encouraging potential employers to work more closely with our schools to help with this. This would also assist employers tracking talented students earlier in the recruitment process. Another area of severe weakness is career advice. I can accept that a teacher can advise a student on the best universities to go to but I have grave doubts that they are able to advise on a particular career to follow. Far too few teachers have ever worked in the 'outside' world. We need more teachers who have worked in industry, business or in the City.

I have found the role of the governing body wonderful to observe and to be a part of personally at KAA, particularly when compared to a company board of directors. Apart from the normal representation such as staff and parents, there is a need for specialist knowledge around the table to deal with finance, marketing, legal, ICT, social media and of course to provide educational challenge. There are also areas such as health and well-being and safeguarding including the recent area of radicalisation. The role of the governing body in an Ofsted inspection is vital and it must demonstrate a high level of challenge to the principal if the school is to achieve an outstanding status. Good governance is both onerous and a high priority. Both within a Multi-academy trust (MAT) and with local governing bodies, trustees and governors need to devote a huge amount of time. It has associated reputational risks and in my view the role of Chair of a MAT will need to attract some form of remuneration. It is important that more people put themselves forward to be governors or trustees. I believe companies should give it equal billing with encouraging senior executives to become non-executive Directors on company boards. It may not be as 'glitzy' a role as being on the Board of a PLC but the impact that you can have on a community is ten times greater. From personal experience of both, I can tell you, the one involving the shaping the lives of young people feels far more rewarding than the other involving corporate life. The problem is that one is a paid role and the other is not.

One aspect of my involvement as a sponsor that I am particularly pleased about and that will differentiate us from other academy chains is the way that we promote education with enterprising attitudes and entrepreneurial thinking. I believe that this will prove to be the driver for many of our students to find success.

At first, I had to explain what I meant by the term 'entrepreneur.' Many parents did not want their sons or daughters to be tainted by making profits at the expense of others, or to risk failure if the business did not work out. For some the only image of an entrepreneurial person was that of Lord Sugar in *The Apprentice* TV programme and the show's contestants – often ruthless wheeler-dealers with little desire to work as a team. Similarly, the *Dragon's Den* TV programme relies on the panel belittling the contestants while playing to the camera rather than encouraging new ideas. So the distorted world of TV entertainment was the only point of reference for most people when it came to entrepreneurial thinking. One of my friends made a telling observation to me about the 'soaps' watched by millions every night. Any entrepreneurial characters in these are usually portrayed as 'sharp' or 'fly' working on shady deals mostly for cash. Even Del Boy from *Only Fools and Horses*, a character that I love, has this image! So no wonder parents were sceptical of the concept.

Fortunately, the desire by young people to become an entrepreneur has come a long way. Recent research has claimed that 15 per cent to 20 per cent of pupils who participate in enterprise activities will later go on to start their own companies, a figure that is three to five times above that of the general population. Another piece of research by *Business Matters* magazine revealed that four out of five young people aged between sixteen and twenty-one in the UK are interested in starting their own business. This figure demonstrates that university does not have to be the only option in the wake of A Level results. The report concluded that this research clearly indicated that a large proportion of young people have entrepreneurial ability most of which is untapped or untested.

The fact is that there is not currently a mainstream education pathway for students to follow which gives them a meaningful qualifications and experiences that develop these entrepreneurial assets. Equally, few teachers that are trained to teach in our secondary schools through conventional teacher training routes are able to advise a student on this or even to recognise the characteristics. This needs to change.

In all of our academies it would not be surprising to be celebrating each term the successes of a dozen or more students who achieve outstanding academic results. Equally, across the school there will be many who will excel at sport or music. My plan is ultimately to be able to celebrate the success of a dozen or more students that have started successful business ventures whilst at the academy.

This will not happen naturally as the education system does not think that way. This is where the change in approach has to come. I am therefore planning my next venture to be building on the work we are doing in our academies to promote these attributes in young people and to raise it as an issue which as a nation we need to address particularly in the wake of BREXIT.

Through the Foundation, we have formed a major partnership with the University of West of England in Bristol to be the home for this work. Working with its Pro-Vice Chancellor of the Business School, Donna Whitehead, we have established the Aldridge Institute for Enterprise and Entrepreneurship to give academic rigour to our thinking. Located in the Business school's brand new £65m-building I am funding the work of the Institute for the first five years by which time we believe its work will be self-financing. We have recently made a great appointment in Gurpreet Jagpal to be the first Professor of the new Institute and to lead its development. Gups, as he is called, is well known from his work at London South Bank University and I am confident will be able to communicate the change in the thinking required on a national and international stage. The intention is to encourage educators to be supportive of the need to transform the skills that young people develop. Quite a challenge, but then I like a challenge – particularly one I am passionate about!

Our approach to enterprise is to base around the development of six key Aldridge Attributes: team-working, risk-taking, passion, problem-solving, creativity and determination. The most important of which I feel is to develop the ability to work as part of a team, for a common cause. It is this skill that employers will look for in staff at all levels. Overall, these traits are very much about developing a mind-set in a young person not to accept the way things are, but to find ways of improving things, both for themselves and for others.

Much of this thinking was applied to the way that I built Capita and was the mind-set we all had working as a team at all levels in growing the business and successfully competing in the market place. I believe each of these strands of thinking can also be developed within an educational environment. Indeed, in our academies students are rewarded for demonstrating these specific attributes in their work, in the way that they act towards others and apply themselves to challenging situations. They are designed to make our students independent and ready for life and work.

These virtues should also be encouraged in school staff, the aim being to create a culture of high aspirations, high motivation and high achievement. This builds a strong community based on fairness and personal responsibility. Embracing these traits demonstrate a personal statement about commitment to personal development as a teacher and leader. These are most definitely attitudes that an Ofsted inspector should increasingly look for in assessing the standard of teaching and learning.

We are embedding the Aldridge Attributes into the school's teaching through a programme developed in Finland called 'Team Academy'. This entrepreneurial education programme was established as a degree course in Finland by an organisation called Akatemia over twenty years ago. It has been highly successful and is now run in 7 universities in the UK including the University of West of England which was a key reason to establish the Institute there. Early in 2018 we reached an agreement with the directors of Akatemia CIC, Robert Goodsell and Alison Fletcher to join forces with the Foundation with the aim of accelerating the development of enterprise and entrepreneurship in education in the UK. This agreement will also bring with it access to a worldwide network covering Finland, Spain, the Netherlands, France and Hungry with coaches being trained for China, India and the USA.

We have taken the methodology utilised at degree level and adapted it for use in a community and school settings with pilots running at Brighton Aldridge Community Academy and the Darwen Aldridge Community academy. Those participating are put into teams and run team companies undertaking a real-life learning approach to delivering entrepreneurial and business education. The initial results in this small cohort are encouraging and improvement in performance is material.

Known as 'Teampreneurs', the students work collaboratively in teams to run a real business or social enterprise. In formal education terms through this approach they make progress towards their core curriculum subjects. How more relevant can you make the sometimes abstract subjects of maths and English than in the development of a business plan that requires numbers in terms of financial projections and the production of a proposal to bid for a contract where the ability to write and express yourself is paramount? The team companies work with business mentors and also reach out to real businesses to help them solve real issues. In this way the model delivers the most profound employer engagement.

I have always been clear that not every student will want to start a business but we are about equipping students with an enterprising mind-set and attributes that will increase their effectiveness in whatever they choose to do. Some will develop entrepreneurial thinking and the desire to take this further and set up and run their own social or commercial enterprise. Above all we believe that the development of non-cognitive skills and an enterprising approach is as important and should be valued in the same way as the pursuit of academic excellence.

In all of our academies we have designed a creative space for small offices or pods where students and people from the community can start businesses. We name this space according to where the academy is based, such as Kensington Creates at Kensington Aldridge Academy. These facilities are where start-up businesses can get hands-on support and mentoring as well as working alongside other start-up entrepreneurs to develop their businesses.

Start-up entrepreneurs who work from these pods are required to give something back to students and school life, helping to run entrepreneur clubs in return for the support that they receive. The academy where this model has operated the longest is in Darwen at DACA where we have eleven business incubation pods. From there we have started almost fifty businesses over the past eight years. The team at the academy has also delivered nearly 500 adult courses on entrepreneurship to members of the community and created 140 work placements for students. The positive impact of this on the students' outlook can be seen in the way that we have record numbers of students going to university, with 70 per cent being the first in their family to do so. This is enormous progress particularly as when we first became the sponsor, there was no Sixth Form for students to progress to.

It has always been my vision for our academies to be seen as community assets and drivers of community regeneration. A large part of this change will come from business start-ups creating local employment. These enterprise zones will link to the Creates space in our academies, enabling businesses that have outgrown our space in schools to move on to the next stage of their journey. The impact of the capital investment of over £300 million we have had from Government to build our family of academies and colleges is more than just an education story, but one of regeneration, creating a massive social return to the community. This will manifest itself through not only creating more employment but also in reducing the long-term cost of social issues that come with crime, drug abuse and general social unrest.

Perhaps unsurprisingly, I can track the Aldridge Attributes in my own family. Everything that I have set out to do in my life has been about my family and providing them with the best options for a fulfilling life. We have come a long way together and are a very close team who have always enjoyed doing things together. We have been fortunate to have experienced some incredible things both here in the UK and on our travels around the world.

We are also a family of individuals, each having different hopes and concerns, interests and aspirations, along with a belief that each should be given the opportunity to pursue our goals. As a family, in seeking to understand the values behind our wish to work in education and with young people, we once sat down with a facilitator to work this through. What transpired was a very telling and accurate picture of the way that we think and act. I wanted to include our deliberations in my book.

We are 'change merchants' who have the ability across the family of making things happen. We are not people who are static or conventional. We definitely challenge the status quo.

We are 'long-term thinkers' who are not a flash in the pan. We want to leave an enduring and positive legacy for future generations. We plan on being here for many generations, hence the importance of the grandchildren, Florence, Atticus and Annie.

We are 'hard workers' and have a strong work ethic. We like to roll up our sleeves, get stuck into the task at hand and stay until the job is done.

We are a family of entrepreneurial, commercially minded

individuals who believe that creating wealth can be a force for good, which will transform lives and build communities. We are 'wealth generators'.

We regard ourselves as being 'carefully confident' being bullish, yet sceptical with our money. We are in the game of reliable, sustainable and long term growth, not speculative, one-off investments. We don't, therefore, take unnecessary risks

We are 'socially responsible', believing that the more fortunate in society have an obligation help those less so.

We are all 'entrepreneurial educators'. By this we believe in the life-changing nature of learning and that the entrepreneurial mind-set can be a tool to educate, empower and inspire.

It was established from our discussion that we are 'stubbornly generous'. By this we mean that we want to help others reach their full potential and that starts with the family. We are hard on ourselves because we want to bring out our best. Similarly, any giving will be associated with deliverable returns and targets.

We value honesty and straight-talking, and are serious about what we do say and do, but never so serious not to enjoy ourselves or to stop smiling.

We are all 'team builders', by this I mean we like to forge relationships, leverage the knowledge and ability of others to create better, more effective outcomes for all involved. We have the ability to build winning teams.

We are 'growth engines' as we don't see growth as a nice to have or an optional pursuit. It is at the core of everything we do. I love this phrase but it is true, we are not in the business of going backwards!

It would seem to me that we are all restless people who are constantly seeking change for the better. We are most definitely 'cause related' and react to social injustice.

It will be interesting to watch if these attributes manifest themselves in my grandchildren, Florence, Atticus and Annie. They will, of course, grow up in entirely different worlds but, as their grandfather, I hope that the family traits hold them in good stead.

I am proud to say that my four children, Debby, Michael, Jennifer and Robert are successful in their chosen ways and have fulfilling lives holding the values that we believe as a family. All have a strong work ethic.

Alongside the Foundation and Aldridge Education, we also have a Family Office, which manages a number of investments that we have made in businesses and projects. The Managing Investment Director of this is Matt Insley. While this is designed to increase the wealth of the family, it is also there to generate funds for the work of our Foundation.

I have been fortunate to build this over the past eight years with the help of my eldest son, Michael, and more recently with his brother Robert's input as well. It has been a very precious time to work with my two sons and something that I never expected to do.

One of our investments is in a company called Sunbird, of which Michael is the co-founder and now CEO. It operates in Eastern and Southern Africa with major offices in Nairobi and Johannesburg. It employs 400 people and provides outsourced services to businesses that operate across sectors such as oil, mining, tourism, and technology. Sunbird markets serviced office space through which it provides a one-stop shop for multinationals looking to expand into eastern and southern Africa.

In late November 2017, Robert and I visited Nairobi, Dar es Salaam and Johannesburg to look at the Sunbird operations there and to attend two sales conferences held for key personnel. It was good spending time with Michael's chairman, John McDonough, with whom I had previously worked on the CBI's Public Services Strategy Board when John was CEO of Carillion. It also gave me the opportunity to meet Michael's management team and to understand more about the business environment. It was a very impressive operation and brought back memories of what it was like when I first started Capita. Yes, it is very hard work building a company and has high risk associated with it, but I was also reminded of the buzz that it gave me, along with the excitement and adrenaline it provides. During one of the conference sessions Michael's team heard of a major sales win, with 'high fives' everywhere. It was good to be a part of that again. I was asked to talk about Capita and how its ethos and values were the basis of its success. It felt surreal for me to listen to Michael holding his team to account for the conversion of sales in the bid pipeline! I will watch how the Sunbird story unfolds with great interest, both as an investor and a proud father.

Sadly, Capita's story has taken a sorry turn. The decline started on 29 September 2016, with the first profits warning to the City issued by Capita in nearly thirty years as a public company. I was away watching the Ryder Cup in the States on the day of the shock announcement when the share price fell by 28 per cent. All I could do was watch from afar the decline of a company that I started and which still means so much to me emotionally. It always will do – it changed my life.

For me, the decline started when Paul Pindar stepped down as CEO in February 2014. Knowing Paul as well as I do, I am sure that he would have had done everything possible to ensure that, on his leaving, the company was in the best possible financial shape. He is one of the most talented individuals I have worked with and we achieved so much together. His departure was followed a year later by Gordon Hurst's retirement as Finance Director which meant that the entire team that had built Capita was no longer there. However, my belief is that the succession planning instigated under Paul's time as CEO was flawed. The Board should have recruited sooner for senior appointments from outside the company in preparation for his departure as the company was continuing to experience substantial growth. This is particularly true at the Chief Operating Officer level. Instead, they placed reliance on the belief that senior people from within the company could step up to take over the mantle of running such a large and complex organisation.

My sense is that the market has changed dramatically, becoming far more competitive with far more players. In some cases this has led to an irresponsible approach to pricing, designed to win contracts at all costs and leading to inevitable consequences. Linked with this trend, the contracts that Capita has bid for and won recently have become far more complex and therefore more risky. It is one thing to outsource the back-office financial services of a local authority, but a completely different level of risk for NHS England to outsource to Capita the administrative support to GPs, dentists, opticians, and pharmacists, including processing of payments, ordering supplies and medical records. I read in a recent National Audit Report that NHS England awarded the contract in the hope of reducing costs by 35 per cent, while Capita planned to make a loss of £64m in its first two years, intending to recoup this later. This a complete change in philosophy, approach and risk profile to that which we applied in our bidding while I was there. It would definitely have resulted in a no-bid for an opportunity loaded with such risks

In City terms, once the first brick is out the wall with a profits warning you have lost the unblemished track record of delivery that took so long to build and you have lost your invincibility and the trust that goes with it. Blame was inevitably placed by the company on the BREXIT vote and the uncertainty that this brought, making customers reluctant to commit to new outsourcing contracts. Concern was expressed by the City over the level of debt on the balance sheet. Even the disposal of the highly valuable competitor to Equiniti in share registration services, Capita Asset Services, for approaching £900m was not sufficient to deal with the issue. Analysts had also begun to comment that some of the accounting treatment adopted by Capita was too aggressive for comfort. The truth of the matter is that the company had lost its way. The culture I had worked hard to instigate and maintain of an open collegiate style of management had been lost.

I subsequently saw it reported that since I left in 2006 the company had made 165 acquisitions of varying size and value. This included for the acquisition of businesses in Germany for the first time, an attempt to broaden the business beyond the UK. With such a large number of people joining Capita through company acquisitions, as well as large contracts wins, integration must have suffered. This is not only about financial integration but about new staff, who may or may not have chosen to work for Capita, being carefully welcomed into the culture in the customary way. Without this many would be left unclear about what sort of organisation they had joined, a particularly dangerous state of play in the case of acquisitions. Capita had become too large and too unwieldy.

A further profits warning followed on 8 December 2016 with

the ultimate ignominy occurring on 1 March 2017 when Capita was relegated from FTSE 100, a privileged position we first achieved in 2000. The irony was that we were replaced by Rentokil Initial who were the golden boys of the City when we first floated. I can recall being at a City lunch to present the Capita story on the very day that the CEO of Rentokil, Sir Clive Thompson, first missed a regularly stated target of his of growing Rentokil at 20 per cent per annum and lost his air of invincibility.

When I think of the detailed preparation and planning that went into the way we communicated with shareholders and the City when I was chairman, it was beyond belief to watch how badly the departure of Andy Parker as CEO was dealt with by the Board. Andy was a great operator at divisional level and a highly intelligent individual, but I believe it was a wrong decision for him to succeed Paul Pindar as CEO of the group. In my view, his approach to team dynamics did not encourage an open style of working and he lacked empathy with clients and shareholders.

It was announced on 2 March 2017 that Andy would leave the group but I believe he was still in the business until September because an interim succession plan could not be agreed by the Board. His replacement as CEO by Jonathan Lewis was not announced until 10 October with a start date for Jonathan of December, meaning that the company was effectively rudderless for 9 months!

From afar, I must ask whatever were the Board thinking of to allow this to happen? They left a company with nearly £5 billion of revenue, running major, long-term contracts and employing 74,000 people, open to all kinds of hostile speculation in the press about the state of the business, encouraging hedge fund activity betting against it.

A third profits warning came on 31 January 2018. Today the Group lies 165th in the list of public companies quoted on the Stock Exchange, valued at £2.5 billion. The situation was made even worse as the latest profits warning came two weeks after the collapse of Carillion, resulting in mistaken attempts to draw a parallel between the two companies. As a result, the share price plunged to a fifteen-year low and Capita became one of the most hedged stocks in the City, with little they could do to stop the decline. It had joined the infamous club of companies that had lost 90 per cent of their value, effectively destroying, in under two years, vast amounts of shareholder value we created over a twenty-nine-year period.

In my twenty-two years at Capita, I never experienced such an adverse chain of events. This situation must have required major work in explaining the position to clients, particularly those within Government. It would also make the winning of new contracts even more difficult. In these circumstances key staff will consider their futures, which may result in many leaving the company.

The recovery began on 23 April 2018 with the announcement of a rights issue for £700m to raise funds from shareholders at a heavily discounted price in order to repair the balance sheet, along with the suspension of dividends to shareholders in the immediate future. The overall strategy appears to be to simplify the business with the main intention for Capita to move to become an international business – a big ask, in my view. This will almost inevitably mean the disposal of companies not considered core to this new strategy, but it will take years to regain the trust of shareholders and the hard-won reputation of dependability.

My seventieth year has proved to be a very eventful and emotional one on a number of levels. On the sporting front there was a major celebration because my real football team (as I still call them) the Seagulls, were promoted to the premiership and will play in the top flight for the first time in thirty-four years. This gave me a conflict of interest with my allegiance to Chelsea but Brighton and Hove Albion will always be the first result that I look for on a Saturday. The thought of Brighton versus Chelsea is something I have waited to see since the days at the Goldstone ground when Chelsea were relegated to the lower division! The AMEX stadium, the home of the Seagulls is right next to Brighton Aldridge Community Academy and I feel that both have played a part in regenerating the community that surrounds the area.

On the golfing front which, over the years, has seen me play in more than twenty different parts of the world, I achieved my lifelong dream. On Monday 17 April I played at Augusta National Golf Club in

Georgia, the home of the Masters. This was just eight days after Sergio Garcia had claimed victory in his first major win. The grandstands and scoreboards were still up around the course, making it a surreal experience. It was made even more special by the fact that I played the course with my son, Robert, who was celebrating his thirtieth birthday, a collective one hundred years playing together! It was a place that both of us always wanted to play but never believed that we would.

I will long remember us arriving at the club and being driven down Magnolia Drive, the iconic entrance to the Club to be welcomed by our host. We had a tour of the historic clubhouse and visited the locker rooms where there is a special area for previous winners – each having their own dedicated locker to store the green jacket they are awarded. The course was immaculately presented with the greens as fast as I have ever experienced. The aroma from the flowers all around the course seemed to follow you everywhere. I will never forget playing Amen Corner, one of the most hallowed series of holes in all of golf, seeing on the thirteenth hole the place from which Phil Mickelson hit that amazing second shot from the trees over water in front on the green to land five feet from the pin and to go to win the Masters in 2010 . I was incredibly nervous not only on the first tee but every tee, although our host and caddies were amazing to us. Robert went round in an incredible seventy-five shots which is just three over par for the course, including birdies on the first two holes. I made ninety, which is in line with my handicap, including a par on one of the most memorable holes on the course, the par-3 16th, named Redbud. As we drove away we both realized what an amazing experience it had been and one which we will relay endlessly to our golfing friends and anyone else who will listen!!

I have made many great friends through golf and have played in some amazing places, including the annual match that Robert and I have at Loch Lomond against my eldest son Michael and his good friend Micky Tudor – R&R versus M&M as we call it. Loch Lomond is a wonderful course in an idyllic setting that has provided many memorable moments for me, including my only hole-in-one on the 8th hole. I happily bought everyone I could find in the clubhouse a drink that evening. My most special regular golfing four-ball friendship has been with Gordon Keith, John York and Dieter May where, over a period of eighteen consecutive years, we had a week's golfing together in places such as Dubai, Turkey, Spain, France, Portugal, Italy, Scotland and Ireland – wonderful memories. I have also been at every Ryder Cup match since 1991, when it was played at Kiwah Island, South Carolina. I have watched many of these events with my two sons, Robert and Michael, along with my good friend Mike Harding. This included witnessing the amazing win at Medinah, Illinois dubbed 'the miracle at Medinah' when, on the Sunday, the Europeans came back from an impossible position to take the trophy.

Unfortunately, prior to my visit to Augusta and in March whilst Carol and I were on holiday in Barbados, we heard that my mother had had a fall at home in her flat. Similar falls had occurred over the years, but she wore a Care Link pendant around her neck at all times – she called it 'my friend'. Simply by activating it an ambulance team arrived to get Mum back on her feet and check that there were no health issues. It was a minor miracle that she had never hit her head as she fell but each incident was clearly further affecting her confidence. I was always contacted by phone as the next of kin and could hear her in the background laughing and chatting up the medics. This time was different. They decided to take Mum into hospital to check her over to see if there were any medical reasons for her fall. When she left her 'lovely flat' as she called it, that day, it transpired that she would never return to it.

Fortunately, Carol and I were returning home to the UK the day following her fall and we went straight to see her at Sussex County Hospital. She was distressed at being in hospital, all the more so as she was looking forward to coming to our house in Oxshott the following weekend to celebrate Mother's Day. Mum was eventually released from hospital after three nights but the hospital insisted that she was moved to a home in Dyke Road, Hove for what they called a 'rehabilitation period'. For the first time I experienced the world of social care. As a result of her fall she had lost her confidence to walk, making a return to her flat impossible. She was there for six weeks before we made the decision to move her to a more permanent care home nearby. It was with her agreement, as she knew in her own mind that It was impossible for her to live without support. A person who had become very important to my mother, Yvonne Allen, who had cleaned my mother's flat for her for over ten years but later effectively became more of a companion, also worked at the Victoria Care Home. This meant in my mother's eyes that it must be a good place for her to go. Yvonne visited her every day after finishing her work and it was a way for us to keep in touch on a daily basis as well as making regular visits. Many family members were tremendously supportive to Mum during this time, in particular Margaret Smith, her cousin; Ann and Peter her brother and sister-in-law; and her nieces and nephew, Andrea, Sonia, Lynn, Keith and Elaine.

On a lighter note, I was able to enjoy some time in Paris with my two daughters in June. Both are great tennis fans and I felt that it was timely for the three of us to do something together, just as I had spent time with the boys playing golf. I arranged for us to see the semi-finals and finals of the French Open, played on the outdoor clay courts of Stade Roland Garros. It was a tremendous experience to relax with my daughters in that wonderful city and to see Rafael Nadal win the final on Sunday 11 June.

Ahead of her 101st birthday on 16 June my mother came to our house to celebrate. It was on a much lesser scale than her 100th celebration but all her grandchildren and great grandchildren were there to share it, along with my Aunt Ann and Uncle Peter. We had two care support staff to look after her but she was clearly in great distress over moving about, particularly getting in and out of bed. I will long remember her yelling my name in agony to help her as she was moved from the bed to her chair via the use of a hoist.

Two days before her birthday, on the morning of Wednesday 14 June, I turned on Sky News and saw to my horror coverage of the massive fire at Grenfell Tower and the tragic events that were unfolding. Kensington Aldridge Academy quite literally sits next door to the Tower. It soon became apparent that every member of the student body and staff were personally affected by the fire, sometimes grievously so. Of the school's current roster of 700 students, eleven lived in the Tower, with another four either ex-pupils or scheduled to join the school in September. Of these, five tragically lost their lives in the fire. Those in the tower itself, and a great number of those who witnessed the terrible events were quite understandably traumatised. The following day I went to visit the staff in the temporary office they had set up a short distance away from the academy. Naturally, people were very subdued and shocked. The immediate impression I was left with was that, no matter where you went, when you looked up the remains of the burnt-out tower confronted you.

The response of the Principal, David Benson, his team and the students was nothing short of awe-inspiring A full curriculum was delivered to everyone by the following Monday, including some students taking their AS Levels the day after the fire. One student even sent her homework in from her hospital bed. Within forty-eight hours the school was holding a series of assemblies at its new temporary home, thanks to the support of the nearby Burlington Danes Academy. It was a cathartic first step on the route back to normality and strangely brought us even closer together as a team. I attended the first of these assemblies. The words expressed by David were perfectly placed. He spoke of resilience. He spoke of students who had lost their lives by saying, 'We loved those students. They were the best of us. They were KAA. We should seek to emulate their behaviours. Each of them, in their own way, represent and symbolised what our great academy is about. What is great about our community.' I circulated his script to my family and to the team at the Foundation. It was just simply brilliant and how David ever managed to deliver it I will never know. But I am sure that the Aldridge Attributes we hold dear for all our students most definitely helped, as did the motto *Intrepidus* meaning undaunted, unshaken and fearless. When David and I were brainstorming this in the board room at our offices in Piccadilly before the academy even opened, trying to settle on a school motto, neither of us thought that *Intrepidus* would be used in such a tragic way.

I returned home from visiting Kensington for the celebration of my mother's actual birthday. This turned out not to be the event I had planned for her as it was clear that her health had deteriorated as a result of the fall. She did, however, have a priceless two hours with her grandchildren and myself talking about the "good old days" and her life with my father. Each of the children spoke of their plans and we had a good laugh together. Mum subsequently remarked to me about how special that time was and how proud she was of her grandchildren.

When she returned to the Victoria Nursing Home in Hove her health visibly declined rapidly and she did less and less each day, not even watching TV or reading her *Hello* magazine that she loved or the local *Argus* newspaper. Eventfully, she made the decision not to get out of bed on a daily basis. It was very distressing to see. The staff at the nursing home were incredibly good to her but this experience confirmed to me that it is important to live life to the full while you can.

Mum sadly passed away on Tuesday 22 August. Carol and I were with her at the time. I was determined that the funeral would be a celebration of her life since, as the Reverend commented in the service, my mother had lived for an incredible 36,898 days – what a full life. All the children took part in the service with Jennifer and Debby both doing readings. Michael and Robert acted as pallbearers. In my eulogy to her, in which I relayed a number of humorous events as well as sad ones, I concluded by saying that as I approached the age of seventy, for the first time in my life I felt incredibly lonely.

In the lead-up to my birthday, Carol had arranged a surprise for me when she invited a number of our close friends, along with the children, to our house in Spain. This place is a very special to both of us as the decision to have a home in Spain was one of the first we made when we got together. Over the past twelve years we have put much effort into developing the house and we always seem to feel able to relax there. So, for me, having a candlelit dinner served by the pool with friends and family was priceless, as was the vista of the Marbella coastline stretching out before us with the coast of Africa and the Rock of Gibraltar in the distance. Carol had also picked up the theme of linking the celebration with Robert's thirtieth birthday, so there were balloons with '70' and '30' on them everywhere.

On 4 November I celebrated my seventieth birthday with a party at the Grosvenor House. It was wonderful putting together the guest list of approaching 300 people for the event. In addition to close friends and family there were people who had been involved from all parts of my life. This included tables consisting of 'the lads' that I went to school with in Portslade over fifty-five years ago, along with the team and colleagues I worked with in my Capita days and currently with the team from The Lowry. The Foundation was well represented, including the principals of our academies. Michael spoke extremely emotionally and articulately about me on behalf of his siblings. Rather than giving a formal speech I had decided to arrange for Naga Munchetty of *BBC News* and *Strictly Come Dancing* fame to interview me on stage. I feel It went well as it enabled me to get over a number of 'thank you' messages in a different way to a speech, but I sense that Naga was very kind to me in her interviewing style!

I have a reputation for my love of giving surprises, particularly at my special birthday parties. So this time, not wishing to disappoint, as the main event of the evening I had organized for Garry Barlow's Take That to perform – they were truly amazing. Only Carol and I knew of it along, of course, with the organizer of the event (Colin of Planned to Perfection) and the hotel staff who had been sworn to secrecy. I had seen Take That perform at Wembley with Robbie Williams but to have them preform for us so 'up close and personal' was very special. Before they came on stage Carol and I met them and they seemed genuinely pleased to be there with one of the band commenting that it was a real treat as 'we rarely get out on a Saturday night.'

A major part of my work going forward will be as the patron to Aldridge Education which will give me the opportunity to visit our academies and spend more time with the students. During the year BACA, DACA and PACA all received a GOOD rating from Ofsted inspections along with, in the case of PACA, record GCSE results in the summer.

However, we received the wonderful news just before Christmas that, after eleven years as a sponsor, we had achieved our first OUTSTANDING judgment from Ofsted and, fittingly, this was Kensington Aldridge Academy. We are still out of the building and now housed in a substantial temporary 'pop up' school designed by the Department of Education. We are, however, to return to 'our home' from September, although none of us will we ever forget the events of 14 June 2017 and those who lost their lives.

I have always believed that a school should have a place at the heart of any community. In the case of KAA it now has an even more pivotal role. There is, naturally, great emotion in the community over the fire and many residents feel they have been dealt with unfairly by the local authority. I believe the healing process will be led by the academy and the young people who are its students.

I began this book by saying how fortunate I felt to have had such a great start in life. I had parents who cared deeply for me. I can only hope that I have achieved the same for my own children. In the case of my childhood, the roles were simple. My father worked hard to bring money into the house to pay for the upkeep and put food on the table. My mother ensured that my father and I had all that we needed every day. My role in this partnership was that they expected me to channel the belief that they had in me to make something special of my life.

As I waited in line at Buckingham Palace at the Investiture for my knighthood, many things were going through my mind, but I recall thinking of both of them and said to myself, 'The boy from Portslade, near Hove actually has come a long way and has delivered what he promised to them.'

I was knighted by HRH Prince of Wales with my mother, Carol and my youngest son, Robert in the front row of the audience in the Ballroom. It was a very proud and special moment in my life. The citation described the reason for my knighthood as 'for services to young people.' This meant a great deal to me as my work is very much about young people – after all, they are our future

I hope that this story is an incentive to others but particularly to young people who are living in challenging circumstances to believe that anything is possible in life with determination and hard work. I would say, always remember your roots, but most importantly it is not where you come from that matters, it is where you want to get to that counts.

Above all, always remember: You're better than they think you are!

INDEX

441